Sources Of American Spirituality

Josiah Royce

SELECTED WRITINGS

Edited by John E. Smith and William Kluback

PAULIST PRESS
New York ♦ Mahwah

Cover art: Detail of *The Three Philosophers*, by Winifred Rieber.
Courtesy of the Harvard University Portrait Collection.

Library of Congress Cataloging-in-Publication Data

Royce, Josiah, 1855–1916.
   [Selections. 1988]
   Josiah Royce : selected writings / edited by John E. Smith and William Kluback.
     p. cm. — (Sources of American spirituality)
   Bibliography: p.
   Includes index.
   ISBN 0-8091-0410-5
   1. Royce, Josiah, 1855–1916—Religion. 2. Religion—Philosophy.
I. Smith, John Edwin. II. Kluback, William. III. Title.
IV. Series.
B945.R61   1988
191—dc19   88-19494
                                                              CIP

Published by Paulist Press
997 Macarthur Boulevard
Mahwah, N.J. 07430

Printed and bound in the United States of America

CONTENTS

*Dedicated to
The Beloved Community
in which man finds
hope and loyalty*

GENERAL INTRODUCTION

Josiah Royce (1855–1916) was a product of a remarkable period that produced some of the finest philosophical minds America has ever known. Born in Grass Valley, California, the son of English-born "forty-niners," he studied at the University of California at Berkeley and later in Germany at Leipzig and Göttingen, before studying for his doctorate at Johns Hopkins University in Baltimore. At Johns Hopkins he began a life-long friendship with William James and was deeply influenced by his *Will to Believe*. During his thirty-three-year career as professor of philosophy at Harvard, he taught with George Santayana and became the admirer and friend of yet another noted contemporary, Charles S. Peirce. Despite the stellar gallery that surrounded him, Royce was able to establish a reputation as one of America's most gifted thinkers and the chief spokesman of the Idealist school.

Royce's age was one of great change. It was a time when people seemed intoxicated with a heady new confidence in their ability to understand and control their environments. Rapid industrial growth tamed the physical world and made it humanity's servant. The extension of liberty and democratic government to the common person through the rise of new republics opened the power to shape society to every citizen. At the heart of it all was the extension of the methods of the new science to all aspects of human knowledge. When applied to history, the new methods yielded the modern historical-critical approach which viewed every aspect of culture, including religion, as essentially historical. When focused on the science of geology, the new scientific method produced a radically different understanding of the creation of the world and the extent of the earth's history. And when turned on questions of human nature it produced, in Darwin's *Origin of Species*, published just five years after Royce's birth, startling ideas about the nature of human life. To extend the empiricism of the new science to a study of the intricacies of human nature was a natural extension of what had been done in the natural sciences, one which was embodied in thinkers like William James, and to no insignificant degree, in Royce himself.

The age, with its new ways of looking at the world and at human nature, also brought fresh ways of thinking about religion. Most especially the question of how humans come to know religious truth was reiterated throughout Royce's life, whether it was in efforts to learn about the history of sacred texts, or to figure the individual into the process of revelation. With this Copernican revolution had to come a rethinking of the relation of philosophy and religion.

Royce understood this as well as any American thinker of his age. He sensed the power of the new mental tools to improve our understanding; but he also was aware of their limits and their abuses, and was eager to avoid those pitfalls. The writings collected in this book are a testimony to the vigor and originality with which he pursued his task. To those remarkable writings, Professors Smith and Kluback have added analyses of subtlety and power which bring into clear focus the extraordinary character of Royce's achievement and its importance for our own day.

John Farina

PREFACE

Two fundamental convictions and commitments lie at the core of this book: the need for the eternal in philosophical thinking and the faith in the objective self as the source of moral responsibility. The following selections from Royce's writings offer the most intense and profound discussion of these convictions. We know how sincerely Royce was committed to a self that is not only interpreted but that infinitely interprets itself and discovers within man the undefinable powers of creation. We believe that by having identified man with the power of interpretation Royce had found that path of humanization in and through which man not only speaks but becomes responsible for what he says. We find agreement with the words of Paul "wherefore let him that speaketh with tongues pray that he may interpret." Although he had a deep sense of the reality of evil and of human waywardness, Royce nevertheless retained an optimism about man's nature in his belief that knowledge would activate our command of self and the realization that this self is ultimately the will to interpretation. The refusal to be no more than the datum of interpretation is man's search to embody this will in community.

Man's realization that he is not only present but past and future lies at the beginning of the existence of community. This idea of community, we believe, is the most precious legacy that Royce conferred on his fellowmen. In this idea of community man renews not only the power of the self, but the *fact* that interpretation is a communal effort, that precious link between the self and the community. Royce reminds us that "life is essentially in its idea, social." The philosophic endeavor is not the fostering of the isolated individual thinker; it is communal responsibility, the sharing of a common past and the hope for a future of deepened communal life. Philosophic life is that love of communal traditions, that intimate sharing of memories, and that intense hope in man's power to

1

comprehend the depths of his individuality in and through the eternal power of the human community.

These values compelled the composition of this book. They are values we believe the reader should again consider and turn to with sympathy and love. Each age needs directions and ideas. We are convinced that the works of Josiah Royce offer these directions to contemporary philosophical discussion. With this conviction we present this book, affirming our faith in the objective self and declaring the eternal to be the beginning of philosophical discourse and community.

W. K.
J. E. S.

INTRODUCTIONS

Josiah Royce, one of the major figures in the so-called golden period of American philosophy, was born in 1855 in Grass Valley, California, a small mining town in the Sierras, a town that Royce was fond of describing as but "slightly older than myself." After graduating from the University of California in 1875, Royce went to Germany to study at the universities of Leipzig and Göttingen and thus began his lifelong attachment to the thought of the German idealists—Kant, Fichte, Hegel, and Schopenhauer. Years later Royce wrote Lectures on Modern Idealism, a work that still stands as one of the clearest and most illuminating accounts in English of the notoriously difficult writings of these German philosophers. The year 1877–1878 found Royce back in America, studying at the Johns Hopkins University where he took his doctor's degree. Returning to his native California in 1878, he taught English at the University of California until 1882. During those four years he became increasingly aware of his lack of a philosophical community and his need to share and compare ideas with other philosophers. He wrote a postal card to the one who was to be his future colleague at Harvard, William James, in which he made the following comment on a philosophical theory he was then teaching: "It was somewhat monstrous, and in this wilderness with nobody to talk about it, I have not the least idea whether it is true or not." One can see, even at this early date, the concern for community that was to reverberate throughout Royce's thought to the end of his life. James responded with sympathy and ultimately arranged for Royce's appointment at Harvard as Instructor of Philosophy in 1882 and helped make this possible by taking a leave of absence himself. Royce became Assistant Professor in 1885 and was finally appointed Alford Professor of Philosophy, a post he held until his death in 1916.

Royce's life was influenced decisively by the religious faith of his

3

mother, Sarah Royce, and while hers was more mystical in temper than that of her son, it is clear that the practical faith that sustained her through the long and perilous journey she undertook from upstate New York to California during the Gold Rush of 1849 made a deep and lasting impression on young Josiah. Fortunately, we do not have to depend on speculation in the matter because we possess a very moving document, A Frontier Lady,* in which Sarah Royce set down, at her son's request, her recollections of the trip. In the 1880s Royce was asked to write what essentially became a history of California and in carrying out the task he asked his mother to write her account of the family's westward trip. In her narrative one can plainly see the force of her triumphant faith that God will deliver those who truly love and trust him. Royce inherited this faith and spent the remainder of his life seeking to make it intelligible by invoking the tradition of philosophical idealism. From The Religious Aspect of Philosophy through The World and the Individual and finally on to The Problem of Christianity, Royce was engaged in a sustained effort to interpret the fundamental religious ideas and to do so in a way that takes full account of the modern temper of mind influenced by science and of the modern temper of life influenced by an advancing technological society. Royce's was no isolated spirituality.

Although Royce was deeply involved in academic life, his thought is not "academic" but reaches down into the important practical problems of human life—social, ethical, and religious. Moreover, he made a great effort to communicate his ideas in language that would make them available to people in all walks of life and not just other philosophers. He was in great demand as a lecturer and was fond of addressing general audiences on topics ranging from the importance of physical education in moral training to the advantages and disadvantages of provincialism and the problems of race relations in the Americas.

ROYCE'S SPIRITUALITY: THE INTEGRATION OF
PHILOSOPHICAL REFLECTION AND RELIGIOUS INSIGHT
BY JOHN E. SMITH

Like St. Augustine before him, Royce was firmly convinced that there can be no finite and particular truths unless there is an Infinite Truth known to an Infinite Thought. More often than not, he envisaged this thought in the form of "the Ideal Judge who knows all Good and Evil,"[1] to whom all

---

*Sarah Royce, *A Frontier Lady: Recollections of the Gold Rush and Early California,* ed. Ralph H. Gabriel (New Haven: Yale University Press, 1932).

hearts are open and all secrets known. Unlike Augustine, however, who sought to recover through a meditative dialectic—"faith seeking understanding"—the presence of the Uncreated Light in the form of first principles (*Sapientia*) in the depths of the created mind, Royce believed that he had a *proof* for the existence of the Infinite Thought so secure that even doubts about the validity of his proof could be made to testify to the existence of that thought. Royce's argument is too detailed and technical to be recounted here, but the gist of it can be made to serve our purposes. In the chapter "The Possibility of Error" in *The Religious Aspect of Philosophy*, Royce argued that the reality of error, of genuine mistakes in thought, can be explained only if there is actually an Infinite Thought in possession of all truth so that this thought, in knowing and embracing error, is able to identify it as such by comparing it with the true state of affairs. Time and again Royce returned to this proof as something accomplished once and for all and, although he was to modify his conception of that Infinite, it remained a cornerstone of his philosophy.

Ever circumspect in his anticipation of criticism, Royce went on to indicate what we are *not* to expect from this thought. It cannot provide us with *a priori* knowledge of any fact or experience, of any general law about nature or the destiny of any individual. It cannot, moreover, fulfill whatever personal demands we make on the world in the presence of the evil that is in it. Above all, we are not to expect from it the answers to special theological questions—who shall be first in the kingdom, how the dead are raised, and so forth. What the Infinite Thought does provide, however, is the comfort that we are *known* in all our strivings, successes, and failures—"For to thee nothing is forgotten."[2] "This thought of the Judge," Royce wrote, "that never ceases to think of us and of all things, never changes, never mistakes and that knows the Good simply because that good is an element of the Truth—perhaps this can sustain us when all else fails."[3] For him only joy and freedom can result from the insight that every individual, every fact has significance in relation to the one organic totality of truth. Our striving is part of the realization of the eternal life of an Infinite Spirit, a point Royce was to stress repeatedly in his philosophy of loyalty and community where he sought to reinterpret the biblical truth "that he who loses his life shall find it." "*Devote yourself to losing yourself in the divine life.*"[4] Here the religious insight completes the moral vision—"In the Divine Thought is perfectly and finally realized the Moral Insight and the Universal Will of our ethical discussion."[5]

Royce was well aware, as many have not been, of the important differences between religion and morality and he also knew how these two closely related spiritual forms have been at war with each other in many historical periods and religious traditions. Consequently, while recognizing their distinctness, Royce made numerous attempts to relate them to each other in a harmonious way. In *The Religious Aspect,* he tried to show how the religious insight completes the moral and in two specific ways. The imperfection of the moral ideal manifests itself first in a certain incompleteness in its definition, and, second, in doubt about its attainability. The overcoming of these imperfections—what the religious adds to the moral—is that the Infinite sees the ideal in its definiteness and knows of its realization. The assurance we gain through the religious insight is not, Royce says, the consolation that the separate individual may seek in his or her own case, but rather the destiny of the moral cause itself. It is enough for each individual to know that he or she is seen and judged truly and justly and indeed Royce regarded this as a test of sincerity, for to love the ideal for its own sake is to rejoice not in our own finite thought but in that of the highest. Howsoever much the world may misjudge us, our character and behavior, we have the consolation that there is the one Judge who knows us truly. The popular image, Royce says, of God as the "big Power" who subjugates all the other powers is mistaken because it sees the world as no more than a heap of powers and "misses the deeper truth of the world as Thought."[6]

Hovering in the background is the nest of problems posed by the reality and mystery of evil; it is to Royce's credit that he never sought to evade that rock which has been called the shipwreck of all theodicy. As is clear from both "The Problem of Job" and the final chapter of *The Religious Aspect,* Royce had fashioned his own solution, which, simply stated, is the claim that the *partial* evil experienced only from the partial insight of the single individual is, from the perspective of the Infinite, universal good. *That* this is so, however, is not yet to know *how* it is so and in this admission Royce pointed to the central problem with which he had to deal. For the partial evil–universal good formula may well be taken to mean no more than that evil is a delusion and that religion comes to no more than the contemplation of God's wisdom. It was just this idea that prompted James to say that Royce's Infinite invites us all to take a "moral holiday"—why fight evil in the world when in the Infinite all is already perfect? Royce was not unaware of the force of this question and he did not try to avoid it, although there is some ambiguity in his response. As will become clear, much depends on the way in which he relocated the problem; evil is to be dealt with not on the basis of God as creator but rather of God as knower.

As regards the ambiguity noted, Royce tells us, on the one hand, that it is superficial for anyone to take him to mean "That thing yonder looks bad, but God must see it to be good."[7] Yet, on the other hand, he says that we must be content to see evil as accidental and opaque and that we have no business murmuring because we know that somehow God experiences the evil as an element in a perfect life. The ground on which Royce sought to distinguish his view from the superficial one is found in the shift from God as creator to God as knower. God, he says, is not the mysterious power who made the things of the world with imperfect means; God is the absolute thought that knows them and howsoever mysterious they may be to us, they are not so to God. Royce saw no difficulty in thus taking the problem out of its traditional setting because he believed that God is not a creator in any ordinary sense, since in his view a creator is finite and would have to be known through experience, whereas the Infinite Thought is not established in that way at all but rather by the rational process exemplified in his theory of error. Here we see Royce's philosophical and theological audacity, a trait we must find exciting whether we agree with him or not. It is as if Royce were saying that God and the world must be what they would have to be in order for his idealism to be true! It is not difficult to see that a position placing such emphasis on truth, knowledge, and meaning must find the category of causality—creating—of far less importance in the interpretation of things than an understanding of their significance in a total pattern of purpose and intelligibility.

Royce was often at his best when he restrained his metaphysical passion and turned instead to the analysis of direct experience. No better illustration could be found than his account of how moral evil, that is, evil in ourselves, is *experienced* as universal good. In fighting evil, he says, "we realize our fragment of the perfect divine life in the moment itself of struggling with the evil."[8] When I find in myself a selfish impulse threatening to destroy the moral insight, I do not look at this evil *objectively* and say, "It is somehow part of the universal good." It is rather that, in the moment of moral *action,* I make it, despite its evil, a part of my good conscience in overcoming it. "The moral insight," he writes, "condemns the evil that it experiences,"[9] and in condemning and conquering the evil, the good will is constituted as an organic unit embracing both itself and the evil. "Only through this inner victory over the evil that is experienced as a conquered tendency," Royce claims, "does the good will have its being."[10] In the doing of the good act there is present in each of us an element of God's life. The emphasis here is clearly not on the explanation of the existence of evil, but on the actual overcoming of evil through willing endeavor. This must be understood against the background of the idea that God is not a separate other to us, but participates in our life as we do in the divine life. Accordingly, Royce could pose the problem of evil with the question, why does God suffer?

For Royce, our individual experience of conquering the evil impulse provides us with a clue to understanding how evil figures in the divine life. Here, as in so many other places, Royce sets forth his view by taking an objection to it and making that objection itself serve as a way of establishing his position. Suppose someone puts forth the following objection: I cannot do evil, for God, as perfect, includes me and cannot be hurt by me, hence whatever I will can only *seem,* but not really *be,* bad, and all evil is illusion. This is, of course, Royce talking to himself, trying out his own doubt, but invariably ready with the answer. The objection, he says, is half-true in that one cannot do an absolute evil, *not* because evil is an illusion, but because the evil intent could be an unmixed evil only if taken as an isolated impulse separated from the organic life of God—which it is not. In that life, the evil impulse forms part of a total good will, just as the evil impulse of the good man is an element in his realization of goodness. We may say that the good will manifests itself in two dimensions; the first is in the *discovery,* which is also the condemnation of the evil; the second is in *overcoming* it; Royce's contention is that unless we are part of the divine life, there would merely be the condemnation following the evil as a separated fact. Another and, perhaps, simpler way of focusing the central point is to say that the good is established only in and through the overcoming of the evil; universal good is the triumph over evil.

No one who has tried to deal seriously with the reality of evil can fail to acknowledge that evil is not exhausted in moral evil; Royce was no exception. Accordingly, he distinguished two classes of evil: There is the ''external seeming'' evil of death, pain, or weakness of character and there is the internal evil or bad will. Because of our limited insight, says Royce, we never know whether evils of the first class are blessings in disguise or expressions of some diabolical will power at work. ''Somehow then,'' he writes, ''we never know exactly how, these seeming great evils must be in God universal good.''[11] As regards the only evil we know as an inner experience—the evil will—however, the situation is quite otherwise, because there we do know its relation to the universal good. Goodness has its life in the exercise of the moral insight when it includes both the evil impulse *and* its correction.

In moral experience, goodness is, as we have seen, the overcoming of experienced evil; in the divine life the realization of goodness must have the same sort of relation to evil as it has in our life. Royce, however, is trying to avoid having his resolution identified as traditional theodicy. It is not that evil *must* exist in order to set off the good by external contrast; ''we say only that the evil will is a conquered element in the good will, and is as such necessary to goodness.''[12] The ''necessary'' here must be taken as a matter of intelligibility and not as a matter of causality meant to explain why evil is there in the first place. Royce's claim is that the evil he envisages is *not* that of the ''partial view'' that in the end makes it an illusion; on the contrary, the evil he means is real, but overcome. Taken as a separate fact, evil would have to be an illusion, but, says Royce, moral experience shows that it is not such a fact but is included in a whole of goodness. Since the entire discussion moves back and forth between idealistic dialectic and an appeal to experience, one is likely to miss the most important points. Underlying Royce's argument is the idea that without the real evil, we would have only *innocence* and not goodness; this is the "necessity" of evil.

Royce repeatedly sought to distinguish his idealism from its older forms which, in his view, rejected both experience and science. Belief in the infinite rationality of things, he claimed, is important but insufficient for reaching the details of situations. In order to realize an ideal, we must know the facts and the appropriate means, hence the need for scientific knowledge. So that even if science is, as Royce says, "the dim shadow of the perfection of the infinite thought,"[13] it is still the only source we have for gaining that knowledge of the world required for the successful pursuit of the moral ideal. Accordingly, he maintained that we are to adopt a realistic attitude toward concrete facts, toward the reality of the world and the deliverances of common sense.

Despite the central place he gave to insight, to understanding, and knowing, Royce never lost sight of the need to relate such insight to religious experience and longing. In seeking to assess the contribution made by religious insight, Royce rejected the view that the world as a whole moves progressively toward goodness and the ultimate disappearance of evil, "leaving the world as innocent and insipid as in the days of Eden."[14] The concept of progress, he says, is as inapplicable as it is superfluous. For moral goodness is the overthrowing of the evil will, not its absence, and hence it is still there as overcome. "Therefore," he concluded, "we have no sympathy with those who expect the future 'salvation' of the world as a whole in time through any all-pervading process."[15] The only experience we have of the destruction of moral evil is the transcendence of the good will over the evil one, and, were that evil to be destroyed, we would have before us not goodness but a vacuous existence. As individuals, however, we still have our own tasks to perform in what Royce did not shrink from calling a "progressive realization of the good," which is at the same time a realization of the life of God in which we are elements. We aim at progress in knowledge, in the discovery of truth and the elimination of error, and at moral progress in the detection of evil and the active overcoming of the evil will. Such progress is not progress for God—"for God this is no real progress"—and indeed Royce concludes in an enigmatic, if not paradoxical, claim that our moral and rational progress are "mere minor facts" or "insignificant elements in the infinite life in which, as a whole, there is and can be no progress."[16]

There is no denying that this conclusion was puzzling to many; how should it happen that Royce's heroic call to the activity of knowing and willing on the part of each individual should result in these becoming "minor facts" and "insignificant elements" in the divine life? Royce had yet to reconcile the importance he was attaching to human activity and creativity with the all-at-once completion in terms of which he understood the nature of God or the Infinite Thought. Somehow at this point in his intellectual development Royce was convinced that it is enough for us to know, in the midst of the real struggles of life, that the victory, the absolute rest, is already achieved in the life of God and that we are *not alone* in our efforts to realize the ideal since there is a righteous Judge who knows and approves of true devotion. How completely Royce was relying on knowledge, the knowledge that the Infinite Thought actually exists, was foreshadowed in an earlier part of his argument when he wrote, "Not Heart, nor Love, though these also are in it and of it; Thought it is, and all things are for Thought, and in it we live and move."[17] There is, however, a spark here that would survive to light a later fire in Royce's mind; the power of the belief that we are not *alone* was to be realized in full force in his later philosophy of loyalty and community. As isolated individuals we are lost, not because we are individuals, but because we are isolated. Royce was later to see the truth in the saying of Jesus that when two or three are gathered together there I am also in the form of the Spirit that makes the many one.

Loyalty, Morality and Religion

Loyalty, both as an idea and as a living spirit in human life, was, for Royce, the cardinal virtue, the basis for morality and religion. He was not unaware that loyalty has often been thought of solely in "martial" terms, involving patriotism and devotion to one's country especially in time of war. While not denying this aspect of the loyal spirit, Royce could not accept such a narrowing down of what he regarded as the most important power in human life. Accordingly, he sought to reinterpret the meaning of loyalty in universal terms and thus to show the central role it plays in all human endeavor. For Royce, loyalty has its own distinguishing marks, which help us in the shaping and directing of our capacity to be loyal. Loyalty is, first, a self-conscious and willing devotion to what he called a "cause" or some aim or goal that many individuals working together are seeking to realize. True, Royce could say that we do not choose our causes but rather that they choose us, but in saying this he also pointed out that we must be, so to speak, accomplices in the process in that we willingly allow ourselves to be chosen by a cause. We say, this cause—the cause of peace, for example—*commands* my loyalty, but then we must be willing to accept and obey the command. Loyalty is also a thoroughgoing commitment and devotion, which means that we make the cause in question a part of our own being, something through which we identify ourselves. Third, loyalty is more than a feeling but must manifest itself in the performance of practical tasks aimed at the realization of the cause. Hence it is not enough merely to express one's "loyalty" in some exalted moment of high resolve; there is work to be done and sentiment alone will not do it. It should be clear that loyalty so understood enters into all the cooperative endeavors in which we engage—scientific, social, religious, political, moral, to name but a few. The success of scientific inquiry depends on loyal adherence to the demands of truth and the procedures through which it is disclosed; the realization of a moral ideal depends on loyalty to the good involved even when this means pain and sacrifice; attaining the goal of religious striving depends on loyalty to those things that are not seen but are eternal.

Royce was well aware of the two most serious objections to his view and he dealt with both at one stroke. Some said that the idea of loyalty is too abstract and vague to provide an individual with adequate guidance in choosing and ordering the many causes that present themselves to us. Others claimed that loyalty is not unambiguously good; there are evil causes based on deceit and treachery, hatred and bigotry, prejudice and racism, and the extent to which they succeed depends on the loyalty of those dedicated to them. Royce's response was to propose the formula "Loyalty to loyalty" as the underlying and basic commitment. Loyalty of a sort is involved in every cause, but not all causes are such as to contribute to the extension of loyalty itself throughout the community of mankind. Hence there are manifestations of loyalty that do *not* at the same time contribute to the increase of loyalty in the world. The Nazi tyranny evoked an enormous and often fanatic loyalty, but who can look upon that program of racial extermination, unspeakable cruelty, and desire for world domination by a "pure" race and believe that it could ever have been aimed at extending the loyal spirit of which Royce wrote? A commitment to loyalty itself, therefore, includes the condemnation and rejection of evil causes whose aims run counter to the cause of civilization. Royce's loyalty is neither uncritical nor sentimental. To take a lesser but still significant example, those whose cause is to carry out a financial swindle and thus to defraud the public will need the loyalty that is said to exist among thieves, but what they aim at is precisely the opposite of the trust, confidence, and commitment to truth that Royce's universal loyalty demands. In response to the charge that the principle of universal loyalty is too abstract and vague to be helpful in individual situations, Royce insisted that, while this cause must enjoin the loyalty of the good person, it can be served only through loyalty to the individual causes that make up the life of each one of us. The reporter who refuses to sacrifice the truth of the matter to the sensational distortions that sell newspapers, the scientist who will not falsify data in the interest of mak-

ing a "discovery" that will enhance his career, the manufacturer who does
not bow to the pressure to shelve evidence that workers in his plant are being
exposed to toxic substances, these are all examples of the loyalty that serves
both the particular cause in which the individual is seeking realization and
the universal cause of extending loyalty among all men. The universal cause
is served and enhanced through the loyalty displayed by individuals in their
various pursuits and vocations.

Royce's most important application of the principle of loyalty to religion is, of course, in the *Problem of Christianity,* where loyalty is transfigured in the love that pervades the beloved community. Prior to this work,
however, Royce was trying to find proper expression for his understanding
of the way in which loyalty might serve to bring the moral insight and the
religious insight into accord with each other. It is as if in *The Philosophy
of Loyalty* he were attempting to deal with the relation of religion to morality
in general terms, reserving for the later work a treatment of the problem in
terms of the biblical tradition.

Those who think vaguely in these matters are likely to conflate the religious and the moral as both having to do with "values" and thus fail to
see that the two, though intimately related, have distinct aims that are not
only not the same but that have led to sometimes bitter conflict, the sort of
conflict, as Royce perceptively noted, that is possible only between near
relations, just as the tragedy of a civil war pits brother against brother. One
of Royce's best insights is that relating science to religion poses a far less
difficult problem than that of relating morality to religion. The reason is
simply that howsoever we may view the supposed conflict between religion
and scientific thought, the latter cannot supplant the former whereas it has
often been claimed that morality is enough and religion is superfluous.
Royce expressed the point in a dialogical form; the proponent of morality
says that the development of conscience and character are sufficient and that
there is no need to become involved in beliefs that may be dubious and superstitious about superhuman realities. The proponent of religion responds
by saying that such a view is "mere" moralism and that while following
the moral ideal may make us good citizens it does not deal at all with the
problem of becoming related in some reconciling way with the unseen order
on which our destiny depends. The conflict is total because each side claims
a self-sufficiency that is meant to exclude the other. Moreover, as Royce
says in citing the prophetic message of Amos declaring the primacy of the
righteousness of God over cultic sacrifice, the conflict becomes more acute
as it manifests itself *within* a religious tradition and not only as a struggle
between the claims of morality and those of religion within a secular society. The problem, in short, has several dimensions and Royce was taking

them into account in his effort to show how loyalty might be the key to a harmonious solution.

Loyalty to a cause provides the purpose of life and is thus a supreme good. As we have seen, there are two elements involved: Our individual, personal causes satisfy the demands of "rational ethical individualism," while loyalty to loyalty itself represents the universal unifying cause. Central to Royce's vision is his belief that, since the good of the cause cannot be verified in the experience of any one person or in the experience of any collection of persons, we are dealing with a spiritual unity that is superhuman. As he was fond of saying, in loyalty we are constantly seeking a "city that is out of sight" and hence requires that we have a will to believe in the Eternal since in our individual loyal acts we seek to manifest the conscious and superhuman unity of life. In daily life we constantly depend on realities just as truly beyond the scope of our ordinary individual experience as any spiritual realm could be. We believe in the reality of our neighbor's mind, we give credit to reports and documents testifying to past and present facts, and we accept as real much that has not been directly experience by us as individuals. Against the view that these beliefs are forced on us by an independent reality, Royce invokes his idealism: There is no wholly independent reality, which is to say that there are no purely theoretical truths unrelated to human purposes and no reality that is foreign to experience. Apart from the superhuman unity of experience, there is no real world and against this background we ask, Where do I as this unique individual stand in that total system of experience?

Against the idea that the superhuman unity of experience is a mere edifying fantasy, Royce tried to show that the same unity present in loyalty is also required for the reality of truth. The loyal are truth-seekers, and the truth-seekers are loyal; in this formula the ethical and the logical are brought together. Is not, Royce now asks, this real world or unity of self-conscious life the same world that religion in its many forms envisages? The answer is yes, and from that it follows that morality and religion are brought into close connection, since both are manifestations of loyalty, which in turn is rooted in the Eternal. An individual life is one that is lived in accordance with a plan or a cause that expresses the purpose of that life. One cannot be loyal without being religious because, while the cause that gives meaning to life is always human, concrete, and practical, it is also *ideal* and a superhuman entity that involves the service of the Eternal. It is the superhuman character of one's cause that forms the bridge between morality and religion. To make the connection more vivid, Royce resorted to his idea of what is meant by a lost cause. The cause of universal loyalty is *for each individual* a lost cause for the reason that it is too good for the present temporal world to express it, and the reason for that in turn is that we as we naturally stand are lost beings. As Royce puts it, "the true cause is indeed real enough, in the higher world, while it is our poor human nature that is lost."[18] Loyalty, however, means a transformation of our nature so that despite grief, suffering, and the loneliness of this life we yet know that we are linked through loyalty to the Eternal. The higher ethical religions, Royce claims, aim at expressing in legend and other symbolic portrayal the basic truth or creed of what he called the "Absolute Religion." In expressing the creed that follows, Royce again shows the boldness of his approach in writing:

> This truth consists in the following facts. *First, the rational unity and goodness of the world-life; next, its true but invisible nearness to us, despite our ignorance; further, its fullness of meaning despite our barrenness of present experience; and yet more, its interest in our personal destiny as moral beings; and finally, the certainty that, through our actual human loyalty, we come, like Moses, face to face with the true will of the world, as a man speaks to his friend.*[19]

It is of the utmost importance to take note of the fact that, in summarizing his view of the coming together of religion and morality in the unity of the world-life, Royce finally came to terms with the problem posed by the seeming incompatibility between his emphasis on the importance of human striving and his insistent belief that the ideal is *already* realized in the superhuman life. Royce put the objection himself, "If the world will attains in its wholeness what we seek, why need we seek that good at all?"[20] and then denounced it as a vain misunderstanding. His claim now is that the world-life includes my individual good *only* if I am loyal. "We have never defined our theory," he writes, "as meaning that the world-life is *first* eternally complete, but then asks us, in an indifferent way, to copy its perfections."[21] This, of course, can only mean that Royce was reconsidering his earlier view and candidly responding to criticism, as becomes plain in his going on to say, "The unity of the world is *not* an ocean in which we are lost, but a life which is and which *needs* all our lives in one."[22] In a veiled response to the criticism of James, Royce adds that "it is no sort of 'moral holiday' that this whole world-life suggests to us."[23] Freeing himself from the image of individuals as "drops" in the ocean of being and from the confines of the Absolute for whom everything is already "all there," Royce was setting the stage for *The Problem of Christianity* and later small writings in which there is more emphasis on *realizing* than on *realized* and a greater attention to what each individual must be doing so that his or her individual contribution will not be lost but will rather become an indispensable element in the divine life.

From the standpoint of religion the interpretation of the divine takes place through parable, historical incidents, and personal experiences portrayed through imagination. In short, religion lives in a world of symbols, but, like Tillich after him, Royce was quick to point out that we are not to say "mere" symbols, because it is *through* them that we see the religious and moral truth they are meant to express. We go astray when we overemphasize the empirical details of these symbols as if we had direct insight into the detailed structure of the divine life. Moreover, a simple, literalistic reading of symbolic expressions—witness those who asked Jesus which husband the twice-married woman would have in the Kingdom of Heaven—makes the mistake of looking for the eternal *within* the realm of human sense experience; it is a looking for the risen Lord in the empty tomb.

Sources of Religious Insight

Royce was well aware of the many sources on which we depend for our understanding of the human situation and of the nature and role of religious faith as it impinges on that situation. For Royce, insight is something deeper and richer than knowledge in the sense of information. A person may know the way to the office where he conducts business, but this is not the same as possessing insight into the nature and strategies of his business. Similarly, one knows the names and faces of his or her acquaintances, but this is not sufficient for insight into their characters. Insight is the sort of knowledge that combines a breadth of range and a wealth of acquaintance or firsthand experience with a certain unity and coherence; insight is seeing many facts in a unity that at once brings us into close personal touch with our object. As Royce points out, unlearned people often have a great deal of insight about matters that concern them intimately, while there are learned people who often attain no insight at all.

Religious insight shares the general character of all insight but it is distinguished by the special object or objects at which it aims. Drawing on Christianity and Buddhism as examples or clues leading to an understanding of religion, Royce laid hold of a most important insight, one that was to serve as his guide in *The Problem of Christianity*. Religion, says Royce, has primarily to do with salvation, a conception he expressed through two basic ideas. There is first the idea that there is some end or aim in human life that is more important than any other and in relation to which all other aims are secondary in importance. Second, there is the idea that man as he naturally is stands in danger of missing this highest aim with the result that life becomes a senseless failure. Anyone who views life in this way has insight into what it means to say that man is in need of salvation and that religion itself is insight into the nature and means of salvation. To this important point we shall return after a brief excursion into Royce's treatment of revelation, an excursion that is necessary because Royce did not include revelation as one among other sources of religious insight since it over-arches all of them and he sought to explain the reason. He was above all seeking to criticize the simplistic view of revelation as an external and fixed authority unrelated to the experience and insight of the individual. To this end he proposed what he called the paradox of revelation, intended, like all paradox, to awaken and even to shock the dormant consciousness. By what marks, he asked, does an individual who accepts what God has revealed to him identify this as revelation? The problem is not unlike that of presenting a personal check at the bank; how is the teller to know that it represents the will of the one who has an account there unless he has on file an authoritative signature with which to compare the signature on the check presented? In short, we would have to know the divine signature and knowing that would lead us into an unending series of revelations, which only postpones and does not solve the problem. What is needed is a revelation that proves its genuineness by appealing to what the interior light and experience of the individual disclose. A new paradox then arises: What light can fallible, individual experience throw on so momentous a problem? Actually, Royce does not mean that any individual has an infallible inner criterion for judging the validity of revelation; such "enthusiasm," as it was called, is a far cry from what Royce had in mind, which was to overcome the *externality* of the relation between a person and revealed truth. "Unless," he writes, "there is something in our individual experience which at least begins to bring us into a genuine touch with the fact that we need salvation and with the marks whereby we may recognize the way of salvation . . . religious insight is impossible, and then no merely external revelation can help us."[24] Royce's insight here is that unless there is a recognition of the reality of our situation and the need for salvation, the revelation that offers the way of overcoming our predicament will appear as external and even irrelevant. As Reinhold Niebuhr once remarked, nothing is more futile than offering a Messiah to those who are not seeking one, or worse, to those who think that none is necessary.

Royce's grasp of the spiritual dimension of life is nowhere more clearly evident than in his schema for representing the universal structure of religion. Contrary to the popular view of religion as a message of triumph, a way of seeing the world in a rosier hue than the facts will bear, Royce set forth a sterner and more realistic conception. According to him, the developed ethical religions exhibit a threefold pattern: First is a vision of human fulfillment and a reconciliation between man and the divine—the ideal; second is the sobering recognition that there is some flaw or defect in our natural existence that stands as an obstacle to the realization of that ideal—the need; finally there is the power not ourselves that works to overcome that flaw—the deliverer. This schema is admirably suited for interpreting the great world religions, for we can ask of any one of them what vision of human fulfillment it holds forth. What conception does it have of the particular defect, the evil or negative factor, that would thwart the realization of the ideal? What is the nature and power of the deliverer to overcome the flaw and bring about both fulfillment and reconciliation? From this vantage point the bewildering variety of belief and practice presented by the plurality of the world religions becomes more intelligible. It is not that all religions "say the same thing," and Royce was well aware that this is not so; it is rather that they speak to the same human predicament and the most significant differences between them can be clearly seen especially when we ask for their diagnoses of the flaw in natural existence. Classical Hinduism sees the flaw in that peculiar ignorance or false knowing—*Maya*—which prevents us from seeing that the soul—*Atman*—and the one Absolute Reality—*Brahman*—are one; Buddhism in its many forms sees the flaw in the boundlessness of desire and the attachment to what is evanescent; the biblical tradition sees the flaw in the rebellious will that would set itself against the sovereignty of God. In all three cases the key to understanding what Royce called the deliverer is found in a grasp of what it is that human beings need to be delivered from. Central to Royce's conception, however, is that religion remains to us a closed book without the recognition of the reality of the flaw in our natural situation. To paraphrase a modern poet, between the promise and the fulfillment stands a shadow, the need that would separate us from the divine life. Royce has taught us that religion is basically concerned with that shadow and how it is to be dispelled through the power embodied in the deliverer.

What then are the sources of religious insight that can throw light on the meaning of the quest for salvation? Royce found these in individual and social experience, in reason, in loyalty, in sorrow, and in the unity of the spirit to which he often referred as the invisible church. In the limited experience of individual life we can come to some understanding of our actual situation and especially of the need in which we are enmeshed. Important, however, as the emphasis on the individual undoubtedly is—Royce was here thinking of the stress placed by James in the *Varieties of Religious Experience* on the individual being "alone with the divine"—Royce was critical of the individual*ism* according to which the problem of salvation takes the form of *my* need as if that were so unique that it had no counterpart in the experience of others. For Royce, religious concern cannot stem from the individual alone and then incidentally take on a social character; the social character of all experience tells us that, while solitude has its own part to play, we cannot be saved alone since we are bound together by spiritual links that cannot be broken. Salvation, says Royce, involves a reconciliation with a social as well as a divine order, "an escape from the wilderness of lonely guilt to the realm where men can understand each other."[25] The social realm, however, has its own shortcomings, for, while it helps us to gain a wider outlook, it still contains the weak mortals who are in need, all the futile conflicts of pride and self-seeking; more importantly, social experience may lead us to the opposite of individualism, namely, to a collectivism in which true individuality is lost. As will become clear, Royce envisaged *community* as that living and spiritual togetherness of individual persons which is beyond the twin evils of individualism and collectivism because it allows for the uniqueness of each individual while uniting all in the one spirit of love.

Royce, always a champion of reason, was concerned to show that the widespread belief that reason is opposed to direct apprehension and to experience—a belief that led many in Royce's day to subscribe to what Hocking called the "retirement of the intellect" in matters of religion—is false; reason is not confined to analysis and the disjoining of what is together, but includes synoptic and synthetic insight as well. Reason is a source of the wider insight we constantly aim at as individuals but can never fully attain. For Royce, all that we think, believe, experience, and do within the limits of our individual situation has a fuller meaning and purpose from the perspective of God, who possesses the synoptic vision. This belief is given dramatic expression in the illustration Royce gave from the experience of one of his students with prayer. This person had given up conventional forms of prayer, and especially petitions for things that he wanted, but in a dark moment he discovered the practical import of the thought that there is a divine wisdom. "When things are too much for me," we read in Royce's paraphrase, "and I am down on my luck, and everything is dark, I go alone by myself, and I bury my head in my hands and I think hard that God must know it all and will see how matters really are, and understands me, and in just that way alone, by understanding me, will help me."[26] Royce saw this as the divine reason literally at work and he was convinced that anyone conceiving of God in this way could not fail to face the world again with renewed courage. How seriously Royce took this insight can be seen in his claim that the seemingly abstract idea of the unity of the world life can never be a merely theoretical affair simply because it impinges on our life at every moment. A truly rational conception of our fragmentary experience is found precisely in our regarding it as a fragment of an experience that is infinitely richer than our own. Once again, there is the desire to know even as we are known, and the thought of this perfected knowledge has its own practical outworkings in experience. Not to be outdone by James, who repeatedly asked what difference will this or that religious or metaphysical belief make to the conduct of my life, Royce boldly declared that *"opinions about the universe are counsels about how to adjust your deeds to the purposes and requirements which a survey of the whole of the life whereto your life belongs shows to be the genuinely rational purposes and requirements."*[27] Rationality not only resides in the wider insight, but it is in the light of that conspectus on our life that our individual wills are to be guided. What the divine wills in willing each individual is that each individual should express his or her own unique choice, the final meaning of which is known to, not a timeless, but a time-inclusive survey. Thus are connected reason and will in both finite and infinite life. The question then arising is, How in fact are we to adjust daily life to this divine will and wisdom? For the answer Royce looked to loyalty.

The principal lesson to be learned from the religion of loyalty is the same as the one that plays so large a part in the discussion of the "moral burden of the individual" in *The Problem of Christianity*. Self-will leads to self-defeat; salvation is essentially bound up with what Royce was fond of calling unity with the brethren, which means all the spiritual bonds that call us back from isolation and loneliness into the mutual understanding and communication of a community of persons. Finding one's way in the world, however, is for Royce no simple affair; on the one hand, we have our own individual conceptions of ourselves and what we are to do, but, on the other, no one of us ever arrives at these conceptions without help from the social relations in which we imitate, contend, cooperate, and interact with other people. Royce's message is not simply that we abandon individual insight and throw ourselves into the hands of the social whole, because that may mean a merely conventional existence; moreover, social experience does not of itself furnish any single ideal or a set of universal rules. While, as we shall see, the solution Royce envisages is found in a certain type of spiritual community, he does not equate that with society in the familiar sense. Consequently, he insisted that we should not seek our will and our aims either in our own individual self or in our ordinary social experience. Something deeper is involved and it sets us on the track of a more reliable principle of life. We escape from thwarting our own will when we have as our aim to act so as never to regret the principle of our action, so that even in adversity we can say, "I have not really failed, for I have acted as I intended, and also as I still intend to act,"[28] whatever others may say of me. For each individual this principle is, as Royce says, a counsel of perfection, but it can find concrete realization in the life of a person who is loyally devoted to a cause in which many individual lives are unified in a common endeavor. Let it be the family, the country, science, art, the relief of the needy, and countless other objectives, the principle is the same: To find yourself is to devote yourself in loyal service to the cause, firm in the knowledge that you are not alone but linked to many other individuals whose service is the same cause. Here it is not a matter of abolishing or sacrificing yourself, but rather of self-realization and devotion to a goal whose meaning transcends the separate meanings of every individual involved. Loyalty, then, moves in a realm that is neither expressive of the merely individual will nor expressive of the society at large; loyalty lives in all the special communities of dedicated persons working together for the realization of a good that far surpasses the experience of any member.

For all of his philosophical idealism, Royce was realistic in the ordinary sense of a person who attends to the facts of the situation and does not ignore the errors, evils, and the failures that occur. True to this spirit, Royce took up the problem of evil again and sought to show what is to be learned from the fact of sorrow and tribulation so prevalent in all that we think and do. Royce saw both the truth and the ambiguity in the essentially moral demand that evil be destroyed. In attempting to fulfill this demand, we often become warriors both with our natural surroundings, in the effort to overcome obstacles and meet our needs, and with our fellow men. Man, as Royce says, is the most destructive of animals and in the struggle with evil it often happens that destruction itself becomes the chief motive. Religion as such, according to Royce, has no quarrel with this moral ideal as long as it does do battle against evil and does not overreach itself. Evil, moreover, has always stood as a stumbling-block to religion chiefly because, from the religious perspective, there is something more in life than the moral struggle against evil; there is also the problem of salvation, which is in turn bound up with the evil in ourselves. Royce's underlying thought is that morality and the quest of the moral ideal is not enough; what is needed in addition is to come in touch with a power or a mind that surveys the real nature of things and accepts us in our conflicts with evil, supporting our efforts in the process. Adapting some features of the biblical story of the laborers in the vineyard to which the master of the vineyard never comes, he likens the moral endeavor to those who work there and discharge their obligations to the best of their ability firm in the belief that what they do is sufficient. Since the master never comes they may even doubt that he exists, but in any case they have no need of him because their moral struggle is sufficient. From the religious standpoint, however, it is not only essential that there be a master, but it is of the utmost importance that an individual become related to him as the one whom he ultimately serves. Royce's conviction is that the moral standpoint can be regarded as sufficient only by those who have not grasped the problem of salvation, something that is not resolved by moral endeavor alone. It is the mission of sorrow and evil in life to teach us that morality, noble as it is, is not enough and that beyond it we need an assurance that there is a reality not ourselves, which is a warrant that our resoluteness will succeed. The very existence of religion itself throughout the entire course of human experience testifies to the religious need, for unless we see ourselves as in danger of missing that good on which our whole life depends, the need for a saving process will not be acknowledged. Royce's insight here is that it is the presence and reality of evil in the world that reveals to us the precariousness of our situation. God can be a helper in time of trouble, but one must have been pierced by sorrow and grief in order to know what that means. Only the wounded, we may say, can serve in God's army. "The ills," Royce wrote, "that we *can* spiritualize and idealize without destroying them hint to us that, despite the uncomprehended chaos of seemingly hopeless tragedy with which for our present view human life seems to be beset, the vision of the spiritual triumph of the good which reason and loyalty present to us need not be an illusion, but is perfectly consistent with the facts."[29] Were the ills of the world and the sorrow they cause to be swept away at a stroke, that would remove from existence the very conditions necessary for the highest good we know. That is the lesson of sorrow and whoever has not learned that lesson knows nothing of salvation either.

The richest source of religious insight comes from what Royce called the "unity of the spirit" or sometimes the "invisible church," and this source points on to his conception of the beloved community, which is the cornerstone of *The Problem of Christianity*. Since Royce regarded salvation as a matter that requires superhuman and supernatural realities, he was at considerable pains to make clear what he meant by these adjectives, fully aware of the confusions surrounding them especially in the popular imagination. To understand any comparison between the human and the superhuman we must have some grasp of what it is to be human, what characterizes our lives as finite beings, and this we can attain through self-reflection. Since, however, our concern is the religious problem of salvation, attention must be given to those features of our natural constitution that give evidence of what Royce called the defect or flaw in our being, which represents what we are seeking to be delivered from. To begin with, our form of consciousness is quite limited; we can attend to and seek to unify only a narrow range of facts and experiences at any given time. Yet we want something more than momentary glimpses of ourselves and the universe; we want to survey life in long stretches, but are at the same time aware that we have little power to enlarge our span of consciousness, with the result that, as Royce says, this limitation is one of the chief causes of human sorrow. We do, however, have the ability to make an *indirect* assault on this limitation in the form of moments that give us some glimpse of what a wider insight might mean. The odor of a flower may bring home to us a meaning that is at the same time the culmination of an entire summer of our life, or the encounter with the wrinkled face of an old man may provide us with the signs that we take to mean the experiences of his lifetime and the personal character he has achieved. Thus, says Royce, despite our narrowness, we live *as if* we saw widely and thereby have an anticipation, as it were, of a view wider than our own present one. Here we have one of Royce's central insights, one to which he appealed ever and again: The meaning of our present experience finally resides in its place in a totality of experience that in the moment we do not actually possess but to which we still appeal in the sense that we believe that if we did possess it we would appreciate the full meaning of that present experience. The parallel with the experience of Job is unmistakable; Job, apart from all arguments about the cause and conditions of his suffering, wants to plead his case filled with the assurance that there is a widest insight, a final justice, in relation to which both his suffering and his response will be understood and in this sense justified.

The value and validity of this indirect approach to the wider vision is grounded in the reality of that inclusive and direct grasp of the whole sense of things. The difference between the human and the superhuman is now before us; the former is partial and limited while the latter is whole and inclusive. The crucial link between the two is found in the idea that whatever real and final meaning our experience has beyond the fragmentary meaning it has in itself depends on the reality of the superhuman consciousness. For Royce, this relation between human and superhuman also appears as a relation between the natural and the supernatural in the sense that if we regard as "natural" all the sorts of things and events studied by the empirical sciences, the underlying claim that the countless collection actually possesses a coherent total sense takes us beyond what any individual ever directly observes. What gives meaning and validity to this natural order is a form of consciousness that can only be described as supernatural. "The unity of the spirit" that Royce set out to define is precisely the meaning possessed by this superhuman consciousness. In this way Royce envisaged the coming together of science, morality, and religion: Reason gives us insight into the need for the superhuman consciousness, loyalty as moral endeavor devotes itself in every sphere to the realization of this consciousness, and salvation means our positive harmony with its purpose.

For Royce all forms of devoted cooperative endeavor manifest the unity of the spirit, whether they be political, scientific, commercial, social, educational, cultural, legal, and the extent to which any one of them approaches the religious domain depends on the extent to which these organizations are aware of and see themselves as devoted to the deeper and larger loyalties that transcend the particular goals at which they aim. Thus, apart from specifically religious communities identified as such, all human communities can take on a religious dimension if they are devoted to the expansion of the spirit of loyalty through whatever their members are engaged in. In addition to the visible churches, there is also an invisible church made up of those who serve the larger loyalty. That this church is invisible is the result of our ignorance and limited vision, for those who serve the larger loyalty may quite literally know not what they do. Whether they know it or not, they live in the Spirit, a real and superhuman organization.

Like Nietzsche, who described modern science as the last of the "ascetic ideals" in his recognition of the discipline, the sacrifice, and the devotion required for the pursuit of scientific knowledge, Royce laid great stress on the community of scientific investigators and the extent to which their enterprise is dependent on the support of every individual, each of whom is dedicated to the pursuit of the same ideal truth and committed to the logical and experimental canons that make this pursuit possible. Again we see that loyalty is the cardinal virtue and that it makes its appearance in all dedicated human endeavor; "wherever two or three are gathered together" and endeavoring to follow the demands of the divine will, there the Spirit is at work. As a transition to *The Problem of Christianity,* Royce concluded his extended discussion of the sources of religious insight by an account of St. Paul's message to the church at Corinth, where he placed Charity—read "Loyalty"—at the head of the gifts of the Spirit. That message was to serve as the foundation for Royce's account of the saving community, the explicitly religious community—the Beloved Community.

Notes

1. *The Religious Aspect of Philosophy* (Boston, 1895; hereafter cited as RAP), p. 436.
2. RAP, p. 440.
3. Ibid.
4. RAP, p. 442.
5. Ibid.
6. RAP, p. 448.
7. RAP, p. 450.
8. RAP, p. 452.
9. Ibid.
10. Ibid.
11. RAP, p. 455.
12. RAP, p. 456.

13. RAP, p. 461.

14. RAP, p. 464.

15. RAP, p. 465.

16. RAP, p. 467.

17. RAP, p. 435.

18. *The Philosophy of Loyalty* (New York, 1908; hereafter cited as PL), p. 388.

19. PL, pp. 390–91.

20. PL, p. 394.

21. Ibid.

22. PL, p. 395; "needs" not italicized in original; "not" is italicized.

23. Ibid.

24. *The Sources of Religious Insight* (New York, 1912; hereafter cited as SRI), p. 26.

25. SRI, p. 71.

26. SRI, p. 133.

27. SRI, p. 159.

28. SRI, p. 189.

29. SRI, p. 237.

THE PROBLEM OF CHRISTIANITY
BY WILLIAM KLUBACK

Our task is to be much more than a funnel through which the thoughts of Royce on community, loyalty, and religion are handed over abstractly to an audience. Philosophy is an interpretive conversation and we offer to the reader the fruits of this conversation. We have decided to discuss in detail Royce, *The Problem of Christianity* (1913), because this work embodies the mature achievement of the philosopher.[1] We make no effort to trace every thought of Royce back to some previous text to give the reader an intellectual history. This would not be an unworthy occupation and it would be helpful for exposition, but it is not the essential concern of philosophy. Its concern is with the exploration of ideas that take place in the perennial conversations among philosophers. Rather than returning to sources, which is presupposed as necessary preparation, we propose a confrontation with Royce through his text. We want to comprehend what Royce said and how it should be understood. With Royce's assumed consent, we want to interpret his words, because to be philosophical is to realize a "will to interpret," to approach the "community of interpretation" that is the philosophical home of those who take their moral burden seriously. In the philosophical community that has existed since man has asked what it means to be both reasonable and rational, we talk to Royce about what he considered to be the primal concern of philosophy: the nature of interpretation.

Royce's Preface deserves particular attention because in it he tells us with care and detail the place of his new work and the theses that underline it. In fact, it is to this Preface that we should return when we finish the book. In reading the "Summary and Conclusion" we think again of the Preface because every genuine philosophical expression is both linear and circular. It is in the circularity of thought that the force and seriousness of interpretation are engendered and realized. In the rethinking and reconstruction we discover the truth that is the foundation of philosophical thinking. One should read Royce's preliminary remarks with a comprehension of the complete text, but we are aware that every reading is only a preparation for that perennial reading which is the demand of every significant text. This is learned from Plato, or from Kant, or, in particular, from Hegel's *Logic*.

From the philosopher's observation there is a consciousness of development. He, like his expositors, seeks to find the "origins" of his achieved expression. Royce noted that "since 1908 my 'philosophy of loyalty' has been growing. Its successive expressions, as I believe, form a consistent body of ethical as well as religious opinion and teaching, verifiable, in its main outlines, in terms of human experience, and capable of furnishing a foundation for a defensible form of metaphysical idealism."[2] The "philosophy of loyalty" is the beginning, the hypothesis, from which we proceed to an interpretation of Christianity. This loyalty is the truth that makes it possible to comprehend the interpretive work of Paul and the primordial idea of community, which Royce believed was Paul's deepest insight and which brought to fruition what was only implied in the teaching of Jesus. Loyalty, community, and interpretation became the fundamental categories of Royce's mature thought. Looking back from this work it would seem that whatever Royce was doing in particular studies and in books matured in the *Problem of Christianity*. This is the advantage of reading back from the end to the beginning. The perspective of the end forces the thinker to comprehend the developmental course of his own thinking, and if it is systematic, to see the necessity of its exposition. Whether Royce had to write the *Problem of Christianity* is beyond our competence to judge, but that he was logically necessitated to expand his category of loyalty into community and into an expanding understanding of the truth of interpretation seems more than probable.

In contrast to James, who worked with the religious experience of individuals, Royce believed that only with the idea of church was it possible to comprehend the individual in a genuine and serious way. The truth of religion lies not in the individual experience, but with the community. In the idea of church Paul achieved Christianity's truth. Royce placed himself in opposition to James and in particular to his failure to grasp the meaning of church or community. In clear and sharp terms Royce stated that James's failure was a "momentous error in the whole religious philosophy of our greatest American master in the study of the psychology of religious experience." "All experience," Royce continued,

> must be *at least* individual experience, but unless it is *also* social experience, and unless the whole religious community which is in question unites to share it, this experience is but as sounding brass, and as a tinkling cymbal. The truth is what Paul saw. This is the rock upon which the truth and ideal church is built. This is the essence of Christianity.[3]

From the opposition to James to the appreciation of Paul's experience and formulation of the idea of church, Royce proceeded to develop and exhibit a philosophy of religion that embodies the idea of loyalty and community in and through which the idea of humanity takes form and content. Although we assume that our reason formulates these ideas, we also know that our formulations are discoveries of truths that think through us. Royce was attracted by the insight of the formula "*Ich denke nicht; sondern es denkt in mir*"[4] (I do not think, but it thinks in and through me) because he had that philosophical insight which told him that thinking depended on an already existent thought.

Continuing his forceful opposition to religious individualism, Royce affirmed that he agreed with those who "held that the Church, rather than the person of the founder, ought to be viewed as the central idea of Christianity."[5] Metaphysical truths surpass what is perceptible. In the reality of church, in its platonic universality, that is, in its catholic essence, we bear witness to such a metaphysical truth. From and through this truth we comprehend individuality. Individuality and community belong to each other as being belongs to nonbeing and reason to violence. From the beginning there was not simply the person of the founder, there was the church or the community, there was interpretation and the community of interpretation. The conclusion that Royce was pleased to reach was that "no individual self can be saved except through ceasing to be a *mere* individual."[6] This attempt to show the inadequacy of the individual is not based on Royce's desire to merge the individual into the whole, but to reach a deeper and more serious concept of individuality.

If Royce was willing to state that it was not through imitating nor yet through loving any mere individual human being that we can be saved, but only through loyalty to the beloved community, then he was willing to show that individuality was not the cause or consequence of community but that it followed from it. Enriched by loyalty to community, which in other terms is commitment to the idea of humanity, individuality is comprehended through universality. The enrichment of individuality in universality removes it from arbitrariness and incoherency. In universality individuality brings the peculiarity and uniqueness of its being to the service of mankind. In the struggle against violence individuality finds its firmest strength in universality. Belief in the beloved community makes it possible to pursue with courage the idea, the nontemporal, nonspatial representation of the idea. In refusing to accept individuality and the relativism of its immediate engagement without universal commitment we reduce man's activity to the uncontrollable character of sense perceptions, to the imaginative absolute of conceptualization freed from the "transcendent" power of the idea. The imaginative flight of conceptualization and the chameleon-like quality of perception are limited by the idea of loyalty and responsibility to the ideal community and its inherent demand for universality.

We should take note of Royce's title, *The Problem of Christianity*, because he asked that this problem be appreciated, investigated, and interpreted seriously. He believed that we are considering "an intensely interesting, life-problem of humanity." He held that such life problems involve "human destiny" and that they require committed philosophical interpretation. This is not a problem of significance, but one of truth. We are concerned not only with the relationship of the individual to the universal but of the universal to both the particular and the individual. The problem is perennial, and when we reflect on the thoughts of Royce we are immediately made aware that the problem was his as a philosopher and is ours in our involvement with philosophy. Royce had always believed that human history was its education. If Christianity has a doctrine that is essential to this education, then it belongs to every age to interpret it. Royce interpreted this doctrine to be "that the human race, taken as a whole, has some genuine and significant spiritual unity, so that its life is no mere flow and strife of opinions, but includes a growth in genuine insight."[7] The problem of Christianity as a living spiritual doctrine is inseparable from the thinking of any being for whom spiritual unity is meaningful. Spiritual unity is the irresistible hypothesis of Royce's writings, because in it he comprehended the essence of philosophical thinking. Fortunately Royce rejected a double truth. Theology and philosophy did not have distinct paths. They paralleled each other with shared serious experiences.

Royce made it clear in the early lectures that his purpose was not a history or a dogmatic discussion of the early church, but an interpretation of the meaning and the truth of three Christian ideas: salvation, the moral burden of the individual, and atonement for sin and guilt. These ideas

should not cause the philosopher to flee because he believes that they belong
to the theologian. He should follow Royce in his discussions to find out why
these ideas are truly philosophical. Royce would ask three questions:
"What is the foundation of this idea? What does it mean? In essence is it a
true idea?"[8] The questions imply that Royce had accepted the reality of
Christianity as expressed both by its founder and by its expositor, Paul.
What we are concerned with is how these ideas can be formulated by reason. They cannot be explained if we mean by explanation a final delinea-
tion. They can be interpreted and comprehended as truths of the human
spirit.

The first idea, that is, salvation, points in the direction of the relationship between the individual and the spiritual community. The second shows
that "of himself and apart from the spiritual community . . . the individual
is powerless to escape from his innate and acquired character, the character
of a lost soul."[9] The third idea, atonement, is the one that Royce thought
would be most difficult for modern man to comprehend, let alone accept.
This idea, he said, is expressed in the statement: "The only escape for the
individual, the only union with the divine spiritual community which he can
obtain, is provided by the divine plan for the redemption of mankind."[10]
These three ideas form a unity in their diversity. No idea can be conceived
without the other. Salvation is dependent on atonement and neither is possible without the moral awareness and will of the individual. The individual, however, belongs from the beginning to the community, in which he
finds salvation, the purpose of his existence. The moral responsibility is
equally inseparable from man's need for atonement, which is related to God
and to the kingdom of heaven. Man's moral burden is his confrontation with
sin and guilt, the realization of his lack of autonomy and his deep dependence on God's grace. This divine dependence is the source of Royce's theistic metaphysics, his unique contribution to a scheme of salvation that
involves "the origin and fate of the whole cosmos." As a theistic meta-
physician Royce weaves these three ideas into an eschatology unique in its
scope and depth. He joined the achievements of Western metaphysics and
Christian eschatology in the cosmic idea of community.

Again and again we read the words *church* and *community*, but there
are difficulties only when we seek precise definitions. In fact, we should
avoid the desire to nail down the terms and be more apt to comprehend fi-
guratively. Royce offered descriptions that defied definition and he was correct. We are dealing with ideas and not with concepts. Concepts do not
necessarily grasp configurations and metaphorical possibilities that lie in
ideas. The true church, Royce was willing to say, "is still a sort of ideal
challenge to the faithful, rather than an already finished institution,—a call
upon men for a heavenly quest rather than a present possession of humanity.

'Create me,'—this is the word that the Church, perceived as an idea, addresses to mankind.''[11] Together with the idea of church as the ideal challenge Royce made a remarkable observation when he stated that the church "is, in a real sense, still to be founded, or rather, to be created.''[12] We have not as yet evolved to an approximation of the idea of community, to the idea of humanity, to the realization that the moral task and purpose of mankind is only just beginning and is to be comprehended as the struggle against violence. We remain in agreement with Royce that "what humanity most needs, it most persistently misunderstands.''[13] The work of philosophy is in the commitment to the idea, to that transcendent vision around which our perceptions and concepts find their purpose and limits.

Royce developed the significance of the future as the source for the hope of humanity; he made it quite clear that his vision of community belongs to a cosmic process in whose center "our planet does not stand, and in whose ages our brief human lives play a part as transient, relatively speaking, as is, for our own eyes, the flickering of the northern lights.''[14] The idea of community and man's salvation belongs to the realization that we are part of an evolutionary process whose reality is in the indefinable future but dependent on our continuous understanding and interpretation. Loyalty to community is the persistent force that brings the idea of community into sharper realization and clarification. The idea is never concrete or given in the concept. It is a vision that is real in every form that is created in loyalty. Reality is not concretization. Where men desire to embody the *true* church, there they deny it. We pay dearly for this misunderstanding. Those who institutionalize man's spiritual revolutions prepare for their degeneration and negation. The idea of community is the principle of hope that drives man beyond the immediate. In its vision man refuses to concretize divinity. The purity of Western monotheism is its negation of idolatry; it is the eternal negation to man's material existence, the challenge the future gives to the past and the present. In man's rational ideal we discover the power in and through which man has changed the course of his individual and societal life.

If community is comprehended through the idea, then loyalty can be described as "active devotion to the community to which the devoted individual belongs.''[15] This devotion must create a new life. It lifts man beyond his individuality; it makes him aware that he is part of a cosmic process to which his loyalty makes a moral contribution. He lives with new visions of purpose and hope. He is fascinated by the demand of the idea. There is in it both the beautiful and the sublime. Royce stated that the community can be for the individual both beautiful and sublime. It can be beautiful because he has discovered what his fellow-man forgot: loyalty, the way to universality. He finds the moral fortitude and strength to subject the demands of immediacy to those of universality. In sublimity he finds the majesty of the idea that only his rational imagination can attempt to formulate. The idea of humanity affects him as sublime in its majesty, as the beautiful is the moral ideal that challenges his individual life. In the beautiful as the moral ideal he finds kinship with those who he knows find in the loyal spirit ways to approach the ideal of the universal community. "To this community, in ideal," Royce believed, all men belong; "and to act as if one were a member of such a community is to win in the highest measure the goal of individual life. It is to win what religion calls salvation."[16] If we assume that the loyal motives are both aesthetic and moral we understand that salvation is not only a moral effort, but also an aesthetic one. Beauty and sublimity accompany the idea as natural expressions of its universality.

Although Royce seemed particularly devoted to the epistles of Paul, he was, nevertheless, not unaware that the history of Israel was a unique community brought into existence through God's promise and covenant. Royce remarked that "the history of the ideals and of the religion of Israel, from the Song of Deborah to the prophets, is a classic instance of the process here in question."[17] The process in question always implied man's continuous interpretation of the meaning of universal loyalty, the unity of the ideal community as a form to which every morally conscious man felt a responsibility in membership. This sense of belonging, through election to the beloved community, lies at the foundation of Israel's experience. It was a tribal experience, but reached out to mankind in its prophetic utterances and reached a new and unique universalism in Paul's vision of the overcoming of both pagan and Jew in the vision of the universal church. This vision Paul knew came forth from the spirit of the risen and ascended God in whom all men are equal and loved. The universal community is not man's creation; it is his perennial discovery. Man reaches the fullness of his being in his loyalty to the idea and membership in community. In fact, what man is, is revealed to him through this loyalty of membership, through the hope that is the community, as is the promise of the redeemed Israel. Man's redemption is not in the economic, political, or social realms; it lies in the transcendent power of the idea. "Serene faith" in the idea expresses man's negation of violence and his struggle for the truth of rational coherency.

As we read Royce's reflections on Paul's unique and peculiar understanding of religious truth we know that we are, at the same time, comprehending Royce's own grasp of philosophic truth. The love for the idea can be as deeply pursued as that for the individual. Royce commented on this when he brought forth what he considered to be the Apostle's most significant discovery: "the truth that a community, when unified by an active indwelling purpose, is an entity, more concrete and, in fact, less mysterious than is any individual man, and that such a community can love and be loved as a husband and wife love; or a father or mother love."[18] This is a peculiar truth because even in the love that remains empirical it is the idea that is embodied in it that evokes our love. What comes forth as the permanent or the essential is what is truly loved and surpasses infatuation or desire. The attachment to the idea is inviolable when in love we are permeated by its truth. The idea grows in intensity as we comprehend its universality and the meaning of its saving grace. When we distance ourselves from the immediacy of the concrete and its incoherency, the ideas emerge as the constant and uncompromisable vision. It is that higher law of divine revelation that indwells in man and community whose loyalty has abandoned the immediate for the universal. Loyalty has consumed love and driven it toward the universal community that embraces all who are devoted to the spirit, to that force of reason that elevates us into a community of thinking, that is, of interpreting. Religion transforms the multiplicity of human communities into a divinely ordained one. This work of transformation is religion's profoundest achievement. With this transformation religion speaks of salvation.

Royce's introduction to the second idea of Christianity, the moral burden of the individual, was expressed in these terms: "The individual human being is by nature subject to some overwhelming moral burden from which, if unaided, he cannot escape. But because of what has technically been called original sin, and because of the sins that he himself has committed, the individual is doomed to a spiritual ruin from which only a divine intervention can save him."[19] From the truth of salvation that linked the individual to the community and the universal there emerged the conceptual dialectic of individual and universal without an indication of the meaning of individuality as both individual and particular. The moral burden of the individual is meaningful from the perspective of the universal that Royce had established with the idea of salvation. From this perspective the individual attempts to comprehend the meaning of his moral burden. Whether he is capable of bearing it as an autonomous being or one who is dependent on the divine is determined. The individual needs to discover the legitimacy of his individuality and he must ask if this legitimacy is not realized in its negation, that is, in the particularity of community and then in universality. The movement—from individuality to community—is one of conflict. Royce saw this conflict as the struggle between individual expression and the "vast organizations of collective powers." Those organizations or bureaucracies are the consequence of man's collective efforts. The inequalities and divisions of power are the results of his "wars" and conquests. They are the fruits of his needs, to which he returns with an ideological idealism to justify the necessary foundation for their protection and perpetuation. Man's moral burden is inseparable from his sin. This sin knows neither worker nor capitalist, conqueror nor conquered, exploiter nor exploited.

Royce turns to a profound biblical question to sum up the pain of man's burden: "Ye shall be as gods." His comments allow us to clearly see how deeply he was opposed to an individualism that knows no mediation. He said: "This is the love of all individualism, and the vice of all our worldly social ambitions. The resulting diseases of self-consciousness are due to the inmost nature of our social race. They belong to its very essence as a social race. They increase with cultivation. The individual cannot escape from the results of them through any deeds of his own."[20] The assumption that Royce makes about man's moral burden, his conflicts with society's bureaucratic powers, the struggle with violence that is the common quality of national and international life, left him not with particular communities, but with the ideal of community as the hope and source of salvation. This hope is dependent on loyalty, and Royce claimed that it "involves an essentially new type of self-consciousness—the consciousness of one who loves a community as a person. Not social training, but the miracle of this love, creates the new type of self-consciousness."[21] Loyalty again comes forth as the fundamental self-consciousness that stands steadfast and persistently against the perpetual warfare that is endemic to human society. Together with the love of community, what we call the struggle for coherent discourse, is the demand of universality as the bulwark against immediacy and self-indulgence, against violence. It refuses the reasonable and the rational discourse and prefers the incoherent and the incommunicable. The ideal of community was always another expression of the idea of humanity that necessarily accepted conflict, but needed to comprehend the coherency of its negation.

What makes it possible to decide for the reasonable, to go beyond the exaggerated and disruptive individualism into which we are naturally born? What makes it possible to ward off the serpent's promise that we shall be like the gods? Nothing seems more enticing than to act and command like gods. Royce used the term *grace*. He spoke of the realm of grace. Is it no longer dependent upon our action and endeavor? Is our moral burden, our sin, to be lifted, at least minutely, only by an irresistible grace? With ease and lambency Royce described the beloved community. "The beloved community embodies, for its lover, *values* which no human individual, viewed as a detached being, could even remotely approach. And in a corresponding way, the love which inspires the loyal soul has been transformed; and is not such as could be given to a detached human individual."[22] The love that attracts the loyal soul, the receptivity he must have for it, is not dependent on his will. The will can long for this love but its reception, the possibility of its embodiment, is the act of grace. Can we explain this force that opens us to this love? Perhaps not if we mean by explanation the possibility of a fixed formula that now can be repeated and provides the necessary label to satisfy our need for precise limitations and explanations. The grace is a *fact,* a fact of reason that we accept and from which we begin. It is the beginning and from it everything else proceeds. Grace is not to be explained, for then it would not be grace; it is accepted.

For man there is no escape from the Pauline conflict between what man wants to do and what he does, between his struggle for power and social influence and his concern for his fellow man. How does man come to terms with his love of individual power and his political and social responsibility? What training or new societal form could overcome this conflict, and if it could be overcome, from where would the power come? Royce referred us to divine grace. Could we remain within the conflict, struggle with the forces that exist, and believe that commitment and opposition do not make a difference? If they do not, our action must necessarily be as if they did. Royce left us with a possible dualism: the realm of grace and the realm of sin. This is a dualism that is transformed into the profoundest conflict of human existence: the challenge of the *ought to be* to what *is.* Royce had already mentioned that the universal community remains the challenge of the future. Loyalty to the idea is the individual's love of a community in which he has embodied what is good, beautiful, and true. The community is lovable because in it the individual has gathered all that is valued and is precious. In relation to this community the individual is educated to the love of humanity and optimism. Since community is both a moral and an aesthetic idea, the education of mankind in goodness and beauty is governed by this ideal of the beloved community. The community is an object of knowledge and beauty because it remains the ideal of coherency and interpretation, never bound completely to conceptualization or to perception, but naturally driven beyond both by the transcendent power of the idea. The idea remains always beyond perception as well as it stands forcefully in defiance of conceptualization.

The love that we have for this community of interpretation is hardly our autonomous choice. From Royce's perspective, "We cannot choose to fall thus in love. Only when once thus in love can we choose to remain lovers."[23] How we come to love this community remains inexplicable. Royce continued his discourse of the beloved community with a reference to Paul:

> The creation of the truly lovable community, and the awakening of the highly trained individual to true love for that community, are, to Paul's mind, a spiritual triumph beyond the wit of man to

devise, and beyond the power of man to accomplish. That which actually accomplishes these triumphs is what Paul means by the divine grace.[24]

If we are committed to reducing the divine human intercourse to explicable schemes, then we are forced to look on Royce's observations as inadequate. From the perspective of those for whom empirical verification is the sole source of truth, there is little to be said in Royce's defense. What Paul and Royce are referring to goes beyond such verification. We speak here of a truth whose significance can be explored only within its dimension of speculative thought. The consequences show the form in which we can comprehend the truth of the idea. For us the beloved community is more than a category; it is the form to which all the others are related and from which they are comprehended. The beloved community is an eternal verity and our speculative consideration of it depends upon our capacity to grasp it as a reality that is always more than itself. In other words, the form or idea of the beloved community is the primal foundation or beginning of reasonable and rational thought. It is the philosophical idea per se. Our continuing interpretation of this idea is possible to the degree that our comprehension is capable of going beyond each point of arrival. What determines this is what we call grace. Grace *is;* we are left with this *fact* because we cannot explain the mystery of mediation. Grace is mediation.

If we explain what we have hinted at philosophically with religious terms we would say with Royce that the master "both knew and loved his community before it existed on earth; for his foreknowledge was one with that of the God whose will he came to accomplish. On earth he called into this community its first members. . . . *He is now identical with the spirit of this community.*"[25] This identity is truly Abrahamic. From the community that grew from Abraham, man's relationship to God assumed the form of a covenant of faith. The radical departure of Abraham from the land of his father and the discovery in and from him of the *communal* relationship between God and his people was the revolutionary contribution of biblical thought. God relates to man not through the individual but through the community. In community man becomes aware of his metaphysical and moral responsibility. Man, in relating to God through community, discovers in the immediacy of his individuality both his uniqueness and the source of its depravation. His individuality is there to be overcome. It is the foundation of the community. It elevates itself to negation of self and discovers in the negation the idea of community. It discovers the community that already was existent in individuality as the negation, but had not achieved self-consciousness. In community individuality is reconciled to its negation. Royce makes the problem simpler. He states that "man, the social being, naturally and in one sense helplessly, depends on his communities. Sundered from them, he has neither worth nor wit, but wanders in waste places, and when he returns, finds the lonely house of his individual life empty, swept, and garnished.''[26] If the faith of Abraham became that of Israel, and in that faith reached its sublime moment, then it is because in this community of faith man discovered the living God. He found in the spirit of the community the deepest expression of mediation and salvation. In community he loses the autonomy of his individuality, but in so doing he gains a higher individuality in relation to God and the other members of the community.

Royce was certain that the identity of divinity and community was the deepest and most enlightening mystery of religious insight and achievement. In this he found the truth of philosophy, the pervading spirit of reason that linked mind to mind in a sacred discourse within the beloved community. Here the divine and the human touched in dialogue and man knew that his destiny was bound neither to perception nor to conceptualization, but that he had a cosmic destiny that tied him to the ideal and the idea. Man discovered in this destiny his fidelity to the transcendent, to the Absolute. Man realized that his human destiny was inseparable from the divine purpose and that the division between the world of God and man's loyalty was imaginative. In man's fidelity to the ideal of the beloved community man rediscovered his primordial belonging to the community from which he fell and which the religious and philosophical life made it possible for him to rejoin. Royce made this clear when he remarked that

> the union of the concrete and the ineffable which hereupon resulted,—the union of what touches the human heart and stirs the soul as only the voice of a living individual leader can touch it— the complete union of this with the greater and most inspiring of human mysteries—the mystery of loving membership in a community whose meaning seems divine—this union became the central interest of Christianity.[27]

Man's membership in this community is the burden of his moral and spiritual life. Royce moved from one description to another of community. He knew that this is the "perennial stone" that is borne in religious commitment and philosophical faith: the eternity of the task and the beautiful pain of the never-ending burden.

Thought, we believe, proceeds from the ideal, from fidelity to the ideal. Thought responds to the force and permanency of the unmoved mover to the receptivity and pervasive activity of the vision of the ideal. We can comprehend what it means to think when we grasp thinking as responding. Thinking begins in response to a purpose, an ideal or an idea. The unmoved mover indicates clearly the *fact* that when we know that truth exists we are necessitated to respond to it. Truth *is* the beginning of philosophical thought. Royce elaborated on this idea by affirming that

> one must regard one's self as a creature with a purpose in living. One must have what they call a "mission" in one's own world. And so, whether one uses philosophical theories or religious beliefs, or does not use them, one must, when one speaks thus, actually have some sort of spiritual realm in which, as one believes, one's moral life is lived, a realm to whose *total* order, as one supposes, one could be false if one chose [and] to view certain at least abstractly possible deeds as moral catastrophes, as creators of chaos, as deeds whereby the self, *if* it choose them, would, at least in so far, banish itself from its own country.[28]

These moral catastrophes bring with them the violence that accompanies every attempt to crush truth and freedom, to destroy the right to moral responsibility and need for critical decision. The violence that myth, ideology, and the corruption of coherent, reasonable discourse brings forth is the chaos of communication that we find in violence as terror. This chaos, however, can be rationally expressed.

Royce was certain and clear in his comprehension of philosophy as fidelity to the ideal, as faith in reason, as commitment to the perennial task of interpretation. Philosophy is the devotion to interpretation because it knows that the world is comprehensible, even if it is not, at the same time, always knowable. The world is meaningful and is, therefore, interpretable. Were the world not meaningful, the work of interpretation would end. In a meaningful world even what is not immediately comprehensible is comprehended as the *yet to be* discovered and possibly known. Royce spoke of a "mission"; we would speak of trust in the idea of humanity, of the struggle of critical thought to overcome violence. Violence is the betrayal of thinking, as it is the renunciation of moral responsibility and community. Violence is the refusal of coherent discourse; it is the acceptance of the language of command, of incoherency and contradiction. Disloyalty to the universal ideal of life is loyalty to its destruction. This loyalty is as forceful as that of its counterpart. We have come to understand that there can be a loyalty to chaos and it can be the consequence of a free, reasonable act. The moral struggle is against the willful acceptance of loyalty to moral catastrophe. Man can choose to be destructive. Royce proclaimed that we should choose our cause and our moral ideal. "What I point out," he said, "is that to so choose is to imply your power to define what, for you, would be the unpardonable sin if you committed it."[29] There is only an "unpardonable sin'' if there is moral awareness. Where there is no such awareness, loyalty or disloyalty means adherence to unquestionable myths whose purpose is the elimination of universal discourse. Whether we call it loyalty or disloyalty, the conflict between moral coherent discourse and the violence that emerges from its refusal remains the characteristic human struggle to realize the universal community.

Man's moral burden is in the awareness that he is capable of being morally indifferent and negative. He is equally capable of being morally committed and forceful. Man the moral traitor had been the natural condition of his being long before Paul formulated this natural treachery. Royce elucidated two conditions of the traitor. He said that ''the first condition is that a traitor is a man who has had an ideal, and who has lived it with all his heart and his soul and his mind and his strength. His ideal must have seemed to him to furnish the cause of his life.'' The second condition would be that ''having thus found his cause, he must, as he now knows, in at least some one voluntary act of his life have been deliberately false to his cause.''[30] We comprehend the traitor because the act of betrayal takes place within the moral dimension. A cause or an ideal can be a tool that is used for self-gratification or for the arbitrary justification of the violent or terroristic act. There is a level of human action where the betrayal would loose its moral significance. There is no betrayal where there is no recognition of the moral act. With the recognition of this refusal philosophy ceases to speak. Here philosophy turns to silence and awaits the destruction of the irrevocable enemy. Betrayal within the moral dimension remains an irreconcilable crime for which there is no atonement. Atonement never erases the act; it elevates it to a deepened moral awareness of inherent evil and the reality of its repetition.

Royce asked the fundamental question about the irreconcilable nature of the immoral act. This problem faces us whenever we turn toward the conflicts of contemporary society. How do we comprehend within the moral discourse the immoral act, the act that tears apart the moral conventions, the act that dehumanizes not the individual alone, but human society? The problem is always the same: How do we think about evil, the holocaust, or does thinking surrender before such events?

Are we left only with feelings and the despair that accompanies a language that is rational and, therefore, falls silent before the nonrational? Royce posed his question differently. He asked: ''Must not the existence of the traitor remain, for the offended community, an evil that is as intolerable and irrevocable and as much beyond its powers of reconciliation as is, for the traitor himself, his own past deed, seen in all the light of its treachery?''[31] The community knows the single unredeemable fact: The evil done cannot be undone. It must be remembered, interpreted and contemplated.

It belongs to human history and as such, is indelible. The human community is the consequence of the evil done as well as the goodness achieved. Without this evil there would be no human community. The evil shatters the community, but awakens it to a deeper and more serious responsibility of its fragility and self-destructiveness. The violence and terror of evil must awaken the atoning power of reason and love. The community, if it is not to perish, must bring forth from itself the capacity to bring evil within the power of the comprehension even if it remains beyond explanation. This power is forged within the unconquerable depths of man's reason whose strength, we believe, withstands those forces of violence against which man wages the eternal struggle for salvation.

Atonement is that power of reason to overcome treason and violence. The overcoming is possible because atonement bears within itself the forces of its negation and it is from these forces that it creates the power to surpass them. Royce remarked that "this triumph [over treason] can only be accomplished by the community, or on behalf of the community, through some steadfastly loyal servant who acts, so to speak, as the incarnation of the very spirit of the community."[32] If we leave aside the personal metaphor, we comprehend the meaning of community as the pervasive discourse of reason that derives its movement from its negation. Royce had developed an eschatology in which philosophy and theology meet in the idea of community. In this idea we embody our hope. We refuse to surrender the vision of utopian thinking. Everything that plagues us politically and socially would mitigate against such visions as illusory and light-minded. This idea, however, is formed in courage and faith and is more creative when negated by empirical reality than if that reality would be conducive to its advancement. Utopian thinking is the "creative deed." Royce would formulate the problem so that we would recognize this deed as the essence of the philosophical act and imagination. Royce said that "*the world, as transformed by this creative deed, is better than it would have been had all else remained the same, but had that deed of treason not been done at all.* That is, the new creative deed has made the new world better than it was before the blow of treason fell."[33] The optimism that fills these words is that of reason, the philosophic faith in the idea of humanity. Pessimism in relationship to reason is antiphilosophical. The greatness of the philosophical thinking is that it reflects on the refusal of thinking to be limited by pessimism that is in the limits of perception or conceptualization. The education of mankind to optimism is in the fidelity to the idea.

Royce was profoundly optimistic simply because he took evil seriously. He is the philosopher of the triumph, the great believer in the ultimate dominance of the spirit of the rational community. In his will to believe he created a philosophical vision that has become the eyes of a humanity struggling to find a utopian thinking capable of lifting it beyond the violence and fatalism of every-day existence. The incarnation of this vision was for Royce in the work of Christ, in the personification of Israel's sacred history. Royce could write that the "atoning work of Christ was for Christian feeling a deed that was made possible only through man's sin, but that somehow was so wise and so rich and so beautiful and divinely fair that, after this work was done, the world was a better world than it would have been had *man* never sinned."[34] In the world without sin man would be in need of neither philosophy nor theology. In the world of sin there could be beauty and sublimity. In this world the beauty of its form and the sublimity of its creative power allows man to find in the work of mediation that divine light which awakens us to our divine partnership and to the traces of God that are expressed in our reason. The mediating power of human reason is the peculiar and unique realization of atonement. This atonement belongs to those distinct human actions that link the human to the divine. We can speak of the tragedy of reason because we know that we can be disloyal to its meaning and defy its command. This command is in the words of Royce: *"No baseness or cruelty of treason so deep or so tragic shall enter our human world, but that loyal love shall be able in due time to oppose to just that deed of treason its fitting deed of atonement."*[35] The dualism of a world of sin and grace is mediated in the act of reason as it is given in divine love. What is love in God is transformed into human deed. In man's rational and reasonable action he finds that path which shows him that perception can never be conceptualized and that conceptualization finds its inadequacy in response to the vision of the idea and its perennial transcendence of the concept: Mediation is the interpreter of human reality as it looses its demand for definition and explanation.

Royce at times liked to interpret biblical parables and parabolic stories. In particular he dealt with the parable of the Prodigal Son and that of Joseph and his brothers. Why does the father rejoice at the return of a son who had left his home to squander his inheritance and return again destitute to his father's home? "The Father," Royce exclaimed, "had won again, not merely his son as a hungry creature who can repent and be fed. The Father has won again the unbroken community of his family. It is the Father's house that rejoices. It is this community which makes merry; and the father is, for the moment, simply the incarnation of the spirit of this community."[36] We appreciate this interpretation when we bear in mind the alienated world of the father-son relationship in Kafka's parables and stories, and famous letter to his father. From this alienation grew a literature, a discourse of reflection on alienation and community in family and society. Man's alienation is his natural condition. His belief and fidelity to community are the sources of his universality. The movement from one to the other exemplifies human history. One without the other is degradation and illusion. Neither is valid alone. In the movement from the one to the other we find that sacred mediation which fulfills man's reason and holds aside the violence of his individuality and the uncontrolled imagination of its illusions.

In the Joseph story Royce found a similar insight. The brothers sell Joseph into slavery from a sense of jealousy. They bring pain to the father, whose love for Joseph was unique in its intensity. The action is treason against the family. Joseph, in the end, forgives his brothers, comforts his father, and reestablishes the unity of the family. What is the atoning work? Royce asked the following question: "Would the mere repentance, or the renewed love of the treacherous brothers for Joseph, or their wish to be forgiven, or their confession of their sin, constitute a sufficient ground for the needed reconciliation in view of their offense against their brother, their father, or their family? If this was all the atonement which Joseph's labors supplied, he failed in his supposed office. Something more is needed to satisfy even the child who enjoys the story."[37] Royce believed that atonement must transform what is evil into what is good not only for the individual or family but for the world. The atoning deed has transfiguring power; it drives the individual act into a universal content. The individual act in its sinfulness cuts man off from the community; the individual is reduced to the privacy of isolation, to that terror which shuts the man off from the community and dehumanizes his person. The work of atonement is the reestablishment of the universal, the opening of the individual to that pervasive spirituality which man shares as a member of the community. The divine dwells in community, in the movement that leads from the privacy of individuality to the universality of community. In community the social and economic differences that separate people from each other are put aside. In man's search for the *imago Dei* he finds that the distinctions are in the realization that each being has his own communal belonging. Man's alienation from this reality is that of a being lost to membership in humanity and to his responsibility for its widening embodiment.

Royce offered a few summary statements that make it possible for us to look back to the beginnings and ask whether the metaphysical idea of community has descended from the vagaries of abstraction to being that mediating power in which man discovers his unique task: the overcoming of his estrangement from his spiritual destiny. Royce made it clear that

> as individuals we are lost; that is, are incapable of attaining the true goal of life. This our loss is due to the fact that we have not loved. So the Master taught. But the problem is also this: For what love shall we seek? What love will save us? Here we restrict our

answer to human objects, and deliberately avoid theology. The Christian answer is: Love the community. That is, be loyal.[38]

These words must be transcribed into ideational form. Philosophy is a pro-creation in beauty. Its motive power is love. Its love is in that mediating power in and through which individuality and universality develop into mutual realities of each other. The truth of individuality is in universality and that of universality in that of individuality. The love of community is the love of the ideal and, at the same time, the realization that the ideal was and is both present and future. The ideal is present in our love and action; it determines our loyalty. The future expresses our hope that what we love as ideal will be transfigured into reality. In the present the community demands our fidelity and as the highest expression of our reason it commands our moral responsibility and action. In community we stand together with those for whom the idea of humanity was worth more than their physical lives. The will to freedom and truth is loyalty to the universal. Freedom forces us to refuse the absolute claim of conceptualization, to go beyond the technical man, to refuse the estrangement of the spirit from the idea.

If again we interpret the Christian doctrine of life we should say: "Let the spirit triumph. Let no evil deed be done so deep in its treachery but that creative love shall find the way to make the world better than it would have been had the evil deed not been done."[39] This supreme confidence in the power of man's spirit to overcome evil is the most sublime moment in Royce's thought. There is no autonomous evil power, no fate, no unre-deemable act, and no pessimism. We live not only in defiance of evil but with a fidelity to reason that is capable of comprehending evil and denying to it the possibility of creating for itself an autonomous realm. The verifi-ability of such a reason is the history of philosophy, the clear refusal of reason to yield or cede to evil or ignorance the right to be more than the momentary depravation of man or a temporary stumbling block in the ad-vancement of knowledge. There *is* only goodness and truth. Making such a statement seems to be folly, but can we philosophically make any other? Empirically the contrary is a deeper reflection of the immediate reality in which we live. The fidelity to goodness and truth is naive and incompre-hensible from the empirical perspective, but this perspective is momentary and in its limitation there is a justifiable vision. There is the philosophical that speaks the truth of the ideal and the universal. The truth does not swing above the perceptible world and refuses to relate to it, but it stands before it as the challenge to its attempted demonic absolutism. It forces upon it limitation and negation. As the transcendent power of the idea, the work of the community of reason is to limit both the unlimited claims of perception and conceptualization. In forcing on them the necessary limitation of their

views, the idea of the community establishes the unique function of the idea
to be the perennial belief in freedom as the deepest expression of the divine-
human mediation. In the words *freedom* and *truth* man discovers the *imago
Dei;* he finds in it the source of his will to seek reality beyond the given.

Although the idea of community is transcendent and is for man a moral
and metaphysical imperative, it is the most deeply felt human reality. Man's
deepest love is the idea; man's deepest infatuation, his material existence.
As the beloved community, the idea is more closely related to man's rational actuality than are the immediacies of his daily life. In our daily existence there are the temptations of compromise and the multiple conditions
for decisions. The loyalty to the community is absolute in its form. It is,
however, an experiential reality. Man's loyalty to the spirit of science is
identical to his belief in the loyalty "to the common insight and to the
growth of knowledge. . . . For the scientific spirit is indeed one of the noblest and purest forms of loyalty."[40] The fact that the idea of community is
the metaphysical foundation of the scientific spirit is another form of
expression that describes the nature of the ideal community. In and through
this foundation the history of thought remains bound to the *Xynon,* the common tie that creates *the* community of coherent discourse. From this primordial form of rational discourse Royce rejected the *idiotes,* the private
man. The individual mystical experience gave to his thinking the deepest
separation from the "original philosophical experience." Philosophy is
cosmic; it thinks "the origin and fate of the whole cosmos." In the cosmic
nature of thinking the individual lost his centricity. We are only brief moments in the ages of the cosmos and "our brief human lives play a part as
brief as transient, relatively speaking, as is, for our own eyes, the flickering
of the northern lights."[41] Need we ask for more to make our contributions?
Would we achieve more if we had remained the "love child" of the cosmos?

Often Royce returned to the opposition between the individual and the
community. He said that "our ethical pluralism makes us proudly declare,
each for himself, 'my deed is my own.' But, our collective life often seems
to advise us to say not 'I act thus' but, 'Thus the community acts in and
through me.' "[42] Abstractly this opposition leads to a conceptual definition
in and through which we reach deeper into the individual, and use higher
levels of abstraction in the conceptual description of community. Through
this growing separability we lose the meaning of both the individual and the
community. In fact, the existential reality of both disappears. Community
is the collective memory of the creative action of individuals. In the collective sense of time the individual comprehends communal historical responsibility, the task that is given in the idea of humanity. In the movement
of time from past to present and to future there develops that broadening

interpenetration of individual and collective responsibility to time, to self, and to community. This collective responsibility built and structured in the history of man's great deeds is recognized in the past as man's civic activity; in the present, as his national and universal obligation; and in the future, as the ideal of the interpretative community, from which the community of mankind stands forth as the challenge to man's loyalty and fidelity. With this ideal man does not overcome violence but faces it on a deeper and far more threatening level.

The idea of community serves the imagination and brings forth from it new terms. We could speak of the "community of memory," and Royce defined it as "constituted by the fact that each of its members accepts, as part of his own individual life and self, the same *past* events that each of his fellow-members accepts."[43] Memory is, however, more than a collective consciousness; it is the recognition that thought is the continuous re-taking and reinterpretation of past categories forcing them to take new directions and to express in different ways perspectives that had been developed in the past, but whose attitudes have not yet been realized. The development of new perspectives takes place within and in opposition to former ones. What we consider to be new is a perspective in opposition to the one that had previously dominated our attempt to comprehend human existence. Memory is the recall of the discourse of categories that man developed to interpret his existence. This discourse founds the community of memory. It preserved the history of the human spirit through which man wrote his autobiography. In this man discovers what it means to think, to grasp, the rational quality of the coherent discourse of categories, to comprehend himself as a being for whom past, present, and future are moments in that beloved community through which his rationality and reasonableness are revealed in discourse.

With clear descriptions of community and self Royce made it possible to clarify more precisely the relationship between self and community. "The first condition upon which the existence of a community, in our sense of the word, depends," he wrote, "is the power of an individual self to extend his life, in ideal fashion, so as to regard it as including past and future events which lie far away in time, and which he does not now personally remember. That this power exists, and that man has a self which is thus ideally extensible in time without any definite limit, we all know."[44] The self, unified by a dominant purpose to which it remains faithful, is a history that embraces time from past to future, that expresses itself in categories, that is formed in the idea, and that is determined through the will to action. The self is community and in this community the self finds its primal condition. This community is created in reason, which every thinking man shares and desires to communicate. The community is never an arbitrary collection of selves. Community is the primal truth of human moral, aesthetic, and intellectual life. Man does not create community; he is created in it. This is man's most painful and sublime discovery. Truth is not his creation, but his discovery. Man must bring into himself what he does not possess but can receive. He can receive only what belongs to his being and must be awakened by a reality that is beyond him but, at the same time, related to him, estranged from him, but not too strange to him. The community is man's extended body and soul. His moral and intellectual life are the inevitable search to find in them a place for his wandering life. All life is a path to the primordial truth of community because only in this community does man find "a love which passes the love wherewith individuals can love one another."[45]

What is significant and unique in Royce's approach to the idea of community is the fact that it is more than the continuous discourse of the mind, but it has a personal and intimate moment that makes it more satisfying than an intellectual experience. Royce remarked that

> the individual coworker not only says: This past and future fortune of the community belong to my life; but also declares: This past and future deed of cooperation belongs to my life. This which none of us could have done alone—this, which all of us together could not have accomplished unless we were ordered and linked in precisely this way,—this we together accomplished, or shall yet accomplish; and this deed of all of us belongs to my life.[46]

This description is vitally important because it goes beyond the phenomenological description into the existential. It speaks of the meaning that community has for present man, how it evokes his feelings of belonging and the satisfaction of needs. It provokes the intimate affection that man has for his spiritual destiny and how this affection is not a passing infatuation, but a pleasure that fulfills the aesthetic and moral need of his being. Man is a being of spiritual needs and the pleasure that satisfies them evokes in him a sense of aesthetic destiny and distinctness. Here we can again speak of the aesthetic dimension, the distinctive pleasure that is derived from that harmony between individuality and universality, a pleasure that emerges as man grasps that tie between his being and that of mankind. Royce knew there was no formula nor a particular way that man knows to find that atonement which lies between the individual and universal. Using the term *love* to express man's longing for community, Royce observed that this "love may be mystical, and work should be directed by clearly outlined intelligence; but the loyal spirit depends upon this union of a longing for unity with a will which needs its own expression of loyal act."[47] The love we develop for the community brings the community into ourselves. In this love we join the community. In it the community is joined to us.

Royce had reached the point that enabled him to answer the question, What is philosophy? He replied with an answering question: "What, however, is any philosophy but an interpretation either of life, or of the universe, or of both? . . . To inquire what the process of interpretation is, takes us at once to the very heart of philosophy, throws a light both on the oldest and on the latest issues of metaphysical thought."[48] Simply stated, Royce would affirm that the main concern of philosophy is interpretation. Philosophy is never perception alone, it can never be satisfied by conceptualization, it peculiarly belongs to the activity of interpretation. Philosophy is the comprehension of the nature and knowledge of the self as it emerges in the perception, conception, interpretation triad. In perception life is reduced to the immediacy of experience; in conceptualization the false assumption is made that this immediacy can be conceptualized. Neither position is valid in the absoluteness of its claim. Both perception and conceptualization are relative sources of knowledge to which the question of meaning and transcendence must always be added. Interpretation is the question of meaning; it is similarly the question of nonmeaning. Refusing to embody the human experience in either perception or conceptualization, we affirm that interpretation touches more deeply the quality of human life than any other attitude or theory of knowledge. If we think of life as moral and intellectual existence, then we seek to discover that community in which the existence has eternal value. We feel called upon to think about the values and purpose of life. We are called upon to join the coherent discourse of a humanity that we are necessitated to bring into existence. We are challenged to it by the act of interpretation. We are commanded to be the watchmen of reason and its universality. In being called to the community of interpretation we link the spirit to the finite, we bring the perspectives of the past into the present, and allow the ideal of the future to drive the present from itself toward new perspectives of thought. From the act of interpretation we find new expressions of mediation. Interpretation is the bridge that forms the discourse of reason drawing the categories of thinking into discourse with each other and in this discourse, in a circular way, reflecting again on the beginnings in which thought found its community and the social quality of its relationship.

We have arrived at the point where we can understand what it means to say that "man is an animal that interprets; and that therefore man lives in communities and depends upon them for insight and for salvation."[49] Man's need for the community of interpretation is fundamental. In it he discovers his humanity and through this humanity he finds what he shares with all other human beings. Rationality is now understood as interpretation. It is not perception nor conceptualization that realizes the idea of humanity, but interpretation. It alone is the bridge between the divine and the human. It reveals the transcendent in the immanent. It is the refusal to absolutize finitude through the concept. Interpretation is the work of the idea, the power to limit the claims of empirical experience and the imperialism of the concept. The idea denies the logic of conceptualization to be the embodiment of the divine human relationship. The love of the idea is man's more sublime fidelity to the ideal. "If love for this community [the community of interpretation] is awakened—then indeed this love is able to grasp, in ideal, the meaning of the Church Universal, or the Church of Saints and of God the Interpreter."[50] The phrase God the Interpreter is, at first, difficult to comprehend unless we grasp the divine as the continuous revelation of divinity itself. Royce would say that "the world is the process of the spirit" into which God is continuously revealing his being. The interpreting power of man is that mediating mystery through which man finds in himself the need for community, by which community is recognized as the primordial metaphysical truth. In this truth man comprehends his philosophical and religious destiny.

Royce clarified this spiritual process with the remark that pointed to "an evolution wherein to every problem corresponds, in the course of the endless ages, its solution, to every antithesis, its resolution, to every estrangement its reconciliation, to every tragedy the atoning triumph which interprets its evil."[51] This is sublime cosmic optimism. The continuous revealing of the divine gives man a moral and aesthetic responsibility that is forever growing and demanding of him a fidelity and hope that is the meaning of philosophy and religion. Royce spoke of new challenges because he believed that it was the philosopher's obligation to set forth to his fellowman and to mankind what he believed was the truth of the spirit, the coherent discourse, and the universal community of interpretation. Philosophy, he knew, was faith in the idea. He asked us to judge every social device, every proposed reform, every national and every local enterprise by the one test: *"Does this help towards the coming of the universal community?"*[52] The imperative is clear, its responsibility difficult, but we comprehend its need and its truth. We demand of ourselves loyalty and we fear the disloyalty of our finitude.

We have attempted to develop the most powerful expression of philosophical optimism in the tradition of American philosophy. The judgement that the times make on such idealism has always been negative. The times are never equal to the idealism of philosophy. Philosophy remains the guardian of the idea and ideal. For them there has been sacrifice. When philosophy is loyal it has the truth to oppose the myths, ideologies, and national gods that have striven to destroy truth and freedom. Philosophy has remained loyal to the universal community and has preserved that fidelity to its metaphysical truth which we call the idea of humanity. Philosophy has joined with religion to comprehend that spirit which is the beloved community, the loyal life, the work of grace, and the mediating power of atonement. The future requires continuing closeness between philosophy and religion. Royce made it possible for us to see how necessary they are to each other. Faith in spirit was Royce's legacy to philosophy. Where it is lost, violence escapes the atoning force of the Spirit and establishes its own realm. There it seeks "to be like the gods." In this search for divinity the Spirit suffers and finally dies; its mediating mystery falls prey to the false absolutism of the finitude of violence.

The problem of Christianity speaks to the salvation of the world. It is the challenge of a metaphysics of community. It reveals to mankind a divine plan that has never been fully interpreted and can never be wholly comprehended at any point in time. It remains an idea and, as an idea, the fundamental problem of our philosophical and religious fidelity.

Notes

1. Josiah Royce, *The Problem of Christianity*, originally published in two volumes in 1913; reprinted in one volume with an introduction by John E. Smith in 1968 (University of Chicago Press). Page numbers in notes following refer to this edition. This book is based on the lectures Royce delivered at Manchester College, Oxford, in 1913.
  2. P. 38.
  3. P. 41.
  4. P. 155.
  5. P. 43.
  6. P. 44.
  7. P. 64.
  8. P. 72.
  9. P. 73.
  10. Ibid.
  11. P. 77.
  12. P. 79.
  13. P. 78.
  14. P. 232.
  15. P. 83.
  16. P. 85.
  17. P. 85.
  18. P. 94.
  19. P. 100.
  20. P. 118.

21. P. 119.
22. P. 125.
23. P. 129.
24. P. 128.
25. P. 131.
26. P. 131.
27. P. 140.
28. Pp. 155–56.
29. P. 158.
30. P. 168.
31. P. 175.
32. P. 180.
33. Ibid.
34. P. 185.
35. P. 186.
36. P. 198.
37. P. 204.
38. P. 206.
39. P. 208.
40. P. 226.
41. P. 232.
42. P. 240.
43. P. 248.
44. P. 253.
45. P. 260.
46. P. 264.
47. P. 268.
48. P. 274.
49. P. 290.
50. P. 319.
51. P. 381.
52. P. 405.

The Religious Aspect of Philosophy

THE POSSIBILITY OF ERROR*

On ne sert dignement la philosophie qu'avec le même feu
qu'on sent pour une maîtresse.—ROUSSEAU, *Nouvelle Helöise.*

We have before us our theorem, and an outline of its proof. We are
here to expand this argument. We have some notion of the magnitude of
the issues that are at stake. We had found ourselves baffled in our search
for a certainty by numerous difficulties. We had found only one way remaining so far quite clear. That was the way of postulating what the moral
consciousness seems to demand about the world beyond experience. For
many thinkers since Kant, that way has seemed in fact the only one. They
live in a world of action. "Doubt," they say, "clouds all theory. One must
act as if the world were the supporter of our moral demands. One must have
faith. One must make the grand effort, one must risk all for the sake of the
great prize. If the world is against us, still we will not admit the fact until
we are crushed. If the cold reality cares naught for our moral efforts, so be
it when we come to know the fact, but meanwhile we will act as if legions
of angels were ready to support our demand for whatever not our selfish
interest, but the great interest of the Good, requires." Such is the view of
the men whose religion is founded upon a Postulate.

We, too, felt that such faith is religious. We were willing to accept it,
if nothing better could be found. But we were not content with it. Life has
its unheroic days, when mere postulates fail us. At such times we grow
weary of toiling, evil seems actually triumphant, and, worse than all, the
sense that there really is any perfect goodness yet unattained, that there is
any worth or reason in our fight for goodness, seems to desert us. And then

---

*From *The Religious Aspect of Philosophy* (Boston: Houghton, Mifflin and Co., 1885).

51

it will indeed be well if we can get for ourselves something more and better than mere postulates. If we cannot, we shall not seek to hide the fact. Better eternal despondency than a deliberate lie about our deepest thoughts and their meaning. If we are not honest, at least in our philosophy, then are we wholly base. To try once more is not dishonest.

So we did make the effort, and, in the last chapter, we sketched a result that seemed nearly within our reach. An unexpected result this, because it springs from the very heart of skepticism itself. We doubted to the last extremity. We let everything go, and then all of a sudden we seemed to find that we could not lose one priceless treasure, try as we would. Our wildest doubt assumed this, namely, that error is possible. And so our wildest doubt assumed the actual existence of those conditions that make error possible. *The conditions that determine the logical possibility of error must themselves be absolute truth,* that was the treasure that remained to us amid all our doubts. And how rich that treasure is, we dimly saw in the last discussion. That dim insight we must now try to make clearer. Perhaps our previous discussion has shown us that the effort is worth making.

Yet of one thing the reader shall be warned. The path that we travel is hereabouts very thorny and stony. It is a path of difficult philosophical investigation. Nobody ought to follow it who does not desire to. We hope that the reader will skip the whole of this chapter unless he wants to find even more of dullness than the rest of this sleepy book has discovered to him. For us, too, the arid way would seem hard, were it not for the precious prize at the end of it.

I

The story of the following investigation shall first be very briefly told. The author had long sought, especially in the discussions of Kant's "Kritik," and in the books of the post-Kantians, for help in seeing the ultimate principles that lie at the basis of knowledge. He had found the old and well-known troubles. Experience of itself can give no certainty about general principles. We must therefore, said Kant, bring our own principles with us to experience. We know then of causation, because causation is a fundamental principle of our thought, whereby we set our experience to rights. And so long as we think, we shall think into experience the connection of cause and effect, which otherwise would not be there. But hereupon the questions arose that have so often been asked of Kant and the Kantians. Why just these principles and no others? "That is inexplicable," replies Kant. Very well, then, suppose we give up applying to experience those arbitrary principles of ours. Suppose we choose to stop thinking of experience as causally connected. What then? "But you cannot stop," says Kant. "Your thought, being what it is, must follow this one fashion forever." Nay, we reply, how knowest thou that, Master? Why may not our thought get a new fashion some day? And then what is now a necessary principle, for example, that every event has a cause, would become unnecessary or even nonsensical. Do we then know *a priori* that our *a priori* principles must always remain such? If so, how come we by this new knowledge?

So Kant leaves us still uncertain about any fundamental principles upon which a sure knowledge of the world can be founded.

Let us, then, examine a little deeper. Are there any certain judgments possible at all? If one is skeptical in a thoroughgoing way, as the author tried to be, he is apt to reach, through an effort to revise Kant's view, a position something like the following—a provisional position of course, but one that results from the effort to accept nothing without criticism: "Kant's result is that our judgments about the real world are founded on an union of thought and sense, thought giving the appearance of necessity to our judgment, sense giving the material. The necessity of any judgment amounts then only to what may be summed up in the words: *So the present union of thought and sense makes things appear.* If either thought or sense altered its character, truth would alter. Hence every sincere judgment is indeed true for the moment in which it is made, but not necessarily true for other moments. We only postulate that it is true for other moments." "And so," to continue this view, "it is only by means of postulates that our thought even seems to have any unity from moment to moment. We live in the present. If our thought has other truth or falsity than this, we do not know it. Past and future exist not for this present. They are only postulated. Save as postulated, they have no present meaning."

When he held and expressed this view, the author is free to admit that he was not always clear whether he ought to call it the doctrine of the relativity of truth or not. It might have avoided the absurdities of total relativity by taking form as a doctrine that the present moment's judgment is really true or false, for a real past and future, but that we, being limited to present moments, can never compare our judgments with reality to find whether our judgments are true or false. But although this interpretation is possible, this view often did express itself for the author as the doctrine of the total relativity of truth. The latter doctrine to be sure has no real meaning, but the author used with many others to fancy that it had.

To apply the view to the case of causal relations. "We continually postulate," the author used to point out, "we demand, without being able to prove it, that nature in future shall be uniform." So, carrying out this thought, the author used to say: "In fact future nature is not given to us, just as the past is not given to us. Sense-data and thought unite at every instant afresh to form a new judgment and a new postulate. Only in the present has any judgment evident validity. And our postulate of causal relation is just a way of looking at this world of conceived past and future *data*. Such postulates avoid being absurd efforts to regulate independent facts of sense, because, and only because, we have in experience no complete series of facts of sense at all, only from moment to moment single facts, about which we make single judgments. All the rest we *must* postulate or else do without them." Thus one reaches a skepticism as nearly complete as is possible to any one with earnest activity of thought in him. From moment to moment one can be sure of each moment. All else is postulate.

From the depths of this imperfectly defined skepticism, which seemed to him provisionally the only view he could adopt, the author escaped only by asking the one question more: "If everything beyond the present is doubtful, then how can even that doubt be possible?" With this question that bare relativity of the present moment is given up. What are the conditions that make doubt logically intelligible? These conditions really transcend the present moment. Plainly doubt implies that the statement doubted may be false. So here we have at least one supposed general truth, namely, "All but the immediate content of the present moment's judgment, being doubtful, we may be in error about it." But *what then is an error?* This becomes at once a problem of exciting interest. Attacking it, the author was led through the wilderness of the following argument.

II

Yet before we undertake this special examination of the nature of error, the reader must pardon us for adding yet another explanatory word. The difficulty of the whole discussion will lie in the fact that we shall be studying the possibility of the plainest and most familiar of commonplaces. Common sense hates to do such things, because common sense thinks that the whole matter is sure from the outset. Common sense is willing to ask whether God exists, but unwilling to inquire how it is possible that there can exist an error about anything. But foreseeing that something is to follow from all this, we must beg common sense to be patient. We have not the shadow of doubt ourselves about the possibility of error. That is the steadfast rock on which we build. Our inquiry, ultra-skeptical as it may at moments seem, is into the question: *How* is the error possible? Or, in other words: *What is an error?* Now there can be little doubt that common sense is not ready with any general answer to such a question. Error is a word with many senses. By error we often mean just a statement that arouses our antipathy. Yet we all admit upon reflection, that our antipathy can neither make nor be used to define real error. Adam Smith declares, with common sense on his side, in his "Theory of the Moral Sentiments,"[1] that: "To approve or disapprove of the opinions of others is acknowledged, by everybody, to mean no more than to observe their agreement or disagreement with our own." Yet no one would accept as a definition of error the statement that: *Error is any opinion that I personally do not like.* Error has thus a very puzzling character. For common sense will readily admit that if a statement is erroneous, it must appear erroneous to every "right mind" that is in possession of the facts. Hence the personal taste of one man is not enough to define it. Else there might be as many sorts of error as there are minds. It is only the "right mind" whose personal taste shall decide what is an error in any particular case. But what then is a normal mind? Who is the right-minded judge? There seems to be danger that common sense shall run at this point into an infinite regress. I say: *That opinion is an error.* What do I mean? Do I mean that I do not like that opinion? Nay, I mean more. I mean that *I ought not to like or to accept it.* Why ought I not? *Because the ideally right-minded person would not,* seeing the given facts, hold that opinion about them. But who is the ideally right-minded person? Well, common sense may answer, *It is my ideal person, the right-minded man as I conceive him.* But why is my ideal the true ideal? *Because I like it?—Nay, because, to the ideal judge, that kind of mind would seem the ideal.* But who is the ideal judge? And so common sense is driven from point to point, unable to get to anything definite.

So much, then, to show in general that common sense does not know what an error is, and needs more light upon the subject. Let common sense not disturb us, then, in our further search, by the constant and indignant protest that error must somehow exist, and that doubt on that subject is nonsense. Nobody has any doubts on that subject. We ask only *how* error exists and how it can exist.

For the rest, what follows is not any effort to demonstrate in fair and orderly array, from any one principle or axiom, what must be the nature of error, but to use every and any device that may offer itself, general analysis, special example, comparison and contrast of cases,—anything that shall lead us to the insight into what an error is and implies. For at last, immediate insight must decide.

We shall study our problem thus. We shall take either some accepted definition of error, or some special class of cases, and we shall ask: How is error in that case, or in accordance with that definition, possible? Since error plainly

---

1. Part I., sec. i., chap. iii., near the beginning.

is possible in some way, we shall have only to inquire: *What are the logical conditions* that make it possible? We shall take up the ordinary suppositions that common sense seems to make about what here determines the possibility of error. We shall show that these suppositions are inadequate. Then the result will be that, on the ordinary suppositions, error would be impossible. But that result would be absurd, if these were the only possible suppositions. Hence the ordinary suppositions must somehow be supplemented. When, therefore, we seem to say in the following that error is impossible, we shall mean only, impossible under the ordinary suppositions of common sense. What supplement we need to these suppositions, our argument will show us. In sum we shall find the state of the case to be this: Common sense regards an assertion as true or as false apart from any other assertion or thought, and solely in reference to its own object. For common sense each judgment, as a separate creation, stands out alone, looking at its object, and trying to agree with it. If it succeeds, we have truth. If the judgment fails, we have error. But, as we shall find, this view of common sense is unintelligible. A judgment cannot have an object and fail to agree therewith, unless this judgment is part of an organism of thought. Alone, as a separate fact, a judgment has no intelligible object beyond itself. And therefore the presuppositions of common sense must be supplemented or else abandoned. Either then there is no error, or else judgments are true or false only in reference to a higher inclusive thought, which they presuppose, and which must, in the last analysis, be assumed as Infinite and all-inclusive. This result we shall reach by no mystical insight, by no revelation, nor yet by any mere postulate such as we used in former discussions, but by a simple, dry analysis of the meaning of our own thought.

The most formidable opponent of our argument will be, after all, however, not common sense, but that thought mentioned in the last chapter,— the thought that may try to content itself with somewhat plausible jargon, and to say that: *"There is no real difference between truth and error at all, only a kind of opinion or consensus of men about a conventional distinction between what they choose to call truth and what they choose to call error."* This view, as the author has confessed, he once tried to hold. Still this meaningless doctrine of relativity is not the same as the view that contents itself with the postulates before discussed. That view might take, and for the author at one time did take, the possible and intelligible form thus expressible: *"Truth and error, though really distinguishable, are for us distinguished only through our postulates, in so far as relates to past and future time."* Such views, while not denying that there is real truth, despair of the attainability for us of more than momentary truth. But the doctrine of Total Relativity, this view above expressed, differs from genuine skepticism. It tries to put even skepticism to rest, by declaring the opinion, *that there is error,* to be itself an error. This is not merely a moderate expression of human limitations, but jargon, and therefore formidable, because jargon is always unanswerable. When the famous Cretan declared all statements made by Cretans to be in all cases lies, his declaration was hard to refute, because it was such honest-seeming nonsense. Even so with the statement that declares the very existence of error to be an erroneously believed fancy. No *consensus* of men can make an error erroneous. We can only find or commit an error, not create it. When we commit an error, we say what was an error already. If our skeptical view in previous chapters seemed to regard truth and error as mere objects of our postulates, that was only because, to our skepticism, the real truth, the real error, about any real past and future, seemed beyond our reach, so that we had to content ourselves with postulates. But that real error exists is absolutely indubitable.

This being the case, it is evident that even the most thorough-going skepticism is full of assumptions. If I say, "There may be no money in that purse yonder," I assume the existence of the purse yonder in order to make just that particular doubt possible. Of course, however, just that doubt may be rendered meaningless by the discovery of the actual non-existence of that particular purse. If there is no purse yonder, then it is nonsensical either to affirm or to deny that it contains money. And so if the purse of which I speak is an hallucination of mine, then the doubt about whether, as an actually existent purse, it has money in it, is deprived of sense. My real error in that case would lie in supposing the purse itself to exist. If, however, I abandon the first doubt, and go on to doubt the real existence of the purse, I equally assume a room, or some other environment, or at all events the universe, as existent, in order to give sense to my question whether the purse has any being in this environment or in this universe. But if I go yet further, and doubt whether there is any universe at all outside of my thought, what does my doubt yet mean? If it is to be a doubt with any real sense, it must be a doubt still with an object before it. It seems then to imply an assumed order of being, in which there are at least two elements, my lonely thought about an universe, and an empty environment of this thought, in which there is, in fact, no universe. But this empty environment, whose nature is such that my thought does wrong to suppose it to be an universe, what is that? Surely if the doubt is to have meaning, this idea needs further examination. The absolute skepticism is thus full of assumptions.

The first European thinker who seems to have discussed our present problem was Plato, in a too-much-neglected passage of the "Theætetus,"[1] where Socrates, replying to the second definition of knowledge given by Theætetus, namely, *knowledge is True Opinion,* answers that his great difficulty has often been to see how any opinion can possibly be false. The

---

1. Plato, *Th.,* p. 187 *sqq.*

conclusion reached by Plato is no very definite one, but the discussion is deeply suggestive. And we cannot do better here than to pray that the shade of the mighty Greek may deign to save us now in our distress, and to show us the true nature of error.

III

Logicians are agreed that single ideas, thoughts viewed apart from judgments, are neither true nor false. Only a judgment can be false. And if a reasoning process is said to be false, the real error lies still in an actual or suppressed assertion. A fallacy is a false assertion that a certain conclusion follows from certain premises. Error is therefore generally defined as a judgment that does not agree with its object. In the erroneous judgment, subject and predicate are so combined as, in the object, the corresponding elements are not combined. And thus the judgment comes to be false. Now, in this definition, nothing is doubtful or obscure save the one thing, namely, the *assumed relation between the judgment and its object*. The definition assumes as quite clear that a judgment has an object, wherewith it can agree or not agree. And what is meant by the agreement would not be obscure, if we could see what is meant by the object, and by the possession of this object implied in the pronoun *its*. What then is meant by *its object?* The difficulties involved in this phrase begin to appear as soon as you look closer. First then the object of the assertion is as such supposed to be neither the subject nor the predicate thereof. It is external to the judgment. It has a nature of its own. Furthermore, not all judgments have the same object, so that objects are very numerous. But from the infinity of real or of possible objects the judgment somehow picks out its own. Thus then for a judgment to have an object, there must be something about the judgment that shows what one of the external objects that are beyond itself this judgment does pick out as its own. But this something that gives the judgment its object can only be the intention wherewith the judgment is accompanied. A judgment has as object only what it intends to have as object. It has to conform only to that to which it wants to conform. But the essence of an intention is the knowledge of what one intends. One can, for instance, intend a deed or any of its consequences only in so far as he foresees them. I cannot be said to intend the accidental or the remote or even the immediate consequences of anything that I do, unless I foresaw that they would follow; and this is true however much the lawyers and judges may find it practically necessary to hold me responsible for these consequences. Even so we all find it practically useful to regard one of our fellows as in error in case his assertions, as we understand them, seem to us to lead to consequences that we do not approve. But our criticisms of his opinions, just like legal judgments of his acts, are not intended to be exact. Common sense will admit that, unless a man is thinking of the object of which I suppose him to be thinking, he makes no real error by merely failing to agree with the object that I have in mind. If the knights in the fable judge each other to be wrong, that is because each knight takes the other's shield to be identical with the shield as he himself has it in mind. In fact neither of them is in error, unless his assertion is false for the shield as he intended to make it his object.

So then judgments err only by disagreeing with their intended objects, and they can intend an object only in so far forth as this object is known to the thought that makes the judgment. Such, it would seem, is the consequence of the common-sense view. But in this case a judgment can be in error only if it is knowingly in error. That also, as it seems, follows from the common-sense suppositions. Or, if we will have it in syllogistic form:—

Everything intended is something known. The object even of an erroneous judgment is intended. ∴. The object even of an error is something known.

Or: Only what is known can be erred about. Nor can we yet be content with what common sense will at once reply, namely, that our syllogism uses *known* ambiguously, and that the object of an erroneous judgment is known enough to constitute it the object, and not enough to prevent the error about it. This must no doubt be the fact, but it is not of itself clear; on the contrary, just here is the problem. As common sense conceives the matter, the object of a judgment is not as such the whole outside world of common sense, with all its intimate interdependence of facts, with all its unity in the midst of diversity. On the contrary, the object of any judgment is just that portion of the then conceived world, just that fragment, that aspect, that element of a supposed reality, which is seized upon for the purposes of just this judgment. Only such a momentarily grasped fragment of the truth can possibly be present in any one moment of thought as the object of a single assertion. Now it is hard to say how within this arbitrarily chosen fragment itself there can still be room for the partial knowledge that is sufficient to give to the judgment its object, but insufficient to secure to the judgment its accuracy. If I aim at a mark with my gun, I can fail to hit it, because choosing and hitting a mark are totally distinct acts. But, in the judgment, choosing and knowing the object seem inseparable. No doubt somehow our difficulty is soluble, but we are here trying first to show that it is a difficulty.

To illustrate here by a familiar case, when we speak of things that are solely matters of personal preference, such as the pleasure of a sleigh-ride, the taste of olives, or the comfort of a given room, and when we only try to tell how these things appear to us, then plainly our judgments, if sincere, cannot be in error. As these things are to us, so they are. We are their measure. To doubt our truthfulness in these cases is to doubt after the fashion of the student who wondered whether the star that the astronomers call Uranus may not be something else after all, and not really Uranus. Surely science does not progress very far or run into great danger of error so long as it employs itself in discovering such occult mysteries as the names of the stars. But our present question is, How do judgments that can be and that are erroneous differ in nature from these that cannot be erroneous? If astronomers would be equally right in case they should agree to call Uranus Humpty Dumpty, why are not all judgments equally favored? Since the judgment chooses its own object, and has it only in so far as it chooses it, how can it be in that partial relation to its object which is implied in the supposition of an erroneous assertion?

Yet again, to illustrate the difficulty in another aspect, we can note that not only is error impossible about the perfectly well-known, but that error is equally impossible, save in the form of direct self-contradiction, about what is absolutely unknown. Spite of the religious awe of some people in presence of the Unknowable, it is safe to say, somewhat irreverently, that about a really Unknowable nobody could make any sincere and self-consistent assertions that could be errors. For self-consistent assertions about the Unknowable would of necessity be meaningless. And being meaningless, they could not well be false. For instance, one could indeed not say that the Unknowable contemplates war with France, or makes sunspots, or will be the next Presidential candidate, because that would be contradicting one's self. For if the Unknowable did any of these things, it would no longer be the Unknowable, but would become either the known or the discoverable. But avoid such self-contradiction, and you cannot err about the Unknowable. For the Unknowable is simply our old friend *Abracadabra,* a word that has no meaning, and by hypothesis never can get any. So if I say that the Unknowable dines *in vacuo* with the chimera, or is Humpty Dumpty, I talk nonsense, and am therefore unable to make a mistake. Nonsense is error only when it involves self-contradiction. Avoid that, and nonsense cannot blunder, having no object outside of itself with which it must agree. But all this illustrates from the other side our difficulty. Is not the object of a judgment, in so far as it is unknown to that judgment, like the Unknowables for that judgment? To be in error about the application of a symbol, you must have a symbol that symbolizes something. But in so far as the thing symbolized is not known through the symbol, how is it symbolized by that symbol? Is it not, like the Unknowable, once for all out of the thought, so that one cannot just then be thinking about it at all, and so cannot, in this thought at least, be making blunders about it? But in so far as the thing symbolized is, through the symbol, in one's thought, why is it not known, and so correctly judged? All this involves that old question of the nature of symbols. They are to mean for us more than we know that they mean. How can that be? No doubt all that is really possible, but how?

IV

We follow our difficulty into another department. Let us attempt a sort of provisional psychological description of a judgment as a state of mind. So regarded, a judgment is simply a fact that occurs in somebody's thought. If we try to describe it as an occurrence, without asking whence it came, we shall perhaps find in it three elements,—elements which are in some fashion described in Ueberweg's well-known definition of a judgment as the "Consciousness about the objective validity of a subjective union of ideas." Our interpretation of them shall be this: The elements are: The *Subject,* with the accompanying shade of curiosity about it; the *Predicate,* with the accompanying sense of its worth in satisfying a part of our curiosity about the subject; and the *Sense of Dependence,* whereby we feel the value of this act to lie, not in itself, but in its agreement with a vaguely felt Beyond, that stands out there as Object.

Now this analysis of the elements of a judgment is no explanation of our difficulties; and in fact for the moment only embarrasses us more. But the nature of the difficulty may come home to us somewhat more clearly, if we try to follow the thread of this analysis a little further. Even if it is a very imperfect account, it may serve to lead us up to the true insight that we seek into the nature of error. Let us make the analysis a little more detailed.

In its typical form then, the judgment as a mental state seems to us to begin with a relatively incomplete or unstable or disconnected mass of consciousness, which we have called the Subject, as it first begins to be present to us. This subject-idea is attended by some degree of effort, namely, of attention, whose tendency is to complete this incomplete subject by bringing it into closer connection with more familiar mental life. This more familiar life is represented by the predicate-idea. If the effort is successful, the subject has new elements united to it, assumes in consciousness a definiteness, a coherency with other states, a familiarity, which it lacked at the outset of the act of judgment; and this coherency it gets through its union with the predicate. All this is accompanied further by what one for short may call a sense of dependence. The judgment feels itself not alone, but looks to a somewhat indefinite object as the model after which the present union of ideas is to be fashioned. And in this way we explain how the judgment is, in those words of Ueberweg's definition, "the consciousness about the objective validity of a subjective union of ideas."

Now as a mere completion of subject-idea through the addition of a predicate-idea, the judgment is simply a mental phenomenon, having interest only to the person that experiences it, and to a psychologist. But as true or as false the judgment must be viewed in respect to the indefinite object of what we have called the sense of dependence, whereby the judgment is accompanied. Seldom in any ordinary judgment does this object become perfectly full and clear; for to make it so would often require many, perhaps an infinite, series of judgments. Yet, for the one judgment, the object, whether full and clear or not, exists as object only in so far forth as the sense of dependence has defined it. And the judgment is true or false only with reference to this undefined object. The intention to agree with the object is contained in the sense of dependence upon the object, and remains for this judgment incomplete, like the object itself. Somewhat vaguely this single act intends to agree with this vague object.

Such being the case, how can the judgment, as thus described, fairly be called false? As mere psychological combination of ideas it is neither true nor false. As accompanied by the sense of dependence upon an object, it would be false if it disagreed with its imperfectly defined object. But, as described, the only object that the judgment has is this imperfectly defined one. With this, in so far as it is for the moment defined, the judgment must needs agree. In so far as it is not defined, it is however not object for this judgment at all, but for some other one. What the imperfect sense of dependence would further imply if it existed in a complete instead of in an incomplete state, nobody can tell, any more than one can tell what towns would grow up by a given rain-pool, if it were no pool, but a great lake. The object of a single judgment, being what it is, namely, a vaguely defined object, present to this judgment, is just what it is for this judgment, and the judgment seems once for all to be true, in case it is sincere.

Some one may here at once answer that we neglect in this description the close interdependence of various judgments. Thought, some one may say, is an organic unity. Separated from all else but its own incompletely defined object, a single judgment cannot be erroneous. Only in the organic unity of a series of judgments, having a common object, is the error of one of them possible. We reply that all this will turn out to be just our result. But the usual supposition at the outset is that any judgment has by itself its own object, so that thereby alone, apart from other judgments, it stands or falls. And thus far we have tried to show that this natural supposition leads us into difficulty. We cannot see how a single sincere judgment should possibly fail to agree with its own chosen object. But enough of our problem in general. We must consider certain classes of errors more in detail. Let us see how, in these special classes of cases, we shall succeed in verifying the natural presupposition of common sense, which regards error as possible only when our object is not wholly present to mind, and which assumes that a judgment can have an object that is yet only partially present to mind. In choosing the classes of cases, we shall first follow common sense as to their definition. We shall take just the assumptions of daily life, and shall show that they lead us into difficulty. We are not for the first bound to explain why these assumptions are made. That common sense makes them is enough.

But let the reader remember: The whole value of our argument lies in its perfect generality. However much we dwell on particular classes of errors, we care nothing for the proof that just those errors are inexplicable, but only for the fact that they illustrate how, without some entirely new hypothesis, absolutely all error becomes impossible. This or that class of judgments may be one in which all the judgments are relative, but the total relativity of our thought implies an incomprehensible and contradictory state of things. Any hypothesis about error that makes total relativity the only admissible view, must therefore give place to some new hypothesis. And our illustrations in the following are intended to show that just what constitutes the difficulty in respect of these illustrations, makes the existence of any error inexplicable without some new hypothesis.

V

The class of errors that we shall first take seems, to common sense, common enough. It is the class known as errors about our neighbor's states of mind. Let us then, for argument's sake, assume without proof that our neighbors do exist. For we are not here concerned to answer Solipsism, but merely to exemplify the difficulties about the nature of error. If our neighbors did not exist, then the nature of the error that would lie in saying that they do exist would present almost exactly the same difficulties. We prefer, however, to begin with the common-sense assumption about ourselves and our neighbors as separate individuals, and to ask how error can then arise in judging of our neighbors' minds.

In the first place then: Who is my neighbor? Surely, on the assumptions that we all make, and that we made all through the ethical part of our discussion, he is no one of my thoughts, nor is any part of him ever any part of my thought. He is not my object, but, in Professor Clifford's phrase, an "eject," wholly outside of my ideas. He is no "thing in my dream," just as I am not in his dream.

Yet I make judgments about him, and he makes them about me. And when I make judgments about him, I do so by having in my thought some set of my own ideas that, although not himself, do yet, as I say, represent him. A kind of dummy, a symbol, a graven image of my own thought's creation, a phantom of mine, stands there in me as the representative of his mind; and all I say about my neighbor's inner life refers directly to this representative. The Scottish philosophy has had much to say to the world about what it calls direct or presentative, as opposed to representative, knowledge of objects. But surely the most obstinate Scottish philosopher that ever ate oatmeal cannot hold so tenaciously by his national doctrine as to say that I have, according to common sense, anything but a representative knowledge of my neighbor's thoughts and feelings. That is the only sort of knowledge that common sense will regard as possible to me, if so much as that is possible. But how I can know about this outside being is not now our concern. We notice only that our difficulty about error comes back to us in a new form. For how can I err about my neighbor, since, for this common-sense view, he is not even partly in my thoughts? How can I intend that as the object of my thought which never can be object for me at all?

But not everybody will at once feel the force of this question. We must be more explicit. Let us take the now so familiar suggestion of our great humorist about the six people that take part in every conversation between two persons. If John and Thomas are talking together, then the real John and Thomas, their respective ideas of themselves, and their ideas of each other, are all parties to the conversation. Let us consider four of these persons, namely, the real John, the real Thomas, John as Thomas conceives him, and Thomas as John conceives him. When John judges, of whom does he think? Plainly of that which can be an object to his thoughts, namely, of *his* Thomas. About whom then can he err? About *his* Thomas? No, for he knows him too well. His conception of Thomas is his conception, and what he asserts it to be, that it is for him. About the real Thomas? No, for it should seem, according to common sense, that he has nothing to do with the real Thomas in his thought, since that Thomas never becomes any part of his thought at all. "But," says one, "there must be some fallacy here, since we are sure that John *can* err about the real Thomas." Indeed he can, say we; but ours is not this fallacy. Common sense has made it. Common sense has said: "Thomas never is in John's thought, and yet John can blunder about Thomas." How shall we unravel the knot?

One way suggests itself. Mayhap we have been too narrow in our definition of *object*. Common sense surely insists that objects are outside of our thought. If, then, I have a judgment, and another being sees both my judgment and some outside object that was not in my thought, and sees how that thought is unlike the object in some critical respect, this being could say that my assertion was an error. So then with John and Thomas. *If Thomas could know John's thoughts about him,* then Thomas could possibly see John's error. That is what is meant by the error in John's thought.

But mere disagreement of a thought with any random object does not make the thought erroneous. The judgment must disagree with *its chosen* object. If John never has Thomas in thought at all, how *can* John choose the real Thomas as his object? If I judge about a penholder that is in this room, and if the next room is in all respects like this, save for a penholder in it, with which my assertion does not agree, who, looking at that penholder in that other room, can say that my judgment is false? For I meant not that penholder when I spoke, but this one. I knew perhaps nothing about that one, had it not in mind, and so could not err about it. Even so, suppose that outside of John there is a real Thomas, similar, as it happens, to John's ideal Thomas, but lacking some thought or affection that John attributes to his ideal Thomas. Does that make John's notion an error? No, for he spoke and could speak only of his idea Thomas. The real Thomas was the other room, that he knew not of, the other side of the shield, that he never could conceive. His Thomas was his phantom Thomas. This phantom it is that he judges and thinks about, and his thoughts may have their own consistency or inconsistency. But with the real other person they have nothing to do. The real other is not his object, and how can he err about what is not object for him?

Absurd, indeed, some one will reply to us. John and Thomas have to deal with representative phantoms of each other, to be sure; but that only makes each more apt to err about the real other. And the test that they can err is a very simple one. Suppose a spectator, a third person, to whom John and Thomas were both somehow directly present, so that he as it were included both of them. Then John's judgment of his phantom Thomas would be by this spectator at once compared with the real Thomas, and even so would Thomas's judgment of John be treated. If now John's phantom Thomas agreed with the real Thomas, then John's ideas would be declared in so far truthful; otherwise they would be erroneous. And this explains what is meant by John's power to err about Thomas.

The explanation is fair enough for its own purpose, and we shall need it again before long. But just now we cannot be content with it. For what we want to know is not what the judgment of a third thinker would be in case these two were somehow not independent beings at all, but things in this third being's thought. For we have started out with the supposition of common sense that John and Thomas are not dreams or thoughts of some higher third being, but that they are independent beings by themselves. Our supposition may have to be given up hereafter, but for the present we want to hold fast to it. And so John's judgment, which we had supposed to be about the independently existing Thomas, has now turned out to be only a judgment about John's idea of Thomas. But judgments are false only in case they disagree with their intended objects. What, however, is the object of

John's judgment when he thinks about Thomas? Not the real Thomas, who could not possibly be an object in another man's thoughts. John's real object being an ideal Thomas, he cannot, if sincere, and if fully conscious of what he means by Thomas, fail to agree in his statements with his own ideal. In short, on this our original supposition, John and Thomas are independent entities, each of which cannot possibly enter in real person into the thoughts of the other. Each may be somehow represented in the other's thoughts by a phantom, and only this phantom can be intended by the other when he judges about the first. For unless one talks nonsense, it should seem as if one could mean only what one has in mind.

Thus, like the characters in a certain Bab ballad, real John, real Thomas, the people in this simple tale, are total strangers to each other. You might as well ask a blind man to make true or false judgments about the real effects of certain combinations of colors, as to ask either John or Thomas, defined as common sense defines them, to make any judgments about each other. Common sense will assert that a blind man can learn and repeat verbally correct statements about color, or verbally false statements about color, but, according to the common-sense view, in no case can he err about color-ideas as such, which are never present to him. You will be quite ready to say that a dog can make mistakes about the odors of the numberless tracks on the highway. You will assure us, however, that you cannot make mistakes about them because these odors do not exist for you. According to the common-sense view, a mathematician can make blunders in demonstrating the properties of equations. A Bushman cannot, for he can have no ideas corresponding to equations. But how then can John or Thomas make errors about each other, when neither is more present to the other than is color to the blind man, the odor of the tracks on the highway to the dog's master, or the idea of an equation to a Bushman? Here common sense forsakes us, assuring us that there is such error, but refusing to define it.

The inconsistency involved in all this common-sense view, and the consequences of the inconsistency, will appear yet better with yet further illustration. A dream is false in so far as it contains the judgment that such and such things exist apart from us; but at least in so far as we merely assert in our dreams about the objects as we conceive them, we make true assertions. But is not our actual life of assertions about actual fellow-beings much like a dream to which there should happen to correspond some real scene or event in the world? Such correspondence would not make the dream really "true," nor yet false. It would be a coincidence, remarkable for an outside observer, but none the less would the dreamer be thinking in his dream not about external objects, but about the things in his dream. But is not our supposed Thomas so and only so in the thought of John as he would be if John chanced to dream of a Thomas that was, to an external spectator, like the real one? Is not then the phantom Thomas, John's only direct object, actually a thing in John's thought? Is then the independent Thomas an object for John in any sense?

Yet again. Let us suppose that two men are shut up, each in a closed room by himself, and for his whole life; and let us suppose that by a lantern contrivance each of them is able at times to produce on the wall of the other's room a series of pictures. But neither of them can ever know what pictures he produces in the other's room, and neither can know anything of the other's room, as such, but only of the pictures. Let the two remain forever in this relation. One of them, A, sees on his wall pictures, which resemble more or less what he has seen in his own room at other times. Yet he perceives these to be only pictures, and he supposes them to represent what goes on in another room, which he conceives as like his own. He is interested, he examines the phenomena, he predicts their future changes, he passes judgment upon them. He may, if you like to continue the hypothesis, find some way of affecting them, by himself acting in a way mysterious to himself so as to produce changes in B's actual room, which again affect the pictures that the real B produces in A's room. Thus A might hold what he would call communication with his phantom room. Even so, B lives with pictures before him that are produced from A's room. Now one more supposition, namely, that A and B have absolutely no other means of communication, that both are shut up altogether and always have been, that neither has any objects before him but his own thoughts and the changing pictures on the wall of his room. In this case what difference does it make whether or no the pictures in A's room are actually like the things that could be seen in B's room? Will that make A's judgments either true or false? Even if A, acting by means that he himself cannot understand, is able to control the pictures on his wall by some alteration that he unconsciously produces in B's room and its pictures, still A cannot be said to have any knowledge of the real B and his room at all. And, for the same reason, A cannot make mistakes about the real room of B, for he will never even think of that real room. He will, like a man in a dream, think and be able to think only of the pictures on his wall. And when he refers them to an outside cause, he does not mean by this cause the real B and his real room, for he has never dreamed of the real B, but only of the pictures and of his own interpretation of them. He can therefore make no false judgments about B's room, any more than a Bushman can make false judgments about the integral calculus.

If to our present world there does correspond a second world somewhere off in space, a world exactly like this, where just the same events at every instant do actually take place, still the judgments that we make about our world are not actually true or false with reference to that world, for we *mean* this world, not that one, when we judge. Why are not John's Thomas and the real Thomas related like this world and that second world in distant space? Why are not both like the relation of A's conceived phantom room and B's real room? Nothing of either real room is ever present to the other. Each prisoner can make true or false judgments if at all, then, only about the pictures on his wall; but neither has even the suggestion that could lead him to make a blunder about the other's real room, of which he has and can have not the faintest idea.

One reason why we fail to see at once this fact lies in the constant tendency to regard the matter from the point of view of a third person, instead of from the point of view that we still implicitly attribute to A and B themselves. If A could get outside of his room once and see B's room, then he could say: "My picture was a good one," or the reverse. But, in the supposed case, he not only never sees B's room, but he never sees anything but his own pictures, never gets out of his room at all for any purpose. Hence, his sole objects of assertion being his pictures, he is innocent of any power to err about B's room as it is in itself, even as the man born blind is innocent of any power to err about the relations of colors.

Now this relation of A and B, as they were supposed to dwell in their perpetual imprisonment, is essentially like the relation that we previously postulated between two independent subjects. If I cannot have you in my thought at all, but only a picture produced by you, I am in respect to you like A confined to the pictures produced from B's room. However much I may fancy that I am talking of you, I am really talking about my idea of you, which for me can have no relation whatever to the real you. And so John and Thomas remain shut up in their prisons. Each thinks of his phantom of the other. Only a third person, who included them both, who in fact treated them as, in the Faust-Epilogue, the *Pater Seraphicus* treats the *selige Knaben* (*Er nimmt sie in sich,* says the stage direction)—only such an inclusive thought could compare the phantoms with the real, and only in him, not in themselves, would John and Thomas have any ideas of each other at all, true or false.

This result is foreign to our every-day thought, because this every-day thought really makes innocent use of two contradictory views of the relations of conscious beings. On the one hand we regard them as utterly remote from one another, as what Professor Clifford called ejects; and then we speak of them as if the thoughts of one could as such become thoughts of the other, or even as if one of them could as an independent being still become object in the thought of the other. No wonder that, with such contradictory assumptions as to the nature of our relations to our neighbors, we find it very easy to make absurd statements about the meaning of error. The contradiction of common sense has in fact just here much to do with the ethical illusion that we called the illusion of selfishness. To clear up this point will be useful to us, therefore, in more ways than one.

VI

Disappointed once more in our efforts to understand how error is possible, we turn to another class of cases, which lie in a direction where, at least for this once, all will surely be plain. Errors about matters of fact or experience are certainly clear enough in nature. And as this class of errors is practically most important, the subtleties of our previous investigation may be dismissed with light heart so soon as we have gotten rid of the few little questions that will now beset us. It is to be noted that all errors about material objects, about the laws of nature, about history, and about the future, are alike errors about our actual or possible experiences. We expect or postulate an experience that at the given time, or under the given conditions, turns out to be other than it was postulated or expected to be. Now since our experiences not now present are objective facts, and capable of clear definition, it would seem clear that error concerning them is an easily comprehensible thing.

But alas! again we are disappointed. That errors in matters of experience are common enough is indubitable, but equally evident becomes the difficulty of defining what they are and how they are possible. Take the case of error about an expected future. What do we mean by a future time? How do we identify a particular time? Both these questions plunge us into the sea of problems about the nature of time itself. When I say, *Thus and so will it be at such and such a future moment,* I postulate certain realities not now given to my consciousness. And singular realities they are. For they have now no existence at all. Yet I postulate that I can err about them. This their non-existence is a peculiar kind of non-existence, and requires me to make just such and such affirmations about it. If I fail to correspond to the true nature of this non-existent reality, I make an error; and it is postulated not merely that my present statement will in that case hereafter turn out false or become false, but also that it is now false, is at this moment an error, even though the reality with which it is to agree is centuries off in the future. But this is not all the difficulty. I postulate also that an error in prediction can be discovered when the time comes by the failure of the prediction to verify itself. I postulate then that I can look back and say: Thus and thus I predicted about this moment, and thus and thus it has come to pass, and this event contradicts that expectation. But can I in fact ever accomplish this comparison at all? And is the comparison very easily intelligible? For when the event comes to pass, the expectation no longer exists. The two thoughts, namely, expectation and actual experience, are separate thoughts, far apart in time. How can I bring them together to compare them, so as to see if they have the same object? It will not do to appeal to memory for the purpose; for the same question would recur about the memory in its relation to the original thought. How can a past thought, being past, be compared to a present thought to see whether they stand related? The past thought lived in itself, had its own ideas of what it then called future, and its own interpretation thereof. How can you show, or intelligently affirm, that the conception which the past expectation had of its future moment is so identical with the conception which this present thought has of this present moment, as to make these two conceived moments one and the same? Here in short we have supposed two different ideas, one of an expected future, the other of an experienced present, and we have supposed the two ideas to be widely separated in time, and by hypothesis they are not together in one consciousness at all. Now how can one say that in fact they relate to the same moment at all? How is it intelligible to say that they do? How, in fine, can a not-given future be a real object of any thought; and how, when it is once the object thereof, can any subsequent moment be identified with this object?

A present thought and a past thought are in fact separate, even as were John and Thomas. Each one means the object that it thinks. How can they have a common object? Are they not once for all different thoughts, each with its own intent? But in order to render intelligible the existence of error about matters of fact, we must make the unintelligible assumption, so it would seem, that these two different thoughts have the same intent, and are but one. And such is the difficulty that we find in our second great class of cases.

                                   VII

So much for the problem, both in general and in some particular instances. But now may not the reader insist, after all, that there can be in this wise no errors whatever? Contradictory as it seems, have we not, after all, put our judgments into a position whence escape for us is impossible? If every judgment is thus by its nature bound up in a closed circle of thought, with no outlook, can any one come afterwards and give it an external object? Perhaps, then, there is a way out of our difficulty by frankly saying that our thoughts may be neither truths nor errors beyond themselves, but just occurrences, with a meaning wholly subjective.

We desire the reader to try to realize this view of total relativity once more in the form in which, with all its inherent absurdities, it now comes back to us for the last time. It says, "Every judgment, *A is B*, in fact does agree and can agree only with its own object, which is present in mind when it is made. With no external object can it agree or fail to agree. It stands alone, with its own object. It has neither truth nor error beyond itself. It fulfills all its intentions, and is true, if it agrees with what was present to it when it was thought. Only in this sense is there any truth or falsity possible for our thought."

But once more, this inviting way out of the difficulty needs only to be tried to reveal its own contradictions. The thought that says, "No judgment is true beyond itself," is that thought true beyond itself or not? If it is true beyond itself, then we have the possibility of other truth than the merely subjective or relative truth. If it is false, then equally we have objective falsity. If it is neither true nor false, then the doctrine of relativity has not been affirmed at all as a truth. One sets up an idea of a world of separate, disorganized thoughts, and then says, "Each of them deals only with its own object, and they have no unity that could make them true or false." But still this world that one thus sets up must be the true world. Else is there no meaning in the doctrine of relativity. Twist as one will, one gets not out of the whirlpool of thought. Error must be real, and yet, as common sense arranges these judgments and their relations to one another, error cannot be real. There is so far no escape.

The perfectly general character of the argument must be understood. One might escape it if it applied to any one class of errors only. Then one would say: "In fact, the class of cases in question may be cases that exclude the possibility of both truth and error." But no, that cannot be urged against us, for our argument applies equally to all possible errors. In short, either no error at all is possible, or else there must be possible an infinite mass of error. For the possibilities of thought being infinite, either all thought is excluded once for all from the possibility of error, or else to every possible truth there can be opposed an infinite mass of error. All this infinite mass is at stake upon the issue of our investigation. Total relativity, or else an infinite possibility of truth and error; that is the alternative before us. And total relativity of thought involves self-contradiction.

Every way but one has been tried to lead us out of our difficulty. Shall we now give up the whole matter, and say that error plainly exists, but baffles definition? This way may please most people, but the critical philosophy knows of no unanswerable problem affecting the work of thought in itself considered. Here we need only patience and reflection, and we are sure to be some day rewarded. And indeed our solution is not far off, but very nigh us. We have indicated it all along. To explain how one could be in error about his neighbor's thoughts, we suggested the case where John and Thomas should be present to a third thinker whose thought should include them both. We objected to this suggestion that thus the natural pre-supposition that John and Thomas are separate self-existent beings would be contradicted. But on this natural presupposition neither of these two sub-jects could become object to the other at all, and error would here be im-possible. Suppose then that we drop the natural presupposition, and say that John and Thomas are both actually present to and included in a third and higher thought. To explain the possibility of error about matters of fact seemed hard, because of the natural postulate that time is a pure succession of separate moments, so that the future is now as future non-existent, and so that judgments about the future lack real objects, capable of identifica-tion. Let us then drop this natural postulate, and declare time once for all present in all its moments to an universal all-inclusive thought. And to sum up, let us overcome all our difficulties by declaring that all the many Be-yonds, which single significant judgments seem vaguely and separately to postulate, are present as fully realized intended objects to the unity of an all-inclusive, absolutely clear, universal, and conscious thought, of which all judgments, true or false, are but fragments, the whole being at once Ab-solute Truth and Absolute Knowledge. Then all our puzzles will disappear at a stroke, and error will be possible, because any one finite thought, viewed in relation to its own intent, may or may not be seen by this higher thought as successful and adequate in this intent.

How this absolute thought is to be related to individual thoughts, we can in general very simply define. When one says: ''This color now before me is red, and to say that it is blue would be to make a blunder,'' one rep-resents an including consciousness. One includes in one's present thought three distinct elements, and has them present in the unity of a single moment of insight. These elements are, first, the perception of red; secondly, the reflective judgment whose object is this perception, and whose agreement with the object constitutes its own truth; and, thirdly, the erroneous reflec-tion, *This is blue,* which is in the same thought compared with the percep-tion and rejected as error. Now, viewed as separate acts of thought, apart from the unity of an including thought, these three elements would give rise to the same puzzles that we have been considering. It is their presence in a higher and inclusive thought that makes their relations plain. Even so we must conceive the relation of John's thought to the united total of thought that includes him and Thomas. Real John and his phantom Thomas, real Thomas and his phantom John, are all present as elements in the including consciousness, which completes the incomplete intentions of both the in-dividuals, constitutes their true relations, and gives the thought of each about the other whatever of truth or of error it possesses. In short, error becomes possible as one moment or element in a higher truth, that is, in a consciousness that makes the error a part of itself, while recognizing it as error.

So far then we propose this as a possible solution for our puzzles. But now we may insist upon it as the only possible solution. *Either there is no such thing as error, which statement is a flat self-contradiction, or else there is an infinite unity of conscious thought to which is present all possible truth.* For suppose that there is error. Then there must be an infinite mass of error possible. If error is possible at all, then as many errors are possible as you please, since, to every truth, an indefinite mass of error may be opposed. Nor is this mere possibility enough. An error is possible for us when we are able to make a false judgment. But in order that the judgment should be false when made, it must have been false before it was made. An error is possible only when the judgment in which the error is to be expressed always was false. Error, if possible, is then eternally actual. Each error so possible implies a judgment whose intended object is beyond itself, and is also the object of the corresponding true judgment. But two judgments cannot have the same object save as they are both present to one thought. For as separate thoughts they would have separate subjects, predicates, intentions, and objects, even as we have previously seen in detail. So that every error implies a thought that includes it and the corresponding truth in the unity of one thought with the object of both of them. Only as present to an including thought are they either true or false. Thus then we are driven to assume an infinite thought, judging truth and error. But that this infinite thought must also be a rational unity, not a mere aggregate of truths, is evident from the fact that error is possible not only as to objects, but as to the relations of objects, so that all the possible relations of all the objects in space, in time, or in the world of the barely possible, must also be present to the all-including thought. And to know all relations at once is to know them in absolute rational unity, as forming in their wholeness one single thought.

What, then, is an error? An error, we reply, is an incomplete thought, that to a higher thought, which includes it and its intended object, is known as having failed in the purpose that it more or less clearly had, and that is fully realized in this higher thought. And without such higher inclusive thought, an assertion has no external object, and is no error.

VIII

If our argument were a Platonic dialogue, there would be hereabouts an interruption from some impatient Thrasymachus or Callicles or Polus, who would have been watching us, threatening and muttering, during all of the latter part of our discussion. At last, perhaps, συστρέψας ἑαυτὸν ὥσπερ θηρίον, he would spring upon us, and would say: "Why, you non-sense-mongers, have you not bethought you of the alternative that represents the reality in this question of yours? Namely, an error is an error, neither to the thought that thinks it, nor of necessity to any higher inclusive thought, but only to a *possible* critical thought that should undertake afterwards to compare it with its object. An error is a thought such that *if* a critical thought *did* come and compare it with its object, it *would be* seen to be false. And it has an object for such a critical thought. This critical thought need not be real and actually include it, but may be only a *possible* judge of its truth. Hence your Infinite all-knower is no reality, only a logical possibility; and your insight amounts to this, that if all *were* known to an all-knower, he *would judge* error to be mistaken. And so error is what he would perceive to be error. What does all that amount to but worthless tautology?''

This argument of our Thrasymachus is the only outwardly plausible objection that we fear to the foregoing analysis, because it is the only objection that fully expresses the old-established view of common sense about such problems. Though common sense never formulates our present difficulty, common sense still dimly feels that to some possible (not actual) judge of truth, appeal is made when we say that a thing is false not merely for us, but in very truth. And this possible judge of common sense we have now unhesitatingly declared to be an Infinite Actuality, absolutely necessary to *constitute* the relation of truth and error. Without it there is for our view no truth or error conceivable. The words, *This is true,* or *This is false,* mean nothing, we declare, unless there is the inclusive thought for which the truth is true, the falsehood false. No barely possible judge, who *would* see the error *if* he were there, will do for us. He must be there, this judge, to constitute the error. Without him nothing but total subjectivity would be possible; and thought would then become purely a pathological phenomenon, an occurrence without truthfulness or falsity, an occurrence that would interest anybody if it could be observed; but that, unfortunately, being only a momentary phantom, could not be observed at all from without, but must be dimly felt from within. Our thought needs the Infinite Thought in order that it may get, through this Infinite judge, the privilege of being so much as even an error.

This, it will be said, is but reassertion. But how do we maintain this view against our Thrasymachus? Our answer is only a repetition of things that we have already had to say, in the argument for what we here reassert. If the judgment existed alone, without the inclusive thought to judge it, then, as it existed alone, it either had an object, or had none. But if it had none, it was no error. If it had one, then either it knew what its object actually was, or it did not know what its object was, or it partially knew and partially did not know what its object actually was. In the first case the judgment must have been an identical one, like the judgment *A pain is a pain.* Such a judgment knows its own object, therefore cannot fail to agree with it, and cannot be an error. If the judgment knew not its own object at all, then it had no meaning, and so could not have failed to agree with the object that it had not. If, however, this separate judgment knew its object enough to intend just that object, but not enough to insure agreement with it, all our difficulties return. The possible judge cannot give the judgment its complete object until he becomes its actual judge. Yet as fair judge he must then give it the object that it already had without him. Meanwhile, however, the judgment remains in the unintelligible attitude previously studied at length. It is somehow possessed of just the object it intends, but yet does not know in reality what it does intend, else it would avoid error. Its object, in so far as unknown to it, is no object for it; and yet only in so far as the object is thus unknown can it be erred about. What helps in all this the barely possible judge? The actual judge must be there; and for him the incomplete intention must be complete. He knows what is really this judgment's object, for he knows what is imperfectly meant in it. He knows the dream, and the interpretation thereof. He knows both the goal and the way thither. But all this is, to the separate judgment as such, a mystery.

In fact, the separate judgments, waiting for the possible judge to test them, are like a foolish man wandering in a wood, who is asked whether he has lost his way. "I may have lost it," he answers. "But whither are you going?" "That I cannot tell?" "Have you no goal?" "I may have, but I have no notion what it is." "What then do you mean by saying that you may have lost the way to this place that you are not seeking? For you seem to be seeking no place; how then can you have lost the way thither?" "I mean that some possible other man, who was wise enough to find whither I am trying to go, might possibly, in his wisdom, also perceive that I am not on the way to that place. So I may be going away from my chosen goal, although I am unaware what goal it is that I have chosen." Such a demented man as this would fairly represent the meaningless claim of the separate judgment, either to truthfulness, or to the chance of error.

In short, though the partial thought may be, as such, unconscious of its own aim, it can be so unconscious only in case it is contained in a total thought as one moment thereof.

It will be seen that wherever we have dealt in the previous argument with the possibility of error as a mere possibility, we have had to use the result of the previous chapter concerning the nature of possibility itself. The idea of the barely possible, in which there is no actuality, is an empty idea. If anything is possible, then, when we say so, we postulate something as actually existent in order to constitute this possibility. The conditions of possible error must be actual. Bare possibility is blank nothingness. If the nature of error necessarily and with perfect generality demands certain conditions, then these conditions are as eternal as the erroneousness of error itself is eternal. And thus the inclusive thought, which constitutes the error, must be postulated as existent.

So, finally, let one try to affirm that the infinite content of the all-including mind does not exist, and that the foregoing idealism is a mere illusion of ours. He will find that he is involved in a circle from which there is no escape. For let him return to the position of total relativity and so say: ''The infinite thought is unreal for me, and hence you are wrong.'' But then also he admits that we are right, for in affirming this infinite we affirm, according to this doctrine of total relativity itself, something that is just as true as it seems to us to be true. The opposing argument is thus at each moment of its progress involved in a contradiction. Or again, let him insist that our doctrine is not only relatively, but really false. Then however he will fail to show us what this real falsity is. In fact he says what all our previous examination shows to mean, this, namely, that an infinite thought does exist, and does experience the truth, and compares our thought with the truth, and then observes this thought of ours to be false, that is, it discovers that itself is non-existent. Whoever likes this result may hold it if he can.

IX

Now that our argument is completed as an investigation, let us review it in another way. We started from the fact of Error. That there is error is indubitable. What is, however, an error? The substance of our whole reasoning about the nature of error amounted to the result that in and of itself alone, no single judgment is or can be an error. Only as actually included in a higher thought, that gives to the first its completed object, and compares it therewith, is the first thought an error. It remains otherwise a mere mental fragment, a torso, a piece of drift-wood, neither true nor false, objectless, no complete act of thought at all. But the higher thought must include the opposed truth, to which the error is compared in that higher thought. The higher thought is the whole truth, of which the error is by itself an incomplete fragment.

Now, as we saw with this as a starting-point, there is no stopping-place short of an Infinite Thought. The possibilities of error are infinite. Infinite then must be the inclusive thought. Here is this stick, this brickbat, this snow-flake: there is an infinite mass of error possible about any one of them, and notice, not merely possible is it, but actual. All the infinite series of blunders that you could make about them not only would be blunders, but in very truth now are blunders, though you personally could never commit them all. You cannot in fact *make* a truth or a falsehood by your thought. You only *find* one. From all eternity that truth was true, that falsehood false. Very well then, that infinite thought must somehow have had all that in it from the beginning. If a man doubts it, let him answer our previous difficulties. Let him show us how he can make an error save through the presence of an actual inclusive thought for which the error always was error and never became such at all. If he can do that, let him try. We should willingly accept the result if he could show it to us. But he cannot. We have rambled over those barren hills already too long. Save for Thought there is no truth, no error. Save for inclusive Thought, there is no truth, no error, in separate thoughts. Separate thoughts as such cannot then know or have the distinction between their own truth and their own falsity in themselves, and apart from the inclusive thought. There is then nothing of truth or of error to be found in the world of separate thoughts as such. All the thoughts are therefore in the last analysis actually true or false, only for the all-including Thought, the Infinite.

We could have reached the same result had we set out from the problem, *What is Truth?* We chose not to do so because our skepticism had the placid answer ready: "No matter *what* truth is, for very likely there is little or no truth at all to be had. Why trouble one's mind to define what a fairy or a brownie is?" "Very well, then," we said to our skepticism, "if that is thy play, we know a move that thou thinkest not of. We will not ask thee of truth, if thou thinkest there is none. We will ask thee of error, wherein thou revelest." And our skepticism very cheerfully, if somewhat incoherently, answers, that, "if there be little or no truth here below, there is at least any amount of error, which as skeptics we have all been detecting ever since we first went to school." "We thank thee for that word, O friend, but now, what is an error?" Blessed be Socrates for that question. Upon that rock philosophy can, if it wants, build we know not yet how much.

It is enough for the moment to sum up the truth that we have found. It is this: "*All reality must be present to the Unity of the Infinite Thought.*" There is no chance of escape. For all reality is reality because true judgments can be made about it. And all reality, for the same reason, can be the object of false judgments. Therefore, since the false and the true judgments are all true or false as present to the infinite thought, along with their objects, no reality can escape. You and I and all of us, all good, all evil, all truth, all falsehood, all things actual and possible, exist as they exist, and are known for what they are, in and to the absolute thought; are therefore all judged as to their real character at this everlasting throne of judgment.

This we have found to be true, because we tried to doubt everything. We shall try to expound in the coming chapter the religious value of the conception. We can however at once see this in it: The Infinite Thought must, knowing all truth, include also a knowledge of all wills, and of their conflict. For him all this conflict, and all the other facts of the moral world, take place. He then must know the outcome of the conflict, that Moral Insight of our first book. In him then we have the Judge of our ideals, and the Judge of our conduct. He must know the exact value of the Good Will, which for him, like all other possible truth, must be an actually realized Fact. And so we cannot pause with a simply theoretical idealism. Our doctrine is practical too. We have found not only an infinite Seer of physical facts, but an infinite Seer of the Good as well as of the Evil. He knows what we have and what we lack. In looking for goodness we are in no wise looking for what the real world does not contain.

This, we say, we have found as a truth, because we tried to doubt everything. We have taken the wings of the morning, and we have fled; but behold, we are in the midst of the Spirit. Truly the words that some people have thought so fantastic ought henceforth to be put in the text-books as commonplaces of logical analysis:—

> "They reckon ill that leave me out;
> When me they fly, I am the wings,
> I am the doubter and the doubt."—

Everything finite we can doubt, but not the Infinite. That eludes even our skepticism. The world-builders, and the theodicies that were to justify them, we could well doubt. The apologetic devices wearied us. All the ontologies of the realistic schools were just pictures, that we could accept or reject as we chose by means of postulates. We tried to escape them all. We forsook all those gods that were yet no gods; but here we have found something that abides, and waxes not old, something in which there is no variableness, neither shadow of turning. No power it is to be resisted, no planmaker to be foiled by fallen angels, nothing finite, nothing striving, seeking, losing, altering, growing weary; the All-Enfolder it is, and we know its name. Not Heart, nor Love, though these also are in it and of it; Thought it is, and all things are for Thought, and in it we live and move.

THE RELIGIOUS INSIGHT

If thou betake thyself to the ever-living and abiding Truth, the desertion or death of a friend shall not make thee sad.—*Imitation of Christ*.

Cum contra sapiens, quatenus ut talis consideratur, vix animo movetur, sed sui et Dei et rerum aeterna quadam necessitate conscius, nunquam esse desinit, sed semper vera animi acquiescentia potitur.—SPINOZA, *Ethica*.

We are in a new world of Divine Life. The dark world of the powers has passed away from our thought. Here is the Eternal, for which all these powers exist, in which they dwell. Here we are in the presence of the Ideal Judge who knows all Good and Evil. From the other side the world as we approached it had seemed so restless, so disheartening, so deaf. The world of our postulates was a brighter one only because we determined to make it so. But there was something lonesome in the thought that the postulates got, as answer from the real world, only their own echo, and not always that. Their world was rather their own creation than an external something that gave them independent support. Sometimes there seemed to be nothing solid that could echo back anything at all. Now we seem to look upon a truth that satisfies indeed no selfish longings of ours, no whims of theological tradition, no demands of our personal narrow lives. We shall not learn in this way who is first in the kingdom of heaven, nor how the dead are raised, nor any answer to any other special demand of any set of men. We learn, however, this at least: *All truth is known to One Thought, and that Infinite*. What does that imply? Let us see.

I

Our argument is somewhat near to the thought that partially satisfied St. Augustine when he found it in his Plato. That there should be a truth at all implies, we have seen, that there should be an Infinite Truth, known to an Infinite Thought; or, in other words, that all is for thought, and without thought is nothing that is. We also are a part of this infinite thought. We know not yet more of the nature of this thought, save that it must be eternal, all-embracing, and One. What then shall we be able further to say about it?

To answer would be to expound a system of philosophy. But we must limit ourselves here to the necessary. And so, for the first, we shall try to point out what this ideal and infinite life of thought that we have found as the eternal truth of things *cannot* be expected to accomplish for the purposes of our religion, and then to consider what we may nevertheless dare to hope from it.

It cannot be expected to furnish us an *a priori* knowledge of any fact of experience, of any particular law of nature, of the destiny of any one finite being. All that remains just as dark as it was before. We neither rejoice in this result, nor lament it. Nobody who wanders into the ideal world may expect to find it ordered for his individual advantage; nor need he try to find there good investments for his money. The Infinite does not wait for his individual approval; although morally speaking he may do well to get the approval of the Infinite. The Infinite was not elected to office by his vote, and he may not impeach it for disregard of his humble petitions for good things, nor threaten it with want of confidence because it does not secure passage for his private bills. In so far as to say this is to condemn the Real, we unhesitatingly do so. But then, as we saw in our ethical discussion, the moral insight is not so much concerned with private bills, as with certain greater matters. If the moral insight wants religious support, possibly the failure of all these personal concerns of ours to find any hint of response from the Absolute, may not render impossible the ethical undertakings of the human spirit. If as individuals we must hear the dreadful words from the spirit of nature: *Du gleichst dem Geist den du begreifst, nicht mir;* still it is possible that with a higher insight, looking upon this same spirit in its eternal and inmost nature, we may yet come with full reason at last to say: *Erhabner Geist, du gabst mir, gabst mir alles, warum ich bat.* For there are demands and demands. Man, as lover, demands success in love, and the course of the world may thwart him; as toiler, he demands for himself personal immortality, and the course of the world may care naught for his individual life; as bereaved, as mourner over his dead, he may demand for his loved ones also this immortality, and the course of the world may leave the fate of all his loved ones mysterious forever; as lover of mankind, he may demand an infinite future of blessed progress for his race, and the law of the dissipation of energy may give him the only discoverable physical answer to his demand; as just man, he may cry aloud that evil shall cease from among men, and the wicked may still laugh in triumph unpunished. And yet for all this he may find some higher compensation. Agnostic as he will remain about all the powers of this world, about the outcome of all finite processes, he will take comfort in the assurance that an Infinite Reason is above all and through all, embracing everything, judging everything, infallible, perfect. To this Thought he may look up, saying: "Thou All-Knowing One seest us, what we are, and how we strive. Thou knowest our frame, and rememberest that we are as dust. In thy perfection is our Ideal. That thou art, is enough for our moral comfort. That thou knowest our evil and our good, that gives us our support in our little striving for the good. Not worthless would we be in thy sight; not of the vile, the base, the devilish party in the warfare of this world. Thou that judgest shalt say that we, even in our poor individual lives, are better than naught. Thou shalt know that in our weakness and blindness, in our pain and sorrow, in our little days, in our dark world, ignorant as to the future, confused with many doubts, beset with endless temptations, full of dread, of hesitation, of sloth, we yet sought, such as we were, to be in our own fashion like thee; to know the truth as thou knowest it, to be full of higher life as thou art full, to be above strife as thou art above it, to be of one Spirit as thou art One, to be perfect as thou art perfect. This thou shalt see in us, and this record shall be eternal, like our knowledge. In thee what we vaguely aim to conceive is clear light. In thee the peace that we strive to find is experienced. And when we try to do right, we know that thou seest both our striving and our successes and our failures. And herein we have comfort. We perish, but thou endurest. Ours is not thy eternity. But in thy eternity we would be remembered, not as rebels against the good, but as doers of the good; not as blots on the face of this part of thy infinite reality, but as healthy leaves that flourished for a time on the branches of the eternal tree of life, and that have fallen, though not into forgetfulness. For to thee nothing is forgotten."

This thought, of the Judge that never ceases to think of us and of all things, never changes, never mistakes, and that knows the Good simply because that Good is an element of the Truth—perhaps this can sustain us when all else fails. Nothing but this may be certain; but this, if it be not all that some people have sought, may be a help to us. This Religion may have no such hot little fires on its altars as we at first longed for; but then it is a very old objection to the stars to say that they bake us no bread, and only glitter up there in the dark to be looked at. Yet even the stars are worth something to us.

II

But if we leave these limitations of our view, and pass to its positive religious value, our first sense is one of joy and freedom to find that our long-sought ideal of a perfect unity of life is here attained. Let us look away for a moment from our finite existence, with its doubts and its problems, to the conception of that infinite life. In that life is all truth, fully present in the unity of one eternal moment. The world is no mass of separate facts, stuck one to another in an external way, but, for the infinite, each fact is what it is only by reason of its place in the infinite unity. The world of life is then what we desired it to be, an organic total; and the individual selves are drops in this ocean of the absolute truth.

Thus then, seen in the light of this our result, the human tasks that we sketched in our ethical discussion find their place in the objective world. Now, and in fact for the first time, we can see what we were really trying to accomplish through our ideal. We were trying in a practical way to realize what we now perceive to be the fullness of the life of God. So that the one highest activity, in which all human activities were to join, is known to us now as the *progressive realization by men of the eternal life of an Infinite Spirit*. So whereas we formerly had to say to men: Devote yourselves to art, to science, to the state, or to any like work that does tend to organize your lives into one life, we may now substitute one absolute expression for all those accidental expressions, and may say: *Devote yourselves to losing your lives in the divine life*. For all these special aims that we have mentioned are but means of accomplishing the knowledge of the fullness of the truth. And Truth is God.

Now this precept is no barren abstraction. It means to take hold of every act of life, however humble and simple. "Where art thou, O man?" our ideal says to us. "Art thou not in God? To whom dost thou speak? With whom dost thou walk? What life is this in whose midst thou livest? What are all these things that thou seemest to touch? Whose is all this beauty that thou enjoyest in art, this unity that thou seekest to produce in thy state, this truth that thou pursuest in thy thought? All this is in God and of God. Thou hast never seen, or heard, or touched, or handled, or loved anything but God. Know this truth, and thy life must be transformed to thee in all its significance. Serve the whole God, not the irrationally separate part that thy delusions have made thee suppose to be an independent thing. Live out thy life in its full meaning; for behold, it is God's life."

So, as it seems, the best that we could have wished from the purely moral side is attained. The Divine Thought it is that actually accomplishes what we imperfectly sought to attain, when we defined for ourselves Duty. In the Divine Thought is perfectly and finally realized the Moral Insight and the Universal Will of our ethical discussion. And this insight and will are not realized as by some Power, that then should set about to accomplish their fulfillment externally. But in the infinite, where all is eternally complete, the insight is both present and fulfilled; the universal will gets what it seeks. There is no lack there, nor hesitation, nor striving, nor doubt, nor weariness; but all is eternally perfect triumph.

Now this, though it sounds mystical enough to our untrained common sense, is no mere poetry of thought. It is the direct philosophical outcome of what we have found by a purely logical process. The driest thought, the simplest fragment of rationality, involves this absolute, infinite, and perfect thought: And this it involves because it involves the possibility of error, and because, as separate from the infinite, this possibility of error in a single thought becomes unintelligible and contradictory. We did all that we could to escape this conclusion. We wandered in the thickets of confusion and contradiction, until there was no chance of finding there a further pathway. And then we turned to see, and behold, God was in this place, though we had known it not. The genuine God that we thus found was no incomplete, struggling God, whom we might pity in his conflict with evil, but the all-embracing thought, in which the truth is eternally finished. And this God it is that we now see as the complete realization of our own ideal, as of all worthy ideals.

For consider if you will this element in our conception of this Thought. Can this infinite know itself as imperfect, or as not possessing some object that it knows to be good? This is impossible, and doubly so. Not only does the conception of an Infinite, in which and for which are all things, wholly exclude the possibility of any good thing beyond the Infinite itself, but also in still another way does the same truth appear. For if you suppose that this infinite thought desires some perfection G, that it has not, then either it is right in supposing this perfection to be truly desirable, or it is wrong. In either case the previous argument of Chapter XI shows us that the truth or the falsity of this judgment of desire about G must exist as known truth or falsity for a higher thought, which, including the thought that desires, and itself actually having this desired good thing, compares the desired object with the conception of the thought that desires it, and judges of them both. Above the desire, then, must in every case exist the satisfaction of the desire in a higher thought. So that for the Infinite there can be no unsatisfied desire. Unsatisfied desire exists only in the finite beings, not in the inclusive Infinite.

The world then, as a whole, is and must be absolutely good, since the infinite thought must know what is desirable, and knowing it, must have present in itself the true objects of desire. The existence of any amount of pain or of other evil, of crime or of baseness in the world as we see it, is, thus viewed, no evidence against the absolute goodness of things, rather a guaranty thereof. For all evil viewed externally is just an evidence to us finite beings that there exists something desirable, which we have not, and which we just now cannot get. However stubborn this evil is for us, that has naught to do with the perfection of the Infinite. For the infinite did not make this evil, but the evil, *together with the making of it,* which indeed was also in its separateness evil,—all this is a phenomenon for the infinite thought, which, in knowing this evil, merely knows the absolute desirableness of that which it also possesses, namely, the absolutely good.

We have used here an argument that could not be used in our study of the "World of Doubt." When we there thought evil to be possible for the world as a whole, we conceived that a being who knew all the world would yet desire something better. But what would this imply? It implies that this being would desire a state of things different from the existing one, and would do so believing that state to be better than the existing one. But would he truly know this desired state to be better, or would he only hope so? Who truly knows the value of a state save the one that possesses it? Knowledge is of the present. Therefore this being would not really know the better state, unless it were already actual for him. But in that case he would include not only the present world, but the perfect world, and his total state could not be one of discontent. So the other alternative remains. Our supposed being would only hope the desired state to be better than what was real already for him. But would his hope be a true one? If so, then it could only be true in case this perfection is already realized in a higher thought. For the Infinite then the question, "Is there anything better than what exists?" must be nonsense. For him the actual and the possible fall together in one truth; and this one truth cannot be evil.

On another side, our conception gives us religious support. The imperfection of the purely moral view lay in part in the fact that there was an inner incompleteness about the very definition of our ideal, as well as a doubt about its attainability. This inner incompleteness must however be removed in and for the Infinite Mind. In dealing with the work of life, we came to a point where we said, thus far we can see our way, but beyond that our ideal remains incomplete. We must have faith, so we implied, that if we attained so much of the ideal social condition, the way from that point onward would become clear. But now we see why the way would of necessity become clear to one whose knowledge of life were broad enough and deep enough. For in the Infinite that includes all life, that rests above all finite strife in the absolute attainment of the ideal, there can be no incompleteness, no torso of an ideal, but a perfect knowledge of what is most excellent. Those faint foreshadowings of a perfect life that art and science and social work show to us, must be for the Infinite no faint foreshadowings, but absolute certainty and perfect clearness. Hence by our religious doctrine we get not merely the assurance that such ideals as we have are realized for the Infinite; but, better than this, we get our first full assurance that our incomplete ideals have an actual completion as ideals. For we thus get our first full assurance that there is in the highest sense any definite ideal at all. Pessimism, as we have seen, implies either doubt about what the ideal state is, or unavoidable lack of that state. And the Infinite can be no Pessimist in either sense.

The religious comfort that a man can get from contemplating all this truth is indeed very different from the consolation of the separate individual as such that many people want their religion to give them. And this very fact furnishes us a good test of moral sincerity. The religious comfort that we find is no comfort save to the truly religious spirit in us. It says to us: "You that have declared your willingness to serve moral ideals because they are such, does this help you to know, not of a goodly place where you personally and individually shall live without tears forever as a reward for your services, but of an eternal Judge that respects in no whit your person, before whom and in whom you are quite open and perfectly known, who now and for all eternity sees your good and your evil, and estimates you with absolute justice? This blaze of infinite light in which you stand, does it cheer you? If it does, then you are glad to learn that above all your struggles there is the eternal Victory, amid all your doubts there is the eternal Insight, and that your highest triumph, your highest conception, is just an atom of the infinite truth that all the time is there. But if all this is true of you, then you do love the ideal for its own sake. Then it is not your triumph that you seek, but the triumph of the Highest. And so it is that you rejoice to learn how this that is best in the world not only will triumph, but always has triumphed, since, as you now learn, for God the highest good is thus a matter of direct experience."

The writer remembers well, how some years since, while all this doctrine seemed to him shrouded in doubt, he heard a very thoughtful and pious friend maintain that the greatest comfort to be got from a belief in God is the sense that however much the world may misjudge us, however much even our best and closest friends may misunderstand us, there is one perfect all-knowing Thought that comprehends us far better than we comprehend ourselves. Goodness is, in that thought, estimated at its full worth. Nothing is hidden from the Judge. And what we are, He knoweth it altogether. The present view seems to the author to meet the conditions that his friend here had in mind. Theism as a doctrine that there is a big power that fights and beats down other powers in the service of the good, is open to all the objections before suggested. This warrior, why does he not win? This slayer of evil things, this binder of Satan, who boasts that all things will yet be put under his feet,—has he not had all eternity in which to put all things under his feet, and has he done it yet? He may be indeed good, but somehow disaster seems to pursue him. Religious comfort in contemplating him you can have if you believe in him, but always you feel that this comfort is shadowed by the old doubt; is he after all what we want him to be, the victorious ruler of the world? But if we leave the eternally doubtful contemplation of the world as a heap of powers, and come to the deeper truth of the world as Thought, then these doubts must disappear.

Yet to show that this is true, we must dwell upon doubts a little longer, and must compare our present view of the solution of the problem of evil with the views condemned in Chap. VIII.

III

So far we have come in joyful contemplation of the Divine Truth. But now is there not a serpent in this Eden also? We have been talking of the infinite goodness; but after all, what shall we still say of that finite "partial evil" of life? We seem to have somehow proved *a priori* that it must be "universal good." For, as we have said, in the Infinite Life of our ideal there can be no imperfection. This, we have said, is the demonstration that we missed all through our study of the world of the Powers. Since we approached that world from without, and never felt the pulse of its heart's blood, we had nothing but doubt after doubt when we contemplated the evil that seemed to be in it. Our efforts to explain evil seemed hollow and worthless. There might be some deeper truth involved in these efforts; but we knew it not. Well, are we right in declaring that we have altogether overcome our difficulty now? Apparently we are as far as ever from seeing *how* the partial evil can be the universal good; we only show, from the conception of the infinite itself, *that* the partial evil must be the universal good. God must see how; and we know this because we know of God. More than this we seem to be unable to suggest.

But will this do? Have we not forgotten one terrible consequence of our doctrine? The partial evil is universal good, is it? There is no evil? All apparent imperfection is an illusion of our partial view? So then *where is the chance to be in a free way and of our own choice better than we otherwise in truth should be?* Is not the arm that is raised to strike down wickedness paralyzed by the very thought that was to give it divine strength? This evil that I fight here in this finite world is a delusion. So then, why fight it? If I do good works, the world is infinitely good and perfect. If I seem to do evil works, the world is in truth no worse. Seeming good is not better than seeming evil, for if it were, then the seeming evil would be a real defect in God, in whose life is everything. If I have never loved aught but God, even so I have never hated aught but God. It is all alike. God does not need just me. Or rather I may say, in so far as he needs me to complete his infinite truth, he already has me from all eternity. I have nothing to do with the business, save to contemplate in dizzy indolence the whirling misty masses of seeming evil, and to say with a sort of amused reverence that they look very ill and opaque to me, but that of course God sees through them clearly enough somehow. The mist is in truth crystalline water, and he has so quick a sense as to look beyond the drops as easily as if they were in the calm unity of a mountain lake. And so, my religion is simply a contemplation of God's wisdom, but otherwise an idle amusement.

So says the man who sees only this superficial view of our doctrine. In so far as, standing once more outside of some evil thing, we say: "That thing yonder looks bad, but God must see it to be good," we do indeed remain indolent, and our religion simply means a sort of stoical indifference to the apparent distinction of good and evil. This is in fact the proper practical attitude of even the most earnest man in the presence of evil that he cannot understand and cannot affect. In such matters we must indeed be content with the passive knowledge. Death and the unavoidable pains of life, the downfall of cherished plans, all the cruelty of fate, we must learn to look at as things to us opaque, but to God, who knows them fully, somehow clear and rational. So regarding them, we must aim to get to the stage of stoical indifference about them. They are to us the accidents of existence. We have no business to murmur about them, since we see that God, experiencing them, somehow must experience them as elements in an absolutely perfect life. For God we regard not as the mysterious power who made them, and who then may have been limited to the use of imperfect means, but as the absolute thought that knows them; so that, however inexplicable they must now be to us, they are in themselves nothing that God vainly wishes to have otherwise, but they are organically joined with the rest of the glorious Whole.

Such is indeed the only present word for us finite minds about many of the shadows of seeming evil that we have to behold in the world of the apparently external facts. Such however is *not* the last word for us about the only evil that has any immediate moral significance, namely, the evil that we see, not as an external, shadowy mist, but as a present fact, experienced in us. Here it is that the objector just mentioned seems really formidable to us. But just here it is that we find the answer to him. For in the world of our own acts we have a wondrous experience. We realize evil, we fight it, and, at the same time, we realize our fragment of the perfect divine life in the moment itself of struggling with the evil. And in this wondrous experience lies the whole solution of the ancient problem of the existence of moral evil. For instance, I find in myself a selfish impulse, trying to destroy the moral insight. Now of this evil impulse I do not say, looking at it objectively: "It is somehow a part of the universal good"; but, in the moment of moral action I *make* it, even in the very moment of its sinfulness, a part of my good consciousness, *in overcoming it*. The moral insight condemns the evil that it experiences; *and in condemning and conquering this evil it forms and is, together with the evil, the organic total that constitutes the good will*. Only through this inner victory over the evil that is experienced as a conquered tendency does the good will have its being. Now since the perfect life of God must have the absolutely good will, therefore it also must be conscious of such a victory. Thus the solution of our difficulty begins to appear. And thus we reap a new religious fruit from our ethical doctrine, to whose main principles we must once more here refer the reader.

When I experience the victory of the moral insight over the bad will, I experience in one indivisible moment both the partial evil of the selfish impulse (which in itself as a separate fact would be wholly bad) and the universal good of the moral victory, which has its existence only in the overwhelming of the evil. So, in the good act, I experience the good as my evil lost in goodness, as a rebellion against the good conquered in the moment of its birth, as a peace that arises in the midst of this triumphant conflict, as a satisfaction that lives in this restless activity of inner warfare. This child of inner strife is the good, and the only moral good, we know.

What I here have present in me when I do a good act is an element of God's life. *I here directly experience how the partial moral evil is universal good;* for so it is a relatively universal good in me when, overcoming myself, I choose the universal will. The bad impulse is still in me, but is defeated. In the choice against evil is the very life of goodness, which would be a pale, stupid abstraction otherwise. Even so, to take another view, in the overcoming of our separateness as individuals lies, as we saw in the previous book, our sense of the worth of the universal life. And what we here experience in the single moment of time, and in the narrowness of our finite lives, God must experience, and eternally. In our single good acts we have thus the specimen of the eternal realization of goodness.

But now how simple becomes the answer to that terrible suggestion of a moment since! How simple also the solution of the problem of evil! "If I want to do evil, I cannot," said the objector; "for God the perfect one includes me with the rest, and so cannot in his perfection be hurt by me. Let me do what I will, my act can only seem bad, and cannot be bad. All evil is illusion, hence there is no moral difference in action possible."

"Right indeed," we answer, but also wrong, because half the truth. The half kills, the whole gives life. Why canst thou not do any absolute evil? Because thy evil intent, which, in its separateness, *would be* unmixed evil, thy selfish will, thy struggle against the moral insight, this evil will of thine is no lonesome fact in the world, but is an element in the organic life of God. *In him thy evil impulse forms part of a total good will, as the evil impulse of the good man forms an element in his realization of goodness.* In God thy separateness is destroyed, and with it thy sin as evil. For good will in the infinite is what the good man finds the good will to be in himself, namely, the organic total whose truth is the *discovery of the evil.* Therefore is God's life perfect, because it includes not only the knowledge of thy finite wicked will, but the insight into its truth as a moment in the real universal will.

If then thou wert good, thou wouldst be good by including the evil impulse in a realization of its evil, and in an acceptance of the higher insight. If thou art evil, then in thyself, as separate being, thou art condemned, and just because thy separate evil is condemned, therefore is the total life of God, that includes thee with thy condemnation and with the triumph over thee, good.

This is the ground for the solution of the problem. To go more into detail: Evil is for us of two classes: the external seeming evil, such as death, pain, or weakness of character; and internal evil, namely the bad will itself. Because we know so little, therefore we can never tell whether those externally seen seeming evils are blessings in disguise, or expressions of some wicked diabolical will-power at work about us. Somehow then, we never know exactly how, these seeming great evils must be in God universal good. But with regard to the only evil that we know as an inward experience, and so as a certain reality, namely, the Evil Will, we know both the existence of that, and its true relation to universal goodness, because and only because we experience both of them first through the moral insight, and then in the good act. Goodness having its very life in the insight and in its exercise, has as its elements the evil impulse *and* its correction. The evil will as such may either be conquered in our personal experience, and then we are ourselves good; or it may be conquered not in our thought considered as a separate thought, but in the total thought to which ours is so related, as our single evil and good thoughts are related to the whole of us. The wicked man is no example of God's delight in wickedness, just as the evil impulse that is an element in the good man's goodness, and a very real element too, is no proof that the good man delights in evil. As the evil impulse is to the good man, so is the evil will of the wicked man to the life of God, in which he is an element. And just because the evil will is the only evil that we are sure of, this explanation is enough.

Thus the distinction between good and evil remains as clear as ever. Our difficulty about the matter is removed, not by any barren external theodicy, such as were the forms of guess-work that we criticised in a previous chapter, but by a plain reflection on the moral experience itself. Goodness as a moral experience is for us the overcoming of experienced evil; and in the eternal life of God the realization of goodness must have the same sort of organic relation to evil as it has in us. Goodness is not mere innocence, but realized insight. To the wicked man we say: God is good because in thinking thee he damns thy evil impulse and overwhelms it in a higher thought of which thou art a part. And in so far as thy will is truly evil, thou art in God just as the evil is in the good man; thou art known only to be condemned and overcome. That is thy blessed mission; and this mission of evil such as thine is indeed an eternal one. So that both things are true. The world is wholly good, and thou, such as thou individually art, mayest be damnably evil if so thou desirest.

We do not say then that evil must exist to set the good off by way of external contrast. That view we long since justly rejected. We say only that the evil will is a conquered element *in* the good will, and is as such necessary to goodness. Our conception of the absolute unity of God's life, and that conception alone, enables us to apply this thought here. No form of dualistic Theism has any chance to apply this, the only satisfactory theodicy. If God were conceived as external to his creatures, as a power that made them beyond himself, the hopeless problems and the unworthy subterfuges of the older theodicies would come back to torment us. As it is, the solution of the problem of evil is given us in the directest and yet in the most unexpected way.

Let us compare this solution with others. Evil, said one thought, before expounded, is an illusion of the partial view, as the shapelessness of the fragment of a statue is no disproof of the real beauty of the whole. We replied in a previous chapter to this notion, by saying that evil seems so positive an element in the world as to make very hard this conception of the partial evil as good universally in the æsthetic sense in which shapelessness of parts may coexist with a total beauty of the statue. For the fragment of the statue is merely an indifferent bit of stone without character. But the evil in the world seems in positive crying opposition to all goodness. Yet now, in the moral experience, we have found a wholly different relation of evil part to good whole. My good act is good just because of the evil that exists in it as conquered element. Without the evil moment *actual* in it, the total act could be at best innocent, not good. It is good by reason of its structure. That structure includes the evil will, but so includes it that the whole act is good. Even so, as we declare, God's life includes, in the organic total of one conscious eternal instant, all life, and so all goodness and evil. To say that God is nevertheless perfectly good is to say, not that God is innocent, knowing of no evil whatever, and including none; but that he so includes the evil will in the structure of his good will, as the good man, in one indivisible moment, includes his evil will in his good will; and that God is good only because he does so.

Again, to pass to another explanation, it has been said that evil exists in the world as a means to goodness. We objected to this that it puts the evil and the good first in separate beings, in separate acts or moments, and then makes the attainment of the good result dependent on the prior attainment of the separate and independently present evil. Now all that explanation could only explain and justify the acts of a finite Power, which, not yet possessing a given good thing, seeks it through the mediation of some evil. In no wise can this explanation apply to God as infinite. He is no finite Power, nor does he make or get things external to himself. Hence he cannot be said to use means for the attainment of ends. But our explanation does not make evil a means to get the separate end, goodness. We say that the connection is one of organic part with organic whole; that goodness has its life only in the instant of the discovery and inner overcoming of the evil will; and that therefore any life is good in which the evil will is present only as overcome, and so as lost in the good will. We appeal to the moral experience to illustrate how, when we do good, the evil will is present as a real fact in us, which yet does not make us as a whole bad, but just because it is present as an overcome element, is, even for that very reason, necessary to make us good. And we go on to say that even so in God the evil will of all who sin is present, a real fact in the Divine Life, no illusion in so far as one sees that it exists in God and nowhere else, but for that very reason an element, and a necessary element, in the total goodness of the Universal Will, which, realized in God, is related to the wills of the sinners as the wills of the good men are related to their evil impulses.

The explanation that evil is needed to contrast with goodness has already been mentioned.

Evil therefore, as a supposed real fact, *separate* from goodness, and a totally independent entity, is and must be an illusion. The objections to this view that we previously urged in Chapter VIII were all applicable to the world of powers, which we viewed and had to view externally. God's life, viewed internally, as philosophy must view it, is not subject to these criticisms. And the moral experience has taught us how we are to explain the existence of the only partial evil that we clearly know to be even a partial evil, namely, the evil will. The explanation is that the good act has its existence and life *in the transcending of experienced present evil*. This evil must not be an external evil, beyond the good will, but must be experienced in the same indivisible moment in which it is transcended. That this wondrous union is possible, we simply find as fact in the moral experience. No genuine moral goodness is possible save in the midst of such inner warfare. The absence of the evil impulse leaves naught but innocence or instinct, morally insipid and colorless. Goodness is this organism of struggling elements. Now, as we declare, in the infinite and united thought of God this unity of goodness is eternally present. God's life is this infinite rest, *not apart from but in the endless strife,* as in substance Heraclitus so well and originally taught.

IV

The problem of the existence of evil thus treated as our limits allow, we must return to a study of the visible world. That we formerly refused to find religious comfort in that world, depended upon our previous manner of approaching it. It was, so approached, the world of doubt; but now it may prove no longer disheartening, so that we may be able to get in it a concrete hold of useful truth. We must briefly sketch the process of return. Our Infinite, once known, is known not as an abstraction, but as an immediately actual object of knowledge. His then is this visible world; and, knowing the fact, we return cheerfully and courageously among the facts that before seemed dead externalities, to find his truth in them. For our general belief in the infinite rationality of things is useless to supersede any jot or tittle of careful scientific study of the common world of experience. Be this aspect of the matter well understood. Some older forms of idealism have looked coldly on experience. Ours does not. To us, if you want to realize your ideal you must know the means, you must study applied ethics as well as the ideal itself; and only from science, from hard, dry, careful collection and collaboration of facts, from cautious generalizations, from endless experiments, observations, calculations, can mankind hope to learn the means of realizing their ideals. Yet more, only from exact science can you get the best concrete examples of that unity of conception, that mastery of complex details, that exhaustive perfection of insight, that we must attribute in an infinitely complete form to our all-embracing Ideal Thought, now that we have got it before us as our Ideal. That all facts and relations of facts should appear in one moment of insight to the all-knowing thought is our postulate, and, as we have shown, it is no mere postulate, but a necessary and absolute principle of philosophy. We must go to exact science to find illustrations of how all this can be in particular cases realized. As the equation of a curve expresses in one thought all the properties of the curve, as the law of a physical process includes all the cases of that process under any of the supposed conditions, as a function of a variable may be the sum of a long series of quantities, each one of which is a derived function of the first multiplied by a particular coefficient, so that the one function is the united expression of the numerous separate functions: even in such wise must the Infinite thought comprehend in some supreme highest unity all the facts and relations of facts that are in the world of truth. For us then the highest achievements of science are the dim shadow of the perfection of the infinite thought. And to science, accordingly, we must go, not for the invention, but for the intellectual illustration of our ideal. And science we must treat as absolute mistress of her own domain. Of the world as a whole, of the eternal as such, of infinite past time, of the inner truth of things, science pretends to tell and can tell nothing. Nor does science invent, nor yet can she prove, her own postulates, as we previously defined them. But in the application of her postulates to the facts, in the discovery of particular laws, science is almighty. To doubt her capacity as highest judge in this field is flagrant contempt of court. Science is just the Infinite Thought as far as it is yet by us realized in the facts of nature. *A priori* we can realize nothing about finite facts, save that they must be *capable* of rational comprehension. We know that the Infinite thinks them, and this is all that we know about them. What they are, experience must tell us.

Such then are some of the restrictions imposed upon our thought. We must now consider more carefully how we must treat the scientific postulates that were our only comfort in studying reality before we reached our present insight.

When we postulated that the world must in the best sense satisfy our fundamental intellectual needs, we assumed what is necessary for science, but what science itself does not satisfactorily explain. Have we now reached any foundation for this theoretical postulate? We have in fact reached one. The postulate of science amounts to this, that the real connections among facts must be such as would be rationally comprehensible if they were known. But we have found in fact that all facts not only must be rationally comprehensible, but are rationally comprehended, in and by the one Divine Mind. The postulate of science expresses therefore in part and as a mere assumption, what we now know as a whole, and as a result of demonstration. The unity of the Divine Thought implies that all facts, if we knew them well enough, would appear rationally interdependent, reducible to unity, a total of realities expressible as one truth. Just as in the one concept of the nature of number is implied all the infinite series of properties that a complete Theory of Numbers would develop, so in the one concept of the universe, which constitutes the Divine Mind, all the facts of all possible experience are comprehended and are reduced to perfect unity. There must be then in fact a universal formula. What this formula is we do not see, and just because we do not see it, we have to look here and there in experience for any traces of the unity and rational connection of facts. Nor can we ever be sure that a connection surmised by us is the really rational connection of things. A law discovered by us is only our attempt to imitate the Divine

Thought. Our attempt may in a given case fail; our induction may be mistaken. But the foundation of our inductive processes is the thought that, since the real world is a perfectly rational and united body of truth, that hypothesis which reduces to relatively rational unity the greatest number of facts is more apt to represent the truth of things than any hypothesis of less scope, and of less rational significance. Just because this natural dualism with which we set out is a blunder, just because in fact the world is not rent in twain by our arbitrary distinction of object and subject, but is in deepest truth one united world, a single thought; therefore it is that when we consider those facts which we have from moment to moment to regard as external, we can be assured that there is a certain and not an arbitrary basis for our views about them. The visible world becomes again hard reality, which we experience and try to comprehend, just because we know that in itself this world is once for all comprehended.

Practically then, in dealing with the world of concrete facts, we must be realistic. It is our duty, for humanity's sake, to study and to believe in this external world, to have faith in the great postulates of common sense, to use all the things of the world. But the basis of this faith common sense can never find. And we have found it in the Absolute.

V

Have we then discovered that something of infinite religious worth of which we went in quest? Or can we say that our life is in vain in such a world? Truly our religious longing has met with a genuine response, but it was not such a response as we at first expected, nor such as most systems appear to desire. Personal needs and hopes apart, most men who make systems to satisfy the impersonal religious longing, seek to prove that the world as a whole progresses towards goodness, so that, in the great consummation of this progress, evil shall certainly and finally disappear, leaving the world as innocent and insipid as in the days of Eden. Now we have found a thought that makes this concept of progress not only wholly inapplicable to the world of the infinite life, but wholly superfluous. If, as we insisted above, moral goodness is not the absence, but the organic subordination, of the evil will, its overthrow in the good will, in which it is still actually present as subdued, then, whenever the world contains any moral goodness, it also, and for that very reason, contains, in its organic unity, moral evil. The world is morally good in spite of the evil will, and yet because of the evil will, since, as every moral experience shows us, the good will is just this triumphant rest in strife above the evil will. Therefore we have no sympathy with those who expect the future "salvation" of the world as a whole in time through any all-pervading process. The only destruction of moral evil that ever takes place or can take place is the transcendence of the evil will by the good will in the very moment of the life of the evil will. If moral evil were to be, as the older systems often expect, absolutely destroyed, and the world so freed therefrom that the evil will was totally forgotten, then what remained would be no moral good any more, only the laziness of an infinitely vacant life. Not indeed to set off the good by any external contrast, but to constitute a moment in the organic unity of the good act, is this evil in the world. And the whole vast trouble about understanding its presence arises because we usually separate it from the very unity with goodness in which we find it whenever we consciously do right ourselves. Then when so separated, as we separated it in a former chapter, moral evil, viewed as an external opaque fact, is inexplicable, disheartening, horrible. Only when we do right ourselves do we practically get the solution of the problem. Only the moral man knows how and why evil exists. For in him the evil will is an essential element of his goodness. The conflicts of morality are and must be eternal.

Our present explanation of evil in the world is, we have seen, the only one that can both give us the absolute religious comfort, and save us from the terrible moral paralysis involved in destroying, for the Infinite, the distinction between good and evil. The moral experience itself contains the miracle of this solution in the simplest and clearest shape. And it relieves us of any need to long for an absolute peace. For in it the distinction of good and evil is the sharpest, the significance of the strife is the most vivid, at the very instant when, in the strife, the evil will, present and real still, is yet conquered by the good will, and so lost in the universal goodness of the total good act. The distinction of good will and evil will becomes thus the greatest possible; and yet only through the reality of this distinction in the unity of the moral life is goodness present and triumphant. Progress in this world as a whole is therefore simply not needed. The good is eternally gained even in and through the evil. How far the actual process of evolution may in our part of the universe extend is a matter for empirical science.

But our own ideal of human life as a "progressive realization of the good,"—what of that? The answer is obvious. The good will that is in us as a temporal fact, not being yet fully realized or triumphant in us *as we are in ourselves as mere finite beings,* must aim at complete expression of itself in time and in us, and through us in those whom we seem to influence. For only *in so seeking* to perfect us in whom it exists, is this good will in us good at all. In so far as we, viewed abstractly, in our separateness from God, are good, we then do indeed try to realize that life of God in which we are all the time an element. For us this is progress. This progress is the form taken temporarily in us by the good will. But for God this is no real progress. Therefore is it indeed true that the moral insight in us must lead us to aim at progress in goodness, just as, on the other side, the rational element in us leads us to aim at progress in knowledge. But, meanwhile, our moral progress and our rational progress, mere minor facts happening at a moment of time, are but insignificant elements in the infinite life in which, as a whole, there is and can be no progress, but only an infinite variety of the forms of the good will and of the higher knowledge.

And so consciousness has given us in concrete form solutions of our two deepest philosophic problems. The possibility of error, necessitating an inclusive thought, is illustrated for us by our own conscious thought, which can include true and false elements in the unity of one clear and true thought at any moment. And the possibility and necessity of moral evil, demanding a real distinction between good and evil, a hateful opposition that seems at first sight fatal to our religious need for the supremacy of goodness in the united world, is illustrated for us in a way that solves this whole trouble, namely, in the unity of the conscious moral act. There at the one moment are good and evil, warring, implacable, yet united in the present momentary triumph of the good will. A world in which this strife, this victory, this absolute rest above the real strife and in the midst of the real strife, is the supreme fact, is the perfect world that religion needs. It is a world of the true Life of God.

VI

And our insight appeals not only to our general religious needs. It comes with its truth home to the individual man. It demands that we consider what our individual life is really worth when it is lived in the presence of this Infinite Judge. O man, what is this thy daily life! Thou livest for the applause or in fear of the blame of thy neighbors. An unkind word cuts thee to the quick. A little public favor, or the approving word of a friend, is worth half thy soul to thee. And all the while thou knowest not that One infinitely greater than multitudes of neighbors is here, not above thee only, nor afar in the heavens, but pervading thy every thought. And that all-pervading Thought judges thee as these neighbors never can. Myriads of their blunders about thee are as nothing to an atom of this infinite Truth. That rain-drop yonder in the sunshine is not more filled with the light, than are all the most hidden recesses of thy heart filled with that Infinite Presence. No one of us is more famous than his neighbor; for no one is known save by God, and to him all alike are known. To be sure, to know this is the same as understanding rightly, that thou art in truth what thou art. All truth is truth because it is known by a conscious Thought: therefore whatsoever thou art, whether it is consciously or unconsciously existent in thee, is known to the all-seeing Universal Consciousness. But commonplace as this seems to the philosopher, is it not more than a mere commonplace to thee, if thou lovest genuine righteousness? For is it not something to feel that thy life is, all of it, in God and for God? No one else knows thee. Alone thou wanderest in a dead world, save for this Presence. These other men, how can they know thee? They love thee or scorn thee or hate thee, but none of them love or scorn or hate thee for what thou art. Whatever they hold of thee, it is an accident. If they knew more of thee, doubtless they would think otherwise of thee. Do they love thee? Then they know thee not well enough, nor do they see thy meanness and thy vileness, thy selfishness and thy jealousy and thy malice. If they saw these, surely they would hate thee. But do they hate thee? Then thou callest them unjust. Doubtless they are so. Some chance word of thine, a careless look or gesture, an accident of fortune, a trifling fault, these they have remembered; and therefore do they hate thee. If they knew better things of thee, perhaps they would love thee.

Thus contradictory is thy life with them. And yet thou must labor that the good may triumph near thee by thy effort. Now in all this work who shall be thy true friend? Whose approval shall encourage thee? Thy neighbor's? Nay, but it is thy duty always to suspect thy neighbor's opinion of thee. He is a corrupt judge, or at best an ignorant judge. He sees not thy heart. He is a respecter of persons. He is too often a bundle of whims. If he also professes to be trying to serve righteousness, it is thy duty to have ready faith in his good intent, if that be possible for thee; but by all means doubt his wisdom about thee, and thine about him. If he praises thee for thy righteousness, listen not willingly to his praise. It will deceive thee. He will most praise thee when thou inwardly art not righteous. If he blames thee for evil, let it warn thee; for if he is not right now, he doubtless soon will be. But take it not too much to heart. He is ignorant of thee. He talks of thee as he might talk of the other side of the moon, unless indeed he talks of thee just as man in general, and not as to thy particular acts. Trust him not in all these things. Realize his needs as thou canst, strive to aid him in being righteous, use him as an instrument for the extension of goodness; but trust not his judgment of thee. Who then is, as the true judge of thy worth, thy only perfect friend?

The Divine Thought. There is the opinion of thee to which thou canst look up. To be sure it is revealed to thee only in thy consciousness of what righteousness is and of what truth is. Nowhere else hast thou a guide that can do more for thee than to help to quicken thy insight. But, then, thy religious comfort is to be, not that the moral law is thundered down from mountain-tops as if some vast town-crier were talking, but that when thou seekest to do right, the Infinite all-seeing One knows and approves thee. If thou lovest righteousness for its own sake, then this will comfort thee. If not, if thou seekest sugar-plums, seek them not in the home of the Infinite. Go among thy fellow-men and be a successful hypocrite and charlatan, and thou shalt have gaping and wonderment and sugar-plums enough.

Herein then lies the invitation of the Infinite to us, that it is, and that it knows us. No deeper sanction is there for true righteousness than this knowledge that one is serving the Eternal. Yet when we say all this, are we simply doing that which we spoke of in the opening chapter of this work? Are we but offering snow to appease the religious hunger? Is this doctrine too cold, too abstract, too far-off? Cold and abstract and far-off is indeed the proof of it. But that was philosophy. That was not the religious aspect of our doctrine, but only the preparation for showing the religious aspect of philosophy. Is the doctrine itself, however, once gained, so remote from the natural religious emotion? What does a man want when he looks to the world for religious support? Does he want such applause as blind crowds give men, such flattery as designing people shower upon them, such sympathy as even the cherished but prejudiced love of one's nearest friends pours out for him? Nay, *if* he seeks merely this, is he quite unselfishly righteous? Can he not get all that if he wants it, wholly apart from religion? And if he looks for reward, can he not get that also otherwise? But what his true devotion to the moral law ardently desires is *not to be alone*. Approval for what really deserves approval he needs, approval from one who truly knows him. Well, our doctrine says that he gets it. Just as deep, as full, as rich, as true approval as expresses the full worth of his act,—this he has for all eternity from the Infinite. To feed upon that truth is to eat something better than snow, but as pure as the driven snow. To love that truth is to love God.

We spoke in the former book of the boundless magnitude of human life as it impresses itself upon one who first gains the moral insight. To many this first devotion to human life seems itself enough for a religion. But then one goes beyond this point, and says that human life has, after all, very much that is base and petty in it. Here is not the ideal. "Would that there were a higher life! To that we would devote ourselves. We will serve humanity, but how can we worship it?" Such is the thought of many an ardent soul that seeks no personal rewards in serving the good, but that does seek some great Reality that shall surely be worthy of service. To such, our religious insight points out this higher reality. You that have been willing to devote yourselves to humanity, here is a Life greater in infinite degree than humanity. And now is it not a help to know that truly to serve humanity is just the same as to serve this Infinite? For whatever had seemed disheartening in the baseness and weakness of man loses its discouraging darkness now that all is transfigured in this Infinite light.

Let us then be encouraged in our work by this great Truth. But let us not spend too much time in merely contemplating this Truth. We, whose lives are to be lived in toil,—it is not good that we should brood over even an infinite Thought. For in our finite minds it will soon become petty, unless we realize it chiefly through our acts. Let us then go about our business. For every man has business and desire, such as they are.

As we turn away then for the time from our contemplation, we have one last word yet as to these practical consequences of our view. If the reader follows us at all in our argument, we want him also to follow us into the practical application of it to life. To work for the extension of the moral insight is, we have said, the chief present duty of man in society. All else is preparation for this work, or else is an anticipation of the higher stage when, if we ever grow up to that level, we shall have our further work to do in the light of the insight itself. But this chief present work of ours, this extension of the moral insight, is best furthered by devotion to our individual vocations, coupled with strict loyalty to the relations upon which society is founded. The work thus set before us demands the sacrifice of many ideal emotional experiences to the service of the Highest. Our comfort however in it all must be that the Highest is there above us, forget it as we may. If the reader accepts all this, then with us he has the assurance that, whatever becomes of the old creeds in the present religious crisis, the foundations of genuinely religious faith are sure.

Whenever we must pause again in our work for religious support, and whenever we are worn out with the jargon of the schools, we can rest once more for a time in this contemplation of the Eternal Truth. *Hic breve plangitur.* But not so is it in God's life. Our problems may be hard, but there all is solved. Our lives may be poor and contemptible, but there all is wealth and fullness of worth. Our efforts may often prove vain, but there naught exists that is vanity. For the imperfection of the finite is but the fragment of the Infinite Whole where there is no true imperfection. Is it not a Religion to feel this? And we shall then turn from such a contemplation once again as we do now, to look with fresher courage at this boundless, tossing sea of human life about us. This is not itself the Divine, but over it all God's winds are blowing. And to our eyes it is boundless. Let us go down into this great sea and toil, fearing no storm, but seeking to find there treasures that shall be copies, however faint, of that which is Eternal.

The World and the Individual

THE HUMAN SELF*

The contrast between Matter and Mind is usually regarded as a serious obstacle in the way of any interpretation of the world of experience in terms of a philosophical Idealism. In the last two lectures we have seen that this contrast is not empirically known to be as absolute as our customary fashions of conception often make it seem. The hypothesis concerning Nature which we suggested was partly intended to illustrate precisely this possibility of reconciling Idealism with the generalizations of our ordinary study of Nature. The hypothesis itself, like any other effort towards a Cosmology, is, in its details, provisional and tentative. Only its general type, as an idealistic hypothesis about Nature, seems to me to be a sure representative of the truth. In its special features it is to be subject to the control of further experience. But it provides in its very terms for such further control. The hypothesis asserts, in fact, that all the theories of the special sciences, together with the general theory of Nature suggested by this very hypothesis itself, must be viewed as incidents in the history of man's effort gradually to comprehend the organization of a realm of Mind, of which man himself is a member. Now every idealist holds that there is no dead matter anywhere in the world, and that all that is, is the expression of the Spirit. But in what way this thesis is to be applied to the detailed interpretation of Nature, cannot be decided in advance of a careful scrutiny of the facts. And the special way suggested at the last time is the one which to me personally seems to promise most. I am sure that in its most general outlines, this hypothesis is sound. But all its details are subject to correction.

---

*From *The World and the Individual* (New York: The Macmillan Co., 1901).

I

Herewith, however, we are led to the threshold of a new enterprise. We have so far stated a general hypothesis regarding Nature. But in forming this hypothesis, I myself have been especially interested in its bearing upon the conception of the place in Nature that is occupied by Man. Now as we know Man, he first of all appears to us as a being whose inner life is that of an individual Self. The Self of each man apparently has had an origin in time, and a development such as makes it dependent, for its contents and its character, upon natural conditions. In its turn, our self-consciousness, when once it has developed, furnishes to us the sort of insight by means of which we may hope for a comprehension of some of the mysteries of Nature. Any deeper criticism of our hypothesis about Nature must therefore depend upon a more exact account of what we mean by the human Self. We must know how we are able, both to conceive this Self as in any sense the outcome of the processes of Nature, and to apply our view of the Self to an explanation of Nature.

My next task must therefore be to state, in outline, a theory of the human Self.

What a man means by himself is notoriously a question to which common sense gives various and ambiguous answers. That by the Self one means a real being, common sense indeed insists. But the nature of this real being forms the topic of the greatest vacillation in all popular metaphysics. The most frequently mentioned doubt is that as to whether the Self is, or at least essentially includes, the bodily organism, or whether the Self is essentially an incorporeal entity. But this is but a single instance of the doubts and hesitancies of the popular doctrine concerning the Ego. And this indefiniteness of customary opinion regarding our problem most of all appears in the practical aspect of the current notions of the Self. If we ask, What is the value of the Self, and what do we gain by cultivating, by knowing, by observing, and by satisfying the Self?—common sense gives contradictory answers which at once show that the very idea of what the Self is, is subject to the most momentous changes as we alter our point of view. Ask the teacher of the people about the value and dignity of the Self at a moment when he is insisting upon the significance and the rights of individuality, and upon the duty of conscious reasonableness, and of moral independence. He will reply, perhaps, in the terms that Burns has made so familiar. ''The man of independent mind'' knows, asserts, expresses, preserves, glorifies the true Self, the moral individual. And the Self which he thus makes central in his moral world is an essentially honorable Self, the determiner of all true values, the despiser of mere externals, the freeman to whom fortune is nothing compared with inner dignity. When one views the moral Self thus, one conceives that the root of all evil and of all baseness must always lie without and beyond the Self. The Self sins not through self-assertion but through self-abandonment. The lost soul is the man who is the slave of fortune. Pleasure, worldly honor, external good,—these may harm the Self, just because they are foreign to its true independence. The ideal lies where the Stoics sought it, in casting off the external bondage. For such a view, every man's Self, if you could only get at the heart of it, and get it to express itself, would appear as essentially good. What corrupts and enchains men is not their innermost selfhood, but the power of an external world of temptations. To assert the true Self, is to be saved.

But even more familiar than this ethical individualism, which so often thrills the hearts of noble youth, and which inspires so many to heroism, is another ancient and, as its history shows, profoundly religious doctrine. This latter doctrine equally appeals to the moral common sense of mankind; it is crystallized, so to speak, in some of the most familiar of our customary phrases; it inspires numerous effective moral appeals; it comes to us with all the weight of the authority of the faith of the fathers. This view is that the Self of man is precisely that which in its original nature is evil, so that it is just our salvation which must to us come from without, and be won through self-abnegation. "By grace ye are saved, and that *not* of yourselves." Self-denial is, for this view, the cardinal virtue. Self-consciousness is even a vice. A man ought to think little of himself, and much of God, of the world, and of his own external business. The central evil of our life is selfishness. Virtue is definable as altruism, *i.e.* as forgetting ourselves in the thought of others. The best eulogy that one can make over the grave of the departed saint is: "He had no thought of Self; he served; he sacrificed himself; he gave himself as an offering for the good of mankind; he lived for others; he never even observed his own virtues; he forsook himself; he asked for nothing but bondage to his duty." And George Eliot sings in praise of the "scorn for miserable aims that end in Self."

Now the opposition just suggested between two views of the value of Self, is so familiar that common sense not only uses these apparently conflicting phrases, but has its own lore regarding various devices by which they are to be reconciled. A man has, as we sometimes learn, two Selves,—the inner and the outer, the nobler and the baser. There is the natural man, who is by his very essence evil; and the spiritual man, who is by nature good. It is to the natural man that the advice about self-abnegation is given; it is to the spiritual Self that the well-known words of Burns make their stirring appeal. The fleshly Self is the root of all evil. The spiritual Self belongs, by origin and by destiny, to a higher realm.

This dualistic way of stating the case, and of attempting to solve the practical problem here at issue, would be more nearly final were it not that in the very effort to carry it out to its consequences, the former ambiguity only arises afresh, in a slightly altered form. The higher Self, the deeper spiritual nature, the individuality which ought to be,—to whom does it originally belong? To the man who finally wins a consciousness that this has become to him his true Self? Or does this higher Self come, as Aristotle said of the Nous, θύραθεν, from without, into the natural man? Does it create for him or in him a new selfhood, so that before the higher selfhood appears in this man, it exists perhaps merely as the intent of God to save this man, or as a selfhood embodied in other men, the teachers, inspirers, guides, of the man who is to be thus brought to the possession of the higher Self in his own person? This question may indeed at first appear an idle subtlety. But as a fact, both common sense and religion, both the teacher's art and the inner consciousness of those who have in any sense passed from death unto life, give this question a very living and practical significance. Our models and our inspirations, the mysterious grace that saves us and the visible social order that moulds us,—these lie at first without the Self. Yet they in such wise determine whatever is best about us that we are all accustomed to nourish the higher selfhood by means of what we find as no creation of the original Self, but as the free gift of the world. And the two doctrines which, in European history, have most insisted upon the duality of our higher and our lower selfhood, viz. the ethical teaching of Plato and the Gospel of the Christian Church, have agreed in insisting that the higher Self is a resultant of influences which belong to the eternal world, and which the individual man himself is powerless to initiate. In Plato's account of the process of the soul's release from its own lower nature, the eternal Ideas appear as the supernatural source of truth and of goodness. In the mythical state of preexistence, the Ideas guided the soul by their visible presence; and the soul's higher nature meant nothing but the contemplation of their uncreated perfection. In this foreign authority the soul found all that was good. And in the present life our higher nature means only our memory of the former presence of the all-powerful truth. This memory guides our awakening reason, controls our irrational passions, binds the lower Self with the might of the eternal, and conducts us back towards that renewed and direct intercourse with the ideal world wherein consists our only higher Selfhood. Christianity, in all its essential teachings, has emphasized a similar source and meaning in speaking of the higher Self. The Divine Spirit enters a man in ways that its own wisdom predetermines, and without the work of God in preparing and accomplishing the plan of salvation, in revealing the truth to man by outward means, and in preparing the heart within for the reception of the truth, the nobler Self of each man not only is unable to win control of the baser Self, but never could come effectively to exist at all. In this sense, then, it is not I who win salvation, but it is God who works in me. The higher Self is originally not myself at all, but the Spirit warring against the Flesh. This spirit is essentially from God. It comes *into* the man like Aristotle's Creative Nous, and is precisely so much of a man as is not his own, but God's.

Now this well-known ambiguity of the traditional doctrines concerning the source and meaning of the higher Self in man, is not, as some have unwisely maintained, a mere consequence of theological and philosophical speculation. On the contrary, it is an expression, in terms of faith, of empirical facts about the Self which common sense everywhere recognizes. The same problems, in other formulation, exist in Hindu philosophy as well as in Plato's; and they are recognized by Buddhism as well as by Christianity. Every watchful parent, and every conscientious teacher, is perfectly well acquainted with facts that illustrate the doctrines of saving grace and of the apparently external source of the higher selfhood, in case of every plastic child. We all of us know, or ought to recognize, how powerless we are, or should have been, to win any higher selfhood, unless influences from without,—whether you know them as mother love, or conceive them as the promptings of the divine Spirit, or view them as the influences of friends and of country,—have brought into us a truth and an ideality that is in no ordinary sense our own private creation. And every man who knows what the wiser humility is, has sometime said: "Of myself I am nothing. It is the truth alone that, coming from without, works in me."

But if you lay aside the problem as to the source of the higher Self, and consider merely the supposed duality of the lower and the higher Self as a given fact, have you in that case even begun to solve the problem as to what the Self of a man actually is? For the Self was to be something unique and individual. But the account here in question makes of it something disintegrated and internally manifold, and threatens to cause the name Self to mean, in case of every individual, a mere general term, applicable to various groups of different facts. For by the same principle whereby you distinguish the lower and the higher Self of a man, you might distinguish, and upon occasion, even in common life, do distinguish, many various selves, all clustered together in what we call the life of a single individual.

For if we are internally in any sense more than one Self, then we consist not merely of the lower and the higher self, but have, in some sense, as many selves as we have decidedly various offices, duties, types of training and of intellectual activity, or momentous variations of mood and condition. Of the man who is once seriously ill, common sense often says that he is no longer himself. If you ask, who then is he, if not himself, you may get the answer that he is another,—a deeply changed,—a strange Self. And if the change has at all the character of a mental derangement, common sense, ever since the savage stage of our social life, has been disposed to conceive the alteration in question as the appearance of an actually foreign and other Self, a new and invading individuality, which the superstitious view as a possession of the man's body by an evil spirit. Such instances are extreme; but health furnishes to us similar, if less unhappy variations, with whose mystery the popular imagination is constantly busy. Deep emotional experiences give the sense of a new or of a wavering selfhood. There are many people, of a fine social sensibility, who are conscious of a strong tendency to assume, temporarily, the behavior, the moods, and in a measure, both the bearing and the accent, both the customs and the opinions of people in whose company they spend any considerable time. I have known amongst such people those who were oppressed by a sense of insincerity in consequence of their own social plasticity. "I almost seem to have no true Self at all," such a sensitive person may say. "I am involuntarily compelled to change my whole attitude towards the most important things whenever I change my company. I find myself helplessly thinking and believing and speaking as the present company want me to do. I feel humiliated by my own lack of moral independence. But I cannot help this fickleness. And the saddest is that I do not know where my true Self lies, or what one amongst all these various selves is the genuine one."

Now such confessions stand again for rather extreme types of variability of the mere sense of selfhood. Yet the experiences of which such less stable souls complain, exist in various degrees in many of us who are merely not sensitive enough, or perhaps not reflective enough, to notice our own actual variations of self-consciousness. I have known very obstinate men, who were full of a consciousness of their own independence and absolute stability of will and character. Yet, as a fact, they were people of very various and complex selfhood, who were, far more than they themselves supposed, the slaves of circumstances and of social influences. Only they regarded themselves as both independent and resolutely fixed in their individuality, merely because their one type of reaction in presence of any other man's opinion was to disagree with that opinion, and their one way of asserting their independence was to insist that their neighbors were wrong, while their fixed device for preserving their independence was to refuse to do whatever external authority desired them to do. But now such resolute opponents of their fellows are as much without a fixed and rational conscious principle of selfhood as their brothers, the self-accused slaves of the passing social situation. For it is as fickle to disagree with everybody as to agree with everybody. And the man who always opposes is as much the slave of external fortune as the man who always agrees. The simply obstinate man, who is said to be set in his own way, but who, in fact, is always set in the way that is opposed to the ways of whoever is just now his fellow,—such a man changes his doctrine whenever his opponent changes; and his teachings, his ideals, and his selfhood play, as it were, puss-in-the-corner with those of his neighbors.

But enough of familiar illustrations of how the mere sense of selfhood may vary, or of how its outer and inner expression may seem dual or multiple. What these facts give us, is not any decision as to the true nature of the Self, but some specification of our problem, and some explanation of the reason why common sense is so uncertain about how to define the true unity of the Self. The inconsistencies of common sense in regard to the Self are, upon their practical side, well summed up in the familiar advice which we are accustomed to give the young. "Forget yourself," we say, "all true success depends upon freedom from yourself." But to the careless youth we sternly say, "What! you *have* forgotten yourself." One sees, it is hard for the poor Self to please common sense. And the reason is that common sense does not in the least know, when it appeals to the Self, whom it is addressing, nor, when it talks of the Self, what object it is meaning.

II

Such considerations ought once for all to give pause to those who have regarded the problem of the true nature of the Self as a matter of direct inner knowledge, or as something to be settled by an appeal to the plain man. But of course these considerations merely indicate a problem, and are by no means decisive as against any metaphysical view which insists upon a true and deeper unity of Selfhood at the basis of all these variations of the apparent Self. But wherein shall our own metaphysical doctrine seek for guidance in this world of complexities?

I reply, The concept of the human Self, like the concept of Nature, comes to us, first, as an empirical concept, founded upon a certain class of experiences. But like the concept of Nature, the concept of the human Self tends far to outrun any directly observable present facts of human experience, and to assume forms which define the Self as having a nature and destiny which no man directly observes or as yet can himself verify. If we consider first the empirical basis of the conception of the Self, and then the motives which lead us beyond our direct experience in our efforts to interpret the Self, we find, as a result of a general survey, three different kinds of conceptions of what it is that one means or ought to mean by the term Self as applied to the individual man. Each of these sorts of conception of the human Self is once more capable of a wide range of variation. Each can be used as a basis of different and, on occasion, of conflicting notions of what the Self is. But the three have their strong contrasts with one another, and each lays stress upon its own aspect of the facts.

First then, there is the more directly empirical way of conceiving the Self. In this sense, by a man's Self, you mean a certain totality of facts, viewed as more or less immediately given, and as distinguished from the rest of the world of Being. These facts may be predominantly corporeal facts, such as not only the man himself but also his neighbors may observe and comment upon. In this sense my countenance and my physical deeds, my body and my clothing,—all these may be regarded as more or less a part of myself. My neighbor so views them. I may and very generally do so view them myself. If you changed or wholly removed such facts, my view of what I am would unquestionably alter. For to my neighbor as to myself, I am this man with these acts, this body, this presence. I cannot see these facts as my neighbor does, nor can he take my view of them. But we all regard such facts, not only as belonging to the Self, but as constituting, in a measure, what we regard as the Self of the present life. In addition to the external or corporeal Self of the phenomenal world, there is the equally empirical and phenomenal Self of the inner life, the series of states of consciousness, the feelings, thoughts, desires, memories, emotions, moods. These, again, both my neighbor and myself regard as belonging to me, and as going to make up what I am. To be sure, within this inner empirical Self, we all make distinctions, now so freely illustrated, between what does and what does not essentially belong to the Self. When a man tells me a piece of interesting news, or expounds to me his opinions, I naturally regard the ideas which then arise in my mind as his and not as mine. I have to reflect in order to observe the somewhat recondite fact that the ideas which he seems to convey to me are in one sense ideas of my own, aroused in me according to laws of association. On the other hand, when I think alone by myself, the ideas which occur to me seem to be primarily mine. I have to reflect in order to remember how largely they have been derived from books, from nature, or from conversation, and how little I can call originally my own. And everywhere in the inner life, as it flits by, I observe a constantly shifting play of what I distinguish as more truly myself, from what I regard as relatively foreign. This feeling or purpose, this mood or this choice, is my own. That other emotion or idea is alien to me. It belongs to another. I do not recognize it as mine. The distinctions, thus empirically made, have no one rational principle. They are often founded upon the most arbitrary and unstable motives. The vacillation of common sense regarding the Self is endlessly repeated in my own inner life. I am constantly sure that there exists a Self, and that there I am, present to my own consciousness as the one whose experiences all these are, and who set myself over against the foreign non-Ego at every moment. But in distinguishing my empirical non-Ego from the Ego, I follow no stateable rule in my inner life from moment to moment. I even voluntarily play with the distinctions of Self and not-Self,—dramatically address myself as if I were another, criticise and condemn myself, and upon occasion observe myself in a relatively impersonal fashion, as if I were a wholly alien personality. On the other hand, there are countless automatic processes that alter or that diminish the immediately given distinctions between Ego and non-Ego. The lover in Locksley Hall somewhat unobservantly tells us how:—

"Love took up the harp of life, and smote on all the chords with
    might;
Smote the chord of Self that trembling, passed in music out of
    sight."

The lover admits that in the state which he thus describes, the Self, if invisible in the inner experience, was still able, most decidedly, to make itself heard. And, as a fact, one may well question whether, in view of what the lover in Locksley Hall tells us, the Self of this lover ever passed beyond his own range of vision at all, or was in the least out of sight. But the happy emotional confusion of self-consciousness here in question is familiar indeed to all who know joyous emotion. And in the sadder emotions one also has endless varieties in the intensity, clearness, and outlines which in our empirical consciousness characterize, from moment to moment, the relations of Self and not-Self.

III

But one may now ask, still dwelling upon the empirical Self, what manner of unity is left, in the midst of all these variations, as the unity that the concept of the Self can still be said to possess in our ordinary experience? And by what marks is the Self to be distinguished from the rest of the world? I reply, by pointing out a fact of central importance for the whole understanding of the empirical Ego. The variations of our experience and of our opinion concerning the empirical Self are countless in number. And no purely rational principle guides us in defining the Self from moment to moment in the world of common sense, or in distinguishing it from the not-Self. But there still does remain *one psychological principle* running through all these countless facts, and explaining, in general, both why they vary, and why yet we always suppose, despite the chaos of experiences, that the Self of our inner and outer life preserves a genuine, although to us hidden unity. This psychological principle is the simple one that, in us men, the distinction between Self and not-Self has a predominantly *Social origin,* and implies a more or less obviously present contrast between what we at any moment view as the life of another person, a fellow-being, or, as you may for short in general call him, an Alter, and the life, which, by contrast with that of the Alter, is just then viewed as the life of the present Ego. To state the case more briefly, I affirm that our empirical self-consciousness, from moment to moment, depends upon a series of contrast-effects, whose psychological origin lies in our literal social life, and whose continuance in our present conscious life, whenever we are alone, is due to habit, to our memory of literal social relations, and to an imaginative idealization of these relations. Herein lies a large part of the explanation of those ambiguities of common sense upon which I have so far insisted.

My proof for this view I cannot here give at length. I have stated the psychological aspects of the whole case pretty extensively elsewhere.[1] My friend, Professor Baldwin of Princeton University, has independently worked out a theory of the psychological origin of Self-Consciousness, and a doctrine about the evolution of the relations of Ego and Alter,—a theory which I am on the whole prepared to accept, and which agrees with the considerations that I myself have been led to develope, and, in the places now referred to, to set forth. Here there is time only for a brief indication of what I mean by this theory of the empirical Ego, of its unity in variety, and of its distinction from the world of the non-Ego.

Nobody amongst us men comes to self-consciousness, so far as I know, except under the persistent influence of his social fellows. A child in the earlier stages of his social development,—say from the end of the first to the beginning of the fifth year of life,—shows you, as you observe him, a process of the development of self-consciousness in which, at every stage, the Self of the child grows and forms itself through Imitation, and through functions that cluster about the Imitation of others, and that are secondary thereto. In consequence, the child is in general conscious of what expresses the life of somebody else, before he is conscious of himself. And his self-consciousness, as it grows, feeds upon social models, so that at every stage of his awakening life his consciousness of the Alter is a step in advance of his consciousness of the Ego. His playmates, his nurse, or mother, or the workmen whose occupations he sees, and whose power fascinates him, appeal to his imitativeness, and set him the copies for his activities. He learns his little arts, and as he does so, he contrasts his own

---

1. See my *Studies of Good and Evil,* especially the essay on the Anomalies of Self-consciousness, *op. cit.,* pp. 169–197. Professor Baldwin's very complete treatment of the topic is to be found in the second volume of his well-known work: *Mental Development in the Child and the Race,* where it dominates the entire discussion.

deeds with those of his models, and of other children. Now contrast is, in our conscious life, the mother of clearness. What the child does instinctively, and without comparison with the deeds of others, may never come to his clear consciousness as his own deed at all. What he learns imitatively, and then reproduces, perhaps in joyous obstinacy, as an act that enables him to display himself over against others,—this constitutes the beginning of his self-conscious life. And in general, thenceforth, social situations, social emotions, the process of peering into the contents of other minds during the child's questioning period, the conflicts of childish sport, the social devices for winning approval,—in brief, the whole life of social harmony and rivalry,—all these things mean an endless series of contrasts between two sets of contents, which retain, amidst all their varieties, *one* psychologically important character. Upon this character the empirical unity and the general continuity of our adult self-consciousness depend.

In any literal social situation, namely, one is aware of ideas, designs, interests, beliefs, or judgments, whose expression is observed in the form of acts, words, looks, and the like, belonging to the perceived organisms of one's fellow-men. In strong contrast, both in the way in which they appear in the field of our sense-perceptions, and in the current interests and feelings with which they are accompanied and blended, are the acts, words, and other expressions, of our own organism, together with the ideas, designs, and beliefs which accompany these acts. Now these two contrasting masses of mental contents simply constitute the Alter and the Ego, the neighbor and the Self, of any empirical instant of our literal social life together. That these sets of contents stand in strong contrast to each other is, for the first, a mere fact of sense and of feeling. One does not reason about this fact from instant to instant. One finds it so. Nor does one appeal to any intuition of an ultimate or of a spiritual Ego, in order to observe the presented fact that my neighbor's words, as he speaks to me, do not sound or feel as my words do when I speak to him, and that the ideas which my neighbor's words at once bring to my consciousness, stand in a strong and presented contrast to the ideas which receive expression in my words as I reply to him. Alter and Ego, in such cases, are found as facts of our direct observation. Were no difference observed between the contents which constitute the observed presence of my neighbor, and the contents which constitute my own life in the same moment, then my sense of my neighbor's presence, and my idea of myself, would blend in my consciousness, and there would be so far neither Alter nor Ego observed.

Now just such social contrast-effects have been occurring in our experience since childhood. The contrasts in question have always retained a certain general similarity, despite wide and countless differences. Just as all color contrasts are in a measure alike, so too are all social contrasts.

Always the contents which constitute the Ego, at the very moment of their contrast with the remaining contents present during the social contrast-effect, have been associated with certain relatively warm and enduring organic sensations, viz. sensations coming from within our own bodies. Always the contents belonging to our consciousness of our neighbors have been relatively free from these accompaniments, and have had the characters belonging to external sense-perceptions. And there are still other empirical similarities present in all social relations. Hence, despite all other changes, the Ego and the Alter have tended to keep apart, as facts of our empirical observation, and each of the two has tended towards its own sort of organization as a mass of observed and remembered empirical facts. The Alter, viewed as a mass of experienced facts,—the words, looks, and deeds and ideas of other people,—differentiates and integrates into all that I call my experience of mankind; the Ego, centred about the relatively constant organic sensations, but receiving its type of unity especially through the social contrast-effects, stands as that totality of inner and outer experience which I recognize as my own, just because it sharply differs from my experience of any of the rest of mankind, and stands in a certain permanent sort of contrast thereto.

In origin, then, the empirical Ego is secondary to our social experience. In literal social life, the Ego is always known as in contrast to the Alter. And while the permanent character of our organic sensations aids us in identifying the empirical Ego, this character becomes of importance mainly because hereby we find ourselves always in a certain inwardly observable type of contrast to the whole of our social world.

Now what literal social life thus trains us to observe, the inner psychological processes of memory and imagination enable us indefinitely to extend and to diversify. The child soon carries over his plays into more or less ideal realms, lives in the company of imaginary persons, and thus, idealizing his social relations, idealizes also the type of his self-consciousness. In my inner life, I in the end learn ideally to repeat, to vary, to reorganize, and to epitomize in countless ways, the situations which I first learned to observe and estimate in literal social relations. Hereby the contrast between Ego and Alter, no longer confined to the relations between my literal neighbor and myself, can be refined into the conscious contrasts between present and past Self, between my self-critical and my naïve Self, between my higher and lower Self, or between my Conscience and my impulses. My reflective life, as it empirically occurs in me from moment to moment, is a sort of abstract and epitome of my whole social life, viewed as to those aspects which I find peculiarly significant. And thus my experience of myself gets a certain provisional unity. But never do I observe my Self as any single and unambiguous fact of consciousness.

IV

The empirical Ego has now been, in outline, characterized. The source of its endless varieties has been sketched. Its unity has been found to be not, in our present form of existence, a fact that gets anywhere fully presented, as a rationally determined whole of life or of meaning. The empirical unity of the Ego depends merely upon a certain continuity of our social and of our inner life of experience and memory. The most stable feature about the empirical Ego, is that *sort of contrast in which it stands to the social world, literal and ideal, in which we live.* But precisely as here upon earth we have no abiding city, just so, in our present human form of consciousness, the Self is never presented except as a more or less imperfectly organized series of experiences, whose contrast with those of all other men fascinates us intensely, but whose final meaning can simply never be expressed in the type of experience which we men now have at our disposal. Were our life not hid in an infinitely richer and more significant life behind the veil, we who have once observed the essential fragmentariness of the empirical Ego would indeed have parted with our hope of a true Selfhood.

But the two other types of conception of the Self remain to be characterized. The one of these types, the second in our list of three, need detain us at this stage but little. The third type we shall at once so sketch as to define the momentous task that yet lies before us in our later lectures.

The second type of the conceptions of the Ego consists of all those views which regard the Self as in some metaphysical sense a real being, without defining the true Being of this Self in strictly idealistic terms. Such conceptions of the human Self as an entity are numerous in the history of philosophy. Their classification and further characterization will receive attention in the next lecture. For the moment I may exemplify them by mentioning as their most familiar examples, those views which conceive the human Self as, in some realistic sense, a distinct and independent entity. For such views the true Self is often essentially a Substance. Its individuality means that in essence it is separable, not only from the body, but from other souls. It preserves its unity despite the chaos of our experiences, just because in itself, and apart from all experience, it *is* One. It lies at the basis of our psychical life; and it must be sharply distinguished from the series of the states of consciousness, and even from their empirical organization. It is the source of all the order of our mental life; and all our self-consciousness is a more or less imperfect indication of its nature.

Such realistic views are well known to you. And you also know now why, without showing the least disrespect to their historical dignity, I can and must simply decline to follow them into their details in these lectures.

They are all founded upon the realistic conception of Being. They must therefore all fall with that conception. Their true spirit indeed is often of far deeper moment than their mere letter. What doctrines of Soul-Substance have often meant to express, namely, a respect for human individuality, and an appreciation of its eternal worth in the life of the Universe, our own theory of the human individual will erelong develope in its own fashion. But taken literally, the doctrine that beneath or behind our conscious life there is a permanent substance, itself never either presented or presentable in consciousness, but real, and real in such wise that its Being is independent of any knowledge that from without refers to it,—this whole doctrine, I say, simply perishes, for the purposes of our argument, together with Realism, and only its revised and purified inner meaning can reappear, in quite another guise, in the world of Idealism. Whatever the Self is, it is not a Thing. It is not, in Aristotle's or in Descartes' sense, a Substance. It is not a realistic entity of any type. Whether we men ever rightly come to know it or not, it exists only as somewhere known, and as a part of the fulfilment of meaning in the divine life. We are spared the trouble of proving this thesis here in detail, simply because our general proof of Idealism has discounted the entire issue. We are not condemning Realism unheard; but only after the most careful analysis of its claims. But with Realism passes away every view which regards the real Self as anything but what every real fact in the universe is: A Meaning embodied in a conscious life, present as a relative whole within the unity of the Absolute life.

Well, there remains the third type of conception of the Self, namely, the strictly idealistic type. And precisely this type it was that I exemplified before, when I spoke of the way in which the Self has been distinguished, even by common sense, into a higher and a lower, a nobler and a baser Self. As stated in ordinary fashion, such concepts, as we saw, remain crude, and lead to frequent inconsistency. Revised with reference to the demands of our Idealism, the concept of the Self will assume a form which will reduce to unity these apparent inconsistencies of ethical common sense, and will also escape from bondage to those empirical complexities forced upon us by the Ego of the passing moment. We shall then see that the concept of the individual Self is, in its higher forms, in large measure an essentially Ethical Conception. And the third type of conceptions of the Ego consists of definitions which have always laid stress upon just this aspect. From this point of view, the Self is not a Thing, but a Meaning embodied in a conscious life. Its individuality, in case of any human being, implies the essential uniqueness of this life. Its unity, transcending as it does what we ever find presented in our present type of consciousness, implies that the true individual Self of any man gets its final expression in some form of consciousness different from that which we men now possess. The empirical variety, complexity, ambiguity, and inconsistency of our present consciousness of the Self, is to be explained as due to the fact that, in the moral order of the universe, no individual Self is or can be isolated, or in any sense sundered from other Selves, or from the whole realm of the inner life of Nature itself. Consequently, even what is most individual about the Self never appears except in the closest connection with what transcends both the meaning and the life of the finite individual. Now, in our present form of conscious existence, we catch mere glimpses of the true meaning of the individual Self, as this meaning gets expressed in our deeds and in our ideals, and we also obtain equally fragmentary glimpses of the way in which this Self is linked to the lives of its fellows, or is dependent for its expression upon its relations to Nature, or is subject to the general moral order of the universe. These various transient flashes of insight constitute our present type of human experience. And it is their variety, their manifoldness, and their fragmentariness, which together are responsible for all those inconsistencies in our accounts of the Self,—inconsistencies which our present discussion has been illustrating. But if you want to free yourself from hopeless bondage to such inconsistencies, you must look, not to some realistic conception of a Soul-Substance, but to some deeper account of the ethical meaning of our present life than we have yet formulated. And from this point of view we get a notion of Selfhood and of individuality which may be summarized at the present stage much as follows.

Our general idealistic theory asserts that the universe in its wholeness is the expression of a meaning in a life. What this view implies about every fragment and aspect of life that your attention may chance to select, or that your human experience may bring before you as the topic of inquiry, we have in former lectures repeatedly pointed out. Any instant of finite consciousness partially embodies a purpose, and so possesses its own Internal Meaning. Any such instant of finite consciousness also seeks, however, for other expression, for other objects, than are now present to just that instant, and so possesses what we have called its External Meaning. Our Idealism has depended, from the first, upon the thesis that the Internal and the External meaning of any finite process of experience are dependent each upon the other, so that if the whole meaning and intent of any finite instant of life is fully developed, and perfectly embodied, this Whole Meaning of the instant becomes identical with the Universe, with the Absolute, with the life of God. Even now, whatever you are or seek, the implied whole meaning of even your blindest striving is identical with the entire expression of the divine Will. And it is in this aspect of the world that we have found the unity of Being. On the other hand, as we have also seen, this unity of the world-life is no simple unity, such as the mystic sought. It is an infinitely complex unity. And of this complexity, of this wealth of life that the complete expression of even your most transient and finite glimpses of meaning implies,—the foregoing facts about the Self are merely instances. If you are in company with a friend, the whole meaning of your thoughts and of your interests while you speak with him, not only requires for its complete expression his inner life as well as yours, and not only requires the genuine and conscious unity of his life and of yours by virtue of the ties of your friendship; but this same meaning also demands that, despite this unity of your life as friends,—yes, even because of this unity, your friend and your-self shall remain also contrasted lives, whose unity includes and presup-poses your variety as these two friends. For a friendship is not a simple unity of conscious life, but the unity of two conscious lives each of which con-trasts itself with the other, and feels in the other's relative independence the fulfilment of its own purpose. And just so, when your meaning is not friendly but hostile, and when you stand in presence of your opponent, your rival, your enemy, your finite conscious meaning still implies, even in the midst of all its confused illusions, the demand that the very life of your enemy shall exist as the expression of your hostile intent to hold him as your real enemy, while nevertheless this life of his, other than your present con-scious experience, and linked with your experience through the ties of meaning, is contrasted with your own life as the life that yours opposes and in so far seeks either to win over to your purposes, or to annul. Finite love and finite hate, and human experience of life in any form, always imply, therefore, that the will now present, but imperfectly expressed, in this pass-ing instant, is genuinely expressed through other conscious life that, from the Absolute point of view, is at once in conscious unity with this instant's purpose, and also in conscious contrast with this instant's purpose.

Primarily then, the contrast of Self and not-Self comes to us as the contrast between the Internal and the External meaning of this present mo-ment's purpose. In the narrowest sense, the Self is just your own present imperfectly expressed pulsation of meaning and purpose,—this striving, this love, this hate, this hope, this fear, this inquiry, this inner speech of the instant's will, this thought, this deed, this desire,—in brief, this idea taken as an Internal Meaning. In the widest sense, the not-Self is all the rest of the divine whole of conscious life,—the Other, the outer World of ex-pressed meaning taken as in contrast with what, just at this instant of our human form of consciousness, is observed, and, relatively speaking, pos-sessed. Any finite idea is so far a Self; and I can, if you please, contrast my present Self with my past or my future Self, with yesterday's hopes or with to-morrow's deeds, quite as genuinely as with your inner life or with the whole society of which I am a member, or with the whole life of which our experience of Nature is a hint, or, finally, with the life of God in its entirety. In every such case, I take account of a true contrast between Self and not-

Self. All such contrasts have a common character, namely, that in them an imperfectly expressed will is set over against its own richer expression, while stress is laid upon the fact,—a perfectly genuine fact of Being,—the fact that the whole expression always retains, and does not merely absorb or transmute, the very contrast between the finite Self and its desired or presupposed Other,—its world of External Meanings. But if you ask how many such contrasts can be made, I reply, An infinite number. In countless ways can the Self of this instant's glimpse of conscious meaning be set into contrast with the not-Self, whose content may be the life of past and future, of friends and of enemies, of the social order and of Nature, of finite life in general, and of God's life in its wholeness.

But if the contrast of Self and not-Self can thus be defined with an infinite variety of emphasis, the unity of each of the two, Self and not-Self, can be emphasized in an equally infinite number of ways, whose depth and whose extent of meaning will vary with the range of life of which one takes account, and with the sort of contrast between Self and not-Self which one leaves still prominent over against the unity. Thus, in the familiar case of our ordinary social self-consciousness, I first view a certain realm of past and future experience as so bound up with the internal meaning of this instant's conscious experience, that I call this temporal whole of life the life of my own human Self, while I contrast this private existence of mine with that of my friends, my opponents, or of my other fellows, or with that of human society in general. The motives that lead to such an identification of the Self of the instant with a certain portion of that which is the instant's not-Self, namely, with a certain portion of past and future experience, are, as we have seen, extremely various, and in our empirical existence, both fickle and transitory. Whoever believes that he has any one rational principle for his usual identification of his past and future with the Self of this instant, has only to consider the psychological variations of self-consciousness before enumerated to discover his error. What will remain, after such an examination of the Self of common sense, will be the really deep and important persuasion that he *ought to possess* or to create for himself, despite this chaos, some one principle, some finally significant contrast, whereby he should be able, with an united and permanent meaning, to identify that portion of the world's life which is to be, in the larger sense, his own, and whereby he should become able to contrast with this, his larger Self, all the rest of the world of life.

And now this very consideration, this fact that one *ought to be able* to select from all the universe a certain portion of remembered and expected, of conceived and of intended life as that of his own true and individual Self, and that one ought to contrast with this whole of life, with this one's larger or truer individuality, the life of all other individual Selves, and the life of the Absolute in its wholeness,—this consideration, I say, shows us at once the sense in which the Self is an Ethical Category. At this instant, as I have said, you can indeed identify the Self, if you please, with just the instant's passing glimpse of Internal Meaning; and in that case you can call all else the not-Self. To do this is to leave the Self a mere thrill of transient life,— a fragment whose deeper meaning is wholly external to itself. But you can, and in general you do, first identify a remembered past, and an intended future, with the Self whose individuality is just now hinted to you; and this enlarged self of memory and purpose you then oppose to a not-Self whose content is first the world of your fellow-men, and then the world of Nature and of the Absolute in its wholeness. Now what justification have you for this view of your larger Self? Apart from the capricious and shifting views of common sense, you can have, I reply, but one justification, namely this: You regard this present moment's life and striving as a glimpse of a certain task now assigned to you, the task of your life as friend, as worker, as loyal citizen, or in general as man, *i.e.* as one of God's expressions in human form. You conceive that, however far you might proceed towards the ful- filment of this task, however rich this individual life of yours might become, it would always remain, despite its unity with the world-life, in some true sense contrasted with the lives of your fellows, and with the life of God, just as now you stand in contrast to both. While your whole meaning is now, and will always remain one with the entire life of God, you conceive that this whole meaning expresses itself in the form of an articulate system of contrasting and cooperating lives, of which one, namely your own individ- ual life, is more closely linked, in purpose, in task, in meaning, with the life of this instant, than is the life of any other individual. Or as you can say: "At this instant I am indeed one with God, in the sense that in him my own absolute Selfhood is expressed. But God's will is expressed in a man- ifold life. And this life is a system of contrasted lives that are various even by virtue of their significant union. For true unity of meaning is best man- ifested in variety, just as the most intimate and wealthy friendship is that of strongly contrasting friends. And in the manifold lives that the world in its unity embodies, there is one, and only one, whose task is here hinted to me as my task, my life-plan,—an ideal whose expression needs indeed the co- operation of countless other Selves, of a social order, of Nature, and of the whole universe, but whose individual significance remains contrasted with all other individual significance. If this is my task, if this is what my past life has meant, if this is what my future is to fulfil, if it is in this way that I do God's work, if my true relation to the Absolute is only to be won through the realization of this life-plan, and through the accomplishment of this unique task, then indeed I am a Self, and a Self who is nobody else, just precisely in so far as my life has this purpose and no other. *By this meaning of my life-plan, by this possession of an ideal, by this Intent always to remain another than my fellows despite my divinely planned unity with them,—by this, and not by the possession of any Soul-Substance, I am defined and created a Self."*

Such, I say, will be your confession, if once you come to define the Self in the only genuine terms,—namely, in ethical terms. If once you choose this definition, then the endless empirical varieties of self-consciousness, and the caprices of common sense, will not confuse you. You will know that since now we see through a glass darkly, you cannot expect at present to experience your human selfhood in any one consistent and final expression. But, too, you will know that you are a Self precisely in so far as you intend to accomplish God's will by becoming one; and that you are an individual precisely in so far as you purpose to do your Father's business in unique fashion, so that in this instant shall begin a work that can be finished only in eternity,—a work that, however closely bound up it may be with all the rest of the divine life, still remains in its expression distinguishable from all this other life. You will indeed recognize that at every moment you receive from without, and from other Selves, the very experiences that give your Selfhood a chance to possess its meaning. You will know that of yourself alone you would be nothing. You will also know that as co-worker with your fellows, and as servant of God, you have a destiny of which our present life gives us but the dimmest hint.

This is in outline, the doctrine of the ethical Self, to whose development and defence our later lectures shall be devoted.

THE PLACE OF THE SELF
IN BEING

In the last lecture, after a study of the various forms which our empirical self-consciousness assumes, we reached an idealistic definition of what we mean by an individual human Self, regarded as a Real Being. During the present lecture I shall, by the term Self, denote, unless I expressly declare to the contrary, the human Self, as thus defined, and not the Absolute Self as the Absolute.

In the present lecture I propose, first, to make some further comparison of our theory of the Self with doctrines that have been maintained in the history of thought, and in this connection to develope our own thesis more fully. Secondly, I shall undertake to consider the relation of our theory of the individual to that Interpretation of Nature which we expounded in our Fourth Lecture, and to discuss the sense in which, from our point of view, new individuals can appear in the course of natural evolution. Thirdly, I intend to consider briefly the question as to the degree to which the Self is causally determined, as to its experience and its will, by its relations to the natural order. Finally, I shall discuss the sense in which the individual Self can possess ethical Freedom, in view of its relation to the divine Will.

I

Historically, there are theories of the Self which correspond to each of the four conceptions of Being. And in the first place, ever since the doctrine of the Sânkhya, that classic instance of early Realism, realistic Metaphysic has been an especially wealthy source of various theories of the Self. Not always has Realism taken the form of the Soul-Substance theory, although, as we saw at the last time, that theory itself is a typical instance of Realism, and is an especially frequent instance of the realistic view of the Self. But any theory of the Self uses the realist's conception of Being, in case this theory views the Self as logically or essentially independent, in its innermost nature, of the fact that other Selves exist, so that you could conceive other Selves vanishing, while this Self still remained, in some innermost core of its Being, unaltered. Leibniz's Monads are realistic selves; and very frequently the extremer forms of ethical individualism, in order to preserve the dignity, or the freedom, or the rights of the Self, have chosen to use a realistic formulation. When thus defined by the more ethical types of individualistic Realism, the Self seems to stand, within its own realm, as a sort of absolute authority, over against any external will or knowledge that pretends to determine its nature, or its precise limits, or its meaning. It is merely what its own substantial nature determines it to be. It is thus a separate entity, in its essence unapproachable, in some sense, by God or man, unconquerable, possessing perhaps its own inalienable rights, the unit of all ethical order, the centre of its own universe. From this point of view, the principal problem, for any such realistic Individualism, always becomes the question how this Self, whose interests are essentially its own, can rationally come to recognize any responsibility to other Selves or to God, or to any absolute Ought, beyond its own caprice. Just because, within its own realm, it is whatever it is in entire indifference to whether you from without know it or not; or to whether your external will approves it or not; the problem at once arises as to why this Self should, in its turn, recognize any authority. In its knowledge of Being, the independent Self of any theoretical form of Realism, when once the independence of this individual Self has come to be recognized, tends to become, in extreme cases, solipsistic. But in its morality, this same Self, in equally extreme forms of ethical Realism, tends to become an anarchist.[1] If, in such extreme and less common forms, Realism, untrue to its usual historical tendencies, throws off its usual and respectable conservatism, that is merely because, in general, extremes easily meet, and because, in the special case of the theory of the Self, Realism deals with a test problem which is peculiarly apt to bring out its deeper inconsistencies. About the world external to all our human Selves, Realism, as it appears in history, is typically submissive, respectable, and conservative, just because it is dealing unreflectively with an unapproachable and absolute Reality beyond our own life. But so soon as Realism attempts to

---

1. Max Stirner's *Der Einzige und Sein Eigenthum* is in the main an example of this type of treatment of the Self. Nietzsche's conception, however, cannot properly be placed here in view of the idealistic element which, as I think, can justly be recognized in his conception of the individual.

apply its categories to the realm within, where its unreflective methods are decidedly not at home, it does not, indeed, become less dogmatic than usual, and not the less disposed to cite tradition, and to hurl its customary pathological epithets at its opponents, but it becomes more manifestly unable, when once it has defined any one of its Independent Beings, to say what link or tie, what law or reason, what obligation or responsibility, can ever bind this Independent Being to any other. Hence the dogmatic anarchists of the history of ethics are often realists in their theory of the Self.

As to the Mystical theory of the Self, we have already followed to the end its account of the problem of life. The Self is the Absolute, the Absolute is simple, and there is neither variety of individuals, nor form nor law of life left. The only word as to the true Self is the Hindu's *Neti, Neti*. Consequently Mysticism simply condemns all finite individuality as an evil dream.

Modern Critical Rationalism also has its own accounts of the Self. These again are manifold. But the Third Conception of Being in general, as we have all along seen, is both reflective and widely observant; and its theories of the Self have, in most cases, their large measure of truth. For Critical Rationalism the Self is no independent entity, nor any mere experience, but a being whose reality involves the validity of a system of laws and relationships. These laws may be viewed in their psychological aspect. In this sense my Self extends as far as my possible memories, or expectations, or definable plans hold valid for the empirical region called my human life. And my existence as a Self means merely that these laws of my memory, of my will, and of my personal experience are valid as long as I live. Or the laws in question may be viewed as those of an ethical interpretation of life. In this case, by the Self, Critical Rationalism means a being defined in the terms of a certain valid system of laws about the rights and the duties of persons. The Self, in the view of such theories, does not first exist as an Independent Being and then either originate, or else acquire, as an external addition, its system of rights and of duties. But, for Critical Rationalism, the ethical Self is defined and exists only through the prior recognition of these valid rights and duties themselves. Whoever has not learned to recognize his office in the world, as a subject of the moral law, or as a member of a social order, is therefore no ethical Self at all. But whoever is a Self, is such by virtue of this recognized validity of law. In the history of recent thought the Kantian conception of the Self, apart from its realistic elements, is, in its consequences, essentially of this third type. Kant's knowing Self exists, from our human point of view, precisely in so far as the Categories, which express its unity in the realm of experience, are valid. Its existence as the Subject of Knowledge, so far as we can know it, thus becomes coextensive with the range of such validity. Kant's ethical

Self exists as the free recognizer of the Moral Law. And in Fichte, who purged Kant's doctrine of its realistic elements, this view of the Self especially comes to light, and contends with the purely idealistic tendencies of Fichte. For Fichte, the Self, although the very principle of Being, rather ought to be than is.

Now the truth, and the practical value of every such doctrine, lies in the fact that it recognizes the valid relations of the Self, and the laws which bind the Self to its fellows, as conditions without which the Self can neither exist nor be conceived. The defect of Critical Rationalism lies in the consequences of its essentially abstract and impersonal view of Being. The Self, in this sense, is a law rather than a life; and a type of existence rather than an Individual. It is precisely the restoration of individuality to the Self which constitutes the essential deed of our Idealism. For us the Self has indeed no Independent Being; but it is a life, and not a mere valid law. It gains its very individuality through its relation to God; but in God it still dwells as an individual; for it is an unique expression of the divine purpose. And since the Self is precisely, in its wholeness, the conscious and intentional fulfilment of this divine purpose, in its own unique way, the individual will of the Self is not wholly determined by a power that fashions it as clay is fashioned and that is called God's will; but, on the contrary, what the Self in its wholeness wills is, just in so far, God's will, and is identical with one of the many expressions implied by a single divine purpose, so that, for the reasons already set forth, in general, in the closing lecture of the foregoing series, the Self is in its innermost individuality, not an independent, but still a Free Will, which in so far owns no external Master, despite its unity with the whole life of God, and despite its dependence in countless ways upon Nature and upon its fellows, for everything except the individuality and uniqueness of its life.

Meanwhile, I cannot too strongly insist that, in our present form of human consciousness, the true Self of any individual man is not a datum, but an ideal. It is true that people at first very naturally, and often very resentfully, reject this interpretation. "Do I not directly know," one insists, "that I am and who I am?" I answer: You indeed know, although never in a merely direct way, *that* you exist. But in the present life you never find out, in terms of any direct experience, *what* you are. I know that I am, as this individual human Self, only in so far as every Internal Meaning, that of my present experience included, sends me elsewhere, or to some Other, for its complete interpretation, while this particular sort of Internal Meaning, such as gets expressed in the Cartesian *cogito ergo sum*, the meaning whereby I come to be aware of myself as this individual different from the rest of the world, implies and demands, for its complete embodiment, some sort of contrast between Self and not-Self. I am assured of myself, then, only in so far as I am assured of the Nature of Being in general. I am indeed right in thus contrasting Self and not-Self; but my certainty regarding the Being of this contrast depends upon the same general assurances that lead to my whole metaphysical view of the nature of Reality.

And now as to the finding out *what* I am, the answer to this question involves, upon its empirical side, all the complications and inconsistencies of common sense which we set forth at the last time. If you take me merely as common sense views me, I am, from moment to moment, whatever social experience or lonely reflection makes me seem. I am, so far, whatever my empirical contrast with you, with society in general, with those whom I love, or with those against whom I contend,—I am, in brief, whatever my remembered or anticipated powers, fortunes, and plans, cause me to regard with emphasis as myself in contrast with the rest of the world. There is no instant in our human experience when I can say, Here I have not merely assumed, or presupposed, or conceived, but actually found in experience the Self, so that I here observe what I finally am.

In what way then can I just now rationally define myself as this actually unique and real person? Already we have seen, in general, the answer to this question. The Self can be defined in terms of an Ideal. If we ask a man to observe once for all what he now is, we call his attention to various empirical accidents of his life,—to his bodily presence, to his organic sensations, to his name, to his social status, and to his memories of the past. But none of these are of any uniquely determined significance; and not thus can we show a man what he is. But when, in vexation at the moral ineffectiveness of a man, we significantly use the imperative mood and say, "Whatever you know or do not know about yourself, at all events *be somebody*,"—we lay stress upon what is, after all, the essential point. What we mean by our words is the exhortation: "Have a plan; give unity to your aims; intend something definite by your life; set before yourself one ideal." We conceive, in such cases, that the Self is definable in terms of purpose, of continuity of life-plan, and of voluntary subordination of chance experiences to a persistently emphasized ideal. If this ideal keeps the individual contrasted with other individuals, as the servant of these masters, or again as the servant, in some unique fashion, of God,—as the friend of these friends, as the teacher of these pupils, as the fellow-worker with these comrades, then the Self which we have defined is the Self of an individual man. It is in so far not to be confounded with their selves just because the ideal, if expressed in a life, would be expressed in constant contrast with these other lives. Our idealistic theory teaches that all individual lives and plans and experiences win their unity in God, in such wise that there is, indeed, but one absolutely final and integrated Self, that of the Absolute. But our idealism also recognizes that in the one life of the divine there is, indeed, articulation, contrast, and variety. So that, while it is, indeed, true that for every one of us the Absolute Self is God, we still retain our individuality, and our distinction from one another, *just in so far as our life-plans, by the very necessity of their social basis, are mutually contrasting life-plans, each one of which can reach its own fulfilment only by recognizing other life-plans as different from its own.* And if from the Absolute point of view, as well as from our own, every individual life that has the unity of a plan, takes its own unique place in the world's life, then for God, as for ourselves, we various human beings live related lives, but still contrasting and various lives, each one of which is an individual life, connected within itself, but distinguishable from all the other lives, precisely as our normal social consciousness makes us seem.

But now, if my human Self can be defined in a single and connected fashion only in terms of such an ideal, we see at once that, in our present human life, no one life-plan ever gets both a precise definition and a complete embodiment; and, therefore, we can say, Never in the present life do we find the Self as a given and realized fact. It is for us an ideal. Its true place is in the eternal world, where all plans are fulfilled. In God alone do we fully come to ourselves. There alone do we know even as we are known.

The conception of the Self thus sketched involves difficulties, and leaves special questions still to be answered, such as I should be the last to ignore. It was for the sake of meeting just such difficulties that our whole previous discussion of the Theory of Being was required as a beginning of our enterprise; and that our Theory of Nature has also been needed as a preliminary to the study of the Self. In general we stated both these difficulties and their answers in dealing with the general problems of Being. But in defining the Self we have already recognized these general problems in a case where, owing to the complex natural relations of the Self, they possess peculiar significance. Nobody can deal with the problem of the Self upon the basis of the empirical facts about human selfhood without seeing, as we saw at the last time, that the Self is in the most intimate relation of dependence upon both natural and social conditions, for every one amongst its attributes that can be defined in general terms. It has an origin in time. It has an hereditary temperament. It is helpless to become anything apart from social training. And, if you remove from its inner consciousness the recognition of its relations of contrast to its literal and to its more or less ideally conceived comrades, rivals, and authorities, it loses at any moment all that makes self-consciousness either worth having, or conceivable. Its whole ethical significance thus depends upon relations to God and to man which, in its capacity as finite being, it can only accept and cannot create. In all these senses the Self temporally appears as a product, a result, a determined creature of destiny. Remove from it the support of the world, and it instantly becomes nothing. Moreover, you in vain endeavor to save the independence of the Self by defining it as a Substance. For all the independence that it ever can even desire to have is a conscious independence, and to this a Soul-Substance contributes nothing. And if your consciousness is merely based upon an existence which lies beneath the consciousness, and which never comes to light as your own present will and meaning, you gain nothing but a name when this unobserved substratum of your personality is called your Soul. The Cartesian *res cogitans* is significant precisely in so far as it is the name for a rational thinking process, but not in so far as it is a *res*. What you want, however, for your Self, is conscious meaning, conscious individuality, and conscious freedom. And the problem is, in view of your unquestionable dependence upon the world for all your endowments, How shall you win this conscious meaning and freedom and individuality; and how is it possible that in any sense you should possess them? Now it is precisely these questions that our Idealism undertakes to answer.

From our point of view, your distinction from the rest of the universe, your contrast with other selves, your uniqueness, your freedom, your individuality, all depend upon one essential principle. This world that we live in is, in its wholeness, the expression of one determinate and absolute purpose, the fulfilment of the divine will. This fulfilment is unique, just because, in the world as a whole, the divine accomplishes its purpose, attains its goal, finds in absolute dominateness what it seeks, and therefore will have no other world than this. Now for this very reason, since the world in its wholeness is unique, every portion of this whole life, every fragment of experience, every pulsation of will in the universe, every intent anywhere partially embodied, is, by virtue of its relation to this unique whole, also unique,—but unique precisely in so far as it is related to the whole, and not in so far as you abstract its various features and endowments from their relation to God, and view them in finite relations. Taken apart from its relation to the whole, the finite fragment appears as something more or less incomprehensible, and therefore as something more or less vaguely general,—a mere case of a type, a member of a series—a temporal expression of dissatisfied will,—a fact that seeks for other facts to explain it,—a bit of experience subject to various psychological laws,—a sort of life that can be interpreted now in this way, and now in that, just as, at the last time, we found the Self subject to the most varying interpretations and estimates.

Yet fear not to find in what manifold ways your life depends upon Nature and Society. It depends upon them for absolutely all of its *general* characters. That is, whatever character it shares with others, implies dependence upon others. If it did not so depend, it would have no intimate share in the common life. But its dependence means precisely that it derives from the other lives everything *except* its uniqueness,—everything *except* its *indi-*

*vidual fashion of acknowledging and taking interest in this its very depend-
ence, and of responding thereto by its deeds.* When, as man, you take your
place amongst men, you thus derive all of your life from elsewhere, *except*
in so far as your life becomes for you your own way of viewing your relation
to the whole, and of actively expressing your own ideal regarding this relation. This *your own way of expressing God's will* is not derived. It is yourself. And it is yours because God worketh in you. The Spirit of God in its
wholeness compels you,—the individual, the Self, the unique personality,
in the sense that it compels you to be an individual, and to be free. Or it
compels your individual will only in so far as you consciously compel yourself.

You indeed find then, as Goethe found in his well-known verses
about heredity, that your dependence on the rest of the world extends
to every character of your nature, precisely in so far as you can define
such a character in general terms. Your temperament you derived from
your ancestors, your training from your social order. Your opinions, as
definable ideas, belong to many of your neighbors also. Your consciousness of yourself, from moment to moment, depends upon social
contrast effects, and varies with them. But your purpose, your life-plan,
just so far as it possesses true rationality of aim, is the purpose to find
for yourself just your own place in God's world, and to fill that place,
as nobody else can fill it. Now this purpose, I maintain, is indeed your
own. As nobody else can share it, so nobody else can create it; and from
no source external to yourself have you derived it. And this I say on
the sole ground that in you, *precisely in so far as you know the world
as one world, and intend your place in that one world to be unique,
God's will is consciously expressed.* And his will is one, and in that will
every life finds its own unique meaning. Hence our theory of the Self
assigns to it the character of the Free Individual but maintains that this
character belongs to it in its true relation to God, and cannot be observed,
at any one instant of time, as an obvious and independent fact.

II

But herewith, having defined what general Form of Being the Self
possesses, we come to a question that in the former lecture was kept
in the background, although it lay very near to us. This is the question
as to the precise relation of our present doctrine about the individual
human Self to our general theory of the process of Evolution in Nature.
If the individual is, within the range of our experience, already known
as a product of Nature, and of his social relations, by so much the more

must his temporal origin, in those aspects of it which escape our direct observation, be viewed as a portion of the vast activities that are hinted to us by our experience of Nature in general. Therefore an effort to bring our theory of the Self into closer relation to our former interpretation of the process of evolution, must form at once the culmination of our doctrine about Nature and a sort of test of our views as to the Self. To such an effort we are now ready to proceed.

As has now been sufficiently shown, a frank admission of the natural origin of the Self, and a study of its relations to the physical world, in no sense involves an abandonment of the idealistic point of view. That the world is the expression of my will, and that nevertheless there has been an infinite past time in which I, the human individual, did not exist—may indeed seem at first a hard saying. But our discussion of the general Categories of Experience, our idealistic theory of Time, and our portrayal of the contrast between the private Self of the human individual and the Absolute Self in its wholeness,—all these preliminaries have cleared the way for an understanding of every such difficulty. In dealing with the categories of the Ought, we saw how and why it is always my will as this human being to acknowledge what is other than the present temporal expression of my will. In our doctrine of Time, we reconciled the fact of our acknowledgment of a remote past time with our assurance that all temporal facts are at once present to the Absolute. In our development of the concept of the human Self, we have shown that we ourselves demand the other individuals, as the very condition of our existence in the Absolute, and that through a wealth of individuality other than our own, and *only* through such variety, is our own life-purpose to be attained. Just as my opponent in a game embodies my will to play with him by opposing me, and gives me an opportunity to be myself through the very fact that he expresses my will in the form of a selfhood whose particular plans are uncontrolled by my private will, while mine are in part uncontrolled by his,—so in general, the private Self is this Self only through contrast with and dependence upon others; and finds its complete Selfhood embodied in other individual life than its own. Moreover, in order that my private will should at this temporal instant form a definite plan, I must always presuppose some world of completed fact as the basis of my present deed; and the realm of that which is viewed as the so far completed expression of the Will, is the temporally Past. The Past too, in its own way, embodies my present will, but embodies it by virtue of the very fact that the Past is the realm of the irrevocable, which I am therefore able to presuppose as a fixed starting-point in forming every new plan. The manifold dependence of my present will upon the social, natural, and temporal order, is thus not only matter of fact, but also a requirement of our idealism.

III

Meanwhile, in order to give full expression to our hypothesis regarding the temporal evolution of new forms of individual selfhood, it will be necessary first to recall some features of our doctrine of the sense in which the Absolute includes a variety of lives, and possesses a temporal expression at all. Only then can we see in detail how what we call novel forms of life can arise in time.

In our criticism of Mysticism, in the former Series of these lectures, we pointed out that a goal which is "a goal of no real process, has as little value as it has content, as little Being as it has finitude." Ever since, in defining the Absolute from our own point of view, we have indeed declared it to be a goal,—*i.e.* a fulfilment of purpose, but have also insisted that, corresponding to each result that is attained in the Absolute, there must also be, in the real world of the Absolute itself, a corresponding purpose or intent, which, just because it is fulfilled in the whole, is at the same time consciously distinguished, as a longing,—a pursuit, a finite idea,—from its own fulfilment. This consideration has constituted, throughout, the ground of our deduction of finitude,—our means of conceiving the union of the One and the Many in the unity of the Absolute Consciousness. For, as a consequence of this principle, the Absolute Life is definable, in the terms of our Supplementary Essay, as a Self-Representative System. Every fact in this system, namely, fulfils a purpose. The consciousness of this purpose is, however, a fact distinct from the fulfilment, and yet correspondent thereto; while, on the other hand, this consciousness itself, as a fact, belonging to the system of the Absolute, is in its own turn the fulfilment of another purpose, which is the consequence, in some degree, of another act that has led up to it; and so on *ad infinitum*. A consciousness of purpose, distinct from fulfilment, is, however, when viewed by itself, a longing, a dissatisfaction, an incompleteness. Hence the Absolute Life includes an infinity of longings, each one of which, in so far as it is taken in itself, is a consciousness of imperfection and finitude seeking its relative fulfilment in some other finite act or state. Only through such consciousness is perfection attainable. The only alternative here is Mysticism, and that is Nothingness. But, as our Supplementary Essay also showed, any system that is self-representative in one way, is self-representative in countless other ways, and the consciousness of the system involved in each one of these ways of self-representation is therefore distinct from the consciousness involved in any of the others, since each way involves a series of voluntary strivings after a goal. In consequence, as the Supplementary Essay also pointed out, whoever conceives the Absolute as a Self, conceives it as in its form inclusive of an infinity of various, but interwoven and so of intercommunicating Selves, each one of which represents the totality of the Absolute in its own way, and with its own unity, so that the simplest conceivable structure of the Absolute Life would be stateable only in terms of an infinitely great variety of types of purpose and of fulfilment, intertwined in the most complex fashions. Apart from any doctrine of evolution, then, we have to regard the Absolute in its wholeness as comprising many Selves, in the most various interrelations.

Now we must urgently insist that, when once we have recognized this variety of finite purposes, and of infinite systems consisting of finite purposes, *within* the Absolute, we are not at all obliged to assume, as many more or less idealistic systems have done, some *further* principle of blind self-differentiation within the Absolute as the ground of the separation or falling away of the finite beings *from* their divine source. Longing, considered as a fact *other than* fulfilment, is, indeed, in its own already distinguished nature, to any extent blind. But, by our hypothesis, longing exists *in* the Absolute Life, and as a significant portion thereof. Any temporal present, taking that word in the ''inclusive'' sense that was defined in our Third lecture of the present Series, contains, as we saw in discussing Time, just such an experience of finitude and of dissatisfaction. Now longing, in itself, means *non*-possession of the goal; and the temporal instance shows us that the proposition: ''To-day the ideal is sought for and *not* found,'' is perfectly consistent with the proposition: ''In eternity the ideal *is* found.'' Nor is it necessary in the least to suppose that if the Absolute is possessed of the eternal point of view, and so is acquainted with the finding of the ideal which *to-day* is sought in vain, the Absolute is therefore *not* directly acquainted with the vain seeking of to-day, or is no sharer therein. Rather, from our point of view, is the very reverse the necessary conclusion. *In order to be possessed of the eternal knowledge of the attainment of the goal, the Absolute insight will actually include all that we experience when to-day we seek the goal in vain.* For the Absolute insight then, as for our own, the seeking of the goal *to-day* will *not* be successful. Just this ill-success of the temporal instant will be the very condition of the success of the eternally expressed Will. For, as we have insisted, without longing, no attainment. Therefore the larger consciousness does noι lose the conscious incompleteness of the lesser, but gives that, just as it is, its place in the completed whole.

The unity of consciousness, even in our own narrow experience, gives us many instances where consciousness either spans in one moment the conflict between two opposing internal tendencies, or embraces in one act the contrasts of longing and fulfilment, of ignorance and knowledge, of defeat and victory. One who, to take a trivial instance, ''expects the unexpected'' (as a sensible man should in dealing with fortune), combines in one consciousness, at the moment when the surprising event occurs, the shock of knowing that event as surprising, and the little triumph of observing that, just because of its surprising character, it meets, in one aspect, his expectations, because he had expected a surprise. Just such expectation of surprises constitutes one of the most cherished joys of the Christmas holidays; and the children, as they fall upon the parcels which contain their presents and open these, have also an instant wherein their temporal span of consciousness, brief as it is, is long enough to embrace ''at once'' (in the sense discussed in our third lecture) the contrast between ignorant suspense and delighted discovery. Now for them, just that is the supreme moment. And it is so because consciousness spans at once the suspense and the solution. Or again, if I have wandered long, thirsty, in a dry land, and find the spring, the most perfect experience is that in which, even while I still am full of thirst, I *also* drink the water for which I have so agonized and wandered. Or still again, a recent psychologist[1] has extensively illustrated the well-known thesis that part of the joy of play lies in the *''bewusste Selbsttäuschung,''* the ''conscious self-deception'' of the player. The delights of the theatre are of this sort; the plays of children and even of puppies and kittens, either exhibit, or at least suggest, the same state of mind. Now ''conscious self-deception'' is a state of mind that more or less definitely spans and includes ignorance and knowledge, blind belief and proud disbelief, in one act. It is only a petty bondage to conventional formulas, and in particular a purely formal and thoughtless use of the phraseology of the principle of contradiction, which makes some of us unwilling to recognize these normal complications that find place in the unity of even our own little consciousness. As a dramatic spectator, I can at once feel with Othello his own strong delusion, and also see with Iago the precise devices that are employed to deceive, and meanwhile, as spectator, can take my critical view of the whole situation. As reasoner, I can (in following the course of an indirect demonstration) appreciate the force of an argument even while I refute it; or can at once hold an opinion, viewed in its unreflective meaning, before my consciousness, even while I also reflect upon it, and so give it a new and a deeper import; or can think the meaning of the separate assertions contained in the antecedent and consequent of a hypothetical judgment, even while I hold in mind the decidedly different meaning involved in their combination in the judgment itself.

Now what these instances illustrate in our own narrow sort of con-

---

1. Groos, in discussing the psychology of Play in his *Spiele der Thiere* and *Spiele des Menschen.* The term *''bewusste Selbsttäuschung''* Groos borrows from K. Lange. See *Spiele der Thiere,* p. 308; *Spiele des Menschen,* p. 164, *sqq.,* p. 499, *sqq.*

sciousness, I apply, in universal terms, to the Absolute. I hold that all finite consciousness, *just as it is in us,*—ignorance, striving, defeat, error, temporality, narrowness,—*is all present from the Absolute point of view, but is also seen in unity with the solution of problems, the attainment of goals, the overcoming of defeats, the correction of errors, the final wholeness of temporal processes, the supplementing of all narrowness.*

Consequently, I see no reason, after once we have found that the Absolute, in order to be complete, must include finitude, to ask yet further, "How then in us does the finitude come to seem to be sundered from the Absolute?" Finitude *means* a sense of sundering, but of a sundering that from the Absolute point of view, also involves union. We, by hypothesis, *are* aware of the longings and of the ignorance. The Absolute, which is our own very selfhood in fulfilment, is aware of all that we are aware of (*i.e.* of the longings and of the ignorance) *and* of the supplement also. If one persists in asking, "But what has sundered us from the Absolute, and narrowed our consciousness as it is narrowed?" my only general answer is, Such narrowness must find its place *within* the Absolute life, in order that the Absolute should be complete. One needs then no new principle to explain why, as Plotinus asked, the souls fell away from God.[1] *From the point of view of the Absolute, the finite beings never fall away.* They are where they are, namely in and of the Absolute Unity. *From their own point of view, they seem to have fallen away,* because (as finite) they are the longing aspect, and *not* the final fulfilment of longing; because they are partial ignorance, and not the fulfilment of knowledge; because they are the expression of an attention to *this* and *this,* and not of that attention to the whole which, in the Absolute, is the corrective and the includer of their inattention; and finally, because they are stages of a temporal process, while the Absolute is possessed of the inclusive eternal insight. The only *general* deduction of their existence is furnished by the fact that, unless they existed, the Absolute Will, which is also their own, could not be expressed.

What we have said of the relation of the Absolute to the various included Individuals, applies also, *within* the world of the various Selves, to the relation in which any larger or including Individual Self stands to the lives of the Individuals which, from our point of view, are included within it. Thus, according to our account, every new Self that arises in time must find its place *within* the life of a larger and inclusive Selfhood. This larger Selfhood indeed permits the included Self, in some aspect of its nature, to become an Individual,—an image of the Absolute,—a will that takes its own individual attitude towards the world. Yet the including Self also in

---

1. Plotinus, *Enn.,* V, 1, at the beginning.

some measure predetermines the character of that which it includes, and limits the latter to a particular place in Being. In our Supplementary Essay we suggested, very inadequately, the variety of internally differentiated structure which any Self-Representative System involves. As a fact, any Self except the Absolute is included within the life of a richer Self, and in turn includes the lives of partial Selves within its own. The consciousness of the included Selves is indeed hereby limited to a particular place in Being, and so constitutes only a particular type of consciousness. At any moment of time the consciousness that embodies a particular stage in the life and self-expression of any Individual, may therefore be limited to an explicit attention to certain facts only,—the "rest of the world" being known to this Individual, just then, only as the undifferentiated background of its consciousness. All such limitations will be expressible in the same general terms. The larger Selfhood involves the inclusion of the partial Self-hood. Therefore the partial Selfhood exists; and one has not to explain by new principles why its consciousness at any temporal instant appears, from its own point of view, as cut off from that which includes it. It is cut off only in so far as it is indeed a partial form of consciousness, which, as this partial form, knows at any time so much of the whole world as just then expresses its stage of life-purpose.

An explanation of the particular existence of *this* finite consciousness can be given therefore, only in one of two forms: first, in terms of universal principles, in so far as without just this finitude, the eternal purpose would not obtain the wealth of individual expression that it actually possesses; or, secondly, in terms of the particular relations of each finite being, in so far as it is what it is in consequence of the presence in the world, and especially in the temporal Past, of other finite beings, whose nature and acts required some aspect of its own life as their resultant.

Consequently, any effort to give an account of the temporal origin and evolution of any particular finite being, such as one of ourselves, must follow the *second* of these forms of explanation, and cannot undertake to give an account of the origin of all finitude. The question about the evolution of new forms of finite life then becomes this: What conditions of the previous finite life of the world explain why, just at this point, a new Self should begin to appear? Or again, to put the question a little more generally, our former theory as to evolution accepted the thesis that humanity, as a whole, has sprung from some non-human process of experience which, before our special type of selfhood appeared, was taking place in the natural world. This previous process, we have said, was no doubt in itself a conscious process, perhaps possessing a type of consciousness whose "temporal span" was more or less different from our own, just because its present interest was always expressed by a longer or shorter series of facts than we now at present take into account. But in any case it was not what we should have called a human process. How came it to give origin to a process of our type? This is the sole question that any philosophical theory of the evolution of the Self can undertake to deal with.

Our answer will take some such form as the following,—a form inevitably hypothetical, but consistent with the facts and theories which we now have at our disposal.

IV

Any form of finite selfhood, just in so far as it is definitely conscious of explicit relations to the divine plan, tends, *ipso facto*, to express itself in an activity that accords with this plan, and that in consequence is one of the stages in that temporal process whereby the divine self-consciousness directly gets its own temporal embodiment.[1] Now since the divine plan of life, in its wholeness, is a self-representative system of longings and attainments, where each act expresses some particular purpose, and accomplishes that purpose, and where to every particular fact there corresponds just the purpose that wins embodiment in this fact, the conscious temporal life of any being who is explicitly aware of his relations to God, who acts accordingly, and who sees his act attaining its goal, must be a Well-Ordered series of deeds and successes, where each step leads to the *next,* where there is so far no wandering or wavering, where novelty results only from recurrent processes, and where plans, as a whole, do not change. We have already seen, especially in our Supplementary Essay, that the process of *counting,* dry and barren as it often seems, is for us, in our ignorance, an admirable example of the mere Form of such a recurrent activity as a being in full control of his own rational processes and of his experience would carry out. For counting produces an endless and, for our reflective investigation, an endlessly baffling wealth of novelties, as the Theory of Numbers proves. And yet this divine wealth of truth is the product of the seemingly so uniform, the unquestionably recurrent process, of counting *again and again.* Give to such a process the concrete content of a life of action in accordance with a principle, and in pursuit of ideals,—and *then* you would have, in the will that expressed itself in this life, a boundlessly wealthy source of constantly novel experience. Such would be the grade of life that we sometimes

---

1. The relation of this thesis to the problem of Free Will, and especially to the question whether the finite being is free to act counter to the divine plan, *i.e.* is free to sin, will find its place in the next lecture.

ascribe to an angel,—a life wherein one is always serving God, unswerv-ingly, and wherein one is nevertheless always doing something new, be-cause at every stage (as in our own number-series) all that has gone before is presupposed in every new deed, and so secures the individuality of that deed.

But now such a finite life as this is, from our point of view, indeed an ideal. We are not such finite beings as this. Nor do we concretely know of any such. The finite beings whom we acknowledge in the concrete, are al-ways, at any temporal moment, such as they are by virtue of an *inattention* which at present blinds them to their actual relations to God and to one an-other. Their acts are limited by reason of this inattention. They are indeed, as finite beings, aware of the world as a whole, as that which they acknowl-edge, and as that to which they ought to react thus or thus. But neither their own will nor their plans of action are at the present temporal instant clear to them. They are also conscious, although imperfectly, of themselves. And their imperfect self-consciousness does indeed show itself in the form of activities which tend to become recurrent, but in a somewhat tentative way. Such partially recurrent activities constitute intelligent habits. Examples of such are: a planful searching after plans, a rational striving to become more concretely rational, and so on. But in such processes these beings are seek-ing further definition of their own life and powers. They are seeking them-selves,—their own purposes, and the means to the execution of these purposes. Now that such imperfect finite beings should be found in God's world at all, is explicable solely on the foregoing general grounds. Igno-rance, error, striving after selfhood,—these are significant, even if, when taken by themselves alone, unintelligible forms of experience. They are, however, intelligible in their relation to the whole. If the divine life did not include them, it could not win the completion of their incompleteness, and so could not attain absolute perfection in the eternal world. We have here then to *presuppose* the occurrence of some such processes of a finite, that is of a longing, dissatisfied, incomplete type. What interests us here is sim-ply the problem: given such forms of finite striving, how could new forms, new Selves, arise from them? What about their nature makes them fruitful of new types of individuality?

To this question, one may next respond with another, viz. What *con-stitutes* a new form of finite life and experience,—a new sort of selfhood? And the answer here is: A new form of selfhood means simply the appear-ance (as in our own case), of a *new type of interest in the world, in God, and in finding the way to self-expression.* A new individual is thus never a new *thing*, but a new kind of life-purpose, finding unique individual em-bodiment in experience by means of definite acts. Now already, in follow-ing the development of the empirical Ego *within* the range of our human experience, we have seen how a new sort of selfhood *can* arise. We have now only to generalize in order to see how a similar process can occur universally, and can lead to a transformation of finite consciousness in the direction of the evolution of new types.

V

It will be remembered that, in our second lecture, we saw how a finite consciousness is led to take a *twofold* view of its relations to the world. In the case of our human interpretation of the nature of things, it was this twofold view that gave us the conception of the contrast between the World of Description and the World of Appreciation. We are at present no longer concerned with the doctrines or theories about the universe which may result, in any finite mind, from the emphasizing now of this and now of that aspect of the contrast here in question; but we are much interested in dwelling, for a moment, upon the fact that this double view of things, which the ignorance of a finite being may lead it to take, has, or tends to have, a very important influence upon the differentiation of new *kinds of activity*. We may remember how the idleness of the cat watching the squirrels reminded us of the contemplative absorption of the men of science in describing phenomena. We easily see how vast an indirect influence upon human life and conduct such absorption in the study of the World of Description has possessed. But there is still another aspect of the tendency here in question which we must at this point emphasize.

In so far as a finite being conceives himself as already knowing enough, in general, for his purposes, he sets about attaining his goal by direct self-expression. That is, he proceeds to react upon his world in a definite way. In so far, however, as although intelligent, he still feels his inability to act in such a more direct way, he falls into that state of watchful discrimination, which looks, as we saw, *for some new object between any pair of objects that has already attracted attention.*[1] Now this search for the *between* is itself a kind of activity, with a recurrent plan. It differs from what we usually call a definite course of action by virtue of the way in which it deals with experience. And, as we saw, it is an activity directed by nothing so much as by *an attention to the contents of experience when once they chance to have been discriminated.* Therefore it is indeed on the whole opposed, by virtue of this attitude, to the more direct plans of action already

---

1. The word *between,* be it noticed, is used here, and in what follows, in the generalized technical sense explained in Lecture II of this series.

present in the life which this love of discriminating novelties interrupts. It emphasizes, in a relatively random way, now this and now that special fact. It tries experiments in the forming of new series of linked contents. Now, in our last lecture, when we followed the genesis of the Empirical Ego, what did we find as the chief source of the new ideas that led to its gradual organization? Imitation. But upon what does all Imitation depend? First, upon an interest *in discriminating between the doings of some other individual and the present deeds of one's own organism;* and, secondly, upon an interest in seeking, through a persistent process of trial and error, to find a new course of action which, when discovered, shall constitute *a modification of the former deeds of one's own organism in the direction of the deeds of one's model.*

It will be seen at once that the accomplishment of an act of imitation, whereby I modify what I formerly could do, so as to be able to conform to my fellow's act, is essentially a construction of something that lies, in a technical sense, *between* the acts of my model, and what were formerly my own acts. Apart from my model, I already tended to act thus or thus. Under the influence of my model, I tend to approach his way of acting. *But I never merely repeat his act.* Imitation is a kind of experimental origination, a trial of a new plan, the initiation of a trial series of acts. The result of imitative efforts is that the world comes to contain a sort of action which lies *between* two former ways of action, in such wise that, if you regarded these two former ways of acting as equivalent to each other, the new way would be equivalent to both. Meanwhile, by being interested in the new act as in something different from both its predecessors, you define for your own consciousness, in a clearer way, the difference of these predecessors from one another. The result is, that the world of your consciousness wins a new expression of the relation of the One and the Many. For here, as in our former discussion of the relation of *between,* it appears that the original, and puzzling, diversity between the imitator and the model has, by the interposition of the imitative act between these prior courses of action, come to appear as a *diversity of stages in the same series.* The triad, formed of the three terms,—(1) the original activities of the imitative being, (2) the activities of the model, and (3) the imitative act itself,—is now a triad of connected members whereof the third lies between the two others. The finite world has hereby won a new consciousness of the unity of its own life.

Any individual Self grows, however, by means of very numerous imitations of many models. Every new act of imitation has this character of interposing a new intermediary between a pair of facts that, apart from the imitation, would have appeared less related. The result is that the new Individual, the life of the empirical human Self, comes to be, in one aspect, *a series of results of intermediation,* a more or less systematic establishment of new terms whereby triads are constituted. Every *result* of imitation tends, however, to the establishment of recurrent processes, whereby the new sort of action, once discovered, tends to repeat itself indefinitely in new acts of the same sort. For the mark of the will that has once discovered its own purpose is that its activities assume the recurrent form. Hence, in initiating new acts, the imitative activity tends to the establishment of new forms of recurrent self-expression.

In addition to this more definite experimental search for new forms of activity by means of imitative adjustments to the social environment, and in addition also to the recurrent activities whereby a growing individual shows that he has discovered *what to do,* and so seeks novelty only in the form of the new terms of a self-representative series, we find, indeed, in the life of any growing self, a still vaguer process of *growth through mere trial and error.* And in the early life of any mind, as well as in our maturer life whenever we are in the midst of very novel conditions, this process plays a large part. In this case, a being, as yet unconscious of a plan, and too ignorant or too unfortunate to find the right social models to guide him, acts *at random* in accordance with his instincts, until by mere happy accident he discovers a plan, which he then begins to pursue in recurrent fashion. This is in a great measure what happens when a child gradually learns to creep, stand, walk. This way of acquiring new habits by a wholly or partly non-imitative adjustment to the environment, has been studied by psychologists even more than the more complex processes of imitation. It is in this way that we vaguely look for new ideas, find our way in new places, help ourselves in learning new arts such as bicycling, and so on. Yet we always prefer the imitation of social models to this vaguer sort of wandering whenever social guidance is possible.

It is to be noted, however, that even here the new adjustment is learned by a process of finding constantly something new that stands *between* our former course of action and our vaguely appreciated goal. We are dissatisfied. That means, so far as we are conscious, that we find ourselves doing something, and conceive vaguely, in the yet unknown future, a way of acting that would satisfy if we could find it. Our course, hereupon, is to seek something *between* that unknown goal, and ourselves as we are. This something, as soon as found, tends to satisfy the will as an effort, even if it leaves us disappointed with the result.

All our finite striving thus includes a creation of new intermediaries between the starting-point and the goal, by imitation where that is possible, by random attention to new facts where such is our only course.

The evolution of a new Self, in the realm of our own conscious life, thus involves, at every step, just the contrast between the two finite ways of viewing the world, and between the two sorts of resulting series,—just the contrast, I say, which we studied so extensively when we compared the structure of the World of Description and the World of Appreciation. *Either,* namely, one has already found out, according to one's lights, what to do, *or else* one is vaguely trying to discriminate, in the vast background which constitutes the world, the facts whose union into series, through the establishment of intermediaries, will give one a comprehension of what one's environment is, a sense of how the One and the Many are related, and so an insight into what one has to do. In the *first* of these two ways of dealing with one's world, one is already, as far as one's consciousness goes, possessed of one's plan as a Self. One's life then consists in *doing again and again* what, according to one's conscious plans, one has to do, and in thereby winning new stages of self-representative life. But in the *second* case, one is receptive, rather than freely constructive; is searching; and succeeds, if at all, only by an experimental interpolation of new terms in given series of discriminated facts. The union of these two tendencies leads to a constant differentiation of new stages of self-consciousness. The principal source of the novel forms of self-expression is the *second* of the two tendencies. The first tendency leads to the sort of novelty in results that the number-series has illustrated.

So much for the two processes, so far as we can observe them within the limits of our human consciousness. I now make the wholly tentative hypothesis that *the process of the evolution of new forms of consciousness in Nature is throughout of the same general type as that which we observe when we follow the evolution of new sorts of plans, of ideas, and of selfhood in our own life.* And, as the general evidence for the worth of such an hypothesis, I point out the following facts.

The types of life that are phenomenally known to us in Nature, form series such as indicate a gradual evolution of new forms from old. A new individual life, so far as we observe, in the outer world, the signs of its presence, is a new way of behavior appearing amongst natural phenomena. This new collection of functions comes to be manifested to us gradually. In the process of heredity, its generation involves, in a vast number of cases, the phenomena which our science interprets as the sexual union of cells that represent previously living individuals. As a result of this union of sexual elements, the cell from which the new organism developes has, in all this class of cases, characters that lie *between* those represented by the parent cells. The resulting organism consequently has characters, and accordingly developes functions, that lie *between* those of formerly existing organisms; and so the new living individual is at once a new link in the series of the possible forms of its type, and an individual variation of its species. In these respects, *sexual generation is analogous to the process of conscious imitation.* For imitation (not, to be sure, in the case of a whole organism, but in the case of a single voluntary function) means that a new process results from the conscious union of the influence of *two* previous processes; and in case of imitation, as we have just seen, the new process lies *between* the original processes. Thus the conscious union of former types of activity, in the very act that, while uniting, discriminates them, results in a new sort of intermediate activity. A corresponding union of *two* elements, with a resultant that lies *between* formerly existent beings, characterizes sexual generation.

But in another class of cases, new living individuals, as they are phenomenally known to us, result *asexually*. Here the processes involved are sufficiently typified, for our present purposes, by the very process of *cell-multiplication* from which any new organism always results. All such processes are, in form, relatively recurrent. Novelty, where it becomes notable at all in the course of such processes, depends upon the massing of the results of former stages of this same recurrent process. So it is, in part, when the multiplying cells of a new organism undergo differentiation just because the newer cells find their places in a whole which is formed of all the previous cells, and so adjust themselves to an environment different from that in which the earlier cells grew. *But this whole process is analogous, in structure and in result, to the recurrent processes of the conscious will that has found what it has to do,* that does it again and again, and that reaches novel results in a way which the counting process has most clearly illustrated for us. Whether such novel results are significant, depends on the grade of significance that the special will, whose expression we observe, has reached. But such recurrent processes are, as we have seen, the normal ones of the World of Appreciation. They are known to us, in our own consciousness, as the source of a particular sort of novelty in the *results* of conduct. They lead to Well-Ordered series of self-expressions.

But further, the new living individuals, in their development, largely illustrate what we call the process of gradual *adaptation to the environment* by novel forms of structure and function. Here again the character of the enormously complicated organic processes involved is still analogous to a process that we observe in consciousness, viz. *to our conscious process of learning new arts through trial and error*. The series of facts that we observe in the living beings are, in this type of instances, on the whole, nonrecurrent. The process is one of interpolating new terms in a series of stages that lie between the original condition of the organism, and a certain ideal goal of perfect adjustment to the environment which the individual organism never reaches.

So far then, for certain analogies between the evolution of new living beings in the phenomenal world, and the evolution of new forms of selfhood in conscious life. But now for one more analogy, and one that relates to that most critical phenomenon, the death of an organism, and to the temporal cessation of a given process of conscious striving.

The discriminating tendency that, in our consciousness, gives rise to the conceptions of the World of Description, is always, as we have seen, one of *two* contrasting tendencies that our finite relation to our world determines. Of these two tendencies, this is the subordinate one, which yields to the tendency to recurrent expression of our already established Purpose, whenever we know what to do. So far as we conceive our world in terms of the will that is now explicit in us, we do not need to give ourselves over to the discrimination of new phenomena, and we do not do so. Descriptive Science is secondary to life, and the scrutiny of that world "in the background," in search of novelties, ceases whenever we are absorbed in what seems to us triumphant self-expression. This is true even when the will which seems to itself clearly conscious of what it has to do, and of how to do it, is in fact of what we have to call a relatively low grade. For in us the will can be base in content, even when it is in form to a great extent of the higher type.

Consequently, our discriminative activities, and also our imitations, our processes of trial and error, and all our tentative seekings after greater clearness, are subject to *the often rigid selection exerted by our already established conscious plans of recurrent action.* Or, as they say, *practical* motives predominate in our life. We make these tentative efforts for the sake of establishing new plans of action wherever we lack plans. But when we have plans, already accepted, the tentative establishment of new courses of action *between* stages already existing, is permitted only in so far as it does not run counter to these already established plans.

Well, just so, in Nature, the variations of organic life that get established by means of the processes analogous (as we have just seen) to those of trial and error, and to those of imitation, are subject to a rigid selection on the part of the "environment." But the "environment," according to our own interpretation of Nature, stands, as an environment with already established characters, *for the expression of such portions of the Nature-life as have already won the habitual, that is, the more or less definitely and permanently recurrent form,* wherein a relatively persistent will to act repeatedly in the same way has become characteristic of the finite consciousness that we suppose to be represented by the natural phenomena in question.

In view of this analogy, I suggest that the evolution of new Selfhood in our own conscious case, and of new forms of life in Nature, is a process subject everywhere to the same sort of selection, whereby new tendencies are accepted or rejected according to their relation to preexistent tendencies. The evolution of new Selfhood, as I conceive the matter, is rendered possible *by the fact that a finite form of conscious life may have a twofold re-lation to the Absolute,* and so may seek the truth and its own self-expression in a twofold way,—a more active and definite course of self-expression, or a more tentative one of discovery. That is, it may grow *either* by perform-ing, in recurrent fashion, over and over, the type of action that it has already come to regard as its own form of Selfhood, *or else* by adopting the dis-criminating attitude that gives us, in our own conscious life, our concep-tions that together make up our view of the World of Description. When a consciousness adopts the latter of these two attitudes, what happens within the unity of its sphere of experience is the appearance of new contents that lie *between* previously recognized contents, or that lie, as tentative expres-sions of its will, between itself and the goal. *These new expressions of pur-pose are tentative, like our trials and errors, or like our imitations.* When they are successful, they so mass themselves as to form definite centres of new experience. By emphasizing the contrast between the Self that has cre-ated or discovered them, and the rest of the world, they then suggest plans of action, which become recurrent, so long as they survive. But when they suggest nothing that permanently accords with the established habits of the Self within which they arise, *they are unadapted to their environment, and so pass away.* A rigid selection presides over their persistence. It is the se-lection established by the more persistent habits, and conscious intents, of the finite Self to which they belong. The portion of Nature where these ten-tatively adopted new forms of life phenomenally appear to us, we call the Organic World.

But now these new creations, if they survive, are not the mere contents of another and larger consciousness. They are also processes occupying time, and embodying will; they are themselves finite conscious purposes, having an inner unity, a relation to the Absolute, of which they also are *ipso facto* partial expressions, and a tendency to adjust themselves to the goal in their own way. If, as in case of the conscious Self of any one of us, they become aware of this their own relation to the Absolute, then they no longer survive or pass away *merely* in so far as they serve the larger purpose that originally invented them as tentative devices of its own. They then, like all finite purposes of self-conscious grade, *define their own lives as individ-ually significant, conceive their goal as the Absolute, and their relations to their natural sources as relations that mean something to themselves also.* Their destiny thus becomes relatively free from that of the finite Self within which they first grew up.

Thus indeed the natural generation of an organism would be the mere phenomenon of a process of creating new stages *within* the life of previously existing Selves. But the new stages might become significant *for* them-selves, with their own time-span, their own relations to the Absolute, and their own sort of selfhood. Originally I, as this Individual, coming into existence at this point of time, might result from an organic process that phenomenally represents how a finite Selfhood, much vaster than mine (let us say the Selfhood of the human race as a whole) established in a tentative and experimental way, within its own conscious life, a new process that was serially interpolated *between* the processes represented by the reproductive cells of my parents. This was, for the race, merely a tentative variation in its life-series, due to the same sort of interest that, in our imitative life, makes us interested in trying the effect of creating a new sort of function intermediate between two previous ones, or to the same sort of scrutiny of the world that leads us to make new experimental discriminations in our scientific thinking. Had this variation been inconsistent with the habits of action already established in Nature, I should not have survived. Just so, a useless imitation, or a new idea inconsistent with established ideas, is erelong abandoned. But having survived, I have entered, with all the instincts of my race, into the social order. On one side of my nature I am thus a resultant. My conscious interests were originally narrowed by the act that determined my place in the series. Hence I am primarily constituted by a series of interests in a small group of facts, and am relatively inattentive to all the rest of the universe. But *within* my narrow span I can still learn about universal truth, because, after all, I am a conscious process, and every such process is really linked to all the world. But when once I become *aware* that my little form of willing also is a hint of an Absolute truth, I know myself as in intent this Individual in the World. And now I have indeed a character that may well survive, that in fact *will* survive, all the organic processes which were originally expressed in my life as this variation of the human stock. For in God, I am this seeker after God, so soon as I know myself as a Self at all, and, as such a seeker after God, I no longer wholly depend on the finite Self *within* which I came into being, just as my organism, even in its physical functions, no longer depends on the parent organisms.

By precisely such processes, the evolution of new life everywhere in Nature would be, upon this hypothesis, explicable. Selves would always originate within Selves, but, as related to the Absolute, would be capable of surviving the finite experimental purposes for which they were originated. Their natural origin would be perfectly consistent with an immortal destiny, just because all facts in the world, however originated, have teleological relations with the Absolute, and because, whatever life includes an explicit seeking for its own selfhood is in *conscious* relations with the Absolute.

The appearance of *new* Individual Selves would be, however, when temporally considered, a genuine fact. And their source would be the one that in ourselves enables us to vary the plans of our Will through the tentative play of the Discriminating Attention. And thus, in completing the sketch of our hypothesis regarding the interpretation of Nature and Evolution, we have brought this hypothesis into definite relation to our former contrast between the World of Description and World of Appreciation. This contrast appears, not merely as a fact of our own consciousness, but as a consequence of a tendency that is responsible, in Nature, for the whole process of Evolution. What in us appears as the conflict between science and practical life, is an example of the struggle for existence in Nature.

VI

That the Self whose natural relations have been so definitely admitted, is, like any other phenomenon in Nature, a proper object for the investigations of any external observer who is interested in explaining the occurrences of his life in terms of Causation, is now plain enough. An external observer of a human Self, as expressed in the behavior of the phenomena of its organism, may be a psychologist. If so, he will be interested in explaining how any human Self appears as a resultant of temperament, heredity, training, and the rest, and how his life is subject to law. To treat the Self thus, is to make its life an object in the psychologist's own World of Description. The undertaking will be as much justified as any other undertaking of science. To an external observer who seeks to win his purposes as a student of science, the individual Self, and all its temporal deeds, must be viewed as facts to be explained, in so far as that is logically possible, through their causal connections with previous facts, and with the whole of Nature. Such an observer, in so far as he deals with the World of Description, can recognize no deed of the Self as a mere outcome of free will. Every describable character of the Self, its temperament, its motives, its impulses, its training, its knowledge, its deeds, will appear to this observer as causally explicable by heredity and by environment. In so far as these aspects of the Self are not yet explained by science, they will still be inevitable and proper *problems* for causal explanation. Science, whether physical or physiological or psychological, will remorselessly and unceasingly pursue the end of making man, the natural being, comprehensible to the understanding of man, the observer of Nature. And this undertaking will be strictly rational. When we admit all this, do we not endanger our own doctrine of the freedom of the Individual Self?

I answer: No, for this very undertaking will have as its sole justification the fact that the teleological structure of Being gives warrant for holding that the true purposes of our descriptive science are, as far as that is logically possible, actually expressed by the universe. Man, as the observer of Nature and of man, has a purpose, and a very profound purpose, in trying thus to comprehend in causal terms his relation to Nature and to his fellows. We know from earlier lectures what this purpose is. This purpose, according to our view, must be capable of some relatively final expression, viz. of the very expression, which our science now begins and unweariedly prosecutes, but which no merely mortal toil will ever finish. Hence it is true that human nature, down to the least externally describable detail of its temporal fashion of expressing itself, is a natural phenomenon, a part of universal Nature, and is as much capable of some kind of explanation in causal terms as is any natural fact. But, on the other hand, this very way of viewing man sets to itself its own limits, viz. the limits of the World of Description. For, in the first place, thus to view man is not to view him as he consciously views his own inner life, that is, as possessing Internal Meaning. To explain man in causal terms is to view him as an external observer sees or might see him; and not as he himself means to be when he expresses his will in his deeds. Hence what you never causally explain about a man is precisely his primary character as a Self, namely, his conscious meaning itself, in so far as it is his. And secondly, all causal explanation has to do with the types and the describable general characters of events, and never with whatever is individual about events. For the individual, as we saw in our foregoing series of lectures, is the indefinable aspect of Being. But what you cannot define, you cannot explain in causal terms.

And so, to sum up,—that I now have this character, and this environment, and that I am subject to these or these consequences of my past experience, you can undertake to explain causally. Yes, whatever about my words, my deeds, my manner, my mood, my feelings, or my plans, is describable as a feature common to me and to any other being in the world,—whatever then there is about me which is expressible in general terms, or which is capable of being externally observed, you can and must undertake, with rationality, to explain causally as due to my ancestry, training, circumstances, environment, and dependence upon Nature in general. But what remains causally inexplicable is precisely my Being as this individual, who am nobody else in God's world. Now my individuality is not in the least separable from what the Scholastics would have called my "common nature." My individuality means simply, that my innumerable common traits are teleologically expressed in this internally determinate but externally undetermined unique life which is now mine, and which, if I have a personal ideal, is to be mine until I have come to my full and final embodiment as this one of God's individuals. And so once more, if you ask me what, in my present consciousness, expresses not the separable portion, but that inseparable *aspect* of my nature which neither God nor man can causally explain, then I answer: *Just my conscious intent to be, in God's world, myself and nobody else*. In this sense alone my life, not as that of an Independent Being, but as the life expressing a rational purpose to win an unique relation to all the universe, an unique contrast with all other Selves, or if you will, an unique instance of dependence upon all the rest, is now, and will always continue to be causally inexplicable and irreducible. For the unique as the unique is not the common nature as such; and only the common nature of things can be causally explicable.

VII

So much then for the causal relations of my Selfhood. "But," you may insist, "is not my unique and individual nature, if not causally determined, still teleologically determined by that very relation to the whole upon which my existence as this individual depends? How can our doctrine speak of the will and of the individuality of the Self as in any sense free, and still recognize that unity of the world and of the divine plan upon which our whole theory depends?"

To answer this objection I must indeed still further repeat considerations sketched in our former series of lectures, and must afresh apply them to the Self. Let us return therefore, as we close, to our former teleological view of the universe, and to the relation between God's inclusive will and the various individual wills. Here I can only emphasize, in the form of replies to objections, a theory whose basis has been fully stated in our general Theory of Being.

In answer, then, to this whole view of mine, you still may say, "In so far as this my will is God's will, and is related to the whole, it is God and not my private Self that wills me to be what I am." I reply, The divine act whereby God wills your individuality to be what in purpose and meaning it is, is identical with your own individual will, and exists not except as thus identical.

"Yet has not the oneness of Being been so explained, by our idealistic theory, as to imply that every life, *i.e.* every fact in the universe, is so related to every other, that no fact in the universe could be altered without some consequent alteration of every other fact? For this was the earliest generalization reached by our Idealism in our criticism of the realistic doctrine. Now if there are thus no Independent Beings, how can there be in any sense Free Beings? And if I am so related to the world that a change in the universe beyond me would alter whatever I am, then am I not dependent upon the rest of the universe for whatever I am? Upon this idealistic theory, is not the teleological determination of every fact in the universe by every other fact a reciprocal determination? But is not such reciprocal determination absolute? Is not then every individual fact in this idealistic world so determined in its purpose by the purpose of every other that nothing undetermined, nothing free, is anywhere left?" So the objector may state his case.

Hereupon I respond, In the very reciprocity of my relations to all else in the universe lies the very assurance that I possess a certain true and significant freedom. The world beyond me can say to me, "Were I to change, you would change, and become in some sense another, both in your experience and in your purpose." All this is true. But in turn I can reply, to the whole universe, natural and spiritual, Aye, but if my individual will changed, if I chose to be another than what I am, you, O world, just because of the universal teleology of your constitution, would be in some wise another, and that in every region of your Being. For you are no more truly independent of me and of my will than I am of you and of your might. However slight the change that I can make, I still do make a difference, by my will, to all beings in heaven and earth. And if I, in my individual capacity as this being, do not create the other beings, just as truly can one say that, in my individual character, they do not create me. Upon precisely such a consideration as this, our whole argument for Idealism itself was founded.

"Yes," you may insist, "but according to this doctrine, God's will creates us all alike, and in some sense (viz. from the Eternal point of view), all *at once,* so that we various beings of the world are equally creatures of the one plan." I respond once more, The very essence of our whole theory, as we already saw in the closing lecture of the foregoing series, is that the categories, whether of causation or of teleological dependence, however they are conceived, are inevitably secondary to the fact that the world exists, in its wholeness and in every fragment and aspect of its life, as the positive embodiment of conscious will and purpose. Now to say that another either causes or teleologically determines me, is to say, at bottom, that my life expresses a purpose that is in some sense different from my purpose, or that is in some sense *not* my own private or individual purpose. But to say this is to point out what indeed is true of every aspect of my life that can be reduced to my relations with Nature and with my fellows, and with whatever else the world beyond me contains. Now all this my dependence upon other beings is not only true, but is desired and intended by my own purpose itself whenever my purpose is rational. For, as our idealistic argument from the very outset has maintained, I can purpose at all only by purposing that my will should find its expression in what is Other than myself, and consequently in what, in some sense, gives my will its own determination as a will that lives in this world of other life than my private life. That I depend for my life and meaning upon life not my own, is as true as that I am I at all. That this dependence involves a temporal origin, is due to the very nature of Time. The question is whether I *wholly* thus depend. And our answer has been that there is that about me which makes my will, as the will of an individual, not wholly the expression of other purposes than my private or individual purpose. This answer has been based upon our whole Theory of Being. If now I, the individual, exist, in one aspect, as the expression of nobody's will but my own, does this assertion in the least conflict with our other assertion that I and all beings exist as the expressions of the divine will? I answer: There is no conflict; for the Divine Will gets expressed in the existence of me the individual only in so far as this Divine Will first not merely recognizes from without, but includes within itself my own will, as one of its own purposes. And since God, for our view, is not an external cause of the world, but is the very existence of the world in its wholeness as the fulfilment of purpose, it follows once more that my existence has its place in the Divine Existence as the existence of an individual will, determined, just in so far as it is this individual will, by nothing except itself.

The problem then of my freedom is simply the problem of my individuality. If I am I and nobody else, and if I am I as an expression of purpose, then I am in so far free just because, as an individual, I express by my existence no will except my own. And that is precisely *how* my existence expresses, or results from, God's Will. That this same existence of mine also has, besides its individuality, its dependence, its natural relations, its temporal origin, means that I am not only I, but also the Self along with all other Selves. But that the One Will of God is expressed through the Many individual wills,—this results from that view of the relation of the One and the Many which our former series so extensively discussed. Simple unity is a mere impossibility. God cannot be One except by being Many. Nor can we various Selves be Many, unless in Him we are One. To know just this is to win the deepest truth that religion has been seeking to teach humanity.

The Sources of Religious Insight

INDIVIDUAL EXPERIENCE
AND SOCIAL EXPERIENCE*

The results of our first lecture appear to have brought the religious problems, so far as we shall attempt to consider them, into a position which in one respect simplifies, in another respect greatly complicates our undertaking.

I

In one way, I say, our undertaking is simplified. For, as we have defined religion, the main concern of any religion that we are to recognise is with the salvation of man, and with whatever objects or truths it is important to know if we are to find the way of salvation. Now the experiences which teach us that we need what I have ventured to call by the traditional name salvation, are, from my point of view, experiences common to a very large portion of mankind. They are great and, in certain respects at least, simple experiences. You can have them and estimate them without being committed to any one form of religious faith, without accepting any special creed about supernatural things, and even without hoping to find out any way of salvation whatever. The essential conditions for discovering that man needs salvation are these: You must find that human life has some highest end; and you must also find that man, as he naturally is, is in great danger of failing to attain this supreme goal. If you discover these two facts (and I personally hold them to be facts whose reality you can experience), then the quest for the salvation of man interests you, and is defined for you in

---

*From *The Sources of Religious Insight* (New York: Charles Scribner's Sons, 1912).

genuinely empirical terms. Given the problem, you may or you may not see how to solve it. You may or you may not appeal to what you suppose to be a revelation to guide you on the way. But in any case, granted these conditions, granted that your experience has shown you your need of salvation—then the problem of religion is upon your hands. Soluble or insoluble, the topic of a revelation from above, or of a scientific inquiry, or of a philosophy, or of a haphazard series of efforts to better your condition, this problem, if it once comes to hold your attention, will make of you a religious inquirer. And so long as this is the case, no degree of cynicism or of despair regarding the finding of the way to salvation, will deprive you of genuinely religious interest. The issue will be one regarding facts of live experience. The concerns that for you will seem to be at stake will be perfectly human, and will be in close touch with every interest of daily life.

To conceive the business of religion in this way simplifies our undertaking, in so far as it connects religion not merely with doubtful dogmas and recondite speculations, but rather with personal and practical interests and with the spirit of all serious endeavour.

Upon the other hand, this way of defining religion does, indeed, also complicate certain aspects of our present task. For if, from our point of view, religion thus becomes, in one way or another, the concern of everybody who has once seen that life has a highest goal, and that we are all naturally in great danger of missing this goal—still any effort to study the nature of religious insight seems to require us to be somehow just to all the endless varieties of human opinion regarding what the highest goal of human life is, and regarding the way to attain that goal after we have once defined it. In some sense, in our further inquiry, nothing human can be alien to us, in case it involves any deep experience of man's purpose in living, or of man's peril as a seeker after the attainment of his purpose; or any assurance regarding the presence or the power which, entering into some sort of union with any man's own spiritual life, seems to that man an apt Deliverer from his evil plight, a genuinely saving principle in his life.

How great the resulting complications that threaten our investigation seem to be the conclusion of our former lecture showed us. Countless souls, trusting to their individual experience, have learned, as we at the last time indicated, to define their ideal, and their need, and, upon occasion, to discover the power that they took to be their saving principle—their deliverer. Who amongst all these were right, either in their judgment as to their need or in their consciousness that they had found the way that leads to peace, to triumph, to union with the goal of human life? Were all of them more or less right? Were any of them wholly deluded? Are there as many supreme aims of life as there are individuals? Are there as many ways of salvation as there are religions that men follow? And by what means shall we decide such questions? Grave and infinitely complicated seem the issues which these queries arouse.

Upon one side, then, our problem is pathetically simple, human, practical, even commonplace. Daily experience, in serious-minded people, illustrates it. The plainest facts of our life exemplify it. It concerns nothing more recondite than that tragedy of natural human failure which you may constantly witness all about you, if not within you. Upon the other side, no questions more bring you into contact with the chaotic variety of human opinion, and with the complexities of the whole universe, than do the religious questions, when thus defined in terms of men's deepest needs and of men's hopes and faiths regarding the possible escape from their most pressing peril of failure.

Our first lecture gave us a glimpse of this simplicity of the main definition of our problem and of this complication with regard to the conflicting proposals that are made toward its special formulation and toward its solution. We have now to study further the sources of insight upon which every solution of our problem must depend.

II

Our present lecture will be devoted to three tasks. First, we shall try to show that the religious consciousness of mankind, when it is concerned with the need and with the way of salvation, must needs appear in many various and apparently conflicting forms, but that, nevertheless, these conflicts need not discourage us. For, as we shall attempt still further to explain, the underlying motives of the higher religions are, after all, much more in agreement than the diversities of creeds and the apparent chaos of religious experiences would lead us to imagine. In order to make this deeper unity of the higher religious life of mankind plain, we shall try to show, more fully than we did in the last lecture, how the consciousness of the ideal of life, and of the need of salvation, naturally arises in the experience of the individual man. The religious paradox, as, in our former lecture, we defined that paradox, depends upon the fact that the principal religious motives are indeed perfectly natural and human motives, which need no mysterious movings from another world to explain their presence in our lives; while, on the other hand, these very motives, when once they appear, force us to seek for relief from spiritual sources that cannot satisfy unless they are far above our natural human level of life—that is, unless they are in some definable sense superhuman. But about superhuman matters it is not surprising that ignorant mortals should widely differ, despite the deeper unity that underlies all our nobler religious needs.

Thus the unity of the religious concerns of mankind is perfectly compatible with the fact that men differ so widely in faith. The mysteries of religion belong to our natural failure to conceive readily and to grasp adequately the religious objects. But our religious need is not a mystery; and our religious interests are as natural as is our ignorance. The higher forms of the religious consciousness are due to perfectly human motives but lead to a stubborn quest for the superhuman. To understand whence the higher religions get their moving principle, you have only to survey our natural life as it is, in all its pathetic and needy fallibility. But if the higher religions are to find what they seek, they call for sources of insight which you cannot define, unless we are able to know a reality that transcends human nature as it is—unless we can come into genuine intercourse with a spiritual realm that is above man. This naturalness of the religious motives, this supernatural and naturally baffling character of the religious objects, I am, then, first to illustrate still further than I at the last time was able to do.

I shall thus be led, in the second place, to the mention of that source of religious insight to which, at the close of the former lecture, I directed your attention, namely, to our social experience. Society, in a certain sense, both includes and transcends the individual man. Perhaps, then, something can be done toward solving the problem of the religious paradox, and toward harmonising the varieties of religious opinion, by considering the religious meaning of our social consciousness. The religious paradox is that the needy and ignorant natural man must somehow obtain the spiritual power to get into a genuine touch with a real life that is above his own level. If he is to be saved, something that is divine must come to be born in the humble manger of his poor natural life. How is this apparition of the divine in the human, of the supernatural in the natural, conceivable? It is that question which most of all divides men into various religious sects. Perhaps a study of our social experience, which, indeed, often tends to mould our naturally narrow selfishness into nobler spiritual forms, may throw light upon this problem. And so I shall, in this second part of the present discourse, state the case for our social experience as a source of religious insight.

We shall, however, no sooner state this case than we shall begin to see how inadequate our ordinary social experience is to give us full religious insight. Therefore, in the third place, I shall try to estimate more critically both the merits and the imperfections of this second source of religious light, and thus I shall be led, as I close, to the mention of a third source, from which, as I hold, we can learn what neither our unaided private experience nor our ordinary social experience ever adequately shows.

III

Let me proceed at once to the first of these three undertakings. I am further to illustrate, on the one hand, the unity and the naturalness of the religious motives; on the other hand, I am to emphasise the mysterious seeming of the religious objects. And I am thus to show the reason why the faiths of men are so diverse but their religious needs so nearly common.

At the last time I tried to define for you, in my own terms, what the supreme purpose of human life is, or, in other words, what that highest good is which we are all in such peril of missing that we need salvation from this peril. My definition was this: We are naturally creatures of wavering and conflicting motives, passions, desires. The supreme aim of life is to triumph over this natural chaos, to set some one plan of life above all the others, to give unity to our desires, to organise our activities, to win, not, indeed, the passionless peace of Nirvana, but the strength of spirit which is above the narrowness of each one of our separate passions. We need to conceive of such a triumphant and unified life, and successfully to live it. That is our goal: Self-possession, unity, peace, and spiritual power through and yet beyond all the turmoil of life— the victory that overcometh in the world.

Now this definition of the ideal life will have seemed to some of you too much a merely philosophical formula. You will say that this is not what plain men have in mind when they ask God's help, or lament their sins, or look to religion for consolation.

I grant you that, since I am here concerned with philosophy and not with preaching, I, of course, prefer, for my present purpose, a formulation of the ideal of life in reflective, in thoughtful terms. But I cannot admit that plain men, in their religious moods, are not concerned with the ideal of life which I thus reflectively formulate. I am trying to formulate the ideal of life that seems to me to underlie all the higher religions. It is one thing, however, to feel an interest and another thing to become conscious of the meaning of the interest. No matter how inarticulate may be a man's sense of his need, that sense, if deep and genuine, may imply a view of life which a whole system of ethics and of metaphysics may be needed to expound. Philosophy ought to be considerate, and to use more or less technical speech, but it need not be on that account inhuman. Its concern is with what common sense means but does not express in clearly conscious terms. It does not want to substitute its formulas for life. It does desire to add its thoughtfulness to the intensity of life's great concerns and to enlighten us regarding what aims life has always really intended to pursue.

My own effort to formulate the supreme end of life does not seem to me to be foreign to common sense. I think that this way of stating the purpose of life may help us to see through many of the apparently hopeless diversities of human opinion regarding what the highest good is.

It is customary to describe that longing for salvation which is, from the point of view of these lectures, the foundation of religion, by saying that the man who begins to get religious interest discovers that when left to himself he is out of harmony with what James calls "the higher powers," that is, with what a Christian calls God. In other words, as a customary formula states the case, the religiously disposed man begins by learning that the chief end of his existence is to come into harmony with God's will. And this discovery, as such a view supposes, teaches him, for the first time, what his ideal of life ought to be. And therefore, as many say, something that is of the nature of a mysterious revelation from without is needed to initiate the religious process and to show us our goal. On the other hand, writers like James, who insist upon interpreting religion, so far as that is possible, in terms of personal experience rather than in terms of external revelation, have nevertheless been led to agree with many of the partisans of revelation in regarding this sense of our disharmony with the "higher powers" as something that must have an essentially superhuman source. For James, our sense of religious need is an experience which mysteriously wells up from the subliminal self, from the soundless depths of our own subconsciousness. James, therefore, conceives it probable that, through the subliminal or subconscious self, we are actually aroused to religious interest by spiritual beings whose level is higher than our own, and whose will, expressed to us through the vague but often intense sense of need which the religiously minded feel, does set for us an ideal task which is of greater worth than our natural desires, and which, when we can get into harmony with these powers through the aid of their subliminal influences, does give a new sense to life.

Now in contrast with such views regarding the origin of that deeper sense of need which is indeed the beginning of religion, I have to insist that the basis of the religious interest is something much less mysterious than James's supposed workings of the "higher powers" through our subliminal selves, and is also something much more universally human than is the opportunity to come under the influence of any one revelation. Men who never heard of Christianity, and men who have never felt conscious of any external revelation from above, as well as men who have had no such sudden uprushes from their own subconscious natures as James's "religious geniuses" have reported, are able to win a genuine religious interest, to be aware of an intense need for salvation, and to set before themselves, in however inarticulate a fashion, the very ideal of life which I have been trying in my own way to formulate. The need and the ideal can come into sight in a manner that indeed does not in the least either exclude or require a belief in one or in another reported revelation, but that links both the need and the ideal to our ordinary personal experience by ties which are not at all mysterious. Let me show you, then, better than my time permitted in the former lecture, how an individual may naturally experience what I have called his need of salvation.

Nothing is more obvious about the natural course of our lives than is the *narrowness* of view to which we are usually subject. We are not only the victims of conflicting motives, but we are often too narrow to know that this is true. For we see our various life interests, so to speak, one at a time. We forget one while we are living out another. And so we are prone to live many lives, seldom noting how ill harmonised they are. Home life, for instance, may be one thing; business life in principle another; sport or social ambition another. And these various lives may be lived upon mutually inconsistent plans. We forget one part of ourselves in our temporary absorption in some other part. And if, as our naturally complex and often conflicting motives determine, these our various lives are out of harmony with one another, we constantly do irrevocable deeds that emphasise and perpetuate the results of this disharmony. And as we grow older our motives alter; yet because of our natural narrowness of interest, we often do not recognise the change. Our youth consequently lays a poor foundation for our age; or perhaps our mature life makes naught of the aspirations of our youth. We thus come to spend a great part of our days thwarting ourselves through the results of our fickleness, yet without knowing who it is that thwarts us. We love, and, like Siegfried, forget our former beloved, and perhaps live to feel the fatal spear-thrust that avenges our treason to our own past. The deeper tragedies of life largely result from this our narrowness of view.

But over against this narrowness of our ordinary activities there, indeed, stand certain moments when we get a wider vision of ourselves, when we review life, or foresee it with a broad outlook. These are, indeed, moments of insight. We all know how tragic they often are, because they show us at a glance how with the left hand we have undone the right hand's work, how we have loved and forgotten, how we have sworn fealty to many masters, and have cheated one while we served another, how absorption in business has made us unworthy of home, or how we have wantonly sacrificed a friend in order to win a game, or gained our bit of the world through what, upon review, we have to call the loss of our souls. Such moments of insight come to us sometimes when our friends die, and when memory reminds us of our neglected debts of love or of gratitude to them, or when worldly defeat reawakens the long-forgotten unworldly aspirations that we abandoned in order to do what has ended in earning the defeat. These are, I repeat, often tragic moments. But they enlighten. And they show us our need. And they arise as naturally as does any other incident of a reasonable life.

What need do they show? I answer, the need to possess what by mere nature we never come to possess, namely, the power to "see life steadily and see it whole," and then to live triumphantly in the light of this vision. Can a plain man who is no philosopher feel this need? I answer, Yes, whenever he has his moments of vision; whenever he feels the longing for the clean, straight, unswerving will, for the hearty whole life; whenever he sees and regrets his fickleness, just because it means self-defeat; whenever he seeks to be true to himself. At such moment his highest aim is the aim that there should be a highest aim in life, and that this aim should win what it seeks. He has the longing, however inarticulate, for integrity of spirit and for success in winning the fruits of integrity.

When the plain man feels what I venture thus to formulate, how will he express his longing? He will, of course, not use my present formulas. He will seize upon whatever expressions the creed or the language of his tribe may suggest to him. He may say, and perhaps truthfully: "This is the ideal that God sets before me. This is the divine will regarding my life." For at such times he conceives of God as the being who has widest vision and who knows him best. Therefore he conceives of God's plan as the fulfilment of his own rational plan. But the interior source of the plain man's view regarding the divine will is simply his better vision of the meaning of his life, the vision that comes at moments when he is not forgetful of the whole; when he does not want to swear fidelity to one beloved, and then, like Siegfried, pursue and win another; when he wants to be true to the whole of himself. No wonder that he, indeed, conceives this supreme goal of life as the goal set for him by some will higher than his own private will. He is right. For, as we shall see, throughout our later study, we are, indeed, helpless either to hold before us this our personal vision of the triumphant life and of the unity of the spirit, or to turn the vision into a practical reality, unless we come into touch and keep in touch with an order of spiritual existence which is in a perfectly genuine sense superhuman, and in the same sense supernatural, and which certainly is not our natural selves.

But in any case the plain man must needs interpret his vision of the ideal in terms of whatever conception of God, or of the triumphant life, or of spiritual power, his traditions and his stage of personal development may suggest to him. Hence the endless varieties in the formulation of the religious ideal. Whatever is suggested to a man, at his moments of wider vision, as a law or as a motive which, *if* it were the ruling motive or the supreme law would make life a consistent whole—

this he takes to be God's will, or the truth that is to save him if, indeed, salvation is possible.

If this account of the sources of the religious motive is right, we need not view the religious interest as the result of an arbitrary intrusion from above—as if the gods loved to disturb us and to trouble our peace. Nor need we, with James, speak of a marvellous and capricious uprush from below the level of our natural consciousness. Yet just as little need we think of religion as having no concern with what is, indeed, superhuman. Religion is, indeed, our own affair; for it grows out of our personal vision of the transformation that a divinely enlarged power to comprehend, to survey, to harmonise, to triumph over our natural life would give. This vision comes to us at moments, in glimpses—and is seen through a glass darkly. Our need is to see face to face and to live in the light thus to be discovered. And so to live would be salvation. The word salvation is fitting, because the need is so great and because the transformation would be so profound. The endlessly various interpretations of this one ideal and of the nature of the saving process are due to the wealth of life and to the imposing multitude of motives and of experiences that the religious consciousness has to consider. But beneath and above all the varieties of religious experience lies the effort to win in reality what the vision of the harmonious and triumphant life suggests to us in our moments of clearness. Since our own natures leave us hopelessly remote from this goal, while our glimpses of spiritual harmony and power reveal to us its preciousness, our religious need is supreme, and is accompanied with the perfectly well-warranted assurance that we cannot attain the goal unless we can get into some sort of communion with a real life infinitely richer than our own—a life that is guided by a perfect and unwavering vision, and that somehow conquers and annuls all fickleness, conflict, and estrangement. Such a life rightly seems to us to be superhuman in its breadth of view and in its spiritual power, if indeed there be such a life at all. If there is no such life, none the less we need it, and so need salvation. If salvation is possible, then there is in the universe some being that knows us, and that is the master of life. And we seek ourselves to know even as we are known and to live as the wise one would have us live.

Thus simple and, for all to whom even the occasional moments of wider vision come, universal are the religious motives. James was wrong when he sought them in any capricious interference of the subliminal self, or of its superhuman controls, with our natural selves. It is we who in our natural lives are capricious and narrowly interfere with our own freedom. It is we who are the disturbers of our own peace. The religious ideal grows out of the vision of a spiritual freedom and peace which are not naturally ours. No two of us get that vision in quite the same way. But all its forms show us the same far-off shining light. The problem of religious insight is the problem whether that light is a mirage.

No wonder, then, that men differ as to their special efforts to solve such a problem. But it is now our task to seek for further sources of insight.

IV

The foregoing discussion may seem to have led us far from the study of our social experience as a source of religious insight. But in fact it is a necessary preliminary to that study and leads us very near to it.

If one principal source of our need of salvation is the natural narrowness of our view of the meaning of our own purposes and motives, and the consequent fickleness and the forgetful inconsistency with which we usually live out our days, it seems right, in searching for a way that may lead toward salvation, to get such help as we can by looking to our normal social experience for whatever guidance it can give. The social world is wide, even if it is still full of conflict. It broadens our outlook at every turn. A man corrects his own narrowness by trying to share his fellow's point of view. Our social responsibilities tend to set limits to our fickleness. Social discipline removes some of our inner conflicts, by teaching us not to indulge caprices. Human companionship may calm, may steady our vision, may bring us into intercourse with what is in general much better than a man's subliminal self, namely, his public, his humane, his greater social self, wherein he finds his soul and its interests writ large. Perhaps, then, whatever the ultimate goal, the way out of the distractions of the natural self, the way toward the divine insight and power that we need, lies through our social experience.

No wonder, then, that in the religious discussions of to-day our social experience is that source of insight upon which a great number of our teachers, whether they are professional religious teachers or not, most frequently insist. Our present time is an age of great concern with social problems and reforms. No wonder, then, that we have all learned to widen our vision, and to control our waywardness, by remembering that man is a being who can be neither understood nor directed in case you try to view him in isolation. As for salvation, many of our most influential leaders now teach us that the problem of our day is the problem of saving, not the individual as an individual, but the social order as a whole. The two tendencies which seem to be most potent in the political realm are the general tendencies known by the admittedly vague names of democracy and socialism. Solidarity, collectivism, the common life—these are the watchwords of some of the most widely influential movements of our time.

And these watchwords have, for many of us, not only a political, but a religious meaning. I need not remind you of the popular influence of such dramas as "The Servant in the House," or of the numbers of clergymen to whom the preaching of religion has come to mean, in the main, the preaching of beneficent social reforms. If teachers who thus view religion as, on the whole, a movement toward the increase of social welfare are asked what their counsel is to the individual regarding the salvation of his soul, they will reply: "If you want to be saved, come out of yourself." Some of them would add: "Forget yourself." But whether they use this latter extremely ambiguous and doubtful form of advice, they very generally agree that to seek to save your own soul by any merely or mainly inward and non-social process is to secure perdition. "It is love that saves," they are fond of telling us. And in this doctrine, as interpreted in the light of our modern social movements, many see the entire essence of Christianity adapted to our present situation.

Nor is the tendency here in question limited to the practical counsels of which I have just reminded you. There are those students of the psychology and the philosophy of religion who are disposed to conceive that the whole essence of the religion of all times, the entire meaning of religious beliefs and practices, can be exhaustively and accurately described in the purely human and social terms which these practical counsels attempt to embody. A recent writer on the psychology of religion defines religion as man's consciousness of his highest social values, and maintains that all religious beliefs are attempts to express this consciousness in whatever terms a given stage of civilisation makes natural and possible.

One can easily suggest to any student of general history some of the facts which such a writer has in mind. Have not the gods often been conceived as tribal deities, and so simply as representatives of the welfare and of the will of the community over against the waywardness and the capriciousness of the individual? Was not the transition from polytheism to the various forms of pantheism and of monotheism determined by the social processes that formed kingdoms or empires, and that finally led over to the modern appreciation of the value of the common interest of an ideally united humanity? Were not the prophets of Israel social reformers? Was not the work of Jesus an anticipation and a prophecy of the coming consciousness of the brotherhood of man, as the lovers of mankind now conceive that brotherhood? What has religion had to teach us, some will insistently ask, more saving, unifying, sustaining, than this love of man for man?

From such a point of view, as you see, our social experience is our principal source of religious insight. And the salvation that this insight brings to our knowledge is salvation through the fostering of human brotherhood. Such salvation accrues to the individual so far as he gives himself over to the service of man, and to mankind in so far as men can only be saved together and not separately.

I am just now depicting, not judging, a view concerning the solution of religious problems which you know to be, in our day, as potent as it is varied and problematic in its teaching. Can this view satisfy? Does this way of stating the case really indicate to us any adequate source of religious insight, any way in which we can define the true salvation of man?

V

We cannot answer this question without taking account of the views of those of our recent teachers to whom this purely social theory of the religious objects and values is indeed profoundly unsatisfactory. That such opponents of the adequacy of the interpretation of religion just suggested are to be found amongst the believers in familiar religious traditions, we need not at any length set forth. The traditions of the great religions of the world do not interpret the old faiths in this way, just because these religious traditions all agree in regarding the human social order as something which exists for the sake of an essentially superhuman order. As these various faiths assert, man can never be saved by purely human means, whether you call these means preventive medicine, or socialism, or universal brotherhood, or even love, so long as love means simply human love. As for Christianity, in all its older forms, it has emphasised the love of man, but always in a certain union with the love of God which tradition could never conceive as adequately expressible in terms of our recent social movements. The ''Servant in the House'' is supposed to be a modern apparition of the Christ; but he is explicitly a heretic regarding the old faith of the church.

But with tradition as tradition, these lectures have to do only by way of occasional illustration. What interests us more, for our present purpose, is the fact that, despite the predominance of the social interpretations of religion of which I have just reminded you, there are still some of our recent teachers who stoutly insist that our social experience does not adequately show us any way of salvation whatever.

And here first I must call attention to certain of the most modern and least theologically disposed of our leaders, namely, to those who emphasise the most characteristic recent forms of individualism. I have mentioned Nietzsche in my former lecture. Surely he stands for opposition to tradition and he expresses tendencies that are potent to-day. But while he lived and wrote, he aspired to be a sort of Antichrist, and preached the doctrine that a religion of love can never save, because, as he insists, what the self needs is power, and power is not to be won by attempting to please a world of slaves. Nietzsche may seem to you, as he has seemed to so many, a hopeless abnormity; but his Titanism is in fact a wayward modern expression of a motive that has always played its notable part in the search for salvation, ever since heroism and the resolute will were first discovered by man. Nietzsche's insight too, such as it is, is a social insight. It comes through noting that, even if the individual needs his social world as a means of grace and a gateway to salvation, the social order, in its turn, needs individuals that are worth saving, and can never be saved unless it expresses itself through the deeds and the inner life of souls deeply conscious of the dignity of selfhood, of the infinite worth of unique and intensely conscious personal life.

As a fact, individualism is as potent an ethical motive in the life of today as is the collectivism just characterised. Each of these tendencies, in our present social order, feeds upon and intensifies the other. Socialism opposes, and yet inevitably encourages, the purposes of the very individual who feels his social ties as a galling restraint. It preaches solidarity and brotherhood and love; but wins a ready hearing from those who view all these tendencies mainly as means whereby they may hope to have their own way, and to become, as Nietzsche's Superman, "beyond good and evil"— masters in the coming world of triumphant democracy. The social experience of our time is full of ambiguous lessons. Its way toward salvation leads not only over the Hill of Difficulty, but both ways around the hill; and it shows us no one straight and narrow road to peace. Whoever would traverse its wilderness and reach salvation needs to supplement his social insight by a use of other and deeper sources.

And as to what these deeper sources of insight are, the teacher whom I have already repeatedly cited—William James—asserts a doctrine that, as you already know, I do not regard as adequate, but that I must again here emphasise, because its contrast with that social theory of religion which I just characterised is so instructive.

James, in his "Varieties of Religious Experience," shows the utmost liberality toward differences of faith, and insists in the opening chapters of his book that religious experience is a field where one must beware of defining sharp boundary lines or of showing a false exclusiveness. Yet *one* boundary line he himself defines with the greatest sharpness; and in respect of *one* matter he is rigidly exclusive. Religious experience, he insists, is, as you will remember from our first lecture, the experience of an individual who feels himself to be "alone with the divine." And the social types of religious experience James rigidly excludes from the "varieties" whereof he takes account. And James's reason for this procedure is explicit. In its social aspects religion, so he insists, always becomes, or has already become, conventional. James no longer finds in the religious life of communities the novelty and independence of vision which he prizes. The essence of true religious experience lies, for him, in its originality, in its spontaneity, and so in the very solitude which is a condition, to James's mind, for the discovery of that which saves.

The words "originality" and "spontaneity" emphasise the features which, as I think, James most meant to emphasise. The problem of salvation, for James, must be an essentially individual problem; for nobody else ever faced *your* need of salvation, or had your personal issues to meet. If you win religious insight, you will have to win it very much as you will have to die—alone. Of course James does not hesitate to test the value of religious experience, in his pragmatic fashion, by its social as well as by its individual consequences. The fruits of the spirit accrue to the general advantage; and the saint, in James's opinion, must indeed undertake to edify, not only himself, but also his brethren. But the effects of religious insight must not be confused with the sources. James insists that the sources are mainly from within the individual and are only incidentally social. A religious discovery has in common with a poetic creation the fact that the religious genius, like the artist, sees his vision, and produces his spiritual miracle, in solitude.

If you ask whether this position which James assumes is anything more than his own private opinion, and if you want to know his grounds for it, a closer examination of his book will show you why he thus deliberately turns his back upon the favourite recent interpretation of religion as an essentially social phenomenon. James, in common with the traditional faiths, although not in conformity with their formulas, always conceived religious experience as an intercourse with objects and with powers that, whatever their deeper bases in our "subliminal" nature, do not adequately express themselves in our everyday, worldly, overt human nature. And in our social life, where the conventional reigns, where man imitates man or contends with man, where crowds bustle and the small-talk or the passionate struggle of the day fill the mind, where lovers pursue their beloved and are jealous of their rivals, and laborers toil and sweat, and worldly authorities display their pomp, you meet not the solution, but the problem of life. James, as man, was full of social interests, and, as psychologist, was fond of studying social processes. But when a man wants peace and spiritual triumph, James observes that, as an empirical fact, he does not readily find them in the market-place, or on the battle-field, or in the law courts, unless, indeed, he comes to these places already full of the light that the saintly souls have often found in the wilderness or in their meditations. In brief, James always emphasises the mystical element in religious experience and is full of the assurance that religion cannot find its food in the commonplace; while our social life is a realm where the commonplace holds sway. Or again, James holds that when the faithful have thought of their religious experience as an intercourse with beings of a level wholly superhuman, they may, indeed, have been wrong in their creeds, but were right in holding that man as he lives in his social world can never save man. Our social consciousness is too barefaced and open in its union of triviality and pathos. What we want as the saving power is, for a teacher such as James, something more mysterious, deep, subconscious or superconscious, and in this sense, indeed, superhuman.

Still I am only depicting, not yet judging. I have now briefly stated opinions that favour and opinions that oppose an interpretation of religious insight in terms of our social experience. But what are the merits of the case? In what sense can there be a religion of the social consciousness?

VI

The answer to this question involves, I think, two considerations, both of them exemplified by the various views here in question, both of them familiar, both of them easily misinterpreted. The first is the very consideration upon which our popular teachers of salvation through love most insist. We ourselves came upon that consideration at the close of our first lecture. Man is, indeed, a being who cannot be saved alone, however much solitude may help him, at times, toward insight. For he is bound to his brethren by spiritual links that cannot be broken. The second consideration is this: So long as man views his fellow-man *merely* as fellow-man, he only complicates his problem, for both he and his fellow equally need salvation. Their plight is common; their very need of salvation chains them together in the prison of human sorrow. If, to adapt the symbolism of ancient stories to our case, the angel of love is to appear in their prison, is to loosen their chains, is to open the doors, it must be, in some wise, as an angel, not as a merely human presence, that love must appear.

Perhaps the best way to indicate wherein lies the strength and the weakness, the irresistible authority and the pathetic limitation of our social experience as a religious guide, and the best way also to indicate its true relations to the religious experience of the human individual, is to remind ourselves of a very few familiar cases in which an individual finds that his own way toward salvation, if any such way is to exist for him at all, lies through his social world, so that he cannot be saved without the help of his fellows.

Our first instance shall be an extreme one, in which the sense of need is intense and the longing for salvation acute, but where there is little or no hope of finding the way, although one knows that if the way could be found it would bring one into touch with a new type of human companionship. We all know how the sense of guilt may take the form of a feeling of overwhelming loneliness. Now the sense of guilt, if deep and pervasive and passionate, involves at least a dim recognition that there is some central aim of life and that one has come hopelessly short of that aim. I may regret a blunder, and yet have no hint that there is any unified and supreme ideal of life. For a blunder is a special affair involving the missing of some particular aim. I may even bitterly repent a fault, and still think of that fault as a refusal to pursue some one separate moral purpose—a violation of this or of that maxim of conduct. But the true sense of guilt in its greater manifestation involves a confession that the whole self is somehow tainted, the whole life, for the time being, wrecked. But the bankruptcy of the self implies that there is one highest purpose which gives the self its value; the sense of total failure is itself a revelation of the value of what was lost. Hence the highly idealising tendency of the great experiences of moral suffering. They lead us to think not of this or of that special good, but of salvation and perdition in their general bearing upon life. The depth of the despair shows the grandeur of what has been missed; and it is therefore not surprising that experiences of this sort have been, for so many, the beginnings of religious insight. To believe that one is cut off from salvation may be the very crisis that in the end saves.

Now some of those who feel this overmastering might of their guilt lay most stress upon their assurance that God has condemned them. And religious tradition has of course emphasised this way of stating the case. But it is perfectly natural, and is surely a humane experience, to feel the sense of guilt primarily in the form of a belief that one is an outcast from human sympathy and is hopelessly alone. The more abnormal types of the sense of guilt, in nervous patients, frequently exemplify this terror of the lonely soul, this inner grief over the homelessness of the remorseful outcast. But actual guilt may be present with or without the more abnormal nervous conditions just mentioned, and, when present, may bring home to the rueful mind the despair of the awakened but forsaken sinner, and may bring it in the form of the feeling of guilty solitude.

A well-known expression of such a mood you find in Kipling's lyric of the "Poor little sheep that have gone astray." In these verses the outcast sons of good families, the "gentlemen-rankers," dwell together in an agonised companionship of common loneliness. Their guilt and their lost homes are for them inseparably associated.

Or again: Beneath all the fantastic imagery of Coleridge's "Ancient Mariner," the poet uses a perfectly recognisable type of the sense of guilt as the means to make his tale of wonders seem, despite all its impossibilities, human and even plausible. The incidents are the miracles of a magic dream; but the human nature depicted is as real as is the torment of any guilty conscience. Somehow—no matter how, or under how arbitrary conditions—the hero has committed a crime without precisely intending it to be a crime. His tale is one of a young man's adventurous insolence. His deed has all the too familiar characters of the typical sins of wayward youth. And that is why the gay young wedding guest must hear his tale. He—the mariner—in his own youth, had consciously meant to be only a little wanton and cruel. He awakened, as many a light-minded youth later awakes, to find that, as a fact, he had somehow struck at the very centre of life, at the heart of love, at the laws that bind the world together, at the spirit of the universe. When one thus awakes, he sees that nature and God are against him. But, worst of all, he has become a curse to his fellows; and in turn they curse him; and then they leave him alone with the nightmare life in death of utter solitude. To his mind there are no living men. He sees about him only "the curse in a dead man's eye." What life he can still see is no longer, to his morbid eyes, really human:

> "The many men, so beautiful!
>   And they all dead did lie;
> And a thousand, thousand slimy things
>   Lived on; and so did I."

The Ancient Mariner's escape from the horrors of this despair, the beginnings of his salvation, date from the first movings of love in his heart toward all living beings. His salvation is won when, at the end, he finds God along with the goodly company at the kirk. In brief, the curse of his guilt is to be "alone on a wide, wide sea." His salvation comes in preaching love and companionship, and in uniting himself hereby to the God who loves all things both great and small.

Now one does not often think of the "Ancient Mariner" as a poem of religious experience; but apart from its brilliant play with natural magic, its human charm actually depends upon this well-founded picture of the loneliness of guilt and of the escape through loving union with one's kind. And the poet deliberately gives to this picture the form and the sense of a religious process of salvation.

If you turn from the dreamy product of Coleridge's youthful fancy to the opposite pole of modern literature, you find an instance of almost the same motives at the basis of that most impressive romance of the Russian Dostoevski: "Crime and Punishment." Dostoevski had himself lived long in what he called "The House of the Dead," in Siberia, before he learned how to write this masterpiece. He had been forced to sojourn amongst the

guilty of the most various grades. He had come to universalise their experiences and to struggle himself with one form of the problem of salvation.
Those who, like Dante, have looked upon hell, sometimes have, indeed,
wonders to tell us. Dostoevski condenses the whole problem of salvation
from guilt in this picture of an individual. Raskolnikow, the hero, after his
thoughtfully conceived crime, and after his laborious effort at self-justifi-
cation, finds himself the prey of a simply overwhelming sense that he walks
alone amongst men, and that, in the crowded streets of the city, he is as one
dead amongst spectres. There is nowhere, I think, a more persuasive picture
of the loneliness of great guilt. Raskolnikow could not be more the victim
of supernatural forces if he were Coleridge's Ancient Mariner. Like the Ancient Mariner, Raskolnikow in the end finds the way to salvation through
love—the love which the martyred Sonia teaches him—herself, as our Russian most persuasively pictures her, at once outcast and saint. The author
uses religious conceptions which are both ancient and, in his use of them,
unconventional. But the central one of these is the familiar conception that
salvation involves a reconciliation both with the social and with the divine
order, a reconciliation through love and suffering—an escape from the wilderness of lonely guilt to the realm where men can understand one another.

In such elemental ways the process of salvation can be made to appear
as essentially a social process, just because its opposite, perdition, seems
to mean banishment from amongst men.

Another group of cases presents to us the same need for human companionship as a means to salvation, but presents it in the winning guise of
salvation beginning through love, without the main stress being laid upon
the previous despair. In such cases the despair may be mentioned but at once
relieved. The religion of friendship and of love is a familiar human experience. James, in his fear of debasing religion by romantic or by grosser
associations, unjustly neglects it in his study of "varieties." In fact, to seem
to find the divine in the person of your idealised friend or beloved is a perfectly normal way of beginning your acquaintance with the means of grace.
You meet, you love, and—you seem to be finding God. Or, to use our present interpretation of what reveals the divine, love seems to furnish you with
a vision of a perfect life, to give you a total survey of the sense of your own
life, and to begin to show you how to triumph. If there be any divine life,
you say, this is my vision of its beauty and its harmony. So the divine appears in one of Browning's later lyrics:

> "Such a starved bank of moss,
>   Till, that May morn,
> Blue ran the flash across;
>   Violets were born!

"Sky—what a scowl of cloud
  Till, near and far,
Ray on ray split the shroud
  Splendid! a star!

"World—how it walled about
  Life with disgrace,
Till God's own smile came out;
  That was thy face!"

In the sonnets of Shakespeare this religion of friendship has found some of its most perfect expressions.

"Haply I think of thee, and then my state,
  Like to the lark's, at break of day arising
From sullen earth, sings hymns at heaven's gate."

And again, in Mrs. Browning's "Sonnets from the Portuguese," the religion of love not only uses speech intensely personal, fond, intimate, but also, and deliberately, accompanies all this with words derived from reflective metaphysics, or from theology, and intended to express the miracle that the nearest movings of affection are also a revelation of the highest powers of the spiritual world.

"How do I love thee? Let me count the ways.
  I love thee to the depth and breadth and height
  My soul can reach, when feeling out of sight
For the ends of Being, and Ideal Grace.
I love thee to the level of everyday's
  Most quiet need, by sun and candle light.
  I love thee freely, as men strive for Right;
I love thee purely, as they turn from Praise;
  I love thee with the passion put to use
In my old griefs, and with my childhood's faith;
  I love thee with a love I seemed to lose
With my lost saints,—I love thee with the breath,
  Smiles, tears, of all my life!—and, if God choose,
I shall but love thee better after death."

Surely one could not better express, than this sonnet does, the naturalness of the religious motive—the mystery of the religious object.

And finally, turning from these cases to those which are social in the larger sense, every patriotic song which deifies one's country, every other form of the religion of patriotism, exemplifies the experience of the devoted lover of his country by teaching that it is "man's perdition to be safe" in case his social world calls for the sacrifice of his life, and that salvation comes through service.

James is indeed wrong then to neglect the social roads that lead toward the experience of what one takes to be divine. There is no love so simple-minded that, if it be true love, the way of salvation may not seem to be opened through it to the lover.

But observe that, as we review these instances, they show us how the social world wherein they bid us seek our salvation is a world whose very essence is transformed by love and by its vision into something that seems to the lover mystical, superhuman, and more than our literal and common-place social life directly exemplifies. Those who have failed to find in their actual social life such inspirations may, indeed, have to look, as the typical mystics have generally done, elsewhere, for their vision of the divine, than in so much of the social world as they know. And such will, indeed, seek their vision of salvation in solitude. When they tell us of their experience, they may well remind the social enthusiast, as well as the lover, that the religion of love is no religion at all, unless it conceives its human object not only as this creature, or as this collection of needy men and women, but as a hint, or revelation, or incarnation of a divine process—of a process which is not only human but superhuman, and which can never be comprehended in the "mart and the crowded street" unless by the soul that is either mystical enough to meet God also "in the bush," or rationally enlightened enough to know that human life is indeed a revelation of something that is also superhuman.

I conclude, then, for the moment, thus: Social experience seems to lie on the way to salvation. Normally the way to salvation, if there be any such way, must lead through social experience. But when our social experience shows us any such way upward it does so, if it truly does so, because human social life is the hint, the likeness, or the incarnation of a life that lies beyond and above our present human existence. For human society as it now is, in this world of care, is a chaos of needs; and the whole social order groans and travails together in pain until now, longing for salvation. It can be saved, as the individual can be saved, only in case there is some way that leads upward, through all our turmoil and our social bickerings, to a realm where that vision of unity and self-possession which our clearest moments bring to us becomes not merely vision, but fulfilment, where love finds its own, and where the power of the spirit triumphs. Of such a realm the lovers dream and the religions tell. Let us appeal to a further source of insight. Concerning the realities that we need, let us next consult our Reason.

THE RELIGIOUS MISSION OF SORROW

It very often happens to us that to reach any notable result, either in life or in insight, is even thereby to introduce ourselves to a new problem. In the present state of the undertaking of these lectures such is our experience. The religious insight whose source is the loyal spirit was our topic in the foregoing lecture. If my own view is correct, this source is by far the most important that we have yet considered. It unites the spirit and the meaning of all the foregoing sources. Rightly interpreted, it points the way to a true salvation.

Yet the very last words of our sketch of the fruits of loyalty were of necessity grave words. Intending to show through what spirit man escapes from total failure, we were brought face to face with the tragedies which still beset the higher life. "Adversity"—poor Griselda faced it in the tale. We left the loyal spirit appearing to us—as it does appear in its strongest representatives, able, somehow, in the power that is due to its insight, to triumph over fortune. But side by side with this suggestion of the nature of that which overcomes the world stood the inevitable reminder of the word: "In this world ye shall have tribulation."

How is tribulation related to religious insight? That is our present problem. It has been forced upon our attention by the study of the place and the meaning of loyalty. Some understanding of this problem is necessary to any further comprehension of the lessons of all the foregoing sources of insight, and is of peculiar significance for any definition of the office of religion.

To nearly all of us, at some time in our lives, and to many of us at all times, the tragic aspect of human life seems to be a profound hindrance to religious insight of any stable sort. I must here first bring more fully to your minds why this is so—why the existence of tragedy in human existence appears to many moods, and to many people, destructive of faith in any religious truth and a barrier against rational assurance regarding the ultimate

173

triumph of anything good. Then I want to devote the rest of this lecture to showing how sorrow, how the whole burden of human tribulation, has been, and reasonably may be, not merely a barrier in the way of insight, but also a source of religious insight. And this is the explanation of the title of the present lecture.

I

We approach our problem fully mindful of the limitations to which the purpose of these lectures confines us. The problem of evil has many metaphysical, theological, moral, and common-sense aspects upon which I can say nothing whatever in the present context. Human sorrow appears in our pathway in these lectures as a topic for us to consider, first, because whatever source of religious insight we have thus far consulted has shown us man struggling with some sort of ill, and, secondly, because there are aspects of this very struggle which will provide us with a new source of religious insight, and which will thus tend to throw new light upon the meaning of all the other sources. A thorough-going study of the problem of evil would require of us a complete philosophy not only of religion but of reality. But we are limiting ourselves, in these discussions, to a survey of certain sources.

The reasons why the existence and the prominence of evil in human life seem to all of us at some times, and to many of us at all times, a hindrance to the acceptance of any religious solution of the problems of life are familiar. I need then only to remind you what they are.

Without going into any subtleties regarding the definition of evil, it is obvious that our first characteristic reaction when we meet with what we take to be an evil is an effort to get rid of it, to shun its presence, or to remove it from existence. Pain, cold, burning heat, disease, starvation, death, our enemies, our dangers, these are facts that, precisely so far as we find them evil, we face with the determination to annul altogether their evil aspect.

A characteristic result of this tendency appears in the fact that man, who of all animals is most clearly aware of the presence of evil in his world, is for that very reason not only an ingenious deviser of new inventions for getting good things and for supplying his needs, but is also the most destructive of animals. He wars with his natural surroundings, and still more with his fellow-men, in ways that show how the instinctive aversions upon which his estimates of evil are founded are reinforced by the habits which he forms in his contests with ill fortune. Man the destroyer of evil thus appears, in much of his life, as a destroyer who is also largely moved by a love of destruction for its own sake. This love plays a great part in the formation of even very high levels of our social and moral consciousness. The heroes of song and story, and often of history as well, are fascinating partly, or chiefly, because they could kill and did so. We love victory over ill. Killing seems to involve such a victory. So we love killing, at least in the hero tales. The result is often a certain inconsistency. The gods offered Achilles the choice between a short life full of the glorious slaying of enemies and a long life of harmless obscurity. He chose the short life; and therefore he is to be remembered forever. For even when he would not fight, his "destructive wrath sent the souls of many valiant heroes to Hades, and left themselves a prey to the dogs and birds of the air." And when he returned to battle, what became of Hector? The song of the Nibelungs opens by assuring us that the old stories tell of many wonders, and of heroes worthy of praise (*von Helden lobebaeren*), and of great labours (*von grosser Arbeit*). These "great labours" consisted mainly in the slaying of other men. And this slaying was obviously "worthy of praise"; for it gave us a model for all our own struggle with evil. As for the heroes of history, of course, we love to dwell upon their constructive labours. But, after all, what sort of comparison is there in what the plain man, apart from a higher enlightenment, usually calls glory, between Washington and Napoleon? No doubt there will always be admirers of Napoleon who will think of him as a misunderstood reformer labouring for the building up of an ideal Europe. But even such admirers will join with the plain man in dwelling, with especial fascination, upon the Napoleon of Austerlitz. And they will not forget even Borodino. No doubt the lovers of Washington find him glorious. But where, in his career, belongs the glory of having put an end to the Holy Roman Empire, or of having destroyed the polity of the Europe of the old maps?

Man the destroyer thus glories in his prowess, and adores the heroes who were the ministers of death. And since, of course, his warfare is always directed against something that he takes to be an evil, the principle which directs his glorious conflicts seems to be one easy of general statement, inconsistent as some of the reasonings founded upon it seem to be. This principle is: "All evil ought to be destroyed. There ought to be none. It should be swept out of existence."

Of course, when the principle of the warfare with evil is thus abstractly stated, it does not tell us what we are to regard as an evil. It leaves the wise estimate of good and evil to be learned through a closer study of the facts of life. No doubt, then, Achilles, and the other heroes of song and story, may have become as glorious as they are by reason of our excessive love of destruction due to some imperfect estimate of the true values of life. And therefore the mere statement of the principle leaves open a very wide range for difference of opinion and for inconsistency of view as to what it is that ought to be destroyed. The natural estimate of the plain man, when he loves the heroes of old, seems to imply that one of the chief ills that man ought to destroy usually takes the form of some other man. And this way of estimating men in terms of their success in killing other men has its obvious inconsistencies. But, after all, as one may insist, much is gained when we have made up our minds as to what ought to be done with evil, whether evil is incorporated in our enemies, in our pains, or in our sins. We may leave to advancing civilisation, or perhaps to some triumph of religion, the correction of our excessive fondness for the destruction of human life. What is essentially important is that it is part of man's mission to destroy evil. And about this general teaching the saints and the warriors, so it seems, may well agree.

Religion, it may be said, can have nothing to urge against this fundamental axiom. So far all appears clear. Evil ought to be driven out of the world. Common sense says this. Every struggle with climate or with disease or with our foes is carried on in this spirit. The search for salvation is itself— so one may insist—simply another instance of this destructive conflict with impending ills. All that is most elemental in our hatreds thus agrees with whatever is loftiest in our souls, in facing evils with our "everlasting No." All the differences of moral opinion are mere differences as to what to destroy. Man is always the destroyer of ill.

II

But if you grant the general principle thus stated, the presence of evil in this world, in the forms that we all recognise, and in the degree of importance that it attains in all our lives, seems, indeed, a very serious hindrance in the way of religious insight. And the reason is plain. Religion, as we have said, in seeking salvation, seeks some form of communion with the master of life. That is, it seeks to come into touch with a power, a principle, or a mind, or a heart, that, on the one hand, possesses, or, with approval, surveys or controls the real nature of things, and that, on the other hand, welcomes us in our conflicts with evil, supports our efforts, and secures our success. I have made no effort, in these lectures, to define a theological creed. Such a creed forms a topic in which I take great interest but which lies beyond the limitations of this discourse. Yet our study of the historical relations between religion and morality, our earlier analysis of the religious need, have shown us that unless you are able to make some sort of effective appeal to principles that link you with the whole nature of things, your religious need must remain unsatisfied, and your last word will have to take, at best, the form of a moral, not a religious doctrine. Religion does not require us to solve all mysteries; but it does require for its stability some assurance that, so far as concerns our need of salvation, and despite the dangers that imperil our salvation, those that are with us, when we are rightly enlightened, are more than those that are against us.

In order to make this fact yet clearer, let us suppose that all such assurance is taken away from us. Review the result. Let it be supposed that we need salvation. Let it be granted that, as we naturally are, in our blindness and narrowness, and in the caprices of our passions, we cannot find the way out unless we can get into touch with some spiritual unity and reasonable life such as the loyal man's cause seems to reveal to him. Let it be further supposed, however, that all human causes are, in their way and time, as much subject to chance and to the capricious blows of fortune as we ourselves individually are. Let it be imagined that the cause of causes, the unity of the whole spiritual world, is, in fact, a mere dream. Let the insight of the reason and of the will, which, when taken in their unity, have been said by me to reveal to us that the universe is in its essence Spirit, and that the cause of the loyal is not only a reality, but *the* reality—let this insight, I say, be regarded as an illusion. Let no other spiritual view of reality prove probable. Then, indeed, we shall be left merely with ideals of life in our hands, but with no assurance that real life, in its wholeness, approves or furthers these ideals. Our need of salvation will then, to be sure, still remain. Our definition of what salvation would be if it should become ours will be unchanged. But, having thus abandoned as illusory or as uncertain all the sources of insight which I have so far been defending, we shall have upon our hands only the moral struggle for the good as our best resource. We shall then hope for no assurance of salvation. We shall abandon religion to the realm of mythical consolations, and shall face a grim world with only such moral courage as we can muster for the uncertain conflict. Our loyalty itself will lose its religious aspect. For the objective goodness of our cause—the divine grace which its presence seems to offer to our life—will no longer mean anything but a faint and uncertain hope, which we shall keep or not according to the caprices of our personal resolutions. Such, I say, would be the outcome of rejecting all sources of religious insight into the real nature of things.

The result, in the case now supposed, will be one which any honest man will indeed accept if he must, but which no one can regard as including any satisfactory religious insight whatever. I certainly do not here present these considerations as in themselves any arguments for religion, or as in themselves furnishing support for our previous arguments regarding the nature and the merits of the sources of insight which we have been reviewing. The case for which I have argued in the foregoing lectures must indeed stand or fall solely upon its own merits. And if the reason and the will, as the spirit of loyalty interprets and unifies their teachings, do *not* really show us any truth about the whole nature of things, I would not for a moment ask to have their teachings tolerated merely because, without such teachings, we should lose our grounds for holding to a religious interpretation of life. If we *must* fall back upon mere moral resoluteness, and abandon any assurance as to the religious objects, and as to the way and the attainment of salvation, I, for one, am quite ready to accept the call of life, and to fight on for a good end so long as I can, without seeking for religious consolations that have once been shown to be mythical. But I have indicated to you, in general, my grounds for holding that our previous sources actually *do* give us an insight which is not only moral but religious, and *do* throw light upon our relations to a reason which moves in all things, to a divine will which expresses itself in all the universe, and to a genuine revelation of its purposes which this makes of itself when it inspires our loyalty. My present purpose is, not to reinforce these grounds by the mere threat that their rejection would involve an abandonment of any well-grounded religious assurance, but to present to you the fact that religion is, indeed, a search for a really divine foundation for the saving process.

Religion differs from morality in looking beyond our own active resoluteness for something—not ourselves—that gives a warrant, founded in the whole nature of things—a warrant for holding that this resoluteness will succeed and will bring us into union with that which saves.

Hence it is, indeed, true that if there is *no* master of life with whom we can come into touch, *no* triumph of the good in the universe, *no* real source of salvation—religion must result in disappointment. And then our only recourse must, indeed, be the moral will. This recourse is one that, as we have seen, many in our time are quite ready to accept. And such, in my own opinion, are for reasons that they do not themselves admit actually well on their way toward real salvation. Only it is useless to attribute to them, in their present stage of conviction, any conscious and assured possession of religious insight. To sum up, then, religion demands the presence of the master of life as a real being, and depends upon holding that the good triumphs.

But if we attempt to combine the two assertions, "All evil ought to be destroyed" and "In the universe as a whole the good triumphs," and hereupon to face the facts of human life as religion finds them, we are at once involved in familiar perplexities. With many of these perplexities the limitations of the present discussion, as already explained, forbid us to deal. I am merely trying to show, for the moment, why the presence of evil in our lives seems to be a hindrance in the way of religious insight. And it is enough if I emphasise at this point what must readily come to the consciousness of all of you when you consider the situation in which our whole argument seems now to have placed us.

The very existence of the religious need itself presupposes not only the presence, but the usual prevalence of very great evils in human life. For unless man is in great danger of missing the pearl of great price, he stands in no need of a saving process. A religious man may come to possess an acquired optimism—the hard-won result of the religious process which seems to him to have pointed out the way of salvation. But a man who begins with the assurance that all is ordinarily well with human nature is precluded from religion, in our sense of the word religion, by his very type of optimism. Such an optimist of the "first intention," such a believer that in the main it is well with human nature, can be, as we have seen, a moralist, although he is usually a very simple-minded moralist, as unaware of the graver moral problems as he is cheerfully indifferent to the hard case in which most of his brethren live. But whoever sees the deep need of human salvation, as the various cynics and rebels and sages and prophets whom we cited in our first lecture have seen it, has begun by recognising the bitterness of human loss and defeat—the gravity of the evil case of the natural man. Were not the world as it now is very evil, what, then, were the call for religion? Religion takes its origin in our sense of deep need—in other words, in our recognition that evil has a very real place in life. "*Tempora pessima*"—"The times are very evil"—is thus no phrase of a merely mediæval type of world-hatred. The woes of man are the presupposed basis of fact upon which the search for salvation rests.

And the further one goes in the pursuit of the sources of religious insight, the more, as we have ourselves found, does one's original recognition of the ill of the human world become both deepened and varied. From the solitude of one's individual sorrows one goes out to seek for religious relief in the social world, only to find how much more manifold the chaos of ordinary social life is than is the conflict of one's private passions. If one asks guidance from reason, reason appears at first as a sort of spirit brooding upon the face of the depths of unreason. When loyalty itself is created, it finds itself beset by adversities. If evil drives us to seek relief in religion, religion thus teaches us to know, better and better, the tragedy of life. Its first word is, thus, about evil and about the escape from evil. But its later words appear to have been a persistent discourse upon our tribulations.

But how can religion, thus presupposing the presence of evil in our life, and illustrating this presence anew at every step, undertake to lead us to any assurance of the triumph of a good principle in the real world, in case, as seems so far obvious, such a triumph of a good principle would mean that all evil is to be simply destroyed and wiped out of existence?

Briefly restating the situation, it is this: If the evils of human life are indeed but transient and superficial incidents, or if—to use a well-known extreme form of statement—evil is an "unreality" altogether—then religion is superfluous. For there is no need of salvation unless man's ordinary case is, indeed, very really a hard case, that is, unless evil is a reality, and a deep-rooted one. But, on the other hand, if evil is thus deep-rooted in the very conditions of human life as they are, and if it persists upon higher levels even of the religious life, religion seems in danger of total failure. For unless goodness is somehow at the real heart of things—is, so to speak, the core of reality—the hope of salvation is a dream, and religion deceives us. But goodness, by the hypothesis that we are just now considering, requires that evil should be wholly abolished. How can that which should not exist at all, namely, evil, be in such wise the expression of the real nature of things that on the one hand religion is needed to save us from evil, and yet is able to do so only by bringing us to know that the real nature of things is good? Here is our problem. And it is a hard one.

In brief, as you may say, religion must take its choice. Either the evil in the world is of no great importance, and then religion is useless; or the need of salvation is great, and the way is straight and narrow; and then evil is deeply rooted in the very nature of reality, and religion seems a failure.

III

I believe that there is some advantage in stating in this somewhat crabbed and dialectical fashion, a problem which most of us usually approach through much more direct and pathetic experience. One advantage in crabbedness and in fondness for dialectic is that it sometimes tends to clear away the clouds with which emotion from moment to moment surrounds certain great problems of life. As I said earlier, in speaking of the office of the reason, abstract ideas are but means to an end. Their end is to help us to a clear and rational survey of the connections of things. When you are to examine the landscape from a height, in order to obtain a wide prospect, you may have to use a glass, or a compass, or some other instrument of abstraction, in order to define what the distance tends to render obscure, or what the manifoldness of the scenery surveyed makes it hard rightly to view in its true relations. And, in such cases, the glass or the compass is but an auxiliary, intended to help in the end your whole outlook. Now the world of good and evil is a world of wide prospects, of vast distances, of manifold features. A bit of dialectics, using abstract and one-sided considerations in succession, may prepare the way for seeing the whole better.

The plain man well knows the problem that I have just been characterising. He knows how it may enter his religious life. Only he does not usually think of it abstractly. It pierces his heart. Stunned by a grief, he may say: "I have trusted God, and now he forsakes me. How can a good God permit this horror in my life?" Yet the plain man, if religiously minded, also knows what is meant by saying, "Out of the depths have I cried." And he knows, too, that part of the preciousness of his very idea of God depends upon the fact that there *are* depths, and that out of them one *can* cry, and that God is precisely a being who somehow hears the cry from the depths. God, "pragmatically viewed," as some of our recent teachers express the matter, is thus often defined for the plain man's religious experience as a helper in trouble. Were there no trouble, there would be, then, it would seem, no cry of the soul for such a being, and very possibly no such being conceived by the soul that now cries. Yet this very God—one cries to him because he is supposed to be all-powerful, and to do all things well, and therefore to be a very present help in time of trouble. All this seems clear enough at the time when one is on the way up, out of the depths, or when one begins to praise God in the Psalmist's words, because, as one now says: "He hath planted my feet upon a rock, and hath established my goings." But how does all this seem at the moment when one suddenly falls into the pit of sorrow, and when one's eyes are turned downward; when he who doeth all things well permits the utmost treachery of fortune, and when the one who can hear every cry seems deaf to one's most heart-rending pleadings? The familiar explanation that all this is a penalty for one's sins may awaken an echo of Job's protest in the mind of the man who knows not how he has deserved this woe, or may arouse the deeper and now consciously dialectical comments on the mystery involved in the fact that God permits sin. "Why was I made thus blind and sinful?" one may cry. And hereupon religious insight becomes, indeed, confused enough, and may turn for relief to that well-known type of defiance which, if not religious, is at least moral; for it is a protest against evil. If at such moments God is, indeed, to our darkened vision, and, for us, who wait for his blessing, as if he were sleeping or on a journey, one can at least, as moral agent, utter this protest against ill, and wonder why his omnipotence does not make it effective. One thus begins, as it were, to try heroically to do the absent God's work for him.

All these are familiar experiences. They find us, too often, unprepared. They find us when emotion tends to cloud every insight. They illustrate a certain dialectical process which belongs to all human life and which plays its part in the whole history of religion. Perhaps it is well to state an aspect of this dialectical process abstractly, crabbedly, and unemotionally, as we have just done, in order that we may make ourselves the more ready to face the issue when life exemplifies it with crushing suddenness, and when

> "The painful ploughshare of passion
> Grinds down to our uttermost rock."

The problem, as just abstractly stated, is this. Religion seems to face this dilemma: Either there are no great and essential ills about human life; and then there is no great danger of perdition, and no great need of salvation, and religion has no notable office; or there are great and essential ills, and man's life is in bitter need of salvation; but in that case evil is deeply rooted in the very nature of the reality from which we have sprung; and therefore religion has no right to assure us of communion with a real master of life who is able to do with evil what not only ought to be done with it, but ought always to have been done with it by any being able to offer man any genuine salvation. For (as we are assuming) what ought to be done, yes, what ought to have been done with evil from the beginning, is and was this: To banish it altogether from existence.

This, I say, is, when abstractly stated, the dilemma in which religion seems to be placed. Of this dilemma the countless struggles of the human soul when, in the spirit of some practical religion, it seeks for salvation and faces its woes are examples. These struggles are infinitely pathetic and in life are often confusing to insight. Is there any value in considering this abstract statement of the principles upon which this dilemma seems to be founded? Possibly there is, if we can hereby be led also to consider—not indeed, in this place, the problems of theology, or the metaphysics of evil, but a new source of insight.

IV

This new source of insight begins to come to us when we observe, as we can often observe if we listen with closer attention to the voices of our own hearts, that the general principle, "Evil ought simply to be put out of existence," does *not* express our whole attitude toward all evils, and gives only an imperfect account either of our more commonplace and elemental or of our more elevated, heroic, and reasonable estimates of life.

The principle: "Evil ought to be simply abolished," is, indeed, one that we unquestionably apply, in our ordinary life, to a vast range of natural ills. But it is not universal. Let us first indicate its apparent range. Physical pain, when sufficiently violent, is an example of an ill that appears to us, in all its greater manifestations, plainly intolerable. So it seems to us to illustrate the principle that "Evil ought to be put out of existence." We desire, with regard to it, simply its abolition. The same is true of what one may call *unassimilated* griefs of all levels—the shocks of calamity at the moment when they first strike, the anguish of loss or of disappointment precisely when these things are new to us and appear to have no place in our life-plan. These are typical ills. And they all illustrate ills that seem to us to be worthy only of destruction. The magnitude of such ills as factors in the individual and in the social world often appears to us immeasurable. Pestilence, famine, the cruelties of oppressors, the wrecks of innocent human lives by cruel fortunes—all these seem, for our ordinary estimates, facts that we can in no wise assimilate, justify, or reasonably comprehend. That is we can see, in the single case, no reason why such events should form part of human life—except that so it indeed is. They seem, to our natural understanding, simply opaque data of experience, to be annulled or removed if we can. And to such ills, from our human point of view, the principle: "They ought to be simply driven out of existence," is naturally applied without limitation. The apparent range of this principle is therefore, indeed, very wide.

Now it forms no part of our present discourse to consider in detail the possible theological or metaphysical basis for a possible explanation of such ills. I have elsewhere written too much and too often about the problem of evil to be subject to the accusation of neglecting the pathos and the tragedy of these massive ills. This, however, I can at once say. *In so far as* ills appear to us thus, they are, indeed, *no* sources of religious insight. On the other hand, even when thus viewed, in all their blackness, they can be, and are, sources of moral enthusiasm and earnestness. Man the destroyer, when, awaking to the presence of such ills in his world, he contends with them, gets a perfectly definite moral content into his life. And he has his right to do so. Whatever his religion, he is morally authorised to labour against these unmediated evils with the heartiest intolerance. When such labour takes on social forms, it helps toward the loftiest humanity. The war with pain and disease and oppression, the effort to bind up wounds and to snatch souls from destruction—all these things constitute some of man's greatest opportunities for loyalty. Nevertheless, when man loyally wars with the ills such as physical anguish and pestilence and famine and oppression, he does *not* thereby tend to discover, through his own loyal act, why such individual ills are permitted in the world. In so far as these evils give him opportunity for service, they appeal to his loyalty as a warrior against them. If his cause includes, for him, activities that enter into this warfare with ills that are to be destroyed, these ills have thus indirectly conduced to his religious life. But it is his loyalty that in such cases is his source of religious insight. The ills themselves that he thus destructively fights remain to him as opaque as before. Why they find their place in the world he does not see. Now that they are found there, he knows what to do with them— namely, to annul them, to put them out of existence, as a part of his loyal service. But if he is religiously minded, he does not for a moment conceive that the ills with which he wars are there simply to give him the opportunity for his service. So far then it is, indeed, true that the ills which we have simply to destroy offer us no source of religious insight.

But now, as I must insist, *not all* the ills that we know are of this na- ture. Wide and deep and terrible as are those conflicts with the incompre- hensible ills of fortune whose presence in the world we do not understand, there are other ills. And toward these other ills we take an attitude which is not wholly destructive. We find them, upon a closer view, inseparably bound up with good—so closely bound up therewith that we could not con- ceive a life wherein this sort of good which is here bound up with this sort of ill could be separated therefrom. In these cases the principle: "Evil should be simply put out of existence," proves to be a palpable falsity. As our knowledge of such ills grows clearer, we commonly find that there is, indeed, something about them, as they at any one moment appear to us, which ought, indeed, to be annulled, set aside, destroyed. But this annulling of one momentary or at least transient aspect of the ill is but part, in such cases, of a constructive process, which involves growth rather than destruc- tion—a passage to a new life rather than a casting wholly out of life. Such ills we remove only in so far as we assimilate them, idealise them, take them up into the plan of our lives, give them meaning, set them in their place in the whole.

Now such ills, as I must insist, play a very great part in life and es- pecially in the higher life. Our attitude toward them constitutes, above all, on the very highest levels of our reasonableness, a very great part of our attitude toward the whole problem of life. In the presence of these idealised evils, man the destroyer becomes transformed into man the creator. And he does so without in the least abandoning his justified moral distinctions, without indulging in any sort of "moral holiday," and without becoming unwilling to destroy when he cannot otherwise rationally face the facts be- fore him than by destroying. He is not less strenuous in his dealing with his moral situation because he has discovered how to substitute growth for de- struction and creative assimilation for barren hostility. He is all the more effectively loyal in the presence of such ills, because he sees how they can become, for his consciousness, parts of a good whole.

Ills of this sort may become, and in the better cases do become, sources of religious insight. Their presence in our world enables us the better to comprehend its spiritual unity. And because they are often very deep and tragic ills, which we face only with very deep and dear travail of spirit, they hint to us how, from the point of view of a world-embracing insight, the countless and terrible ills of the other sort, which we *cannot* now understand, and which, at present, appear to us merely as worthy of utter destruction, may still also have their places, as stages and phases of expression, in the larger life to which we belong. In our own power to assimilate and spiritualise our own ills, we can get at times a hint of such larger spiritual processes. In these very processes we also, through our loyal endeavour, can act our own real part; although *what* the larger processes are we cannot expect at present to comprehend better than a sympathising dog, whose master is devoting his life to furthering the highest spiritual welfare of a nation or of all mankind, can know why his master's face is now grief-stricken and now joyous.

In other words, the ills that we *can* spiritualise and idealise without merely destroying them hint to us that, despite the uncomprehended chaos of seemingly hopeless tragedy with which for our present view human life seems to be beset, the vision of the spiritual triumph of the good which reason and loyalty present to us need not be an illusion, but is perfectly consistent with the facts. The world is infinite. With our present view we could not expect to grasp directly the unity of its meaning. We have sources of insight which tend to our salvation by showing us, in general, although certainly not in detail, the nature of the spiritual process which, as these sources of insight persistently point out, constitutes the essence of reality. Whether these sources are themselves valid and trustworthy is a question to be considered upon its own merits. I have stated my case so far as our brief review requires it to be stated. I must leave to your own considerateness the further estimate of what these sources teach, both as to the reality of the master of life and as to the nature of the process of salvation. My present concern is simply with the cloud that the presence of evil seems to cause to pass over the face of all these sources. I cannot undertake wholly to dispel this cloud by showing you in detail why pestilences or why broken hearts are permitted to exist in this world. But I can show you that there are, indeed, ills, and very dark ills in life, which not only are there, but are essential to the highest life. I do not exaggerate our power to solve mysteries when I insist that *these* ills constitute not an opaque hindrance to insight, not a cloud over the sun of reason and of loyalty, but rather a source of insight. And, as I insist, they constitute such a source without being in the least an excuse for any indolence in our moral struggle with precisely those aspects of such ills as we ought to destroy. They show us how the triumph of the moral will over such adversities is perfectly consistent with the recognition that the most rational type of life demands the existence of just such adversities. Their presence in our world does not excuse sloth, does not justify a "moral holiday," does not permit us to enjoy any mere luxury of mystical contemplation of the triumph of the divine in the world, without ourselves taking our rational and strenuous part in the actual attainment of such triumph. But what these forms of ill show us is that there are accessible cases in which if—but only if—one does the divine will—one can know of the doctrine that teaches how the divine will can and does become perfect, not through the mere abolition of evil, but through suffering. Such cases of ill are true sources of insight. They reveal to us some of the deepest truths about what loyalty, and spiritual triumph, and the good really are. They make for salvation. They drive away clouds and bring us face to face with the will of the world.

I have so far spoken of evil in general. For the present purpose I need a name for the ills that one rationally faces only when one, through some essentially active, constructive, moral process, creatively assimilates and idealises them, and thus wins them over to be a part of good—not when one merely drives them out of existence. One name for such ills is Griselda's name: "Adversities." But I have chosen, in the title of this lecture, to use the vaguer untechnical name: Sorrow. A great physical pain, you in general cannot, at least at the moment, idealise. You then and there face it only as something intolerable, and can see no good except through its mere abolition. The same is true of any crushing blow of fortune, precisely in so far as it crushes. All such things you then and there view narrowly. Their mystery lies in the very fact that they are thus, for the moment, seen only narrowly. Hence, they are *ipso facto* hindrances to insight. But a sorrow—when you use the word you have already begun to assimilate and idealise the fact that you call a sorrow. That you have begun to idealise it, the very luxury of deep grief often vaguely hints, sometimes clearly shows. For sorrows may have already become tragically precious to you. Would you forget your lost love, or your dead, or your "days that are no more," even if you could? Is mere destruction, then, your *only* tendency in the presence of such sorrows? A closer view of your attitude toward such sorrows shows that they are not only clouding but revealing. They begin, they may endlessly continue, to show you the way into the spiritual realm and the nature of this realm.

By sorrow, then, I here mean an experience of ill which is not wholly an experience of that which as you then and there believe ought to be simply driven out of existence. The insight of which sorrow is the source, is an insight that tends to awaken within you a new view of what the spiritual realm is. This view is not in the least what some recent writers have blindly proclaimed it to be—a philosopher's artificial abstraction—a cruel effort to substitute a "soft" doctrine of the study for a moral and humane facing of the "hard" facts of human life. No, this view is the soul of the teaching of all the world's noblest and most practical guides to the most concrete living. This view faces hardness, it endures and overcomes. Poets, prophets, martyrs, sages, artists, the heroes of spirituality of every land and clime, have found in it comfort, resolution, and triumph. The philosopher, at best, can report what these have seen. And "soft," indeed, is the type of thoughtful effort which declines to follow with its ideas what all these have learned to express in their lives and in their religion.

V

Because I am here not stating for you a merely speculative doctrine concerning the place of evil in a good and rational spiritual world, I once more need, at this point, to appeal as directly as I can to life. Let me present to you, from recent literature, a noteworthy instance of the use of our present source of insight. The instance is confessedly one where no complete and determinate religious creed is defended as the result of the use of the insight in question. And an actually eternal truth about the spiritual world— a very old truth in the lore of the wise, but a deeply needed truth for our own day—is illustrated by the instance which the tale portrays.

I refer to a recent short story, published in the *Atlantic Monthly* for November, 1910, and written by Cornelia A. P. Comer. It is entitled "The Preliminaries." It is, to my mind, an impressive union of a genuinely effective realism and a deep symbolism. The characters are very real human beings. Their problem is one of the most familiar problems of daily life— the problem as to the advisability of the proposed marriage of two young lovers. The conditions of the problem are hard facts, of a general type that is unfortunately frequent enough under our confusing modern conditions. These facts are viewed in the tale as such people might well view them. And yet the issues involved are, like all the problems of young lovers, issues that are bound up with all the interests of religion and with the whole problem of the reality of a spiritual world. These issues are treated as they truly are, with a result that is fairly supernatural in its ancient but always new appeal to a source of insight that we can reach only through sorrow.

Since the question inevitably concerns the prospects of the proposed marriage, the first statement of the problem is fully in harmony with the spirit of recent pragmatism. The truth of the assertion: "We ought to marry," is surely a truth that, as the pragmatists would say, the young lovers who make the assertion should regard as quite inseparable from the probable results to which this marriage will lead in concrete life. Such a truth then is, one would say, wholly empirical. A marriage proposal, to use the favourite phrase of pragmatism, is a "working hypothesis." Such hypotheses must be submitted to the test of experience. No such test, it would seem, would be absolute. What does poor humanity know as to the real values of our destiny? Meanwhile the whole problem of good and evil is in question. Marriage, especially under certain conditions, will lead to one or another sorrow. Can one face sorrow with any really deeper trust in life? Is life really a good at all, since there is so much sorrow in it? Must not any prudent person be afraid of life? Ought the lovers to defy fortune and to ignore obvious worldly prudence?

Such is the first statement of the problem. Its treatment in this admirable sketch shows an insight into the nature of good and evil which I had myself come to regard as very little present to the minds of the story-tellers of to-day, who are so often dominated by the recent love of power, by the tedious blindness of modern individualism, by false doctrines as to the merely temporal expediency of truth, and by the merely glittering show of unspiritual worldly efficiency. I rejoice to find that, in a literature which has been, of late, so devastated by a popularly trivial interpretation of pragmatism, and by an equally trivial disregard for the "rule of reason," there is still place for so straightforward and practical a recognition of eternal truth as the wise woman who has written this short story exemplifies.

The issue regarding this particular marriage proposal is stated at once in the opening words of the tale:

"Young Oliver Pickersgill was in love with Peter Lannithorne's daughter. Peter Lannithorne was serving a six-year term in the penitentiary for embezzlement."

The young hero is depicted as a high-minded youth of unquestionable and prosperous social position in his community. His beloved is a loyal daughter who is convinced that her father's crime was due solely to a momentary and benevolent weakness, and to a mind confused by care for the needs and too importunate requirements of his own family. Not unjustly attributing the father's final downfall to the impatience, to the agonising discontent, and to the worldly ambition of her own mother, the daughter with spirit replies to the lover's proposal by saying plainly: "I will never marry any one who doesn't respect my father as I do." The lovers somewhat easily come to terms, at least apparently, as to this sole present ground for disagreement. The youth, not without inward difficulty, is ready to accept the daughter's version of her father's misadventure. In any case, love makes him indifferent to merely worldly scruples, and he has no fear of his own power to face his community as the loving husband of a convict's daughter; though there is, indeed, no doubt as to the father's actual guilt, and although Lannithorne is known to have admitted the justice of his sentence.

But to love, and to be magnanimously hopeful—this is not the same as to convince other people that such a marriage is prudent, or is likely, as the pragmatists would say, to have "expedient workings." Young Oliver has to persuade Ruth's mother on the one hand, his own father on the other, that such a marriage is reasonable. Both prove to be hard to convince. To the ordinary scruples of worldly prudence which young lovers generally have to answer, they easily add seemingly unanswerable objections. The mother—the convict's wife—now a brilliantly clear-witted but hopelessly narrow-minded invalid—a broken woman of the world—pragmatically enlightened, in a way, by the bitter experience of sorrow, but not in the least brought thereby to any deeper insight, faces the lover as an intruder upon her daughter's peace and her own desolation. She has known, she says, what the bitterness of an unhappy marriage can be and is. If she herself has had her share of blame for her husband's downfall, that only the more shows her such truth as, in this dark world, she still can grasp. "I do not want my daughters to marry"—this is, to her, the conclusion of the whole matter. The bitterness of her own marriage has taught her this lesson, which she expounds to the lover with all the passion of wounded pride and the dear-bought lore of life as she has learned it. But of course, as she admits, she may be wrong. Let the lover consult her husband at the jail. He—the convict—is a well-meaning man, after all. He fell; but he is not at heart a criminal. Let him say whether he wants his daughter to take up the burden of this new tragedy. So the mother concludes her parable.

The lover, baffled, but still hopeful, next turns to his own father for consent and encouragement. But now he has to listen to the teachings of a loftier yet to him profoundly discouraging prudence. Oliver's father is a truly high-minded man of the world, with a genuinely religious feeling in the background of his mind, and is intensely devoted to his son. But from this proposed match he recoils with a natural horror. The world is full of good girls. Why not choose one who brings no such sorrow with her? Peter Lannithorne was in his crime no worse, indeed, than many other men who are not in jail. He even meant on the whole well, and blundered, until at last from blunder he drifted into crime. He then took his penalty like a man, and owned that it was just. But, after all, he was found out. Such a taint lasts. It cannot be removed by repentance. The proposed marriage can only lead to misery. Peter Lannithorne himself, who, after all, "knows what's what," would be the first to admit this fact, if one asked his advice. If the son must persist in making light of a loving father's wisdom—well, let him then consult Peter Lannithorne himself. Ask the convict in his prison what a man needs and expects in the family of the woman whom he is to marry. This is the father's firm but kindly ultimatum.

Terrified by the gravity of repeated warnings, and dispirited by having to leave his dearest problem to the decision of the convict himself, Oliver determines to face the inevitable. He arranges for the interview at the jail, and is left by the warden alone with the prisoner in the prison library. Suddenly, as he faces his man, the youth finds himself in the presence of one who has somehow been transformed as if by a supernatural power. As for the convict's person—

> His features were irregular and unnoticeable; but the sum-total of them gave the impression of force. It was a strong face, yet you could see that it had once been a weak one. It was a tremendously human face, a face like a battleground, scarred and seamed and lined with the stress of invisible conflicts . . . Not a triumphant face at all, and yet there was peace in it. Somehow, the man had achieved something, arrived somewhere, and the record of the journey was piteous and terrible. Yet it drew the eyes in awe as much as in wonder, and in pity not at all.

Oliver, reassured by the new presence, and glad to find himself at last facing a man who has nothing left to fear in life, states as well as possible his main problem. The father of his beloved listens, first with surprise at the news, then with seriousness. Oliver finds himself forced to cut deep when he repeats his own father's appeal to know the convict's opinion about what a man expects to meet in his future wife's family, and then pauses with a keen sense of the cruelty of his own position. But Lannithorne, who has long since become accustomed to feeling the ploughshare of passion grind down to his uttermost rock, is perfectly ready with his response. As the youth pauses and then begins a new appeal—

> The man looked up and held up an arresting hand. "Let me clear the way for you a little," he said. "It was a hard thing for you to come and seek me out in this place. I like your coming. Most young men would have refused, or come in a different spirit. I want you to understand that if in Ruth's eyes, and my wife's, and your father's, my counsel has value, it is because they think I see things as they are. And that means, first of all, that I know myself for a man who committed a crime and is paying the penalty. I am satisfied to be paying it. As I see justice, it is just. So, if I seem to wince at your necessary allusions to it, that is part of the price. I don't want you to feel that you are blundering or hurting me more than is necessary. You have got to lay the thing before me as it is."
> Something in the words, in the dry, patient manner, in the

endurance of the man's face, touched Oliver to the quick and made him feel áll manner of new things: such as a sense of the moral poise of the universe, acquiescence in its retributions, and a curious pride, akin to Ruth's own, in a man who could meet him after this fashion, in this place.

Hereupon, fully aroused, the youth tells with freedom why the problem seems so hard for the young people, and how their elders all insist upon such frightful discouragements, and how much he longs to know the truth about life, and whether all such doubts and scruples as those of his own father and of Ruth's mother are well founded. At last the prisoner begins his reply:

> "They haven't the point of view," he said. "It is life that is the great adventure. Not love, not marriage, not business. They are just chapters in the book. The main thing is to take the road fearlessly—to have courage to live one's life."
>
> "Courage?"
>
> Lannithorne nodded.
>
> "That is the great word. Don't you see what ails your father's point of view, and my wife's? One wants absolute security in one way for Ruth; the other wants absolute security in another way for you. And security—why, it's just the one thing a human being can't have, the thing that's the damnation of him if he gets it! The reason it is so hard for a rich man to enter the Kingdom of Heaven is that he has that false sense of security. To demand it just disintegrates a man. I don't know why. It does."
>
> Oliver shook his head uncertainly.
>
> "I don't quite follow you, sir. Oughtn't one to try to be safe?"
>
> "One ought to try, yes. That is common prudence. But the point is that, whatever you do or get, you aren't after all secure. There is no such condition, and the harder you demand it, the more risk you run. So it is up to a man to take all reasonable precautions about his money, or his happiness, or his life, and trust the rest. What every man in the world is looking for is the sense of having the mastery over life. But I tell you, boy, there is only one thing that really gives it!"
>
> "And that is—?"
>
> Lannithorne hesitated perceptibly. For the thing he was about to tell this undisciplined lad was his most precious posses-

sion; it was the price of wisdom for which he had paid with the years of his life. No man parts lightly with such knowledge.

"It comes," he said, with an effort, "with the knowledge of our power to endure. That's it. *You are safe only when you can stand everything that can happen to you.* Then, and then only! Endurance is the measure of a man! . . . Sometimes I think it is harder to endure what we deserve, like me," said Lannithorne, "than what we don't. I was afraid, you see, afraid for my wife and all of them. Anyhow, take my word for it. Courage is security. There is no other kind."

"Then—Ruth and I—"

"Ruth is the core of my heart!" said Lannithorne thickly. "I would rather die than have her suffer more than she must. But she must take her chances like the rest. It is the law of things. If you know yourself fit for her, and feel reasonably sure you can take care of her, you have a right to trust the future. Myself, I believe there is some One to trust it to."

The speaker of this hard-won wisdom, after this appeal to the eternal, utters his last tremulous word as from a father's loving heart, and then the interview must end. The author concludes:

Finding his way out of the prison yard a few minutes later, Oliver looked, unseeing, at the high walls that soared against the blue spring sky. He could not realise them, there was such a sense of light, air, space, in his spirit.

Apparently, he was just where he had been an hour before, with all his battles still to fight, but really he knew they were already won, for his weapon had been forged and put in his hand. He left his boyhood behind him as he passed that stern threshold, for the last hour had made a man of him, and a prisoner had given him the master-key that opens every door.

VI

Now this, I insist, is insight. It is no "soft" doctrine. It is far beyond the sort of pragmatism that accepts the test of momentary results. As far as it goes, it is religious insight. It is insight, moreover, into the nature of certain ills which cannot, yes, which in principle, and even by omnipotence, could not, be simply removed from existence without abolishing the conditions which are logically necessary to the very highest good that we know. Life in the spirit simply presupposes the conditions that these ills exemplify.

What sorrow is deeper than the full recognition of one's own now irrevocable deed, if one has, hereupon, fully to confess that this deed is, from one's own present point of view, a crime? Yet how could such ills be simply removed from existence if any range of individual expression, of freedom, of power to choose is to be left open at all? How can one possess spiritual effectiveness—the privilege that youth most ardently demands—without assuming the risk involved in taking personal responsibility for some aspects of the lives of our fellows? As for our blunders, what more precious privilege do we all claim than the privilege of making our own blunders, or at least a due proportion of them? When we act, every act is done for eternity, since it is irrevocable. When we love, we ask the privilege to bind up other destinies with our own. The tragedies of such a world as ours are, therefore, not such as could be simply wiped out of existence, unless one were ready to deprive every individual personality both of its range of free choice and of its effectiveness of action. When we suffer, then, in such a world, we know indeed that there need have been no such suffering had there been no world at all. But precisely when our ills are most bound up with our own personal wills, we know that no mere removal of such ills could have occurred without the abolition of all the conditions which our spiritual freedom, our longing for effectiveness, and our love for union with other personalities make us regard as the conditions of the highest good. No God could conceivably give you the good of self-expression without granting you the privilege, not only of choosing wrongly, but of involving your brethren in the results of your misdeed. For when you love your kind, you aim to be a factor in their lives; and to deprive you of this privilege would be to insure your total failure. But if you possess this privilege, you share in a life that, in proportion to its importance and depth and range and richness of spiritual relations, is full of the possibilities of tragedy.

Face such tragedy, however, and what does it show you? The possibility, not of annulling an evil, or of ceasing to regret it, but of showing spiritual power, first, through idealising your grief, by seeing even through this grief the depth of the significance of our relations as individuals to one another, to our social order, and to the whole of life; secondly, through enduring your fortune; and thirdly, through conquering, by the might of the spirit, those goods which can only be won through such sorrow. What those goods are, the convict has just, if only in small part, told us. Griselda told us something about them which is much deeper still. For adversity and loyalty are, indeed, simply inseparable companions. There could not be loyalty in a world where the loyal being himself met no adversities that personally belonged to and entered his own inner life. That this is true, let every loyal experience bear witness.

Now such sorrows, such idealised evils, which are so interwoven with good that if the precious grief were wholly removed from existence, the courage, the fidelity, the spiritual self-possession, the peace through and in and beyond tribulation which such trials alone make possible, would also be removed—they surely show us that the abstract principle: "Evil ought to be abolished," is false. They show us that the divine will also must be made perfect through suffering. Since we can comprehend the meaning of such experiences only through resolute action, through courage, through loyalty, through the power of the spirit, they in no wise justify sloth, or mere passivity, or mystical idleness. The active dealing with such sorrow gives, as James himself once well asserts, a new dimension to life. No experiences go further than do these to show us how, in our loyalty and in our courage, we are becoming one with the master of life, who through sorrow overcomes.

Let man, the destroyer, then remember that there is one ill which he could not destroy, even if he were God, without also destroying all the spiritual prowess in which all those rejoice who, inspired by an ambition infinitely above that of Achilles, long to be one with God through bearing and overcoming the sorrows of a world.

We have thus indicated a source of insight. To tell more about what it reveals would at once lead me, as you see, close to the most vital of all Christian teachings, the doctrine of the Atonement. But such a study belongs elsewhere.

THE UNITY OF THE SPIRIT
AND THE INVISIBLE CHURCH

My present and concluding lecture must begin with some explanations of what I mean by the term "The Unity of the Spirit." Then I shall have to define my use of the term "The Invisible Church." Thereafter, we shall be free to devote ourselves to the consideration of a source of religious insight as omnipresent as it is variously interpreted by those who, throughout all the religious world, daily appeal to its guidance. The outcome of our discussion may help some of you, as I hope, to turn your attention more toward the region where the greatest help is to be found in the cultivation of that true loyalty which, if I am right, is the heart and core of every higher religion.

I

In these lectures I have repeatedly called the religious objects, that is, the objects whereof the knowledge tends to the salvation of man, "superhuman" and "supernatural" objects. I have more or less fully explained, as I went, the sense in which I hold these objects to be both superhuman and supernatural. But every use of familiar traditional terms is likely to arouse misunderstandings. I have perfectly definite reasons for my choice of the traditional words in question as adjectives wherewith to characterise the religious objects. But I do not want to leave in your minds any doubts as to what my usage is deliberately intended to imply. I do not want to seem to make any wrong use of the vaguer associations which will be in your minds when something human is compared with something superhuman, and when the natural and the supernatural are contrasted. This

195

closing lecture, in which I am to deal with an aspect of spiritual life which we have everywhere in our discourse tacitly presupposed, but which now is to take its definitive place on our list of sources of religious insight, gives me my best opportunity to forestall useless misunderstandings by putting myself upon record as to the precise sense in which both the new source itself and everything else superhuman and supernatural to which religion has a rational right to appeal is, to my mind, a reality, and is a source or an object of human insight. I shall therefore explain the two adjectives just emphasised by giving you a somewhat fuller account of their sense than I have heretofore stated. If the new account touches upon technical matters, I hope that, by our long list of illustrations of the superhuman and of the supernatural, we have now sufficiently prepared the way.

In my general sketch of the characteristics of human nature which awaken in us the sense of our need for salvation, I laid stress, both in our first and in our second lectures, upon our narrowness of outlook as one principal and pervasive defect of man as he naturally is constituted. I illustrated this narrowness by some of its most practically noteworthy instances. Repeatedly I returned, in later discussions, to this same feature of our life. Now man's narrowness of natural outlook upon life is first of all due to something which I have to call the "form" of human consciousness. What I mean by this form, I have already illustrated to you freely by the very instances to which I have just referred. But technical clearness as to such topics is hard to attain. Allow me, then, to insist with some care upon matters which are as influential in moulding our whole destiny as they are commonly neglected in our discussions of the problems of life and of reality.

Man can attend to but a very narrow range of facts at any one instant. Common-sense observation shows you this. Psychological experiment emphasises it in manifold ways. Listen to a rhythmic series of beats—drum beats—or the strokes of an engine, or the feet of horses passing by in the street. You cannot directly grasp with entire clearness more than a very brief sequence of these beats, or other sounds, or of rhythmic phrases of any kind. If the rhythm of a regularly repeated set of sounds is too long, or too complex, it becomes confused for you. You cannot make out by your direct attention what it is at least until it has by repetition grown familiar. Let several objects be brought before you at once. You can attend to one and then to another at pleasure if only they stay there to be attended to. But only a very few distinct objects can be suddenly seen at once, and at a single glance, and recognised, through that one instantaneous presentation, for what they are. If the objects are revealed to you in the darkness by an electric spark, or are seen through a single slit in a screen that rapidly moves before your eyes—so that the objects are exposed to your observation only during the extremely brief time when the slit passes directly between them and your eyes—this limit of your power to grasp several distinct objects at once, upon a single inspection, can be experimentally tested. The results of such experiments concern us here only in the most general way. Enough—as such tests show—what one may call the *span* of our consciousness, its power to grasp many facts in any one individual moment of our lives, is extremely limited. It is limited as to the number of simultaneously presented facts that we can grasp at one view, can distinguish, and recognise, and hold clearly before us. It is also limited with regard to the number and the duration of the successive facts that we can so face as directly to grasp the character of their succession, rhythmic or otherwise.

Now this limitation of the span of our consciousness is, I repeat, an ever-present defect of our human type of conscious life. That is why I call it a defect in the "form" of our conscious life. It is not a defect limited to the use of any one of our senses. It is not a failure of eyes or of ears to furnish to us a sufficient variety of facts to observe. On the contrary, both our eyes and our ears almost constantly rain in upon us, especially during our more desultory waking life, an overwealth of impressions. If we want to know facts, and to attain clearness, we have to pick out a few of these impressions, from instant to instant, for more careful direct inspection. In any case, then, this limitation is not due to the defects of our senses. It is our whole conscious make-up, our characteristic way of becoming aware of things, which is expressed by this limitation of our conscious span. On this plan our human consciousness is formed. Thus our type of awareness is constituted. In this way we are all doomed to live. It is our human fate to grasp clearly only a few facts or ideas at any one instant. And so, being what we are, we have to make the best of our human nature.

Meanwhile, it is of our very essence as reasonable beings that we are always contending with the consequences of this our natural narrowness of span. We are always actively rebelling at our own form of consciousness, so long as we are trying to know or to do anything significant. We want to grasp many things at once, not merely a few. We want to survey life in long stretches, not merely in instantaneous glimpses. We are always like beings who have to see our universe through the cracks that our successive instants open before us, and as quickly close again. And we want to see things, *not* through these instantaneous cracks, but without intervening walls, with wide outlook, and in all their true variety and unity. Nor is this rebellion of ours against the mere form of consciousness any merely idle curiosity or peevish seeking for a barren wealth of varieties. Salvation itself is at stake in this struggle for a wider clearness of outlook. The wisest souls, as we have throughout seen, agree with common-sense prudence in the desire to see at any one instant greater varieties of ideas and of objects than our form of consciousness permits us to grasp. To escape from the limitations imposed upon us by the natural narrowness of our span of consciousness—by the form of consciousness in which we live—this is the common interest of science and of religion, of the more contemplative and of the more active aspects of our higher nature. *Our form of consciousness is one of our chief human sorrows.*

By devices such as the rhythmic presentation of facts to our attention we can do something—not very much—to enlarge our span of consciousness. But for most purposes we can make only an *indirect,* not a *direct,* escape from our limitations of span. Our salvation depends upon the winning of such indirect successes. Indirectly we escape, in so far as we use our powers of habit-forming, of memory, and of abstraction, to prepare for us objects of momentary experience such as have come to acquire for us a wide range of meaning, so that, when we get before our momentary attention but a few of these objects at once, we still are able to comprehend, after our human fashion, ranges and connections and unities of fact which the narrow form of our span of consciousness forbids us to grasp with directness. Thus, the repetition of similar experiences forms habits such that each element of some new instant of passing experience comes to us saturated with the meaning that, as we look back upon our past life, we suppose to have resulted from the whole course of what has happened. And through such endlessly varied processes of habit-forming, we come to reach stages of insight in which the instantaneous presentation of a few facts gets for us, at a given moment, the value of an indirect appreciation of what we never directly grasp—that is, the value of a wide survey of life. All that we usually call knowledge is due to such indirect grasping of what the instant can only hint to us, although we usually feel as if this indirect presentation were itself a direct insight. Let me exemplify: The odour of a flower may come to us burdened with a meaning that we regard as the total result of a whole summer of our life. The wrinkled face of an old man reveals to us, in its momentarily presented traces, the signs of what we take to have been his lifetime's experience and slowly won personal character. And, in very much the same way, almost any passing experience may seem to us to speak with the voice of years, or even of ages, of human life. To take yet another instance: a single musical chord epitomises the result of all our former hearings of the musical composition which it introduces.

In this way we live, despite our narrowness, *as if* we saw widely; and we constantly view *as if it were* our actual experience, a sense and connection of things which actually never gets fully translated in any moment of our lives, but is always simply presupposed as the interpretation which a wider view of life *would* verify. Thus bounded in the nutshell of the passing instant, we count ourselves (in one way or another, and whatever our opinions), kings of the infinite realm of experience, or would do so were it not that, like Hamlet, we have so many "bad dreams," which make us doubt the correctness of our interpretations, and feel our need of an escape from this stubborn natural prison of our own form of consciousness. We therefore appeal, in all our truth-seeking, to a wider view than our own present view.

Our most systematic mode of indirect escape from the consequences of our narrow span of consciousness, is the mode which our thinking processes, that is, our dealings with abstract and general ideas exemplify.

Such abstract and general ideas, as we earlier saw, are means to ends— never ends in themselves. By means of generalisation or abstraction we can gradually come to choose signs which we can more or less successfully substitute for long series of presented objects of experience; and we can also train ourselves into active ways of estimating or of describing things—ways such, that by reminding ourselves of these our active attitudes toward the business of life, we can seem to ourselves to epitomise in an instant the sense of years or even of ages of human experience. Such signs and symbols and attitudes constitute our store of general and abstract ideas. Our more or less systematic and voluntary thinking is a process of observing, at one or another instant, the connections and the meanings of a very few of these our signs and attitudes at once. We actively put together these ideas of ours, and watch, at the instant, the little connections that then and there are able to appear, despite the narrowness of our span of consciousness. That, for instance, is what happens when we add up columns of figures, or think out a problem, or plan our practical lives. But because each of the ideas used, each of these signs or symbols or attitudes, can be more or less safely substituted for some vast body of facts of experience, what we observe only in and through our narrow span can indirectly help us to appreciate something whose real meaning only a very wide range of experience, a consciousness whose span is enormously vaster than ours, could possibly present directly.

Thus, confined to our own form and span of consciousness as we are, we spend our lives in acquiring or devising ways to accomplish indirectly what we are forbidden directly to attain, namely, the discovery of truth and of meaning such as only a consciousness of another form than ours can realise. Now, as I maintained in our third and fourth lectures, *the whole validity and value of this indirect procedure of ours depends upon the principle that such a wider view of things, such a larger unity of consciousness, such a direct grasp of the meanings at which we indirectly but ceaselessly aim is a reality in the universe.* As I there maintained, *the whole reality of the universe itself must be defined, in terms of the reality of such an inclusive and direct grasp of the whole sense of things.* I can here only repeat my opinion that this thesis is one which nobody can deny without self-contradiction.

Now the difference between the narrow form of consciousness that we human beings possess and the wider and widest forms of consciousness whose reality every common-sense effort to give sense to life, and every scientific effort to discover the total verdict of experience presupposes—the difference, I say, between these two forms of consciousness is *literally* expressed by calling the one form (the form that we all possess) *human,* and by calling the other form (the form of a wider consciousness which views experience as it is) *superhuman.* The wider conscious view of things that we share only indirectly, through the devices just pointed out, is certainly not human; for no mortal man ever directly possesses it. It is real; for, as we saw in our study of the reason, if you deny this assertion in one shape, you reaffirm it in another. For you can define the truth and falsity of your own opinions only by presupposing a wider view that sees as a whole what you see in fragments. That unity of consciousness which we presuppose in all our indirect efforts to get into touch with its direct view of truth is above our level. It includes what we actually get before us in our form of consciousness. It also includes all that we are trying to grasp indirectly. Now what is not human, and is above our level, and includes all of our insight, but transcends and corrects our indirect efforts by its direct grasp of facts as they are, can best be called superhuman. *The thesis that such a superhuman consciousness is a reality is a thesis precisely equivalent to the assertion that our experience has any real sense or connection whatever* beyond the mere fragment of connectedness that, at any one instant, we directly grasp.

Furthermore, to call such a larger consciousness—inclusive of our own, but differing from ours, in form, by the vastness of its span and the variety and completeness of the connections that it surveys—to call it, I say, a *supernatural* consciousness is to use a phraseology that can be very deliberately and, if you choose, technically defended. By "natural" we mean simply: Subject to the laws which hold for the sorts of beings whose character and behaviour our empirical sciences can study. If you suddenly found that you could personally and individually and clearly grasp, by an act of direct attention, the sense and connection of thousands of experiences at once, instead of the three or four presented facts of experience whose relations you can now directly observe in any one of your moments of consciousness, you would indeed say that you had been miraculously transformed into another type of being whose insight had acquired an angelic sort of wealth and clearness. But whenever you assert (as every scientific theory, and every common-sense opinion, regarding the real connections of the facts of human experience requires you to assert), that not only thousands, but a countless collection of data of human experience actually possess a perfectly coherent total sense and meaning, such as no individual man ever directly observes, this your assertion, which undertakes to be a report of facts, and which explicitly relates to facts of experience, implies the assertion that there exists such a superhuman survey of the real nature and connection of our own natural realm of conscious life. We ourselves are strictly limited by the natural conditions that determine our own form of consciousness. And no conditions can be regarded by us as more characteristically natural than are these. For us human beings to transcend those conditions, by surveying countless data at once, would require an uttermost exception to the natural laws which are found to govern our human type of consciousness. To believe that any man ever had accomplished the direct survey of the whole range of the physical connections of the solar and stellar systems at once—in other words, had grasped the whole range of astronomical experience in a single act of attention—would be to believe that a most incredible miracle had at some time taken place—an incredible miracle so far as any knowledge that we now possess enables us to foresee what the natural conditions under which man lives, and is, in human form, conscious, permit. But, on the other hand, to accept, as we all do, the validity of that scientific interpretation of the data of human experience which astronomy reports is to acknowledge that such an interpretation more or less completely records a system of facts which are nothing if they are not in some definite sense empirical, although, in their wholeness, they are experienced by no man. That is, the acceptance of the substantial truth of astronomy involves the acknowledgment that some such, to us simply superhuman, consciousness is precisely as real as the stars are real, and as their courses, and as all their relations are real. Yet, of course, we cannot undertake to investigate any process such as would enable us to define the natural conditions under which any such superhuman survey of astronomical facts would become psychologically possible.

The acceptance of our natural sciences, as valid interpretations of connections of experience which our form of consciousness forbids us directly to verify, logically presupposes, at every step, that such superhuman forms and unities of consciousness are real. For the facts of science are indefinable except as facts in and for a real experience. But, on the other hand, we can hope for no advance in physical or in psychological knowledge which would enable us to bring these higher forms of consciousness under what we call natural laws. So the superhuman forms of consciousness remain for us also supernatural. *That* they are, we must acknowledge, if any assertion whatever about our world is to be either true or false. For all assertions are made about experience, and about its real connections, and about its systems. But *what* conditions, *what* natural causes, bring such superhuman forms of consciousness into existence we are unable to investigate. For every assertion about nature or about natural laws presupposes that natural facts and laws are real only in so far as they are the objects known to such higher unities of consciousness. The unities in question are themselves no natural objects; while all natural facts are objects for them and are expressions of their meaning.

Thus definite are my reasons for asserting that forms of consciousness superior to our own are real, and that they are all finally united in a single, world-embracing insight, which has also the character of expressing a world-will. Thus definite are also my grounds for calling such higher unities of consciousness both superhuman and supernatural. By the term "The unity of the spirit" I name simply *the unity of meaning which belongs to these superhuman forms of consciousness.* We ourselves partake of this unity, and share it, in so far as, in our lives also, we discover and express, in whatever way our own form of consciousness permits, truth and life that bring us into touch and into harmony with the higher forms of consciousness, that is, with the spirit which, in its wholeness, knows and estimates the world, and which expresses itself in the life of the world.

Thus near are we, in every exercise of our reasonable life, to the superhuman and to the supernatural. Upon the other hand, there is positively no need of magic, or of miracle, or of mysterious promptings from the subconscious, to prove to us the reality of the human and of the supernatural, or to define our reasonable relations with it. And the essential difference between our own type of consciousness and this higher life is a difference of form, and is also a difference of content precisely in so far as its wider and widest span of conscious insight implies that the superhuman type of consciousness possesses a depth of meaning, a completeness of expression, a wealth of facts, a clearness of vision, a successful embodiment of purpose which, in view of the narrowness of our form of consciousness, do not belong to us.

Man needs no miracles to show him the supernatural and the superhuman. You need no signs and wonders, and no psychical research, to prove that the unity of the spirit is a fact in the world. Common-sense tacitly presupposes the reality of the unity of the spirit. Science studies the ways in which its life is expressed in the laws which govern the order of experience. Reason gives us insight into its real being. Loyalty serves it, and repents not of the service. Salvation means our positive harmony with its purpose and with its manifestation.

II

Amongst the sources of insight which bring us into definite and practical relations with that spiritual world whose nature has now been again defined, one of the most effective is the life and the word of other men who are minded to be loyal to genuine causes, and who are already, through the service of their common causes, brought together in some form of spiritual brotherhood. The real unity of the life of such fellow-servants of the Spirit is itself an instance of a superhuman conscious reality; and its members are devoted to bringing themselves into harmony with the purposes of the universe. Any brotherhood of men who thus loyally live in the Spirit is, from my point of view, a brotherhood essentially religious in its nature, precisely in proportion as it is practically moved by an effort to serve—not merely the special cause to which its members, because of their training and their traditions, happen to be devoted, but also the common cause of all the loyal. Such a brotherhood, so far as it is indeed human, and, therefore narrow, may not very expressly define what this common cause of all the loyal is, for its members may not be thoughtfully reflective people. But if, while rejoicing in their own perfectly real fraternal unity, they are also practically guided by the love of furthering brotherhood amongst men in general; if they respect the loyalty of other men so far as they understand that loyalty; if they seek, not to sow discord amongst the brethren of our communities, but to be a city set on a hill, that not only cannot be hid, but is also a model for other cities—a centre for the spreading of the spirit of loyalty—then the members of such an essentially fruitful brotherhood are actually loyal to the cause of causes. They are a source of insight to all who know of their life, and who rightly appreciate its meaning. And of such is the kingdom of loyalty. And the communities which such men form and serve are essentially religious communities. Each one is an example of the unity of the Spirit. Each one stands for a reality that belongs to the superhuman world.

Since the variety of social forms which appear under human conditions is an unpredictably vast variety, and since the motives which guide men are endlessly complex, different communities of loyal people may possess such a religious character and value in the most various degrees. For it results from the narrowness of the human form of consciousness that men, at any one moment, know not the whole of what they mean. No sharp line can be drawn sundering the brotherhoods and partnerships, and other social organisations which men devise, into those which for the men concerned are consciously religious, and those which, by virtue of their absence of interest in the larger and deeper loyalties are secular. The test whereby such a distinction should be made is in principle a definite test. But to apply the test to every possible case requires a searching of human hearts and a just estimate of deeds and motives whereto, in our ignorance, we are very generally inadequate.

A business firm would seem to be, in general, no model of a religious organisation. Yet it justly demands loyalty from its members and its servants. If it lives and acts merely for gain, it is secular indeed. But if its business is socially beneficent, if its cause is honourable, if its dealings are honest, if its treatment of its allies and rivals is such as makes for the confidence, the cordiality, and the stability of the whole commercial life of its community and (when its influence extends so far) of the world, if public spirit and true patriotism inspire its doings, if it is always ready on occasion to sacrifice gain for honour's sake—then there is no reason why it may not become and be a genuinely and fervently religious brotherhood. Certainly a family can become a religious organisation; and some of the most ancient traditions of mankind have demanded that it should be one. There is also, and justly, a religion of patriotism, which regards the country as a divine institution. Such a religion serves the unity of the spirit in a perfectly genuine way. Some of the most momentous religious movements in the world's history have grown out of such an idealised patriotism. Christianity, in transferring local names from Judea to a heavenly world, has borne witness to the sacredness that patriotism, upon its higher levels, acquires.

In brief, the question whether a given human brotherhood is a religious institution or not is a question for that brotherhood to decide for itself, subject only to the truth about its real motives. Has its cause the characters that mark a fitting cause of loyalty? Does it so serve its cause as thereby to further the expression of the divine unity of the spirit in the form of devoted human lives, not only within its own brotherhood, but as widely as its influence extends? Then it is an essentially religious organisation. Nor does the extent of its worldly influence enable you to decide how far it meets these requirements. Nor yet does the number of persons in its membership form any essential criterion. Wherever two or three are gathered together, and are living as they can in the Spirit that the divine will (which wills the loyal union of all mankind) requires of them—there, indeed, the work of the Spirit is done; and the organisation in question is a religious brotherhood. It needs no human sanction to make it such. Though it dwell on a desert island, and though all its members soon die and are forgotten of men, its loyal deeds are irrevocable facts of the eternal world; and the universal life knows that here at least the divine will is expressed in human acts.

But so far as such communities both exist and are distinctly recognisable as religious in their life and intent, they form a source of religious insight to all who come under their influence. Such a source acts as a means whereby any or all of our previous sources may be opened to us, may become effective, may bear fruit. *Hence, in this new source, we find the crowning source of religious insight.*

This last statement is one which is accepted by many who would nevertheless limit its application to certain religious communities, and to those only; or who, in some cases, would limit its application to some one religious community. There are, for instance, many who say, for various special reasons, that the crowning source of religious insight is the visible church. By this term those who use it in any of its traditional senses, mean one religious institution only, or at most only a certain group of religious organisations. The visible church is a religious organisation, or group of such organisations, which is characterised by certain traditions, by a certain real or supposed history, by a more or less well-defined creed, and by further assertions concerning the divine revelation to which it owes its origin and authority. With the doctrinal questions involved in the understanding of this definition, these lectures, as you now well know, have no direct concern. It is enough for our present purpose to say that the visible church thus defined is indeed, and explicitly, and in our present sense, a religious organisation. In all those historical forms which here concern us, the visible church has undertaken to show men the way to salvation. It has carried out its task by uniting its members in a spiritual brotherhood. It has in ideal extended its interest to all mankind. It has aimed at universal brotherhood. It has defined and called out loyalty. It has conceived this loyalty as a service of God and as a loyalty to the cause of all mankind. Its traditions, the lives of its servants, its services, its teachings, have been and are an inexhaustible source of religious insight to the vast multitudes whom it has influenced and, in its various forms and embodiments, still influences. Not unnaturally, therefore, those who accept its own doctrines regarding its origin and history view such a visible church not only as by far the most important source of religious insight, but also as a source occupying an entirely unique position.

The deliberate limitations of the undertaking of these lectures forbid me, as I have just reminded you, to consider in any detail this supposed uniqueness of the position which so many of you will assign to some form of the historical Christian church. After what I have said as to the nature and the variety of the forms which the spiritual life has taken, and still takes, amongst men, you will nevertheless not be surprised if, without attempting to judge the correctness of the traditions of the visible church, I forthwith point out that, to the higher religious life of mankind the life of the visible church stands related as part to whole; and that very vast ranges of the higher religious life of mankind have grown and flourished outside of the influence of Christianity. And when the religious life of mankind is viewed in its historical connections, truth requires us to insist that Christianity itself has been dependent for its insight and its power upon many different sources, some of which assumed human form not only long before Christianity came into being, but in nations and in civilisations which were not dependent for their own spiritual wealth upon the Jewish religious traditions that Christianity itself undertook to transform and to assimilate. Christianity is, in its origins, not only Jewish but Hellenic, both as to its doctrines and as to its type of spirituality. It is a synthesis of religious motives which had their sources widely spread throughout the pre-Christian world of Hellenism. Its own insight is partly due to the non-Christian world.

As a fact, then, the unity of the Spirit, the religious life which has been and is embodied in the form of human fraternities, is the peculiar possession of no one time, or nation, and belongs to no unique and visible church. Yet such an unity is a source of religious insight. We have a right to use it wherever we find it and however it becomes accessible to us. As a fact, we all use such insight without following any one principle as to the selection of the historical sources. Socrates and Plato and Sophocles are religious teachers from whom we have all directly or indirectly learned, whether we know it or not. Our own Germanic ancestors, and the traditions of the Roman Empire, have influenced our type of loyalty and have taught us spiritual truth that we should not otherwise know.

Moreover, that which I have called the cause of all the loyal, the real unity of the whole spiritual world, is not merely a moral ideal. It is a religious reality. Its servants and ministers are present wherever religious brotherhood finds sincere and hearty manifestation. In the sight of a perfectly real but superhuman knowledge of the real purposes and effective deeds of mankind, *all the loyal, whether they individually know the fact or not, are, and in all times have been, one genuine and religious brotherhood*. Human narrowness and the vicissitudes of the world of time have hidden, and still hide, the knowledge of this community of the loyal from human eyes. But indirectly it comes to light whenever the loyalty of one visible spiritual community comes, through any sort of tradition, or custom, or song or story, or wise word or noble deed, to awaken new manifestations of the loyal life in faithful souls anywhere amongst men.

I call the community of all who have sought for salvation through loyalty the Invisible Church. What makes it invisible to us is our ignorance of the facts of human history and, still more, our narrowness in our appreciation of spiritual truth. And I merely report the genuine facts, human and superhuman, when I say that *whatever any form of the visible church has done or will do for the religious life of mankind, the crowning source of religious insight is, for us all, the actual loyalty, service, devotion, suffering, accomplishment, traditions, example, teaching, and triumphs of the invisible church of all the faithful.* And by the invisible church I mean the brotherhood consisting of all who, in any clime or land, live in the Spirit.

Our terms have now been, so far as my time permits, sharply defined. I am here not appealing to vague sentiments about human brotherhood, or to merely moral ideals about what we merely hope that man may yet come to be. And I am not for a moment committing myself to any mere worship of humanity, so long as one conceives humanity as the mere collection of those who are subject to the natural laws that govern our present physical and mental existence. Humanity, viewed as a mere product of nature, is narrow-minded and degraded enough. Its life is full of uncomprehended evils and of mutual misunderstandings. It is not a fitting object of any religious reverence. But it needs salvation. It has been finding salvation through loyalty. And the true cause, the genuine community, the real spiritual brotherhood of the loyal is a superhuman and not merely a human reality. It expresses itself in the lives of the loyal. In so far as these expressions directly or indirectly inspire our own genuine loyalty, they give us insight. Of such insight, whatever you may learn from communion with any form of the visible church, is an instance—a special embodiment. The invisible church, then, is no merely human and secular institution. It is a real and superhuman organisation. It includes and transcends every form of the visible church. It is the actual subject to which belong all the spiritual gifts which we can hope to enjoy. If your spiritual eyes were open, no diversity of human tongues, no strangeness of rites or of customs or of other forms of service, no accidental quaintnesses of tradition or of symbols or of creeds, would hide from your vision its perfections. It believes everywhere in the unity of the Spirit, and aims to save men through winning them over to the conscious service of its own unity. And it grants you the free grace of whatever religious insight you can acquire from outside yourself. If you are truly religious, you live in it and for it. You conceive its life in your own way and, no doubt, under the limitations of your own time and creed. But you cannot flee from its presence. And your salvation lies in its reality, in your service, and in your communion with its endlessly varied company of those who suffer and who in the might of the spirit overcome.

Let me tell you something of this life of the invisible church.

III

And first let me speak of its membership. We have now repeatedly defined the test of such membership. The invisible church is the spiritual brotherhood of the loyal. Only a searcher of hearts can quite certainly know who are the really loyal. We can be sure regarding the nature of loyalty. That loyalty itself should come to men's consciousness in the most various forms and degrees, and clouded by the most tragic misunderstandings, the narrow form of human consciousness, and the blindness and variety of human passion, make necessary.

If one is loyal to a narrow and evil cause, as the robber or the pirate may be loyal to his band or to his ship, a conscious effort to serve the unity of the whole spiritual world may seem at first sight to be excluded by the nature of the loyalty in question. But what makes a cause evil, and unworthy of loyal service, is the fact that its service is destructive of the causes of other men, so that the evil cause preys upon the loyalty of the spiritual brethren of those who serve it, and so that thereby the servants of this cause do actual wrong to mankind. But this very fact may not be understood by the individual robber or pirate. He may be devoted with all his heart and soul and mind and strength to the best cause that he knows. He may therefore sincerely conceive that the master of life authorises his cause. In that case, and so far as this belief is sincere, the robber or pirate may be a genuinely religious man.

Does this statement seem to you an absurd quibble? Then look over the past history of mankind. Some at least of the Crusaders were genuinely religious. That we all readily admit. But they were obviously, for the most part, robbers and murderers, and sometimes pirates, of what we should now think the least religious type if they were to-day sailing the Mediterranean or devastating the lands. Read in "Hakluyt's Voyages" the accounts of the spirit in which the English explorers and warriors of the Elizabethan age accomplished their great work. In these accounts a genuinely religious type of patriotism and of Christianity often expresses itself side by side with a reckless hatred of the Spaniard and a ferocity which tolerates the most obvious expressions of mere natural greed. These heroes of the beginnings of the British Empire often hardly knew whether they were rather the adventurous merchants, or the loyal warriors for England, or the defenders of the Christian faith, or simply pirates. In fact they were all these things at once. Consider the Scottish clans as they were up to the eighteenth century. The spirit that they fostered has since found magnificent expression in the loyalty of the Scottish people and in its later and far-reaching service of some of the noblest causes that men know. Yet these clans loved cattle-thieving and tortured their enemies. When did they *begin* to be really patriots and servants of mankind? When did they begin to be truly and heartily religious? Who of us can tell?

Greed and blindness are natural to man. His form of consciousness renders him unable, in many cases, to realise their unreasonableness, even when he has already come into sincerely spiritual relations with the cause of all the loyal. What we *can* know is that greed and blindness are never of themselves religious, and that the way of salvation is the way of loyalty. But I know not what degrees of greedy blindness are consistent with an actual membership in the invisible church, as I have just defined its membership. When I meet, however, with the manifestations of the spirit of universal loyalty, whether in clansman, or in crusader, or in Elizabethan and piratical English defender of his country's faith, or in the Spaniard whom he hated, I hope that I may be able to use, not the greed or the passions of these people, but their religious prowess, their free surrender of themselves to their cause, as a source of insight.

Membership in the invisible church is therefore not to be determined by mere conventions, but by the inward spirit of the faithful, as expressed in their loyal life according to their lights. Yet of those who seem to us most clearly to belong to the service of the spirit, it is easy to enumerate certain very potent groups, to whose devotion we all owe an unspeakably great debt. The sages, the poets, the prophets, whose insight we consulted in our opening lecture, and have used throughout these discourses, form such groups. It is indifferent to us to what clime or land or tongue or visible religious body they belonged or to-day belong. They have sincerely served the cause of the spirit. They are to us constant sources of religious insight. Even the cynics and the rebels, whom we cited in our opening lecture, have been, in many individual cases, devoutly religious souls who simply could not see the light as they consciously needed to see it, and who loyally refused to lie for convention's sake. Such have often served the cause of the spirit with a fervour that you ill understand so long as their words merely shock you. They often seem as if they were hostile to the unity of the spirit. But, in many cases, it is the narrowness of our nature, the chaos of our unspiritual passions, the barren formalism of our conventions that they assail. And such assaults turn our eyes upward to the unity of the spirit from whence alone consolation and escape may come. Indirectly, therefore, such souls are often the misunderstood prophets of new ways of salvation for men. When they are loyal, when their very hardness is due to their resolute truthfulness, they are often amongst the most effective friends of a deeper religious life.

A notable criterion whereby, quite apart from mere conventions, you may try the spirits that pretend or appear to be religious, and may discern the members of the invisible church from those who are not members, is the criterion of the prophet Amos: "Woe unto them that are at ease in Zion." This, as I said earlier, is one of the favourite tests applied by moralists for distinguishing those who serve from those who merely enjoy. That it is also a religious test, and *why* it is a religious test, our acquaintance with the spirit of loyalty has shown us. Religion, when triumphant, includes, indeed, the experience of inward peace; but the peace which is not won through strenuous loyal service is deceitful and corrupting. It is the conquest over and through tribulation which saves. Whoever conceives religion merely as a comfortable release from sorrows, as an agreeable banishment of cares, as a simple escape from pain, knows not what evil is, or what our human nature is, or what our need of salvation means, or what the will of the master of life demands. Therefore, a visible church that appears simply in the form of a cure for worry, or a preventive of trouble, seems to me to be lacking in a full sense of what loyalty is. Worry is indeed, in itself, not a religious exercise. But it is often an effective preliminary, and is sometimes, according to the vicissitudes of natural temper, a relatively harmless accompaniment, to a deeply religious life. Certainly the mere absence of worry, the mere attainment of a sensuous tranquillity, is no criterion of membership in the invisible church. Better a cynic or a rebel against conventional religious forms, or a pessimist, or a worrying soul, if only such a being is strenuously loyal according to his lights, than one to whom religion means simply a tranquil adoration without loyalty. But, of course, many of the tranquil are also loyal. When this is true we can only rejoice in their attainments.

If we look for other examples still of types of spirituality which seem to imply membership in the invisible church, I myself know of few better instances of the genuinely religious spirit than those which are presented to us, in recent times, by the more devoted servants of the cause of any one of the advancing natural sciences. And such instances are peculiarly instructive, because many great men of science, as a result of their personal temperament and training, are little interested in the forms of the visible church, and very frequently are loath to admit that their calling has religious bearings. But when the matter is rightly viewed, one sees that the great scientific investigator is not only profoundly loyal, but serves a cause which, at the present time, probably does more to unify every sort of wholesome human activity, to bind in one all the higher interests of humanity, to bring men of various lands and races close together in spirit than does any other one special cause that modern men serve. The cause of any serious scientific investigator is, from my point of view, a superhuman cause, for precisely the reasons which I have already explained to you.

The individual scientific worker, uninterested as he usually is in metaphysics, and unconcerned as he often is about the relation of his task to the interests of the visible church, knows indeed that with all his heart, and soul, and mind, and strength he serves a cause that he conceives to be worthy. He knows, also, that this cause is beneficent, and that it plays a great part in the directing of human activities, whether because his science already has practical applications, or because the knowledge of nature is in itself an elevating and enlarging influence for mankind. The scientific investigator knows also that, while his individual experience is the source to which he personally looks for new observations of facts, his private observations contribute to science only in so far as other investigators can verify his results. Hence his whole scientific life consists in submitting all his most prized discoveries to the rigid test of an estimate that belongs to no individual human experience, but that is, or that through loyal efforts tends to become, the common possession of the organised experience of all the workers in his field. So far the devoted investigator goes in his own consciousness as to his work.

Beyond this point, in estimating his ideals and his value, he sometimes seems not to wish to go, either because he is unreflective or because he is modest. But when we remember that the unity of human experience, in the light of which scientific results are tested, and to whose growth and enrichment the scientific worker is devoted, is indeed a superhuman reality of the type that we have now discussed; when we also recall the profound values which the scientific ideal has for all departments of human life in our day; when, further, we see how resolutely the true investigator gives his all to contribute to what is really the unity of the spirit, we may well wonder who is in essence more heartily religious than the completely devoted scientific investigator—such a man, for instance, as was Faraday.

When I have the fortune to hear of really great scientific workers who are as ready to die for their science (if an experiment or an observation requires risk) as to live for it through years of worldly privation and of rigid surrender of private interests to truth, and when I then by chance also hear that some of them were called, or perhaps even called themselves, irreligious men, I confess that I think of the little girl who walked by Wordsworth's side on the beach at Calais. The poet estimated her variety of religious experience in words that I feel moved to apply to the ardently loyal hero of science:

> "Thou dwellest in Abraham's bosom all the year,
> And worship'st at the temple's inmost shrine,
> God being with thee when we know it not."

There also exists a somewhat threadbare verse of the poet Young which tells us how "the undevout astronomer is mad." I should prefer to say that the really loyal scientific man who imagines himself undevout is not indeed mad at all, but, like Wordsworth's young companion at Calais, unobservant of himself and of the wondrous and beautiful love that inspires him. For he is, indeed, inspired by a love for something much more divine than is that august assemblage of mechanical and physical phenomena called the starry heavens. The soul of his work is the service of the unity of the spirit in one of its most exalted forms.

That all who, belonging to any body of the visible church, are seriously loyal to the divine according to their lights, are members also of the invisible church, needs, after what I have said, no further explanation.

But if, surveying this multitude that no man can number from every kindred, and tribe, and nation, and tongue, you say that entrance to the invisible church is guarded by barriers that seem to you not high enough or strong enough, I reply that this membership is indeed tested by the severest of rules. Do you serve with all your heart, and soul, and mind, and strength a cause that is superhuman and that is indeed divine? This is the question which all have to answer who are to enter this the most spiritual of all human brotherhoods.

IV

The invisible church is to be to us a source of insight. This means that we must enter into some sort of communion with the faithful if we are to enjoy the fruits of their insight. And, apart from one's own life of loyal service itself, the principal means of grace—that is, the principal means of attaining instruction in the spirit of loyalty, encouragement in its toils, solace in its sorrows, and power to endure and to triumph—the principal means of grace, I say, which is open to any man lies in such communion with the faithful and with the unity of the spirit which they express in their lives. It is natural that we should begin this process of communion through direct personal relations with the fellow-servants of our own special cause. Hence whatever is usually said by those who belong to any section of the visible church regarding the spiritual advantages which follow from entering the communion of their own body may be accepted, from our present point of view, as having whatever truth the devotion and the religious life of any one body of faithful servants of the unity of the spirit may give to such statements when applied precisely to their own members. But to us all alike the voice of the invisible church speaks—it sustains us all alike by its counsels, not merely in so far as our own personal cause and our brethren of that service are known to us, but in so far as we are ready to understand the loyal life, and to be inspired by it, even when those who exemplify its intents and its values are far from us in their type of experience and in the manner of their service.

You remember the rule of loyalty: "So serve your cause that if possible through your service everybody whom you influence shall be rendered a more devoted servant of his own cause, and thereby of the cause of causes—the unity of all the loyal." Now the rule for using the invisible church as a source of insight is this: "So be prepared to interpret, and sympathetically to comprehend, the causes and the service of other men, that whoever serves the cause of causes, the unity of all the loyal, may even thereby tend to help you in your personal service of your own special cause." To cultivate the comprehension and the reverence for loyalty, however, and wherever loyalty may be found, is to prepare yourself for a fitting communion with the invisible church.

And in such communion I find the crowning source of religious insight. What I say is wholly consistent then with the recognition of the preciousness of the visible church to its members. Once more, however, I point out the fact that the visible church is as precious as it is because it is indeed devoted to the unity of the spirit, that is, because it is a part and an organ of the invisible church.

V

I cannot close this extremely imperfect sketch of our crowning source of insight without applying to our present doctrine of the invisible church, the eternally true teaching of St. Paul regarding spiritual gifts.

As Paul's Corinthians, in their little community, faced the problem of the diversity of the gifts and powers whereby their various members undertook to serve the common cause—as this diversity of gifts tended from the outset to doctrinal differences of opinion, as the differences threatened to confuse loyalty by bringing brethren into conflict—even so, but with immeasurably vaster complications, the whole religious world, the invisible community of the loyal, has always faced, and still faces, a diversity of powers and of forms of insight, a diversity due to the endlessly various temperaments, capacities and sorts and conditions of men. The Corinthian church, as Paul sketched its situation, was a miniature of religious humanity. All the ways that the loyal follow lead upward to the realm of the spirit, where reason is at once the overarching heaven and the all-vitalising devotion which binds every loyal individual to the master of life. But in our universe the one demands the many. The infinite becomes incarnate through the finite. The paths that lead the loyal to the knowledge of the eternal pass for our vision, with manifold crossings and with perplexing wanderings, through the wilderness of this present world. The divine life is won through suffering. And religious history is a tale of suffering—of mutual misunderstanding amongst brethren who have from moment to moment been able to remember God only by narrowly misreading the hearts of their brethren. The diversity of spiritual gifts has developed, in religious history, an endless war of factions. The invisible church has frequently come to consciousness in the form of sects that say: "Ours alone is the true spiritual gift. Through our triumph alone is the world to be saved. Man will reach salvation only when our own Jerusalem is the universally recognised holy city."

Now it is useless to reduce the many to the one merely by wiping out the many. It is useless to make some new sect whose creed shall be that there are to be no sects. *The unity of the visible church, under any one creed,*

*or with any one settled system of religious practices, is an unattainable and
undesirable ideal.* The varieties of religious experience in James's sense of
that term are endless. The diversity of gifts is as great as is the diversity of
strong and loyal personalities. What St. Paul saw, in the miniature case presented to him by the Corinthian church, was that all the real gifts, and all
the consequently inevitable differences of approach to the religious problems, and all the differences of individual religious insight were necessary
to a wealthy religious life, and might serve the unity of the spirit, if only
they were conceived and used subject to the spiritual gift which he defined
as Charity.

Now the Pauline Charity is simply *that* form of loyalty which should
characterise a company of brethren who already have recognised their
brotherhood, who consciously know that their cause is one and that the spirit
which they serve is one. For such brethren, loyalty naturally takes the form
of a self-surrender that need not seek its own, or assert itself vehemently,
because the visible unity of the community in question is already acknowledged by all the faithful present, so that each intends to edify, not himself
alone, but his brethren, and also intends not to convert his brother to a new
faith, but to establish him in a faith already recognised by the community.
Yet since the Corinthians, warring over their diversity of gifts, had come
to lose sight of the common spirit, Paul simply recalls them to their flag,
by his poem of charity, which is also a technically true statement of how
the principle of loyalty applies to a brotherhood fully conscious of its common aim.

But the very intimacy of the Pauline picture of charity makes it hard
to apply this account of the loyalty that should reign within a religious family to the problems of a world where faith does not understand faith, where
the contrasts of opinion seem to the men in question to exclude community
of the spirit, where the fighting blood even of saintly souls is stirred by
persecutions or heated by a hatred of seemingly false creeds. And Paul himself could not speak in the language of charity, either when he referred to
those whom he called "false brethren" or characterised the Hellenic-Ro-
man spiritual world to whose thought and spirit he owed so much. As the
Corinthians, warring over the spiritual gifts, were a miniature representation of the motives that have led to religious wars, so St. Paul's own failure
to speak with charity as soon as certain matters of controversy arose in his
mind, shows in miniature the difficulty that the visible church, in all its
forms, has had to unite loyal strenuousness of devotion to the truth that one
sees with tolerance for the faiths whose meaning one cannot understand.

And yet, what Paul said about charity must be universalised if it is true.
When we universalise the Pauline Charity, it becomes once more the loyalty
that, as a fact, is now justified in seeking her loyal own; but that still, like

charity, rejoices in the truth. Such loyalty loves loyalty even when race or creed distinctions make it hard or impossible for us to feel fond of the persons and practices and opinions whereby our more distant brethren embody their spiritual gifts. Such loyalty is tolerant. Tolerance is what charity becomes when we have to deal with those whose special cause we just now cannot understand. Loyalty is tolerant, *not* as if truth were indifferent, or as if there were no contrast between worldliness and spirituality, but is tolerant precisely in so far as the best service of loyalty and of religion and of the unity of the spirit consists in helping our brethren not to our own, but to *their* own. *Such loyalty implies genuine faith in the abiding and supreme unity of the spirit.*

Only by thus universalising the doctrine which Paul preached to the Corinthians can we be prepared to use to the full this crowning source of insight—the doctrine, the example, the life, the inspiration, which is embodied in the countless forms and expressions of the invisible church.

The work of the invisible church—it is just that work to which all these lectures have been directing your attention. The sources of insight are themselves the working of its spirit in our spirits.

If I have done anything (however unworthy) to open the minds of any of you to these workings, my fragmentary efforts will not have been in vain. I have no authority to determine your own insight. Seek insight where it is to be found.

The Problem of Christianity

THE IDEA OF THE UNIVERSAL COMMUNITY*

In accordance with the plan set forth at the close of our first lecture, we begin our study of the Problem of Christianity by a discussion of the Christian idea of the Church, and of its universal mission.

I

The Kingdom of Heaven, as characterized in the Sermon on the Mount and in the parables, is something that promises to the individual man salvation, and that also possesses, in some sense which the Master left for the future to make clearer, a social meaning. To the individual the doctrine says, "The Kingdom of Heaven is within you." But when in the end the Kingdom shall come, the will of God, as we learn, is to be done on earth as it is in heaven. And therewith the kingdoms of this world the social order as it now is and as it naturally is—will pass away. Then there will come to pass the union of the blessed with their Father, and also, as appears, with one another, in the heavenly realm which the Father has prepared for them.

This final union of all who love is not described at length in the recorded words of the Master. A religious imagery familiar to those who heard the parables that deal with the end of the world was freely used; and this imagery gives us to understand that the consummation of all things will unite in a heavenly community those who are saved. But the organization, the administration, the ranks and dignities, of the Kingdom of Heaven the Master does not describe.

When the Christian Church began, in the Apostolic Age, to take visible form, the idea of the mission of the Church expressed the meaning which

---

*From *The Problem of Christianity* (New York: The Macmillan Co., 1913).

219

the Christian community came to attach to the social implications of the founder's doctrine. What was merely hinted in the parables now became explicit. The Kingdom of Heaven was to be realized in and through and for the Church,—in the fellowship of the faithful who constituted the Church as it was on earth; through the divine Spirit that was believed to guide the life of the Church; and for the future experience of the Church, whenever the end should come, and whenever the purpose of God should finally be manifested and accomplished.

Such, in brief, was the teaching of the early Christian community. Unquestionably this teaching added something new to the original doctrine of the Kingdom. But this addition, as we shall later see, was more characteristic of the new religion than was any portion of the sayings that tradition attributed to the Master, and was as inseparable from the essence of primitive Christianity as the belief of the disciples themselves was inseparable from their very earliest interpretations of the person and the mission of their leader.

It is useless, I think, for the most eager defender and expounder of primitive Christianity in its purity to ignore the fact that, whatever else the Christian religion involves, some sort of faith or doctrine regarding the office and the meaning of the Church was an essential part of the earliest Christianity that existed after the founder had passed from earth.

Since our problem of Christianity involves the study of the most vital Christian ideas, how can we better begin our task than by asking what this idea of the Church really means, and what value and truth it possesses? Not only is such a beginning indeed advisable, but, at first sight, it seems especially adapted to enable us to use the manifold and abundant aids which, as we might suppose, the aspirations of all Christian ages would furnish for our guidance.

For, as you may naturally ask, is not the history of Christianity, viewed in at least one very significant way, simply the history of the Christian Church? Is not the idea of the Church, then, not only essential and potent, but one of the most familiar of the religious ideas of Christendom? Must not the consciousness of all really awakened Christian communities whose creeds are recorded stand ready to help the inquirer who wants to interpret this idea? May we not then begin this part of our enterprise with high hope, sure that, as we attempt to grasp and to estimate this first of our three essential Christian ideas, we shall have the ages of Christian development as our helpers? So, I repeat, you may very naturally ask. But the answer to this question is not such as quite fulfils the hope just suggested.

II

As a fact, the idea and the doctrine of the Christian Church constitute indeed a vital and permanent part of Christianity; and a study of this idea is a necessity, and may properly be the first part of our inquiry into the Problem of Christianity.

But we must not begin this inquiry without a due sense of its difficulty. We must remember at the very outset the fact that all the Christian ages, up to the present one, unite, not to present to us any finished interpretation of the idea of the Church, but rather to prove that this idea is as fluent in its expression as it is universal in its aim; and is as baffling, by reason of the conflicts of its interpreters, as it is precious in the longings that constitute its very heart.

If this idea comforts the faithful, it is also a stern idea; for it demands of those who accept it the resolute will to face and to contend against the greatest of spiritual obstacles, namely, the combined waywardness of the religious caprices of all Christian mankind. For the true Church, as we shall see, is still a sort of ideal challenge to the faithful, rather than an already finished institution,—a call upon men for a heavenly quest, rather than a present possession of humanity. "Create me,"—this is the word that the Church, viewed as an idea, addresses to mankind.

Meanwhile the contrast between the letter and the spirit of a fundamental doctrine is nowhere more momentous and more tragic than in the case of the doctrine of the nature and the office of the Christian Church. The spirit of this doctrine consists, as we have already seen, in the assertion that there is a certain divinely ordained and divinely significant spiritual community, to which all must belong who are to attain the true goal of life; that is, all who, to use the distinctly religious phraseology, are to be saved.

How profoundly reasonable are the considerations upon which this doctrine is based we have yet to see, and can only estimate in the light of a due study of all the essential Christian ideas. To my own mind these considerations are such as can be interpreted and defended without our needing, for the purposes of such interpretation and defence, any acceptance of traditional dogmas. For these considerations are based upon human nature. They have to do with interests which all reasonable men, whether Christian or non-Christian, more or less clearly recognize, in proportion as men advance to the higher stages of the art of life.

The spirit, then, of the doctrine of the Church is as reasonable as it is universal. It is Christian by virtue of features which, when once understood, also render it simply and impressively human. This, I say, is what our entire study of the three Christian ideas will, in the end, if I am right, bring to our attention.

III

But the letter of the doctrine of the Church has been subject to fortunes such as, in various ways and degrees, attend the visible embodiment of all the great ideals of humanity; only that, as I have just said, the resulting tragedy is, in no other case in which spirit and letter are in conflict, greater than in this case.

In general the risks of temporary disaster which great ideals run appear to be directly proportioned to the value of the ideals. The disasters may be destined to give place to victory; but great truths bear long sorrows. What humanity most needs, it most persistently misunderstands. The spirit of a great ideal may be immortal; its ultimate victory, as we may venture to maintain, may be predetermined by the very nature of things; but that fact does not save such an ideal from the fires of the purgatory of time. Its very preciousness often seems to insure its repeated, its long-enduring, effacement. The comfort that it would bring if it were fully understood and accepted may make all the greater the sorrow of a world that still waits for the light.

In case of the history of the essential idea of the Church, the complications of dogma, the strifes of the sects, the horrors of the religious wars in former centuries, the confusions of controversy in our own day, must not make us despair. Such is the warfare of ideals. Such is this present world.

Least of all may we attempt, as many do, to accuse this or that special tendency or power in the actual Church, past or present, of being mainly responsible for this failure to appreciate the ideal Church. The defect lies deeper than students of such problems usually suppose. Human nature,—not any one party,—yes, the very nature of the processes of growth themselves, and not any particular form of religious or of moral error, must be viewed as the source of the principal tragedies of the history of all the Christian ideals.

In fact, the true idea of the Church has not been forsaken; it is, in a very real sense, still to be found, or rather, to be created. We have to do, in this case, not so much with apostasy as with evolution. To be sure, at the very outset, the ideal of the Church was seen afar off through a glass, darkly. The well-known apocalyptic vision revealed the true Church as the New Jerusalem that was yet to come down from heaven. The expression of the idea was left, by the early Church, as a task for the ages. The spirit of that idea was felt rather than ever adequately formulated, and the vision still remains one of the principal grounds and sources of the hope of humanity.

IV

Such doctrines, and such conflicts of spirit and letter, cannot be understood unless our historical sense is well awakened. On the other hand, they cannot be understood *merely* through a study of history. The values of ideals must be ideally discerned. If viewed without a careful and critical reflection, the history of such processes as the development of the idea of the Church presents a chaos of contending motives and factions. Apart from some understanding of history, all critical reflection upon this idea remains an unfruitful exercise in dialectics. We must therefore first divide our task, and then reunite the results, hoping thereby to win a connected view of the ideal that constitutes our present problem.

Let us, then, first point out certain motives which, when considered quite apart from any specifically Christian ideas or doctrines, may serve to make intelligible the ideal which is here in question. Then let us sketch the way in which the idea of the Christian Church first received expression.

This first expression of the idea of the Church, as we shall find, transformed the very teaching which it most eloquently reenforced and explained, namely, the teaching which the parables of the founder had left for the faith of the Christian community to interpret. This was the teaching about the office and the saving power of Christian love. For such, as we shall see, was the first result of the appearance of the idea of the Church in Christian history.

By sketching, then, some non-Christian developments and then a stage of early Christian life, we shall get two aspects of the ideal of the universal community before us. Hereby we shall not have reached any solution of our problem of Christianity; but we shall have brought together in our minds certain Christian and certain non-Christian ideas whose interrelations will hereafter prove to be of the utmost importance for our whole enterprise.

Next in order, then, comes a brief review of some of those motives which, apart from Christian history and Christian doctrine, make the ideal of the universal community a rationally significant ideal. These motives, in their turn, are of two kinds. Some of them are motives derived from the natural history of mankind. Some of them are distinctively ethical motives. We must become acquainted, through a very general summary, with both of these sorts of motives. Both sorts have interacted. The nature of man as a social being suggests certain ethical ideals. These ideals, in their turn, have modified the natural history of society.

V

As an essentially social being, man lives in communities, and depends upon his communities for all that makes his civilization articulate. His communities, as both Plato and Aristotle already observed, have a sort of organic life of their own, so that we can compare a highly developed community, such as a state, either to the soul of a man or to a living animal. A community is not a mere collection of individuals. It is a sort of live unit, that has organs, as the body of an individual has organs. A community grows or decays, is healthy or diseased, is young or aged, much as any individual member of the community possesses such characters. Each of the two, the community or the individual member, is as much a live creature as is the other. Not only does the community live, it has a mind of its own,—a mind whose psychology is not the same as the psychology of an individual human being. The social mind displays its psychological traits in its characteristic products,—in languages, in customs, in religions,— products which an individual human mind, or even a collection of such minds, when they are not somehow organized into a genuine community, cannot produce. Yet language, custom, religion are all of them genuinely mental products.

Communities, in their turn, tend, under certain conditions, to be organized into composite communities of still higher and higher grades. States are united in empires; languages cooperate in the production of universal literature; the corporate entities of many communities tend to organize that still very incomplete community which, if ever it comes into existence, will be the world-state, the community possessing the whole world's civilization.

So far, I have spoken only of the natural history of the social organization, and not of its value. But the history of thought shows how manifold are the ways in which, if once you grant that a community is or can be a living organic being, with a mind of its own, this doctrine about the natural facts can be used for ideal, for ethical, purposes. Few ideas have been, in fact, more fruitful than this one in their indirect consequences for ethical doctrines as well as for religion.

It is no wonder, then, that many object to every such interpretation of the nature of a community by declaring that, whatever our ethical ideals may demand, a community really has no mind of its own at all, and is no living organism. All the foregoing statements about the mind of a community (as such objectors insist) are metaphorical. A community is a collection of individuals. And the comparison of a community to an animal, or to a soul, is at best a convenient fiction.

Other critics, not so much simply rejecting the foregoing doctrine as hesitating, remark that to call a community an organism, and to speak of its possession of a mind, is to use some form of philosophical mysticism. And such mysticism, they say, stands, in any case, in need of further interpretation.

To such objectors I shall here only reply that one can maintain all the foregoing views regarding the real organic life and regarding the genuine mind of a community, without committing one's self to any form of philosophical mysticism, and without depending upon mere metaphors. For instance, Wundt, in his great book entitled "Völkerpsychologie," treats organized communities as psychical entities. He does so deliberately, and states his reasons. But he does all this purely as a psychologist. Communities, as he insists, behave as if they were wholes, and exhibit psychological laws of their own. Following Wundt, I have already said that it is the community which produces languages, customs, religions. These are, all of them, intelligent mental products, which can be psychologically analyzed, which follow psychological laws, and which exhibit characteristic processes of mental evolution,—processes that belong solely to organized groups of men. So Wundt speaks unhesitatingly of the *Gesammtbewusstsein,* or *Gesammtwille,* of a community; and he finds this mental life of the community to be as much an object for the student of the natural history of mind, as is the consciousness of any being whose life a psychologist can examine. His grounds are not mystical, but empirical,—if you will, pragmatic. A community behaves like an entity with a mind of its own. Therefore it is a fair "working hypothesis" for the psychologist to declare that it is such an entity, and that a community has, or is, a mind.

VI

So far, then, I have merely sketched what, in another context, will hereafter concern us much more at length. For in later lectures we shall have to study the metaphysical problems which we here first touch. A community can be viewed as a real unit. So we have seen, and so far only we have yet gone.

But we have now to indicate why this conception, whether metaphysically sound or not, is a conception that can be ethical in its purposes. And here again only the most elementary and fundamental aspects of our topic can be, in this wholly preparatory statement, mentioned. To all these problems we shall have later to return.

We have said that a community can behave like an unit; we have now to point out that an individual member of a community can find numerous very human motives for behaving towards his community as if it not only were an unit, but a very precious and worthy being. In particular he—the individual member—may love his community as if it were a person, may be devoted to it as if it were his friend or father, may serve it, may live and die for it, and may do all this, not because the philosophers tell him to do so, but because it is his own heart's desire to act thus.

Of such active attitudes of love and devotion towards a community, on the part of an individual member of that community, history and daily life present countless instances. One's family, one's circle of personal friends, one's home, one's village community, one's clan, or one's country may be the object of such an active disposition to love and to serve the community as an unit, to treat the community as if it were a sort of super-personal being, and as if it could, in its turn, possess the value of a person on some higher level. One who thus loves a community, regards its type of life, its form of being, as essentially more worthy than his own. He becomes devoted to its interests as to something that by its very nature is nobler than himself. In such a case he may find, in his devotion to his community, his fulfilment and his moral destiny. In order to view a community in this way it is, I again insist, not necessary to be a mystic. It is only necessary to be a hearty friend, or a good citizen, or a home-loving being.

Countless faithful and dutifully disposed souls, belonging to most various civilizations,—people active rather than fanciful, and earnest rather than speculative,—have in fact viewed their various communities in this way. I know of no better name for such a spirit of active devotion to the community to which the devoted individual belongs, than the excellent old word "Loyalty,"—a word to whose deeper meaning some Japanese thinkers have of late years recalled our attention.

Loyalty, as I have elsewhere defined it, is the willing and thoroughgoing devotion of a self to a cause, when the cause is something which unites many selves in one, and which is therefore the interest of a community. For a loyal human being the interest of the community to which he belongs is superior to every merely individual interest of his own. He actively devotes himself to this cause.[1]

Loyalty exists in very manifold shapes, and belongs to no one time, or country, or people. Warlike tribes and nations, during the stages of their life which are intermediate between savagery and civilization, have often developed a high type of the loyal consciousness, and hence have defined their virtues in terms of loyalty. Such loyalty may last over into peaceful stages of social life; and the warlike life is not the exclusive originator of the loyal spirit. Loyalty often enters into a close alliance with religion, and

---

1. See Lecture I of the "Philosophy of Loyalty" (New York, 1908).

from its very nature is disposed to religious interpretations. To the individual the loyal spirit appeals by fixing his attention upon a life incomparably vaster than his own individual life,—a life which, when his love for his community is once aroused, dominates and fascinates him by the relative steadiness, the strength and fixity and stately dignity, of its motives and demands.

The individual is naturally wayward and capricious. This waywardness is a constant source of entanglement and failure. But the community which he loves is rendered relatively constant in its will by its customs; yet these customs no longer seem, to the loyal individual, mere conventions or commands. For his social enthusiasm is awakened by the love of his kind; and he glories in his service, as the player in his team, or the soldier in his flag, or the martyr in his church. If his religion comes into touch with his loyalty, then his gods are the leaders of his community, and both the majesty and the harmony of the loyal life are thus increased. The loyal motives are thus not only moral, but also æsthetic. The community may be to the individual both beautiful and sublime.

Deep-seated, then, in human nature are the reasons that make loyalty appear to the individual as a solution for the problem of his personal life. Yet these motives tend to still higher and vaster conquests than we have here yet mentioned. Warlike tribes and nations fight together; and in so far loyalty contends with loyalty. But on a more highly self-conscious level the loyal spirit tends to assume the form of chivalry. The really devoted and considerate warrior learns to admire the loyalty of his foe; yes, even to depend upon it for some of his own best inspiration. Knighthood prizes the knightly spirit. The loyalty of the clansmen breeds by contagion a more intense loyalty in other clans; but at the same time it breeds a love for just such loyalty. Kindred clans learn to respect and, ere long, to share one another's loyalty. The result is an ethical motive that renders the alliance and, on occasion, the union of various clans and nationalities not only a possibility, but a conscious ideal.

The loyal are, in ideal, essentially kin. If they grow really wise, they observe this fact. The spirit that loves the community learns to prize itself as a spirit that, in all who are dominated by it, is essentially one, despite the variety of special causes, of nationalities, or of customs. The logical development of the loyal spirit is therefore the rise of a consciousness of the ideal of an universal community of the loyal,—a community which, despite all warfare and jealousy, and despite all varieties of gods and of laws, is supreme in its value, however remote from the present life of civilization.

The tendency towards the formation of such an ideal of an universal community can be traced both in the purely secular forms of loyalty, and in the history of the relations between loyalty and religion in the most varied civilizations. In brief, loyalty is, from the first, a practical faith that communities, viewed as units, have a value which is superior to all the values and interests of detached individuals. And the sort of loyalty which reaches the level of true chivalry and which loves the honor and the loyalty of the stranger or even of the foe, tends, either in company with or apart from any further religious motive, to lead men towards a conception of the brotherhood of all the loyal, and towards an estimation of all the values of life in terms of their relation to the service of one ideally universal community. To this community in ideal all men belong; and to act as if one were a member of such a community is to win in the highest measure the goal of individual life. It is to win what religion calls salvation.

When thus abstractly stated, the ideal of an universal community may appear far away from the ordinary practical interests of the plain man. But the history of the spirit of loyalty shows that there is a strong tendency of loyalty towards such universal ideals. Some such conception of the ideal community of all mankind, actually resulting from reflection upon the spirit of loyalty, received an occasional and imperfect formulation in Roman Stoicism. In this more speculative shape the Stoic conception of the universal community was indeed not fitted to win over the Roman world as a whole to an active loyalty to the cause of mankind.

Yet the conception of universal loyalty, as devotion to the unity of an ideal community, a community whereof all loyal men should be members, has not been left merely to the Stoics, nor yet to any other philosophers to formulate. The conception of loyalty both springs from practical interests and tends of itself, apart from speculation, towards the enlargement of the ideal community of the loyal in the direction of identifying that community with all mankind. The history of the ideals and of the religion of Israel, from the Song of Deborah to the prophets, is a classic instance of the process here in question.

VII

We have thus indicated some of the fundamentally human motives which the ideal of the universal community expresses. We have next to turn in a wholly different direction and to remind ourselves of the way in which this ideal found its place in the early history of the Christian Church.

I cannot better introduce this part of my discussion than by calling attention to a certain contrast between the reported teaching of the Master regarding the Kingdom of Heaven, and some of the best-known doctrines of the Apostle Paul. This contrast is as obvious and as familiar as it has been neglected by students of the philosophy of Christianity. Every word that I can say about it is old. Yet a survey of the whole matter is not common, and I believe that this contrast has never more demanded a clear restatement than it does to-day.

The particular contrast which I here have in mind is *not* the one which both the apologists and the critics of Pauline Christianity usually emphasize. It is a contrast which does not directly relate to Paul's doctrine of the person and mission of Christ; and nevertheless it is a contrast that bears upon the very core of the Gospel. For it is a contrast that has to do with the doctrine about the nature, the office, the saving power of Christian love itself. I say that just this contrast between Paul's doctrine and the teachings of Jesus, although perfectly familiar, has been neglected by students of our problem. Let me briefly show what I have in mind.

The best-known and, for multitudes, the most directly moving of the words which tradition attributes to Jesus, describe the duty of man, the essence of religion, and the Kingdom of Heaven itself, in terms of the conception of Christian love. I have not here either the time or the power adequately to expound this the chief amongst the doctrines which tradition ascribes directly to Jesus. I must pass over what countless loving and fit teachers have made so familiar. Yet I must remind you of two features of Christ's doctrine of love which at this point especially concern our own enterprise.

First, it is needful for me to point out that, despite certain stubborn and widespread misunderstandings, the Christian doctrine of love, as that doctrine appears in the parables and in the Sermon on the Mount, involves and emphasizes a very positive and active and heroic attitude towards life, and is not, as some have supposed, a negative doctrine of passive self-surrender. And secondly, I must also bring to your attention the fact that the Master's teaching about love leaves unsolved certain practical problems, problems which this very heroism and this positive tendency of the doctrine make by contrast all the more striking.

These unsolved problems of the reported teaching of Jesus about love seem to have been deliberately brought before us by the Master, and as deliberately left unsolved. The way was thus opened for a further development of what the Master chose to teach. And such further development was presumably a part of what the founder more or less consciously foresaw and intended.

The grain of mustard seed—so his faith assured him—must grow. To that end it was planted. Now a part of the new growth, a contribution to the treatment of the problems which the original teaching about love left unsolved, was, in the sequel, due to Paul. This sequel, whether the Master foresaw it or not, is as important for the further office of Christianity as the original teaching was an indispensable beginning of the process. Jesus awaited in trust a further revelation of the Father's mind. Such a new light came in due season.

Two features, then, of the doctrine of love as taught by Jesus,—its impressively positive and active character, and the mystery of its unsolved problems,—these two we must next emphasize. Then we shall be ready to take note of a further matter which also concerns us,—namely, Paul's new contribution to the solution of the very problems concerning love which the parables and the sayings of Jesus had left unsolved. This new contribution,—Paul himself conceived not as his own personal invention. For he held that the new teaching was due to the spirit of his risen and ascended Lord. What concerns us is that Paul's additional thought was a critical influence in determining both the evolution and the permanent meaning of Christianity.

VIII

The love which Jesus preached has often been misunderstood. Critics, as well as mistaken friends of the Master's teachings, have supposed Christian love to be more or less completely identical with self-abnegation,— with the amiably negative virtue of one who, as the misleading modern phrase expresses the matter, "has no thought of self." Another modern expression, also misleading, is used by some who identify Christian love with so-called "pure altruism." The ideal Christian, as such people interpret his virtue, "lives wholly for others." That is what is meant by the spirit which resists not evil, which turns the other cheek to the smiter, which forgives, and pities, and which abandons all worldly goods.

Now, against such misunderstandings, many of the wiser expounders of Christian doctrine, both in former times and in our own, have taken pains to show that love, as the Jesus of the sayings and of the parables conceived it, does *not* consist in mere self-abnegation, and is not identical with pure altruism, and is both heroic and positive. The feature of the Master's doctrine of love which renders this more positive and heroic interpretation of the sayings inevitable, is the familiar reason which is laid at the basis of his whole teaching. One is to love one's neighbor because God himself, as Father, divinely loves and prizes each individual man. Hence the individual man has an essentially infinite value, although he has this value only in and through his relation to God, and because of God's love for him. Therefore mere self-abnegation cannot be the central virtue. For the Jesus of the sayings not only rejoices in the divine love whereof every man is the object, but also invites every man to rejoice in the consciousness of this very love, and to delight also in all men, since they are God's beloved. The man whom this love of God is to transform into a perfect lover cannot henceforth merely forget or abandon the self. The parable of the servant who, although himself forgiven by his Lord, will not forgive his fellow-servant, shows indeed how worthless self-assertion is when separated from a sense that all are equally dependent upon God's love. But the parable of the talents shows with equal clearness how stern the demands of the divine love are in requiring the individual to find a perfectly positive expression of the unique value which it is his office, and his alone, to return to his Lord with usury. Every man, this self included, has just such an unique value, and must be so viewed. Hence the sayings are full of calls to self-expression, and so to heroism. Love is divine; and therefore it includes an assertion of its own divinity; and therefore it can never be mere self-abnegation. Christian altruism never takes the form of saying, "I myself ought to be or become nothing; while only the others are to be served and saved." For the God who loves me demands not that I should be nothing, but that I should be his own. Love is never merely an amiable tolerance of whatever form human frailty and folly may take. To be sure, the lover, as Jesus depicts him, resists not evil, and turns his cheek to the smiter. Yes, but he does this with full confidence that God sees all and will vindicate his servant. The lover vividly anticipates the positive triumph of all the righteous; and so his love for even the least of the little ones is, in anticipation, an active and strenuous sharing in the final victory of God's will. His very non-resistance is therefore inspired by a divine contempt for the powers of evil. Why should one resist who always has on his side and in his favor the power that is irresistible, that loves him, and that will triumph even through his weakness?

Such a spirit renders pity much more than a mere absorption in attempting to relieve the misery of others. Sympathy for the sufferer, as the sayings of Jesus depict it, is but an especially pathetic illustration of one's serene confidence that the Father who cares for all triumphs over all evil, so that when we feel pity and act pitifully, we take part in this divine triumph. Hence pity is no mere tenderness. It is a sharing in the victory that overcomes the world.

Such, then, in brief, is the doctrine of Christian love as the sayings and the parables contain it,—a doctrine as positive and strenuous as it is humane, and as it is sure of the Father's good will and overruling power. So far I indeed merely remind you of what all the wiser expounders of Christian doctrine, whatever their theology or their disagreements, have, on the whole, and despite popular misunderstandings, agreed in recognizing. And hereupon you might well be disposed to ask: Is not this, in spirit and in essence, the deepest meaning,—yes, is it not really the whole of Christianity? What did Paul do, what could he do, when he spoke of love, but repeat this, the Master's doctrine?

IX

In answer to this question, we must next note that, over against this clear and positive definition of the spiritual attitude that Jesus attributes to the Christian lover, there stand certain problems which come to mind when we ask for more precise directions regarding what the lover is to do for the object of his love. Love is concerned not only with the lover's inner inspiration, but with the services that he is to perform for the beloved. Now, in the world in which the teaching of Jesus places the Christian lover, love has two objects,—God and one's neighbor. What is one to do in order to express one's love for each of these objects?

So far as concerns the lover's relation to God, the answer is clear, and is stated wholly in religious terms. Purity of heart in loving, perfect sincerity and complete devotion, the heroism of spirit just described,—these, with complete trust in God, with utter submission to the Father's will,—these are the services that the lover can render to God. In these there is no merit; for they are as nothing in comparison with one's debt to the Father. But they are required. And in so far the doctrine of love is made explicit and the rule of righteousness is definite.

But now let us return to the relation of love to the services that one is to offer to one's neighbor. What can the lover,—in so far as Jesus describes his task,—what can he do for his fellow-man?

To this question it is, indeed, possible to give one answer which clearly defines a duty to the neighbor; and this duty is emphasized throughout the teaching of Jesus. This duty is the requirement to use all fitting means,— example, precept, kindliness, non-resistance, heroism, patience, courage, strenuousness,—all means that tend to make the neighbor himself one of the lovers. The first duty of love is to produce love, to nourish it, to extend the Kingdom of Heaven by teaching love to all men. And *this* service to one's neighbor is a clearly definable service. And so far the love of the neighbor involves no unsolved problems.

But in sharp contrast with this aspect of the doctrine of love stands another aspect, which is indeed problematic. In addition to the extension of the loving spirit through example and precept, the lover of his neighbor has on his hands the whole problem of humane and benevolent practical activity,—the problem of the positively philanthropic life.

The doctrine of love,—so positive, so active, so resolute in its inmost spirit,—might naturally be expected to give in detail counsel regarding what to do for the personal needs of the lover's fellow-man. But, at this point, we indeed meet the more baffling side of the doctrine of love. Jesus has no system of rules to expound for guiding the single acts of the philanthropic life. Apart from insisting upon the loving spirit, apart from the one rule to extend the Kingdom of Heaven and to propagate this spirit of love among men, the Master leaves the practical decisions of the lover to be guided by loving instinct rather than by a conscious doctrine regarding what sort of special good one can do to one's neighbor.

Thus the original doctrine of love, as taught in the parables, involves no definite programme for social reform, and leaves us in the presence of countless unsolved practical issues. This is plainly a deliberate limitation to which the Master chose to subject his explanations about love.

Jesus tells us of many conditions that appear necessary to the practical living of the life of love for one's neighbor. But when we ask: Are these conditions not only necessary but sufficient? we are often left in doubt. Love relieves manifest suffering, when it can; love feeds the hungry, clothes the naked;—in brief, love seems, at first sight, simply to offer to the beloved neighbor whatever that neighbor himself most desires. It is easy to interpret the golden rule in this simple way. Yet we know, and the author of the parables well knows and often tells us, that the natural man desires many things that he ought not to desire and that love ought not to give him. Since the life is more than meat, it also follows that feeding the hungry and clothing the naked are not acts which really supply what man most needs. The natural man does not know his own true needs. Hence the golden rule does not tell us in detail what to do for him, but simply expresses the spirit of love. What is sure about love is that it indeed unites the lover, in spirit, to God's will. What constitutes, in this present world, the pathos, the tragedy of love, is that, because our neighbor is so mysterious a being to our imperfect vision, we do not now know how to make him happy, to relieve his deepest distresses, to do him the highest good; so that most loving acts, such as giving the cup of cold water, and helping the sufferer who has fallen by the wayside, seem, to our more thoughtful moods, to be mere symbols of what love would do if it could,—mere hints of the active life that love would lead if it were directly and fully guided by the Father's wisdom.

Modern philanthropy has learned to develop a technically clearer consciousness about this problem of effective benevolence, and has made familiar the distinction between loving one's neighbor, and finding out how to be practically useful in meeting the neighbor's needs. Hence, sometimes, the modern mind wonders how to apply the spirit of the parables to our special problems of benevolence, and questions whether, and in what sense, the original Gospel furnishes guidance for our own modern social consciousness.

The problems thus barely suggested are indeed in a sense answered, so far as the originally reported teaching of Jesus is concerned, but are answered by a consideration which awakens a new call for further interpretation. The parables and the Sermon on the Mount emphasize, in the present connection, two things: First, that it is indeed the business of every lover of his neighbor to help other men by rendering them also lovers; and secondly that, as to other matters, one who tries to help his neighbor must leave to God, to the all-loving Father, the care for the true and final good of the neighbor whom one loves. Since the judgment day is near, in the belief of Jesus and of his hearers, since the final victory of the Kingdom will erelong be miraculously manifested, the lover, so Jesus seems to hold, can wait. It is his task to use his talent as he can, to be ready for his Lord's appearance, and to be strenuous in the spirit of love. But the God who cares for the sparrows will care for the success of love.

It is simply not the lover's task to set this present world right; it is his only to act in the spirit that is the Father's spirit, and that, when revealed and triumphant, at the judgment day, will set all things right. In this way the heroism of the ideal of the Kingdom is perfectly compatible, in the parables, with an attitude of resignation with regard to the means whereby the ideal is to be accomplished. Serene faith as to the result, strenuousness as to the act, whatever it is, which the loving spirit just now prompts: this is the teaching of the parables.

I have said that the world of the parables contains two beings to whom Christian love is owed: God and the neighbor. Both, as you now see, are mysterious. The serene faith of the Master sets one mystery side by side with the other, bids the disciple lay aside all curious peering into what is not yet revealed to the loving soul, and leaves to the near future,—to the coming end of the world,—the lifting of all veils and the reconciliation of all conflicts.

X

Such, then, are the problems of the doctrine of love which the Master brings to light, but does not answer. Our next question is: What does Paul contribute to this doctrine of love?

Paul indeed repeated many of his Master's words concerning love; and he everywhere is in full agreement with their spirit. And yet this agreement is accompanied by a perfectly inevitable further development of the doctrine of Christian love,—a development which is due to the fact that into the world of Paul's religious life and teaching there has entered, not only a new experience, but a new sort of being,—a real object whereof the Master had not made explicit mention.

God and the neighbor are beings whose general type religion and common sense had made familiar long before Jesus taught, mysterious though God and one's neighbor were to the founder's hearers, and still remain to ourselves. Both of them are conceived by the religious consciousness of the parables as personal beings, and as individuals. God is the supreme ruler who, as Christ conceives him, is also an individual person, and who loves and wills. The neighbor is the concrete human being of daily life.

But the new, the third being, in Paul's religious world, seems to the Apostle himself novel in its type, and seems to him to possess a nature involving what he more than once calls a "mystery." To express, so far as he may, this "mystery," he uses characteristic metaphors, which have become classic.

This new being is a corporate entity,—the body of Christ, or the body of which the now divinely exalted Christ is the head. Of this body the exalted Christ is also, for Paul, the spirit and also, in some new sense, the lover. This corporate entity is the Christian community itself.

Perfectly familiar is the fact that the existence and the idea of this community constitute a new beginning in the evolution of Christianity. But neglected, as I think and as I have just asserted, is the subtle and momentous transformation, the great development which this new motive brings to pass in the Pauline form of the doctrine of Christian love.

What most interests us here, and what is least generally understood, I think, by students of the problem of Christianity, is the fact that this new entity, this corporate sort of reality which Paul so emphasizes, this being which is not an individual man but a community, does not, as one might suppose, render the Apostle's doctrine of love more abstract, more remote from human life, less direct and less moving, than was the original doctrine of love in the parables. On the contrary, the new element makes the doctrine of love more concrete, and, as I must insist, really less mysterious. In speaking of this corporate entity, the Apostle uses metaphors, and knows that they are metaphors; but, despite what the Apostle calls the new "mystery," these metaphors explain much that the parables left doubtful. These metaphors do not hide, as the Master, in using the form of the parable, occasionally intended for the time to hide from those who were not yet ready for the full revelation, truths which the future was to make clearer to the disciples. No, Paul's metaphors regarding the community of the faithful in the Church bring the first readers of Paul's epistles into direct contact with the problems of their own daily religious life.

The corporate entity—the Christian community—proves to be, for Paul's religious consciousness, something more concrete than is the individual fellow-man. The question: Who is my neighbor? had been answered by the Master by means of the parable of the Good Samaritan. But that question itself had not been due merely to the hardness of heart of the lawyer who asked it. The problem of the neighbor actually involves mysteries which, as we have already seen and hereafter shall still further see, the parables deliberately leave, along with the conception of the Kingdom of Heaven itself, to be made clearer only when the new revelation, for which the parables are preparing the way, shall have been granted. Now Paul feels himself to be in possession of a very precious part of this further revelation. He has discovered, in his own experience as Apostle, a truth that he feels to be new. He believes this truth to be a revelation due to the spirit of his Lord.

In fact, the Apostle has discovered a special instance of one of the most significant of all moral and religious truths, the truth that a community, when unified by an active indwelling purpose, is an entity more concrete and, in fact, less mysterious than is any individual man, and that such a community can love and be loved as a husband and wife love; or as father or mother love.

Because the particular corporate entity whose cause Paul represents, namely, the Christian community, is in his own experience something new, whose origin he views as wholly miraculous, whose beginnings and whose daily life are bound up with the influence which he believes to be due to the spirit of his risen and ascended Lord, Paul indeed regards the Church as a "mystery." But, as a fact, his whole doctrine regarding the community has a practical concreteness, a clear common sense about it, such that he is able to restate the doctrine of Christian love so as to be fully just to all its active heroism, while interpreting much which the parables left problematic.

XI

What can I do for my neighbor's good? The parables had answered: "Love him, help him in his obvious and bitter needs, teach him the spirit of love, and leave the rest to God." Does Paul make light of this teaching? On the contrary, his hymn in honor of love, in the first epistle to the Corinthians, is one of Christianity's principal treasures. Nowhere is the real consequence of the teaching of Jesus regarding love more completely stated. But notice this difference: For Paul the neighbor has now become a being who is primarily the fellow-member of the Christian community.

The Christian community is itself something visible; miraculously guided by the Master's spirit. It is at once for the Apostle a fact of present experience and a divine creation. And therefore every word about love for the neighbor is in the Apostle's teaching at once perfectly direct and human in its effectiveness and is nevertheless dominated by the spirit of a new and, as Paul believes, a divinely inspired love for the community.

Both the neighbor and the lover of the neighbor to whom the Apostle appeals are, to his mind, members of the body of Christ; and all the value of each man as an individual is bound up with his membership in this body, and with his love for the community.

Jesus had taught that God loves the neighbor,—yes, even the least of these little ones. Paul says to the Ephesians: "Christ loved the church, and gave himself up for it, that he might sanctify it; . . . that he might present the church to himself a glorious church, not having spot: . . . but that it should be holy and without blemish." One sees: The object of the divine love, as Paul conceives it, has been at once transformed and fulfilled.

In God's love for the neighbor, the parables find the proof of the infinite worth of the individual. In Christ's love for the Church Paul finds the proof that both the community, and the individual member, are the objects of an infinite concern, which glorifies them both, and thereby unites them. The member finds his salvation only in union with the Church. He, the member, would be dead without the divine spirit and without the community. But the Christ whose community this is, has given life to the members,—the life of the Church, and of Christ himself. "You hath he quickened, which were dead in trespasses and sins."

In sum: Christian love, as Paul conceives it, takes on the form of Loyalty. This is Paul's simple but vast transformation of Christian love.

Loyalty itself was, in the history of humanity, already, at that time, ancient. It had existed in all tribes and peoples that knew what it was for the individual so to love his community as to glory in living and dying for that community. To conceive virtue as faithfulness to one's community, was, in so far, no new thing. Loyalty, moreover, had long tended towards a disposition to enlarge both itself and its community. As the world had come together, it had gradually become possible for philosophers, such as the later Stoics, to conceive of all humanity as in ideal one community.

Although this was so far a too abstract conception to conquer the world of contending powers, the spirit of loyalty was also not without its religious relationships, and tended, as religion tended, to make the moral realm appear, not only a world of human communities, but a world of divinely ordained unity. Meanwhile, upon every stage, long before the Christian virtues were conceived, loyalty had inspired nations of warriors with the sternest of their ideals of heroism, and with their noblest visions of the destiny of the individual. And the prophets of Israel had indeed conceived the

Israel of God's ultimate triumph as a community in and through which all men should know God and be blessed.

But in Paul's teaching, loyalty, quickened to new life, not merely by hope, but by the presence of a community in whose meetings the divine spirit seemed to be daily working fresh wonders, keeps indeed its natural relation to the militant virtues, is heroic and strenuous, and delights to use metaphors derived from the soldier's life. It appears also as the virtue of those who love order, and who prefer law to anarchy, and who respect worldly authority. And it derives its religious ideas from the prophets.

But it also becomes the fulfilment of what Jesus had taught in the parables concerning love. For the Apostle, this loyalty unites to all these stern and orderly and militant traits, and to all that the prophets had dreamed about Israel's triumph, the tenderness of a brother's love for the individual brother. Consequently, in Paul's mind, love for the individual human being, and loyalty to the divine community of all the faithful; graciousness of sentiment, and orderliness of discipline; are so directly interwoven that each interprets and glorifies the other.

If the Corinthians unlovingly contend, brother with brother, concerning their gifts, Paul tells them about the body of Christ, and about the divine unity of its spirit in all the diversity of its members and of their powers. On the other hand, if it is loyalty to the Church which is to be interpreted and revivified, Paul pictures the dignity of the spiritual community in terms of the direct beauty and sweetness and tenderness of the love of brother for brother,—that love which seeketh not her own.

The perfect union of this inspired passion for the community, with this tender fondness for individuals, is at once the secret of the Apostle's power as a missionary and the heart of his new doctrine. Of loyalty to the spirit and to the body of Christ, he discourses in his most abstruse as well as in his most eloquent passages. But his letters close with the well-known winning and tender messages to and about individual members and about their intimate personal concerns.

As to the question: "What shall I do for my brother?" Paul has no occasion to answer that question *except* in terms of the brother's relations to the community. But just for that reason his counsels can be as concrete and definite as each individual case requires them to be. Because the community, as Paul conceives it,—the small community of a Pauline church,— keeps all its members in touch with one another; because its harmony is preserved through definite plans for setting aside the differences that arise amongst individuals; because, by reason of the social life of the whole, the physical needs, the perils, the work, the prosperity of the individual are all made obvious facts of the common experience of the church, and are all just as obviously and definitely related to the health of the whole body,—Paul's gospel of love has constant and concrete practical applications to the life of those whom he addresses. The ideal of the parables has become a visible life on earth. So live together that the Church may be worthy of Christ who loves it, so help the individual brother that he may be a fitting member of the Church. Such are now the counsels of love.

All this teaching of Paul was accompanied, of course, in the Apostle's own mind, by the unquestioning assurance that this community of the Christian faith, as he knew it and in his letters addressed its various representatives, was indeed a genuinely universal community. It was already, to his mind, what the prophets had predicted when they spoke of the redeemed Israel. By the grace of God, all men belonged to this community, or would soon belong to it, whom God was pleased to save at all.

For the end of the world was very soon to come, and would manifest its membership, its divine head, and its completed mission. According to Paul's expectation, there was to be no long striving towards an ideal that in time was remote. He dealt with the interests of all mankind. But his faith brought him into direct contact with the institution that represented this world-wide interest. What loyalty on its highest levels has repeatedly been privileged to imagine as the ideal brotherhood of all who are loyal, Paul found directly presented, in his religious experience, as his own knowledge of his Master's purpose, and of its imminent fulfilment.

This vision began to come to Paul when he was called to be an apostle; and later, when he was sent to the Gentiles, the ideal grew constantly nearer and clearer. The Church was, for Paul, the very presence of his Lord.

Such, then, was the first highly developed Christian conception of the universal community. That which the deepest and highest rational interests of humanity make most desirable for all men, and that which the prophets of Israel had predicted afar off, the religious experience of Paul brought before his eyes as the daily work of the spirit in the Church. Was not Christ present whenever the faithful were assembled? Was not the spirit living in their midst? Was not the day of the Lord at hand? Would not they all soon be changed, when the last trumpet should sound?

Our sketch, thus far, of the spirit of the ideal of the universal community, solves none of our problems. But it helps to define them. This, the first of our three essential ideas of Christianity, is the idea of a spiritual life in which universal love for all individuals shall be completely blended, practically harmonized, with an absolute loyalty for a real and universal community. God, the neighbor, and the one church: These three are for Paul the objects of Christian love and the inspiration of the life of love.

Paul's expectations of the coming judgment were not realized. Those little apostolic churches, where the spirit daily manifested itself, gave place to the historical church of the later centuries, whose possession of the spirit has often been a matter of dogma rather than of life, and whose unity has been so often lost to human view. The letter has hidden the spirit. The Lord has delayed his coming. The New Jerusalem, adorned as a bride for her husband, remains hidden behind the heavens. The vision has become the Problem of Christianity.

Our sketch has been meant merely to help us towards a further definition of this problem. To such a definition our later lectures must attempt still further to contribute. We have a hint of the sources of the first of our three essential ideas of Christianity. We have still to consider what is the truth of this idea. And in order to move towards an answer to this question, we shall be obliged, in our immediately subsequent lectures, to attempt a formulation of the two other essential ideas of Christianity named in our introductory statement.

THE MORAL BURDEN OF THE INDIVIDUAL

"All things excellent," says Spinoza, "are as difficult as they are rare"; and Spinoza's word here repeats a lesson that nearly all of the world's religious and moral teachers agree in emphasizing. Whether such a guide speaks simply of "excellence," or uses the distinctively religious phraseology and tells us about the way to "salvation," he is sure, if he is wise, to recognize, and on occasion to say, that whoever is to win the highest goal must first learn to bear a heavy burden. It also belongs to the common lore of the sages to teach that this burden is much more due to the defects of our human nature than to the hostility of fortune. "We ourselves make our time short for our task": such comments are as trite as they are well founded in the facts of life.

I

But among the essential ideas of Christianity, there is one which goes beyond this common doctrine of the serious-minded guides of humanity. For this idea defines the moral burden, to which the individual who seeks salvation is subject, in so grave a fashion that many lovers of mankind, and, in particular, many modern minds, have been led to declare that so much of Christian doctrine, at least in the forms in which it is usually stated, is an unreasonable and untrue feature of the faith. This idea I stated at the close of our first lecture, side by side with the two other ideas of Christianity which I propose, in these lectures, to discuss. The idea of the Church,—of the universal community,—which was our topic in the second lecture, is expressed by the assertion that there is a real and divinely significant spiritual community to which all must belong who are to win the true goal of life. The idea of the moral burden of the individual is expressed by maintaining that (as I ventured to state this idea in my own words): "The individual human being is by nature subject to some overwhelming moral burden from which, if unaided, he cannot escape. Both because of what has technically been called original sin, and because of the sins that he himself has committed, the individual is doomed to a spiritual ruin from which only a divine intervention can save him."

This doctrine constitutes the second of the three Christian ideas that I propose to discuss. I must take it up in the present lecture.

II

To this mode of continuing our discussion you may object that our second lecture left the idea of the Church very incompletely stated, and, in many most important respects, also left that idea uninterpreted, uncriticised, and not yet brought into any clear relation with the creed of the modern man. Is it well, you may ask, to discuss a second one of the Christian ideas, when the first has not yet been sufficiently defined?

I answer that the three Christian ideas which we have chosen for our inquiry are so closely related that each throws light upon the others, and in turn receives light from them. Each of these ideas needs, in some convenient order, to be so stated and so illustrated, and then so made the topic of a thoughtful reflection, that we shall hereby learn: First, about the basis of this idea in human nature; secondly, about its value,—its ethical significance as an interpretation of life; and thirdly, about its truth, and about its relation to the real world. At the close of our survey of the three ideas, we shall bring them together, and thus form some general notion of what is essential to the Christian doctrine of life viewed as a whole. We shall at the same time be able to define the way in which this Christian doctrine of life expresses certain actual needs of men, and undertakes to meet these needs. We shall then have grounds for estimating the ethical and religious value of the connected whole of the doctrines in question.

There will then remain the hardest part of our task: the study of the relation of these Christian ideas to the real world. So far as we are concerned, this last part of our investigation will involve, in the main, metaphysical problems; and the closing lectures of our course will therefore contain an outline of the metaphysics of Christianity, culminating in a return to the problems of the modern man.

Such is our task. On the way toward our goal we must be content, for a time, with fragmentary views. They will, ere long, come into a certain unity with one another; but for that unity we must wait, until each idea has had its own partial and preliminary presentation.

Of the idea of the universal community we have learned, thus far, two things, and no more. First, we have seen that this idea has a broad psychological basis in the social nature of mankind, while it gets its ethical value from its relations to the interests and needs of all those of any time or nation who have learned what is the deeper meaning of loyalty. By loyalty, as you remember, I mean the thoroughgoing, practical, and loving devotion of a self to an united community.

Secondly, we have seen that, in addition to its general basis in human nature, this idea has its specifically Christian form. The significance of this form we have illustrated by the way in which the original doctrine of Christian love, as Jesus taught it in his sayings and parables, received not only an application, but also a new development in the consciousness of the apostolic churches, when the Apostle Paul experienced and moulded their life.

The synthesis of the Master's doctrine of love with the type of loyalty which the life of the spirit in the Church taught Paul to express, makes concrete and practical certain more mysterious aspects of the doctrine of love which the Master had taught in parables, but had left for a further revelation to define. And herewith the spirit of the Christian idea of the universal community entered, as a permanent possession, into the history of Christianity.

This preliminary study of the idea of the universal community leaves us with countless unsolved problems. But it at least shows us where some portion of our main problem lies. The dogmas of the historical Church concerning its own authority we have so far left, in our discussion, almost untouched. That the spirit and the letter of this first of our Christian ideas are still very far apart, all who love mankind, and who regard Christianity wisely, well know. We have not yet tried to show how spirit and letter are to be brought nearer together. It has not been my privilege to tell you where the true Church is to-day to be found. As a fact, I believe it still to be an invisible Church. And I readily admit that a disembodied idea does not meet all the interests of Christianity, and does not answer all the questions of the modern man.

But we have yet, in due time, to consider whether, and to what extent, the universal community is a reality. That is a problem, partly of dogma, partly of metaphysics. It is not my office to supply the modern man, or any one else, with a satisfactory system of dogmas. But I believe that philosophy has still something to say which is worth saying regarding the sense in which there really is an universal community such as expresses what the Christian idea means. I shall hereafter offer my little contribution to this problem.

III

Let us turn, then, to our new topic. The moralists, as we have already pointed out, are generally agreed that whoever is to win the highest things must indeed learn to bear a heavy moral burden. But the Christian idea now in question adds to the common lore of the moralists the sad word: "*The individual cannot bear this burden.* His tainted nature forbids; his guilt weighs him down. If by salvation one means a winning of the true goal of life, the individual, unaided, cannot be saved. And the help that he needs for bearing his burden must come from some source entirely above his own level,—from a source which is, in some genuine sense, divine."

The most familiar brief statement of the present idea is that of Paul in the passage in the seventh chapter of the epistle to the Romans, which culminates in this cry: "Oh, wretched man that I am!" What the Apostle, in the context of this passage, expounds as his interpretation both of his own religious experience and of human nature in general, has been much more fully stated in the form of well-known doctrines, and has formed the subject-matter for ages of Christian controversy.

In working out his own theory of the facts which he reports, Paul was led to certain often cited statements about the significance and the effect of Adam's legendary transgression. And, as a consequence of these words and of a few other Pauline passages, technical problems regarding original sin, predestination, and related topics have come to occupy so large a place in the history of theology, that, to many minds, Paul's own report of personal experience, and his statements about plain facts of human nature, have been lost to sight (so far as concerns the idea of the moral burden of the individual) in a maze of controversial complications. To numerous modern minds the whole idea of the moral burden of the individual seems, therefore, to be an invention of theologians, and to possess little or no religious importance.

Yet I believe that such a view is profoundly mistaken. The idea of the moral burden of the individual is, as we shall see, not without its inherent complications, and not without its relation to very difficult problems, both ethical and metaphysical. Yet, of the three essential ideas of Christianity which constitute our list, it is, relatively speaking, the simplest, and the one which can be most easily interpreted to the enlightened common sense of the modern man. Its most familiar difficulties are due rather to the accidents of controversy than to the nature of the subject.

The fate which has beset those who have dealt with the technical efforts to express this idea is partly explicable by the general history of religion; but is also partly due to varying personal factors, such as those which determined Paul's own training. This fate may be summed up by saying that, regarding just this matter of the moral burden of the individual, those who, by virtue of their genius or of their experience, have most known what they meant, have least succeeded in making clear to others what they know.

Paul, for instance, grasped the essential meaning of the moral burden of the individual with a perfectly straightforward veracity of understanding. What he saw, as to this matter, he saw with tragic clearness, and upon the basis of a type of experience that, in our own day, we can verify, as we shall soon see, much more widely than was possible for him. But when he put his doctrine into words, both his Rabbinical lore, and his habits of interpreting tradition, troubled his speech; and the passages which embody his theory of the sinfulness of man remain as difficult and as remote from his facts, as his report of these facts of life themselves is eloquent and true.

Similar has been the fortune of nearly all subsequent theology regarding the technical treatment of this topic. Yet growing human experience, through all the Christian ages, has kept the topic near to life; and to-day it is in closer touch with life than ever. The idea of the moral burden of the individual seems, to many cheerful minds, austere; but, if it is grave and stern, it is grave with the gravity of life, and stern only as the call of life, to any awakened mind, ought to be stern. If the traditional technicalities have obscured it, they have not been able to affect its deeper meaning or its practical significance. Rightly interpreted, it forms, I think, not only an essential feature of Christianity, but an indispensable part of every religious and moral view of life which considers man's business justly, and does so with a reasonable regard for the larger connections of our obligations and of our powers.

IV

If we ourselves are to see these larger connections, we must, for the time, disregard the theological complications of the history of doctrine concerning original sin, and must also disregard the metaphysical problems that lie behind these complications. We must do this; but not as if these theological theories were wholly arbitrary, or wholly insignificant. We must simply begin with those facts of human nature which here most deeply concern us.

These facts have a metaphysical basis. In the end, we ourselves shall seek to come into touch with so much of theology as most has to do with our problem of Christianity. We cannot tell, until our preliminary survey is completed, and our metaphysical treatment of our problem is reached, what form our sketch of a theology will assume. We must be patient with our fragmentary views until we see how to bring them together.

But, for the time being, our question relates not to the legend of Adam's fall, nor to something technically called original sin, but to man as we empirically know him. We ask: How far is the typical individual man weighed down, in his efforts to win the goal of life, by a burden such as Paul describes in his epistle to the Romans? And what is the significance of this burden?

Here, at once, we meet with the obvious fact, often mentioned, not only in ancient, but also in many modern, discussions of our topic,—with the fact that there are, deep-seated in human nature, many tendencies that our mature moral consciousness views as evil. These tendencies have a basis in qualities that are transmitted by heredity.

Viewed as an observant naturalist,—as a disinterested student of the life-process views them, all our inherited instincts are, in one sense, upon a level. For no instincts are, at the outset of life, determined by any purpose,—either good or evil,—of which we are then conscious. But, when trained, through experience and action, our instincts become interwoven into complex habits, and thus are transformed into our voluntary activities. What at the beginning is an elemental predisposition to respond to a specific sensory stimulus in a more or less vigorous but incoherent and generalized way, becomes, in the context of the countless other predispositions upon which is based our later training, the source of a mode of conduct,—of conduct that, as we grow, tends to become more and more definite, and that may be valuable for good or for ill. And, as a fact, many of our instinctive predispositions actually appear, in the sequel, to be like noxious plants or animals. That is, to use a familiar phrase, they "turn out ill." They are expressed in our maturer life in maladjustments, in vices, or perhaps in crimes.

Now Paul, like a good many other moralists, was impressed by the number and by the vigor of those amongst our instinctive predispositions which, under the actual conditions of human training, "turn out ill," and are interwoven into habits that often lead the natural man into baseness and into a maze of evil deeds. Paul summarizes this aspect of the facts, as he saw them, in his familiar picture, first, of the Gentile world, and then of the moral state of the unregenerate who were Jews. This picture we find in the opening chapters of his epistle to the Romans.

The majority of readers appear to suppose that the essential basis of Paul's theory about the moral burden of the individual is to be found in these opening chapters, and in the assertion that the worst vices and crimes of mankind are the most accurate indications of how bad human nature is. For such readers, whether they agree with Paul or not, the whole problem reduces to the question: "Are men, and are human traits and tendencies, naturally as mischievous; are we all as much predisposed to vices and to crimes as Paul's dark picture of the world in which he lived bids us believe that all human characters are? Is man,—viewed as a fair observer from another planet might view him,—is man by nature, or by heredity, predominantly like a noxious plant or animal? Unless some external power, such as the power that Paul conceives to be Divine Grace, miraculously saves him, is he bound to turn out ill,—to be the beast of prey, the victim of lust, the venomous creature, whom Paul portrays in these earlier chapters of his letters to the Romans?"

You well know that, as to the questions thus raised, there is much to be said, both for and against the predominantly mischievous character of the natural and instinctive predispositions of men; and both for and against the usual results of training, in case of the people who make up our social world. Paul's account of this aspect of the life of the natural man has both its apologists and its critics.

I must simply decline, however, to follow the usual controversies as to the natural predispositions of the human animal any further in this place. I have mentioned the familiar topic in order to say at once that none of the considerations which the opening chapters of the epistle to the Romans suggest to a modern reader regarding the noxious or the useful instinctive predispositions of ordinary men, or even of extraordinarily defective or of exceptionally gifted human beings, seem to be of any great importance for the understanding of the genuine Pauline doctrine of the moral burden of the individual.

Paul opened the epistle to the Romans by considerations which merely prepared the way for his main thesis. His argument in the earlier chapters is also chiefly preparatory. But his main doctrine concerning our moral burden depends upon other considerations than a mere enumeration of the vices and crimes of a corrupt society. It depends, in fact, upon considerations which, as I believe, are almost wholly overlooked in most of the technical controversies concerning original sin, and concerning the evil case of the unregenerate man.

I shall venture to translate these more significant considerations which Paul emphasizes into a relatively modern phraseology. I believe that I shall do so in a way that is just to Paul's spirit, and that will enable us soon to return to the text of the seventh chapter of his epistle with a clearer understanding of the main issue.

V

Whoever sets out to study, as psychologist, the moral side of human nature, with the intention of founding upon that study an estimate of the part which good and evil play in our life, must make clear to his mind a familiar, but important, and sometimes neglected distinction. This is the distinction between the conduct of men, upon the one hand, and the grade or sort of consciousness with which, upon the other hand, their conduct, whatever it is, is accompanied.

Conduct, as we have already mentioned, results from the training which our hereditary predispositions, our instinctive tendencies, get, when the environment has played upon them in a suitable way, and for a sufficient time. The environment which trains us to our conduct may be animate or inanimate; although in our case it is very largely a human environment. It is not necessary that we should be clearly aware of what our conduct in a given instance is or means, just as it is not necessary that one who speaks a language fluently should be consciously acquainted with the grammar of that language, or that one who can actually find the way over a path in the mountains should be able to give directions to a stranger such as would enable the latter to find the same way.

In general, it requires one sort of training to establish in us a given form of conduct, and a decidedly different sort of training to make us aware of what that form of conduct is, and of what, for us ourselves, it means.

The training of all the countless higher and more complex grades and types of knowledge about our own conduct which we can find present in the world of our self-knowledge, is subject to a general principle which I may as well state at once. Conduct, as I have just said, can be trained through the action of any sort of tolerable environment, animate or inanimate. But the higher and more complex types of our consciousness about our conduct, our knowledge about what we do, and about why we do it,—all this more complex sort of practical knowledge of ourselves, is trained by a specific sort of environment, namely, by a social environment.

And the social environment that most awakens our self-consciousness about our conduct does so by opposing us, by criticising us, or by otherwise standing in contrast with us. Our knowledge of our conduct, in all its higher grades, and our knowledge of ourselves as the authors or as the guides of our own conduct, our knowledge of how and why we do what we do,—all such more elaborate self-knowledge is, directly or indirectly, a social product, and a product of social contrasts and oppositions of one sort or another. Our fellows train us to all our higher grades of practical self-knowledge, and they do so by giving us certain sorts of social trouble.

If we were capable of training our conduct in solitude, we should not be nearly as conscious as we now are of the plans, of the ideals, of the meaning, of this conduct. A solitary animal, if well endowed with suitable instincts, and if trained through the sort of experimenting that any intelligent animal carries out as he tries to satisfy his wants, would gradually form some sort of conduct. This conduct might be highly skilful. But if this animal lived in a totally unsocial, in a wholly inanimate, environment, he would meet with no facts that could teach him to be aware of what his conduct was, in the sense and degree in which we are aware of our own conduct. *For he, as a solitary creature, would find no other instance of conduct with which to compare his own.* And all knowledge rests upon comparison. It is my knowledge of my fellows' doings, and of their behavior toward me,—it is this which gives me the basis for the sort of comparison that I use whenever I succeed in more thoughtfully observing myself or estimating myself.

If you want to grasp this principle, consider any instance that you please wherein you are actually and clearly aware of how you behave and of why you behave thus. Consider, namely, any instance of a higher sort of skill in an art, in a game, in business,—an instance, namely, wherein you not only *are* skilful, but are fully observant of what your skill is, and of why you consciously prefer this way of playing or of working. You will find that always your knowledge and your estimate of your skill and of your own way of doing, turn upon comparing your own conduct with that of some real or ideal comrade, or fellow, or rival, or opponent, or critic; or upon knowing how your social order in general carries on or estimates this sort of conduct; or, finally, upon remembering or using the results of former social comparisons of the types mentioned.

I walk as I happen to walk, and in general, if let alone, I have no consciousness as to what my manner of walking is; but let my fellow's gait or pace attract my attention, or let my fellow laugh at my gait, or let him otherwise show that he observes my gait; and forthwith, if my interest is stirred, I may have the ground for beginning to observe what my own gait is, and how it is to be estimated.

In brief, it is our fellows who first startle us out of our natural unconsciousness about our own conduct; and who then, by an endless series of processes of setting us attractive but difficult models, and of socially interfering with our own doings, train us to higher and higher grades and to more and more complex types of self-consciousness regarding what we do and why we do it. Play and conflict, rivalry and emulation, conscious imitation and conscious social contrasts between man and man,—these are the source of each man's consciousness about his own conduct.

Whatever occurs in our literal social life, and in company with our real fellows, can be, and often is, repeated with endless variations in our memory and imagination, and in a companionship with ideal fellow-beings of all grades of significance. And thus our thoughts and memories of all human beings who have aroused our interest, as well as our thoughts about God, enrich our social environment by means of a wealth of real and ideal fellow-beings, with whom we can and do compare and contrast ourselves and our own conduct.

And since all this is true, this whole process of our knowledge about our own doings, and about our plans, and about our estimates of ourselves, is a process capable of simply endless variation, growth, and idealization. Hence the variations of our moral self-consciousness have all the wealth of the entire spiritual world. Comparing our doings with the standards that the social will furnishes to us, in the form of customs and of rules, we become aware both of what Paul calls, in a special instance, "the law," and of ourselves either as in harmony with or opposed to this law. The comparison and the contrast make us view ourselves on the one side, and the social will,—that is, "the law,"—on the other side, as so related that, the more we know of the social will, the more highly conscious of ourselves we become; while the better we know ourselves, the more clearly we estimate the dignity and the authority of the social will.

So much, then, for a mere hint of the general ways in which our moral self-consciousness is a product of our social life. This self is known to each one of us through its social contrasts with other selves, and with the will of the community. If these contrasts displease us, we try to relieve the tension. If they fascinate, we form our ideals accordingly. But in either case we become conscious of some plan or ideal of our own. Our developed conscience, psychologically speaking, is the product of endless efforts to clear up, to simplify, to reduce to some sort of unity and harmony, the equally endless contrasts between the self, the fellow-man, and the social will in general,—contrasts which our social experience constantly reveals and renders fascinating or agonizing, according to the state of our sensitiveness or of our fortunes.

VI

These hints of the nature of a process which you can illustrate by every higher form and gradation of the moral consciousness of men have now prepared us for one more observation which, when properly understood, will bring us directly in contact with Paul's own comments upon the moral burden of any human being who reaches a high spiritual level.

Our conduct may be, according to our instincts and our training, whatever it happens to be. Since man is an animal that is hard to train, it will often be, from the point of view of the social will of our community, more or less defective conduct. But it might also be fairly good conduct; and, in normal people of good training, it often is so. In this respect, then, it seems unpsychological to assert that the conduct of all natural men is universally depraved,—however ill Paul thought of his Gentiles.

Let us turn, however, from men's conduct to their consciousness about their conduct; and then the simple and general principles just enunciated will give us a much graver view of our moral situation. Paul's main thesis about our moral burden relates not to our conduct, but to our consciousness about our conduct.

Our main result, so far, is that, from a purely psychological point of view, my consciousness about my conduct, and consequently my power to form ideals, and my power to develop any sort of conscience, are a product of my nature as a social being. And the product arises in this way: Contrasts, rivalries, difficult efforts to imitate some fascinating fellow-being, contests with my foes, emulation, social ambition, the desire to attract attention, the desire to find my place in my social order, my interest in what my fellows say and do, and especially in what they say and do with reference to me,— such are the more elemental social motives and the social situations which at first make me highly conscious of my own doings.

Upon the chaos of these social contrasts my whole later training in the knowledge of the good and the evil of my own conduct is founded. My conscience grows out of this chaos,—grows as my reason grows, through the effort to get harmony into this chaos. However reasonable I become, however high the grade of the conscientious ideals to which, through the struggle to win harmony, I finally attain, all of my own conscientious life is psychologically built upon the lowly foundations thus furnished by the troubled social life, that, together with my fellows, I must lead.

VII

But now it needs no great pessimism to observe that our ordinary social life is one in which there is a great deal of inevitable tension, or natural disharmony. Such tension, and such disharmony, are due not necessarily to the graver vices of men. The gravest disharmonies often result merely from the mutual misunderstandings of men. There are so many of us. We naturally differ so much from one another. We comprehend each other so ill, or, at best, with such difficulty. Hence social tension is, so to speak, the primary state of any new social enterprise, and can be relieved only through special and constantly renewed efforts.

But this simple observation leads to another. If our social life, owing to the number, the variety, and the ignorance of the individuals who make up our social world, is prevailingly or primarily one in which strained social situations,—forms of social tension,—social troubles, are present, and are constantly renewed, it follows that every individual who is to reach a high grade of self-consciousness as to his own doings, will be awakened to his observation of himself by one or another form or instance of social tension. As a fact, it is rivalry, or contest, or criticism that first, as we have seen, naturally brings to my notice what I am doing. And the obvious rule is that, within reasonable limits, the greater the social tension of the situation in which I am placed, the sharper and clearer does my social contrast with my fellows become to me. And thus, the greater the social tension is, the more do I become aware, through such situations, both about my own conduct, and about my plans and ideals, and about my will.

In brief, my moral self-consciousness is bred in me through social situations that involve,—not necessarily any physical conflict with my fellows,—but, in general, some form of social conflict,—conflict such as engenders mutual criticism. Man need not be, when civilized, at war with his fellows in the sense of using the sword against them. But he comes to self-consciousness as a moral being through the spiritual warfare of mutual observation, of mutual criticism, of rivalry,—yes, too often through the warfare of envy and of gossip and of scandal-mongering, and of whatever else belongs to the early training that many people give to their own consciences, through taking a more or less hostile account of the consciences of their neighbors. Such things result from the very conditions of high grades of self-consciousness about our conduct and our ideals.

The moral self, then, the natural conscience, is bred through situations that involve social tension. What follows?

VIII

It follows that such tension, in each special case, indeed seems evil to us, and calls for relief. And in seeking for such relief, the social will, in its corporate capacity, the will of the community, forms its codes, its customary laws; and attempts to teach each of us how he ought to deal with his neighbors so as to promote the general social harmony. But these codes,—these forms of customary morality,—they have to be taught to us as conscious rules of conduct. They can only be taught to us by first teaching us to be more considerate, more self-observant, more formally conscientious than we were before. But to accomplish this aim is to bring us to some higher level of our general self-consciousness concerning our own doings.

And this can be done, as a rule, only by applying to us some new form of social discipline which, in general, introduces still new and more complex kinds of tension,—new social contrasts between the general will and our own will, new conflicts between the self and its world.

Our social training thus teaches us to know ourselves through a process which arouses our self-will; and this tendency grows with what it feeds upon. The higher the training and the more cultivated and elaborate is our socially trained conscience,—the more highly conscious our estimate of our own value becomes, and so, in general, the stronger grows our self-will.

This is a commonplace; but it is precisely upon this very commonplace that the moral burden of the typical individual, trained under natural social conditions, rests. If the individual is no defective or degenerate, but a fairly good member of his stock, his conduct may be trained by effective social discipline into a more or less admirable conformity to the standards of the general will. But his conduct is not the same as his own consciousness about his conduct; or, in other words, his deeds and his ideals are not necessarily in mutual agreement. Meanwhile, his consciousness about his conduct, his ideals, his conscience, are all trained, under ordinary conditions, by a social process that begins in social troubles, in tensions, in rivalries, in contests, and that naturally continues, the farther it goes, to become more and more a process which introduces new and more complex conflicts.

This evil constantly increases. The burden grows heavier. Society can, by its ordinary skill, train many to be its servants,—servants who, being under rigid discipline, submit because they must. But precisely in proportion as society becomes more skilled in the external forms of culture, it trains its servants by a process that breeds spiritual enemies. That is, it breeds men who, even when they keep the peace, are inwardly enemies one of another; because every man, in a highly cultivated social world, is trained to moral self-consciousness by his social conflicts. And these same men are inwardly enemies of the collective social will itself, because in a highly cultivated social order the social will is oppressively vast, and the individual is trained to self-consciousness by a process which shows him the contrast between his own will and this, which so far seems to him a vast impersonal social will. He may obey. That is conduct. But he will naturally revolt inwardly; and that is his inevitable form of spiritual self-assertion, so long as he is trained to self-consciousness in this way, and is still without the spiritual transformations that some higher form of love for the community,—some form of loyalty, and that alone,—can bring.

This revolt will tend to increase as culture advances. High social cultivation breeds spiritual enmities. For it trains what we in our day call individualism, and, upon precisely its most cultivated levels, glories in creating highly conscious individuals. But these individuals are brought to consciousness by their social contrasts and conflicts. Their very consciences are tainted by the original sin of social contentiousness. The higher the cultivation, the vaster and deeper are precisely the more spiritual and the more significant of these inward and outward conflicts. Cultivation breeds civilized conduct; it also breeds conscious independence of spirit and deep inner opposition to all mere external authority.

Before this sort of moral evil the moral individual, thus cultivated, is, if viewed merely as a creature of cultivation, powerless. His very conscience is the product of spiritual warfare, and its knowledge of good and evil is tainted by its origin. The burden grows; and the moral individual cannot bear it, unless his whole type of self-consciousness is transformed by a new spiritual power which this type of cultivation can never of itself furnish.

For the moral cultivation just described is cultivation in "the law"; that is, in the rules of the social will. But such cultivation breeds individualism; that is, breeds consciousness of self-will. And the burden of this self-will increases with cultivation.

As we all know, individualism, viewed as a highly potent social tendency, is a product of high cultivation. It is also a relatively modern product of such cultivation. Savages appear to know little about individualism. Where tribal custom is almighty, the individual is trained to conduct, but not to a high grade of self-consciousness. Hence the individual, in a primitive community, submits; but also he has no very elaborate conscience. Among most ancient peoples, individualism was still nearly unknown.

Two ancient peoples, living under special conditions and possessing an extraordinary genius, developed very high grades of individualism. One of these peoples was Israel,—especially that fragment of later Israel to which Judaism was due. Paul well knew what was the nature and the meaning of just that high development of individuality which Judaism had in his day made possible.

The other one of these peoples was the Greek people. Their individualism, their high type of self-consciousness regarding conduct, showed what is meant by being, as every highly individualistic type of civilization since their day has been, characteristically merciless to individuals. Greek individualism devoured its own children. The consciousness of social opposition determined the high grade of self-consciousness of the Greek genius. It also determined the course of Greek history and politics; and so the greatest example of national genius which the world has ever seen promptly destroyed its own life, just because its self-consciousness was due to social conflicts and intensified them. The original sin of its own cultivation was the doom of that cultivation.

In the modern world the habit of forming a high grade of individual consciousness has now become settled. We have learned the lesson that Israel and Greece taught. Hence we speak of personal moral independence as if it were our characteristic spiritual ideal. This ideal is now fostered still more highly than ever before,—is fostered by the vastness of our modern social forces, and by the way in which these forces are to-day used to train the individual consciousness which opposes itself to them, and which is trained to this sort of opposition.

The result is that the training of the cultivated individual, under modern conditions, uses, on the one hand, all the motives of what Paul calls "the flesh,"—all the natural endowment of man the social being,—but develops this fleshly nature so that it is trained to self-consciousness by emphasizing every sort and grade of more skilful opposition to the very social will that trains it. Our modern world is therefore peculiarly fitted to illustrate the thesis of Paul's seventh chapter of the epistle to the Romans. To that chapter let us now, for a moment, return.

IX

The difficulty of the argument of Paul's seventh chapter lies in the fact that in speaking of our sinful nature, he emphasizes three apparently conflicting considerations: First, he asserts that sinfulness belongs to our elemental nature, to our flesh as it is at birth; secondly, he insists that sin is not cured but increased by cultivation, unless the power of the Divine Spirit intervenes and transforms us into new creatures; thirdly, he declares that our sinfulness belongs not to especially defective or degenerate sinners, but to the race in its corporate capacity, so that no one is privileged to escape by any good deed of his own, since we are all naturally under the curse.

To the first consideration many modern men reply that at birth we have only untrained instinctive predispositions, which may, under training, turn out well or ill, but which, until training turns them into conduct, are innocent.

This comment is true, but does not touch Paul's main thesis, which is that, being as to the flesh what we are,—that is, being essentially social animals,—all our natural moral cultivation, if successful, can only make us aware of our sinfulness. "Howbeit, I had not known sin but for the law." It is precisely this thesis which the natural history of the training of our ordinary moral self-consciousness illustrates. This training usually takes place through impressing the social will upon the individual by means of discipline. The result must be judged not by the accidental fortunes of this or of that formally virtuous or obviously vicious individual. The true problem lies deeper than we are accustomed to look. It is just that problem which Paul understands.

Train me to morality by the ordinary modes of discipline and you do two things: First, and especially under modern conditions, you teach me so-called independence, self-reliance. You teach me to know and to prize from the depths of my soul, my own individual will. The higher the civilization in which this mode of training is followed, the more I become an individualist among mutually hostile individualists, a citizen of a world where all are consciously free to think ill of one another, and to say, to every external authority: ''My will, not thine, be done.''

But this teaching of independence is also a teaching of distraction and inner despair. For, if I indeed am intelligent, I also learn that, in a highly cultivated civilization, the social will is mighty, and daily grows mightier, and must, ordinarily and outwardly, prevail unless chaos is to come. Hence you indeed may discipline me into obedience, but it is a distracted and wilful obedience, which constantly wars with the very dignity of spirit which my training teaches me to revere. On the one hand, as a reasonable being, I say: ''I ought to submit; for law is mighty; and I would not, if I could, bring anarchy.'' So much I say, if I am indeed successfully trained. But I will not obey with the inner man. For I am the being of inalienable individual rights, of unconquerable independence. I have my own law in my own members, which, however I seem to obey, is at war with the social will. I am the divided self. The more I struggle to escape through my moral cultivation, the more I discern my divided state. Oh, wretched man that I am!

Now this my divided state, this my distraction of will, is no mishap of my private fortune. It belongs to the human race, as a race capable of high moral cultivation. It is the misfortune, the doom of man the social animal, if you train him through the discipline of social tension, through troubles with his neighbors, through opposition and through social conflict, through what Whistler called ''the gentle art of making enemies.'' This, apart from all legends, is Paul's thesis; and it is true to human nature. The more outer law there is in our cultivation, the more inner rebellion there is in the very individuals whom our cultivation creates. And this moral burden of the individual is also the burden of the race, precisely in so far as it is a race that is social in a human sense.

Possibly all this may still seem to you the mere construction of a theorist. And yet an age that, like our own, faces in new forms the conflicts between what we often name individualism and collectivism,—a time such as the present one, when every new enlargement of our vast corporations is followed by a new development of strikes and of industrial conflicts,—a time, I say, such as ours ought to know where the original sin of our social nature lies.

For our time shows us that *individualism and collectivism are tendencies, each of which, as our social order grows, intensifies the other*. The more the social will expresses itself in vast organizations of collective power, the more are individuals trained to be aware of their own personal wants and choices and ideals, and of the vast opportunities that would be theirs if they could but gain control of these social forces. The more, in sum, does their individual self-will become conscious, deliberate, cultivated, and therefore dangerously alert and ingenious.

Yet, if the individuals in question are highly intelligent, and normally orderly in their social habits, their self-will, thus forcibly kept awake and watchful through the very powers which the collective will has devised, is no longer, in our own times, a merely stupid attempt to destroy all social authority. It need not be childishly vicious or grossly depraved, like Paul's Gentiles in his earlier chapters of the epistle to the Romans. It is a sensitive self-will, which feels the importance of the social forces, and which wants them to grow more powerful, so that haply they may be used by the individual himself.

And so, when opportunity offers, the individual self-will casts its vote in favor of new devices to enrich or to intensify the expression of the collective will. For it desires social powers. It wants them for its own use. Hence, in its rebellion against authority, when such rebellion arises, it is a consciously divided self-will, which takes in our day no form more frequently than the general form of moral unrest, of discontent with its own most ardent desires. It needs only a little more emphasis upon moral or religious problems than, in worldly people, in our day, it displays, in order to be driven to utter from a full heart Paul's word: "Oh, wretched man that I am!"

For the highly trained modern agitator, or the plastic disciple of agitators, if both intelligent and reasonably orderly in habits, is intensely *both* an individualist and a man who needs the collective will, who in countless ways and cases bows to that will, and votes for it, and increases its power. The individualism of such a man wars with his own collectivism; while each, as I insist, tends to inflame the other. As an agitator, the typically restless child of our age often insists upon heaping up new burdens of social control,—control that he indeed intends to have others feel rather than himself. As individualist, longing to escape, perhaps from his economic cares, perhaps from the marriage bond, such a highly intelligent agitator may speak rebelliously of all restrictions, declare Nietzsche to be his prophet, and set out to be a Superman as if he were no social animal at all. Wretched man, by reason of his divided will, he is; and he needs only a little reflection to observe the fact.

But note: These are no mere accidents of our modern world. The division of the self thus determined, and thus increasing in our modern cultivation, is not due to the chance defects of this or of that more or less degenerate individual. Nor is it due merely to a man's more noxious instincts. This division is due to the very conditions to which the development of self-consciousness is subject, not only in our present social order, but in every civilization which has reached as high a grade of self-consciousness as that which Paul observed in himself and in his own civilization.

X

The moral burden of the individual, as Paul conceives it, and as human nature makes it necessary, has now been characterized. The legend of Adam's transgression made the fall of man due to the sort of self-consciousness, to the knowledge of good and evil, which the crafty critical remarks of the wise serpent first suggested to man, and which the resulting transgression simply emphasized. What Paul's psychology, translated into more modern terms, teaches, is that the moral self-consciousness of every one of us gets its cultivation from our social order through a process which begins by craftily awakening us, as the serpent did Eve, through critical observations, and which then fascinates our divided will by giving us the serpent's counsels. "Ye shall be as gods." This is the lore of all individualism, and the vice of all our worldly social ambitions. The resulting diseases of self-consciousness are due to the inmost nature of our social race.

They belong to its very essence as a social race. They increase with cultivation. The individual cannot escape from the results of them through any deed of his own. For his will is trained by a process which taints his conscience with the original sin of self-will, of clever hostility to the very social order upon which he constantly grows more and more consciously dependent.

What is the remedy? What is the escape? Paul's answer is simple. To his mind a new revelation has been made, from a spiritual realm wholly above our social order and its conflicts. Yet this revelation is, in a new way, social. For it tells us: "There is a certain divinely instituted community. It is no mere collection of individuals, with laws and customs and quarrels. Nor is its unity merely that of a mighty but, to our own will, an alien power. Its indwelling spirit is concrete and living, but is also a loving spirit. It is the body of Christ. The risen Lord dwells in it, and is its life. It is as much a person as he was when he walked the earth. And he is as much the spirit of that community as he is a person. Love that community; let its spirit, through this love, become your own. Let its Lord be your Lord. Be one in him and with him and with his Church. And lo! the natural self is dead. The new life takes possession of you. You are a new creature. The law has no dominion over you. In the universal community you live in the spirit; and hence for the only self, the only self-consciousness, the only knowledge of your own deeds which you possess or tolerate: these are one with the spirit of the Lord and of the community.''

Translated into the terms that I ventured to use in our last lecture, Paul's doctrine is that salvation comes through loyalty. Loyalty involves an essentially new type of self-consciousness,—the consciousness of one who loves a community as a person. Not social training, but the miracle of this love, creates the new type of self-consciousness.

Only (as Paul holds) you must find the universal community to which to be loyal; and you must learn to know its Lord, whose body it is, and whose spirit is its life.

Paul is assured that he knows this universal community and this Lord. But, apart from Paul's religious faith, the perfectly human truth remains that loyalty (which is the love of a community conceived as a person on a level superior to that of any human individual)—loyalty,—and the devotion of the self to the cause of the community,—loyalty, is the only cure for the natural warfare of the collective and of the individual will,—a warfare which no moral cultivation without loyalty can ever end, but which all cultivation, apart from such devoted and transforming love of the community, only inflames and increases.

Thus the second of the essential ideas of Christianity illustrates the first, and is in turn illumined by the first. This, I believe is the deeper sense and truth of the doctrine of the inherent moral taint of the social individual.

THE COMMUNITY AND
THE TIME-PROCESS

The present situation of the Philosophy of Religion is dominated by motives and tendencies which are at once inspiring and confusing. It is the task of a student of this branch of philosophy to do whatever he can towards clarifying our outlook. Some of our recent leaders of opinion have turned our attention to new aspects of human experience, and have enriched philosophy with a wealth of fascinating intuitions. These contributions to the philosophy of our time have obvious bearings upon the interests of religion. If religion depended solely upon intuition and upon novelty, our age would already have proved its right to be regarded as a period of great advances in religious insight.

In fact, however, religion is concerned, not merely with our experience, but also with our will. The true lover of religion needs a conscience, as well as a joy in living—a coherent plan of action as well as a vital impulse. Now, in the present phase of the philosophy of religion, the religious aspect of the conscience is, as I believe, too seldom made a central object of inquiry. The interests of a coherent plan of life are too much neglected. I believe that both our ethical and our distinctly religious concerns tend to suffer in consequence of these tendencies of recent thought to which I thus allude. I believe that much can be done to profit by the novelties and by the intuitions of our day, without losing ourselves in the wilderness of caprices into which recent discussion has invited us to make the future home of our philosophy.

I

Because I view the problems of the philosophy of religion in this general way, I have undertaken, in the foregoing lectures, a study of the prob-

260

lem of Christianity which has been intended to accomplish three distinct, but closely connected tasks:—

First, in a fashion that has shown, as I hope, some genuine sympathy with the tendencies now prevalent, both in the whole field of philosophy, and, in particular, in the study of religion, I have tried to interpret some of the more obviously human and practical aspects of the religious beliefs of our fathers. In other words, I have approached the problem of Christianity from the side, not of metaphysics and of traditional dogmas, but of religious life and of human experience.

Secondly, even in using this mode of approach, I have laid stress upon the fact that Christianity—viewed as a doctrine of life—is not merely a religion of experience and of sentiment, but also a religion whose main stress is laid upon the unity and the coherence of the common experience of the faithful, and upon the judgment which a calm and far-seeing conscience passes upon the values of life. The freedom of spirit to which Christianity, in the course of its centuries of teaching, has trained the civilizations which it has influenced, has been the freedom which loves both a wide outlook and a well-knit plan of action. In brief, I have insisted that Christianity, whatever its metaphysical basis may be, and however rich may be the wealth of intuitions which it has opened to its followers, has all the seriousness of purpose, and all the strenuousness of will, which make it indeed a religion of loyalty.

Thirdly, I have, from the outset, said that our view of the mission and the truth of the Christian doctrine of life would not be complete without a study of the metaphysical basis of the Christian ideas.

In the last two lectures we have considered how the modern mind stands related to the human interests which the Christian doctrine of life expresses. Our fathers, however, held Christianity to be, not merely a plan for the salvation of man, but a revelation concerning the origin and fate of the whole cosmos. From this point onwards, in our study, we must face anew the problem which the old faith regarded as solved. We, too, must take account of the universe. We must consider what is the consistent position for the modern mind to accept when the inquiry arises: Has the Christian doctrine of life a more than human meaning and foundation? Does this doctrine express a truth, not only about man, but about the whole world, and about God?

II

The modern man has long since learned not to confine himself to a geocentric view of the universe, nor to an anthropocentric view of the affairs of this planet of ours. For minds trained as ours now are, it has become inevitable to imagine how human concerns would seem to us if we heard of them from afar, as dwellers in other solar or stellar systems might be supposed to hear of them. We have been taught to remember that at some time,—a time not nearly so distant from us in the future as the Miocene division of the Tertiary period is now distant from us in the past, man will probably be as extinct as is now the sabre-toothed tiger. But such considerations as these arouse further queries about Christian doctrine—queries which no modern mind can wholly ignore. Let all be admitted which we urged at the last time regarding the close relation of the Christian doctrine of life to the deepest needs of humanity. Then this will indeed show that Christianity, viewed simply *as* such a doctrine of life, need not fear social changes, so long as civilized man endures; and will remain as a spiritual guide of future generations, however vast the revolutions to which they may be subject, so long as the future generations view life largely and seriously.

But such considerations will not meet all the legitimate questions of a philosophy of religion. For religion, although it need not depend for its appeal to the human heart upon solving the problems of the cosmos, inevitably leads to a constantly renewed interest in those problems. Let it be granted that the salvation of mankind indeed requires some form of religion whose essential ideas are in harmony with the Christian ideas which we have examined; still, that fact will not quite supply an answer to our natural inquiries, if indeed mankind is destined simply to fail,—as the sabre-toothed tiger failed. And if mankind, in the vast cosmos, is as much alone amongst the beings that people the universe as the earth seems to be alone amongst the countless worlds,—what shall it profit us if we seem to be saving our own souls for a time, but actually remain, after all, what we were before,— utterly insignificant incidents in a world-process that neither needs men nor heeds them?

Traditional theology could long ignore such considerations, because it could centre all the universe about the earth and man. But the modern man must think of his kind as thus really related to an immeasurably vast cosmic process, at whose centre our planet does not stand, and in whose ages our brief human lives play a part as transient, relatively speaking, as is, for our own eyes, the flickering of the northern lights.

The task to which we must now devote ourselves is thus determined, for our age, and for the modern man, by the enlarged perspective in which we have to view human history. Our doctrine of life is not so readily to be connected with our picture of the universe as would be the case if we still lived under the heavenly spheres of an ancient cosmology. Yet we shall find that the difference which is here in question will not prove to be so great in its meaning as the quantitative differences between the ancient and modern world seem, at first, to imply. Our fathers also faced the problem of the infinity of the universe, much as they often tried to ignore or to minimize that problem. And, in the spiritual world, mere quantity, however vast, is not the hardest of obstacles to overcome.

III

In any case, however, the part of our undertaking upon which we thus enter, corresponds to those chapters of traditional theology which dealt with the existence and nature of God, and with God's relation to the world, and with the origin and destiny of the human individual. Our own attempt to study these well-worn problems begins with one, and perhaps with only one, advantage over the best-known traditional modes of expounding a philosophical theology. We, namely, set out under the guidance of our foregoing study of the Christian ideas. Central among these ideas is that of the Universal Community. For us, then, theology, if we are to define any theology at all, must depend upon the metaphysical interpretation and foundation of the community. If that ideal of one beloved and united community of all mankind whose religious value we have defended, has a basis, not merely in the transient interests of us mortals, but also in whatever is largest and most lasting in the universe, then indeed the doctrine of the community will prove to be a doctrine about the being and nature and manifestation of God; and our estimate of the relation of the modern mind to the spirit of a Christian creed will be altered and completed accordingly. This one doctrine will indeed not suffice to make us literal followers of tradition; but it will bring us into a sympathy with some of the most essential features of the Christian view of the divine being.

IV

What interests are at stake when this aspect of the problems of theology is emphasized, I can best remind you by recalling the fact which we mentioned in comparing Buddhism and Christianity in a former lecture. The most characteristic feature by which the Christian doctrine of life stands contrasted with its greatest religious rival, we found to be the one summarized in the words of the creed: "I believe in the Holy Ghost, the Holy Catholic Church, the communion of saints." In our former lecture, when we commented upon these words, we laid no stress upon the special traditions of the historical Church. We considered only the universally human significance of the ideal which has always constituted the vital principle of the historical Church,—far away as the adequate embodiment of that ideal in any visible human institution still seems to be. At the present stage of our inquiry,—since we are, of necessity, entering for the time the world of metaphysical abstractions, we have also to abstract from still another aspect of the meaning which the words of the creed intend to convey. For neither the historical Church, nor the distinctively human ideal which it expresses, shall be, in these metaphysical lectures, at the centre of our attention. We are here to ask: For what truth, if any, regarding the whole nature of things, does that article of the creed stand? Our answer must be found, if at all, in some metaphysical theory of the community and of its relation, if such relation it possesses, to the divine being. In other words, the central problem in our present attempt at a theology must be that problem which traditional Christian theology has so strangely neglected,—the problem of what the religious consciousness has called the Holy Spirit.

v

The philosophy of religion, in dealing with the problem of Christianity, has often elaborately expounded and criticised the arguments for the existence of God. Such philosophical arguments have in general to do with the concept of the Deity viewed quite apart from the Christian doctrine of the Trinity. In other cases, and for obvious historical reasons, the philosophy of religion has had much to say about the doctrine of the Logos. This doctrine, when treated as a part of Christian theology, is usually taken to be the theory of the second person of the Trinity. But the traditional doctrine of the Holy Spirit, neglected by the early theologians of the Church, even when the creeds were still in the formative period of their existence, has remained until this day in the background of inquiry, both for the theologians and for the philosophers. A favorite target for hostile, although often inarticulate, criticism on the part of the opponents of tradition, and a frequent object of reverential, but confessedly problematic and often very vague, exposition on the part of the defenders of the faith,—the article of the creed regarding the Holy Spirit is, I believe, the one matter about which most who discuss the problem of Christianity have least to say in the way of definite theory.

Yet, if I am right,—this is, in many respects, the really distinctive and therefore the capital article of the Christian creed, so far as that creed suggests a theory of the divine nature. This article, then, should be understood, if the spirit of Christianity, in its most human and vital of features, is to be understood at all. And this article should be philosophically expounded and defended, if any distinctively Christian article of the creed is to find a foundation in a rationally defensible metaphysical theory of the universe.

Apart from the doctrine of the ideal community, and of the divine Spirit as constituting the unity and the life of this community, Theism can be, as for many centuries it has been, defined and defended. But such theism, which "knows not so much as whether there is any Holy Ghost," is not distinctively Christian in its meaning. And the Logos-doctrine, except when viewed in unity with the doctrine of the Spirit, is indeed what some of its recent hostile critics (such as Harnack) have taken it to be,—a thesis of Greek philosophy, and not a characteristically Christian opinion. The Logos-doctrine of the Fourth Gospel, as we earlier saw, is indeed no mere following of Greek metaphysics; for the Fourth Gospel identifies the Logos with the spirit of the community. Here, then, in this doctrine of the spirit, lies the really central idea of any distinctively Christian metaphysic.

To approach the problems of the philosophy of religion from the side of the metaphysical basis of the idea of the community is therefore, I believe, to undertake a task as momentous as it is neglected.

VI

Moreover, as we shall soon find, this mode of beginning the metaphysical part of our task promises to relieve us, for the time, from the need of using some terms and of repeating some discussions, which recent controversy may well have made wearisome to many of us. The altogether too abstractly stated contrast between Monism and Pluralism—a contrast which fills so large a place in the polemical metaphysical writings of the day, does not force itself to the front, in our minds and in our words, when we set out to inquire into the real basis of the idea of the community. For a community immediately presents itself to our minds both as one and as many; and unless it is both one and many, it is no community at all. This fact does not, by itself, solve the problem of the One and the Many. But it serves to remind us how untrue to life is the way in which that problem is frequently stated.

In fact, as I believe, the idea of the community, suggested to us by the problems of human social life, but easily capable of a generalization which possesses universal importance, gives us one of our very best indications of the way in which the problem of the One and the Many is to be solved, and of the level of mental life upon which the solution is actually accomplished.

So much may serve as a general indication of the nature of our undertaking. Let me next attempt to define the problem of the community more precisely.

VII

Motives which are as familiar as they are hard to analyze have convinced us all, before we begin to philosophize, that our human world contains a variety of individually distinct minds or selves, and that some, for us decisively authoritative, principle of individuation, keeps these selves apart, and forbids us to regard their various lives merely as incidents, or as undivided phases of a common life. This conviction—the stubborn pluralism of our present and highly cultivated social consciousness—tends indeed, under criticism, to be subject to various doubts and modifications,—the more so as, in case we are once challenged to explain who we are, none of us find it easy to define the precise boundaries of the individual self, or to tell wherein it differs from the rest of the world, and, in particular, from the selves of other men.

But to all such doubts our social common sense replies by insisting upon three groups of facts. These facts combine to show that the individual human selves are sundered from one another by gaps which, as it would seem, are in some sense impassable.

First, in this connection, our common sense insists upon the empirical sundering of the feelings,—that is, of the immediate experiences of various human individuals. One man does not feel, and, speaking in terms of direct experience, cannot feel, the physical pains of another man. Sympathy may try its best to bridge the gulf thus established by nature. Love may counsel me to view the pangs of my fellow *as if they were* my own. But, as a fact, my sensory nerves do not end in my fellow's skin, but in mine. And the physical sundering of the organisms corresponds to a persistent sundering of our streams of immediate feeling. Even the most immediate and impressive forms of sympathy with the physical pangs of another human being only serve the more to illustrate how our various conscious lives are thus kept apart by gulfs which we cannot cross. When a pitiful man shrinks, or feels faint, or is otherwise overcome with emotion, at what is called "the sight" of another's suffering,—how unlike are the sufferings of the shrinking or terrified or overwhelmed spectator, and the pangs of the one with whom he is said to sympathize. As a fact, the sympathizer does not feel the sufferer's pain. What he feels is his own emotional reverberation at the sight of its symptoms. That is, in general, something very different, both in quality and in intensity, from what the injured man feels.

We appear, then, to be individuated by the diversity and the separateness of our streams of immediate feeling. My toothache cannot directly become an item in my neighbor's mind. Facts of this sort form the first group of evidences upon which common sense depends for its pluralistic view of the world of human selves.

The facts of the second group are closely allied to the former, but lie upon another level of individual life,—namely, upon the level of our more organized ideas.

"One man," so says our social common sense, "can only indirectly discover the intentions, the thoughts, the ideas, of another man." Direct telepathy, if it ever occurs at all, is a rare and, in most of our practical relations, a wholly negligible fact. By nature, every man's plans, intents, opinions, and range of personal experience are secrets, except in so far as his physical organism indirectly reveals them. His fellows can learn these secrets only through his expressive movements. Control your expression, keep silence, avoid the unguarded look and the telltale gesture; and then nobody can discover what is in your mind. No man can directly read the hearts of his fellows. This seems, for our common sense, to be one of the deepest-seated laws of our social experience. It is often expressed as if it were not merely an empirical law, but a logical necessity. How could I possibly possess or share or become conscious of the thoughts and purposes of another mind, unless I were myself identical with that mind? So says our ordinary common sense. The very supposition that I could be conscious of a thought or of an intent which was all the while actually present to the consciousness of another individual man, is often regarded as a supposition not only contrary to fact, but also contrary to reason. Such a supposition, it is often said, would involve a direct self-contradiction.

Otherwise expressed, the facts of this second group, and the principles which they exemplify, are summed up by asserting, as our social common sense actually asserts: We are individuated by the law that our trains of conscious thought and purpose are mutually inaccessible through any mode of direct intuition. Each of us lives within the charmed circle of his own conscious will and meaning,—each of us is more or less clearly the object of his own inspection, but is hopelessly beyond the direct observation of his fellows.

Of separate streams of feeling,—of mutually inaccessible and essentially secret trains of ideas,—we men are thus constituted. By such forms and by such structure of mental life, by such divisions which no human power can bring into one unity of insight, individual human minds are forced to exist together upon terms which make them, in so far, appear to resemble Leibnizian monads. Their only windows appear to be those which their physical organisms supply.

The third group of facts here in question is the group upon which our cultivated social common sense most insists whenever ethical problems are in question; and therefore it is precisely this third group of facts which has most interest in its bearings upon the idea of the community.

"We are all members one of another." So says the doctrine of the community. "On the contrary," so our social common sense insists: "We are beings, each of whom has a soul of his own, a destiny of his own, rights of his own, worth of his own, ideals of his own, and an individual life in which this soul, this destiny, these rights, these ideals, get their expression. No other man can do my deed for me. When I choose, my choice coalesces with the voluntary decision of no other individual." Such, I say, is the characteristic assertion to which this third group of facts leads our ordinary social pluralism.

In brief: We thus seem to be individuated by our deeds. The will whereby I choose my own deed, is not my neighbor's will. My act is my own. Another man can perform an act which repeats the type of my act, or which helps or hinders my act. But if the question arises concerning any one act: Who hath done this?—such a question admits of only one true answer. Deeds and their doers stand in one-one correspondence. Such is the opinion of our cultivated modern ethical common sense.

Upon this individuation of the selves by their deeds appear to rest all the other just mentioned ethical aspects of our modern social pluralism. As we mentioned in an earlier lecture, primitive man is not an individualist. The clear consciousness of individual rights, dignity, worth, and responsibility seems to be a product of that moral cultivation of which we have now frequently spoken. According to the primitive law of blood revenge, it is the community and not the individual that suffers for a deed. The consciousness that my deed is peculiarly my own also forms the basis for that cultivated idea of sin of which we found Paul making use. At all events, this ethical aspect of individual self-consciousness is frequently used by common sense as one of the most impressive grounds for doubting any philosophy which appears to make light of the distinctness of the social individuals.

VIII

Nevertheless, all these varieties of individual experience, these chasms which at any one present moment seem to sunder mind and mind, and these ethical considerations which have taught us to think of one man as morally independent of another, do not tell us the whole truth about the actual constitution of the social realm. There are facts that seem to show that these many are also one. These, then, are facts which force upon us the problem of the community.

As we have now repeatedly seen, social cooperation unquestionably brings into existence languages, customs, religions. These, as Wundt declares, are indeed psychological creations. Yet a language, a custom, or a religion is not a collection of discrete psychological phenomena, each of which corresponds to some separate individual mind to which that one mental fact belongs, or is due. Thus, the English language is a mental product,—and a product possessing intelligent unity. Its creator must be regarded as also, in some sense, a single intelligence. But the creator of the English language was no mere collection of Englishmen, each of whom added his word or phrase or accent, or other linguistic fact. The creator of English speech is the English people. Hence the English people is itself some sort of mental unit with a mind of its own.

The countless phenomena which Wundt in his Völkerpsychologie brings to our attention, constitute a philosophical problem which ought to be only the more carefully studied in case one regards the facts upon which our ordinary social pluralism rests as both unquestionable and momentous.

For if indeed men are sundered in their individual lives by the chasms which our social common sense seems to make so obvious; if they live in mutually inaccessible realms of conscious solitude; how comes it to pass that, nevertheless, in their social life, large and small bodies of men can come to act as if one common intelligence and one common will were using the individuals as its almost helpless instruments? Here is indeed a great problem. The theories of Wundt's type have the advantage of emphasizing and defining that problem.

Our ordinary social pluralism leads us to conceive the individual streams of consciousness as if they were unable to share even a single pang of pain. No one of them, we have said, can directly read the secret of a single idea that floats in another stream. Each conscious river of individual life is close shut between its own banks, like the Oregon of Bryant's youthful poem that rolls, "and hears no sound but his own waves."

But in our actual social life,—in the market-place, or at the political gathering, or when mobs rage and imagine a vain thing, in the streets of a modern city, the close shut-in streams of consciousness now appear as if they had lost their banks altogether. They seem to flow together like rivers that are lost in the ocean, and to surge into tumultuous unity, as if they were universal tides.

Or, again, our ordinary social pluralism makes us view the individual selves as if they were Leibnizian monads that had no windows. The social phenomena of the lives of communities, on the contrary, make these monads appear as if they had no walls, or as if they became mere drops that coalesce. Our ethical pluralism makes us proudly declare, each for himself, "My deed is my own." But our collective life often seems to advise us to say, not, "I act thus"; but, "Thus the community acts in and through me." Or again, our cultivated independence declares, "I think thus and thus." But, when the ethnologist Bastian uses the formula, "Ich denke nicht; sondern es denkt in mir,'' the social facts, especially of primitive human thought, go far to give this formula a meaning. In Europe the discovery of individual thinking began in some sense with the early Greek philosophers. Before them, tribes and communities did the thinking.

Now such considerations are emphasized by the theories of the type which Wundt favors.

Such theories, without being able to tell us all that we should like to know regarding what constitutes the unity of a community, have in common the tendency to insist that in many cases a community behaves as an unit, and therefore must be an unit, however its inner coherence may be constituted. If, however, we admit the facts which Wundt emphasizes, it is natural to seek for some further and perhaps more concrete way of conceiving what the mental life of a community may be, and how its unity is constituted. Wundt himself has hardly done all, I think, that we could desire in this direction, and it is natural to supplement his views by others.

Such a further approach towards an insight into the problem of the community is suggested by William James's discussion of what, in his lectures here at Oxford on ''The Pluralistic Universe,'' he called the ''compounding of consciousness.''

The main interests which guided James in the lectures to which I refer were indeed not the interests which I have emphasized in the early part of this course. James was not dealing with the problems which Christianity presents; nor was he interested in the idea of the community, in the form in which I am approaching that problem. But he was concerned with general religious and metaphysical issues; and questions relating to pluralism were explicitly in the foreground of his inquiry. He was also led to take account of manifold motives which tend to show that our mental world does not merely consist of sundered fields or streams of consciousness with barriers that part them.

Those who hear me will well remember how James emphasized, in the course of his argument, the difficulties which, as he explained, had so long held him back from any form of philosophy which should involve believing that a ''compounding of consciousness'' occurs, or is real. How should any one conscious mind be inclusive of another, or such that it was compounded with that other? This question, as James declared, had long seemed to him incapable of any answer in terms which should involve admitting the possibility of such ''co-consciousness,'' if indeed our philosophy were to be permitted to remain rational at all. But James actually reached at length a point in his own reflections where, as he said, this compounding of consciousness, this Bergsonian interpenetration of the various selves, came to appear to him in certain cases an empirically verifiable fact,—or, at all events, an irresistible hypothesis. When this point was reached, James felt that, for him, a philosophical crisis had come.

James faced and passed this crisis. He did so upon the basis of his own well-known anti-intellectualism. The mental world, he said, must not be interpreted in rational terms. If the compounding of consciousness occurs, it is irrational, although real. James was rejoiced, however, to feel that, in this matter, he stood in alliance with Bergson. And so, henceforth, for James, the many selves interpenetrated, or, at all events, might do so. It was merely the sterile intellect (so he now affirmed) which was responsible for the conceptual abstractions that had seemed to sunder various minds, not only empirically, but absolutely, and to make the compounding of consciousness impossible. It still remained for James true that we are indeed many. But this assertion no longer implied: We are sundered from one another by divisions that are absolutely impassable. We may be many selves; and yet, from these many selves, a larger self may be compounded,—a self such as one of Fechner's planetary consciousnesses was, or such as some still vaster cosmical form of mental life may be. This larger self may from above, as it were, bridge what is for us an impassable chasm. Interpenetration, which for us seems impossible, may come to pass for some higher sort of intuition.

With this treatment of the problem of the one and the many in the form in which social psychology presents it to our attention, James's account of the great cosmological questions and of their religious bearings came to an end,—just at the point where we all most needed to know what his next step in philosophy would be.

In substance, this outcome of a long series of efforts to deal with the problems of the one and the many in the world of the mental beings was based, in the case of James, partly upon empirical phenomena, of the type reported in his "Varieties of Religious Experience," and partly upon hypothetical extensions of these empirical phenomena. These hypothetical extensions themselves were again suggested to him, partly by Fechner's speculations on the cosmical enlargements of consciousness; partly by the general voluntaristic tendencies which so long characterized James's religious thought; and partly by Bergson's use of the new category of "interpenetration" as the one especially suited to aid us in the perception of the mental world. The results brought James, at the very close of his career, into new relations with the idealistic tradition in philosophy,—a relation which I ought not here to attempt to characterize at all extensively.

But in any case, the sort of compounding of consciousness which James favored differed in many respects from what I have in mind when I speak of the idea of the community. When the minds of James's world began to interpenetrate in earnest, as they did in this last phase of his religious speculation, they behaved much like drops of mercury that, falling, may form a pool, until, moved by one impulse or another, they break away from their union again, and flow and glitter until the next blending occur. Paul's conception of the spirit in the Church never appealed, I think, to James's mind.

But, in any case, James's final opinions, although only indirectly bearing upon our own main problem, tended to show, better than would otherwise have been possible, where the true problem lies.

IX

We may be aided in making a more decisive advance towards understanding what a community is by emphasizing at this point a motive which we have not before mentioned, and which no doubt plays a great part in the psychology of the social consciousness.

Any notable case wherein we find a social organization which we can call, in the psychological sense, either a highly developed community or the creation or product of such a community, is a case where some process of the nature of a history—that is, of coherent social evolution—has gone on, and has gone on for a long time, and is more or less remembered by the community in question. If, ignoring history, you merely take a cross-section of the social order at any one moment; and if you thus deal with social groups that have little or no history, and confine your attention to social processes which occur during a short period of time,—for example, during an hour, or a day, or a year,—what then is likely to come to your notice takes either the predominantly pluralistic form of the various relatively independent doings of detached individuals, or else the social form of the confused activities of a crowd. A crowd, whether it be a dangerous mob, or an amiably joyous gathering at a picnic, is not a community. It has a mind, but no institutions, no organization, no coherent unity, no history, no traditions. It may be an unit, but is then of the type which suggests James's mere blending of various consciousnesses,—a sort of mystical loss of personality on the part of its members. On the other hand, a group of independent buyers at market, or of the passers-by in a city street, is not a community. And it also does not suggest to the onlooker any blending of many selves in one. Each purchaser seeks his own affairs. There may be gossip, but gossip is not a function which establishes the life of a community. For gossip has a short memory. But a true community is essentially a product of a time-process. A community has a past and will have a future. Its more or less conscious history, real or ideal, is a part of its very essence. A community requires for its existence a history and is greatly aided in its consciousness by a memory.

If you object that a Pauline church, such as I have so often used as an ideal instance of a community, was an institution that had been but very recently founded when the apostle wrote his epistles, then I reply at once that a Pauline church was instructed by the apostle to regard its life as a phase in the historical process of the salvation of mankind. This process, as conceived by Paul and his churches, had gone on from Adam unto Moses, from Moses unto Christ; and the very life of the community was bound up with its philosophy of history. That the memory of this community was in part legendary is beside the point. Its memory was essential to its life, and was busy with the fate of all mankind and with the course of all time.

The psychological unity of many selves in one community is bound up, then, with the consciousness of some lengthy social process which has occurred, or is at least supposed to have occurred. And the wealthier the memory of a community is, and the vaster the historical processes which it regards as belonging to its life, the richer—other things being equal—is its consciousness that it *is* a community, that its members are somehow made one in and through and with its own life.

The Japanese are fond of telling us that their imperial family, and their national life, are coeval with heaven and earth. The boast is cheerfully extravagant; but its relation to a highly developed form of the consciousness of a community is obvious. Here, then, is a consideration belonging to social psychology, but highly important for our understanding of the sense in which a community is or can be possessed of one mental life.

X

If we ask for the reason why such a real or fancied history, possessing in general a considerable length and importance, is psychologically needed in case a group consisting of many individual human beings is to regard itself as an united community, our attention is at once called to a consideration which I regard as indeed decisive for the whole theory of the reality of the community. Obvious as it is, however, this consideration needs to be explicitly mentioned, because the complexity of the facts often makes us neglect them.

The rule that time is needed for the formation of a conscious community is a rule which finds its extremely familiar analogy within the life of every individual human self. Each one of us knows that he just now, at this instant, cannot find more than a mere fragment of himself present. The self comes down to us from its own past. It needs and is a history. Each of us can see that his own idea of himself as this person is inseparably bound up with his view of his own former life, of the plans that he formed, of the fortunes that fashioned him, and of the accomplishments which in turn he has fashioned for himself. A self is, by its very essence, a being with a past. One must look lengthwise backwards in the stream of time in order to see the self, or its shadow, now moving with the stream, now eddying in the currents from bank to bank of its channel, and now strenuously straining onwards in the pursuit of its own chosen good.

At this present moment I am indeed here, as this creature of the moment,—sundered from the other selves. But nevertheless, if considered simply in this passing moment of my life, I am hardly a self at all. I am just a flash of consciousness,—the mere gesticulation of a self,—not a coherent personality. Yet memory links me with my own past,—and not, in the same way, with the past of any one else. This joining of the present to the past reveals a more or less steady tendency,—a sense about the whole process of my remembered life. And this tendency and sense of my individual life agree, on the whole, with the sense and the tendencies that belong to the entire flow of the time-stream, so far as it has sense at all. My individual life, my own more or less well-sundered stream of tendency, not only is shut off at each present moment by various barriers from the lives of other selves,—but also constitutes an intelligible sequence in itself, so that, as I look back, I can say: "What I yesterday intended to pursue, that I am to-day still pursuing." "My present carries farther the plan of my past." Thus, then, I am one more or less coherent plan expressed in a life. "The child is father to the man." My days are "bound each to each by mutual piety."

Since I am this self, not only by reason of what now sunders me from the inner lives of other selves, but by reason of what links me, in significant fashion, to the remembered experiences, deeds, plans, and interests of my former conscious life, I need a somewhat extended and remembered past to furnish the opportunity for my self to find, when it looks back, a long process that possesses sense and coherence. In brief, my idea of myself is an interpretation of my past,—linked also with an interpretation of my hopes and intentions as to my future.

Precisely as I thus define myself with reference to my own past, so my fellows also interpret the sense, the value, the qualifications, and the possessions of my present self by virtue of what are sometimes called my antecedents. In the eyes of his fellow-men, the child is less of a self than is the mature man; and he is so not merely because the child just now possesses a less wealthy and efficient conscious life than a mature man possesses, but because the antecedents of his present self are fewer than are the antecedents of the present self of the mature man. The child has little past. He has accomplished little. The mature man bears the credit and the burden of his long life of deeds. His former works qualify his present deeds. He not only possesses, but in great part is, for his fellow-men, a record.

These facts about our individual self-consciousness are indeed well known. But they remind us that our idea of the individual self is no mere present datum, or collection of data, but is based upon an interpretation of the sense, of the tendency, of the coherence, and of the value of a life to which belongs the memory of its own past. And therefore these same facts will help us to see how the idea of the community is also an idea which is impressed upon us whenever we make a sufficiently successful and fruitful effort to interpret the sense, the coherent interest, and the value of the relations in which a great number of different selves stand to the past.

XI

Can many different selves, all belonging to the present time, possess identically the same past as their own personally interesting past life? This question, if asked about the recent past, cannot be answered in the affirmative, unless one proposes either to ignore or in some way to set aside the motives which, in our present consciousness, emphasize, as we have seen, the pluralism of the social selves. Quite different, however, becomes the possible answer to this question if, without in the least ignoring our present varieties and sunderings, one asks the question concerning some past time that belongs to previous generations of men. For then each of two or more men may regard the same fact of past life as, in the same sense, a part of his own personal life. Two men of the present time may, for instance, have any number of ancestors in common. To say this is not to ignore the pluralistic view of the selves, but only to make mention of familiar facts of descent. But now if these men take great interest in their ancestors, and have a genuine or legendary tradition concerning the ancestors, each of the two men of the present time may regard the lives, the deeds, the glory, and perhaps the spiritual powers or the immortal lives of certain ancestors, now dwelling in the spirit-world, as a part of his own self. Thus, when the individual Maori, in New Zealand, in case he still follows the old ways, speaks of the legendary canoes in which the ancestors of old came over from the home land called Hawaiki to New Zealand, he says, choosing the name of the canoe according to his own tribe and tradition, "*I* came over in the canoe Tai-Nui." Now any two members of a tribe whose legendary ancestors came over in Tai-Nui, possess, from their own point of view, identically the same past, in just this respect. Each of the two men in question has the same reason, good or bad, for extending himself into the past, and

for saying, "I came over in that canoe." Now the belief in this identity of
the past self of the ancestor of the canoe, belonging to each of the two New
Zealanders, does not in the least depend upon ignoring, or upon minimiz-
ing, the present difference between these two selves. The present consciousnesses do not in the least tend to interpenetrate. Neither of the two
New Zealanders in question need suppose that there is now any compounding of consciousness. Each may keep aloof from the other. They may be
enemies. But each has a reason, and an obvious reason, for extending himself into the ancestral past.

My individual self extends backwards, and is identified with my remembered self of yesterday, or of former years. This is an interpretation of
my life which in general turns upon the coherence of deeds, plans, interests,
hopes, and spiritual possessions in terms of which I learn to define myself.
Now my remembered past is in general easily to be distinguished from the
past of any other self. But if I am so interested in the life or in the deeds of
former generations that I thus extend, as the Maori extends, my own self
into the ancestral past, the self thus extended finds that the same identical
canoe or ancestor is part of my own life, and also part of the ideally extended
life of some fellow-tribesman who is now so different a being, and so
sharply sundered from my present self.

Now, in such a case, how shall I best describe the unity that, according
to this interpretation of our common past, links my fellow-tribesmen and
myself? A New Zealander says, "We are of the same canoe." And a more
general expression of such relations would be to say, in all similar cases,
"We are of the same community."

In this case, then, the real or supposed identity of certain interesting
features in a past which each one of two or of many men regards as belonging to his own historically extended former self, is a ground for saying
that all these many, although now just as various and as sundered as they
are, constitute, with reference to this common past, a community. When
defined in such terms, the concept of the community loses its mystical
seeming. It depends indeed upon an interpretation of the significance of
facts, and does not confine itself to mere report of particulars; but it does
not ignore the present varieties of experience. It depends also upon an interpretation which does not merely say, "These events happened," but adds,
"These events belong to the life of this self or of this other self." Such an
interpretation we all daily make in speaking of the past of our own familiar
individual selves. The process which I am now using as an illustration,—
the process whereby the New Zealander says, "I came over in that canoe,"—extends the quasi-personal memory of each man into an historical
past that may be indefinitely long and vast. But such an extension has motives which are not necessarily either mystical or monistic. We all share

those motives, and use them, in our own way, and according to our ideals, whenever we consider the history of our country, or of mankind, or of whatever else seems to us to possess a history that is significantly linked with our personal history.

XII

Just as each one of many present selves, despite the psychological or ethical barriers which now keep all of these selves sundered, may accept the same past fact or event as a part of himself, and say, "That belonged to my life," even so, each one of many present selves, despite these same barriers and sunderings, may accept the same future event, which all of them hope or expect, as part of his own personal future. Thus, during a war, all of the patriots of one of the contending nations may regard the termination of the war, and the desired victory of their country, so that each one says: "I shall rejoice in the expected surrender of that stronghold of the enemy. That surrender will be my triumph."

Now when many contemporary and distinct individual selves so interpret, each his own personal life, that each says of an individual past or of a determinate future event or deed: "That belongs to my life"; "That occurred, or will occur, to me," then these many selves may be defined as hereby constituting, in a perfectly definite and objective, but also in a highly significant, sense, a community. They may be said to constitute a community *with reference* to that particular past or future event, or group of events, which each of them accepts or interprets as belonging to his own personal past or to his own individual future. A community constituted by the fact that each of its members accepts as part of his own individual life and self the same *past* events that each of his fellow-members accepts, may be called a *community of memory*. Such is any group of persons who individually either remember or commemorate the same dead,—each one finding, because of personal affection or of reverence for the dead, that those whom he commemorates form for him a part of his own past existence.

A community constituted by the fact that each of its members accepts, as part of his own individual life and self, the same expected *future* events that each of his fellows accepts, may be called a *community of expectation,* or upon occasion, a *community of hope.*

A community, whether of memory or of hope, exists relatively to the past or future facts to which its several members stand in the common relation just defined. The concept of the community depends upon the interpretation which each individual member gives to his own self,—to his own past,—and to his own future. Every one of us does, for various reasons, extend his interpretation of his own individual self so that from his own point of view, his life includes many far-away temporal happenings. The complex motives of such interpretations need not now be further examined. Enough,—these motives may vary from self to self with all the wealth of life. Yet when these interests of each self lead it to accept any part or item of the same past or the same future which another self accepts as its own,— then pluralism of the selves is perfectly consistent with their forming a community, either of memory or of hope. How rich this community is in meaning, in value, in membership, in significant organization, will depend upon the selves that enter into the community, and upon the ideals in terms of which they define themselves, their past, and their future.

With this definition in mind, we see why long histories are needed in order to define the life of great communities. We also see that, if great new undertakings enter into the lives of many men, a new community of hope, unified by the common relations of its individual members to the same future events, may be, upon occasion, very rapidly constituted, even in the midst of great revolutions.

The concept of the community, as thus analyzed, stands in the closest relation to the whole nature of the time-process, and also involves recognizing to the full both the existence and the significance of individual selves. In what sense the individual selves constitute the community we can in general see, while we are prepared to find that, for the individual selves, it may well prove to be the case that a real community of memory or of hope is necessary in order to secure their significance. Our own definition of a community can be illustrated by countless types of political, religious, and other significant communities which you will readily be able to select for yourselves. Without ignoring our ordinary social pluralism, this definition shows how and why many selves may be viewed as actually brought together in an historical community. Without presupposing any one metaphysical interpretation of experience, or of time, our definition shows where, in our experience and in our interpretation of the time-process, we are to look for a solution of the problem of the community. Without going beyond the facts of human life, of human memory, and of human interpretation of the self and of its past, our definition clears the way for a study of the constitution of the real world of the spirit.

PERCEPTION, CONCEPTION,
AND INTERPRETATION

In defining what constitutes a community I have repeatedly mentioned processes of Interpretation. The word ''interpretation'' is well known; and students of the humanities have special reasons for using it frequently. When one calls an opinion about the self an interpretation, one is not employing language that is familiar only to philosophers. When a stranger in a foreign land desires the services of an interpreter, when a philologist offers his rendering of a text, when a judge construes a statute, some kind of interpretation is in question. And the process of interpretation, whatever it is, is intended to meet human needs which are as well known as they are vital. Such needs determine, as we shall see, whatever is humane and articulate in the whole conduct and texture of our lives.

I

Yet if we ask, What is an interpretation?—the answer is not easy. Nor is it made much easier by stating the question in the form: What does one desire who seeks for an interpretation? What does one gain, or create, or acknowledge who accepts an interpretation?

Our investigation has reached the point where it is necessary to face these questions, as well as some others closely related to them. For, as a fact, to inquire what the process of interpretation is, takes us at once to the very heart of philosophy, throws a light both on the oldest and on the latest issues of metaphysical thought, and has an especially close connection with the special topics to which this course is devoted.

279

II

First, then, let me briefly recall the ways in which we have already been brought into contact with questions involving the nature of interpretation.

Our whole undertaking is an effort to interpret vital features of Christianity. Each of the three ideas which I have viewed as essential to the Christian doctrine of life had to be interpreted first for itself, and then in its connection with the others. You might have supposed that, when we turned to our metaphysical problems, we should henceforth have to do with questions of fact, and not with interpretations. But we have found that we could not decide how the Christian doctrine of life is related to the real world without defining what we mean by a community. A community, as we have seen, depends for its very constitution upon the way in which each of its members interprets himself and his life. For the rest, nobody's self is either a mere datum or an abstract conception. A self is a life whose unity and connectedness depend upon some sort of interpretation of plans, of memories, of hopes, and of deeds. If, then, there are communities, there are many selves who, despite their variety, so interpret their lives that all these lives, taken together, get the type of unity which our last lecture characterized. Were there, then, no interpretations in the world, there would be neither selves nor communities. Thus our effort to study matters of fact led us back to problems of interpretation. These latter problems obviously dominate every serious inquiry into our problem of Christianity.

What, however, is any philosophy but an interpretation either of life, or of the universe, or of both? Does there exist, then, any student of universally interesting issues who is not concerned with an answer to the question, What is an interpretation?

Possibly these illustrations of our topic, few as they are, seem already so various in their characters as to suggest that the term "interpretation" may be too vague in its applications to admit of precise definition. A rendering of a text written in a foreign tongue; a judge's construction of a statute; a man's interpretation of himself and of his own life; our own philosophical interpretation of this or of that religious idea; and the practical interpretation of our destiny, or of God, which a great historical religion itself seems to have taught to the faithful; or, finally, a metaphysical interpretation of the universe,—what—so you may ask—have all these things in common? What value can there be in attempting to fix by a definition such fluent and uncontrollable interests as inspire what various people may call by the common name interpretation?

III

I reply that, beneath all this variety in the special motives which lead men to interpret objects, there exists a very definable unity of purpose. Look more closely, and you shall see that to interpret, or to attempt an interpretation, is to assume an attitude of mind which differs, in a notable way, from the other attitudes present in the intelligent activities of men; while this attitude remains essentially the same amidst very great varieties, both in the individual interpreters and in the interpretations which they seek, or undertake, or accept. Interpretation, viewed as a mental process, or as a type of knowledge, differs from other mental processes and types of knowledge in the objects to which it is properly applied, in the relations in which it stands to these objects, and in the ends which it serves.

In order to show you that this is the case, I must summarize in my own way some still neglected opinions which were first set forth, in outline, more than forty years ago by our American logician, Mr. Charles Peirce, in papers which have been little read, but which, to my mind, remain of very high value as guides of inquiry, both in Logic and in the Theory of Knowledge.[1]

Mr. Charles Peirce has become best known to the general public by the part which William James assigned to him as the inventor of the term "Pragmatism," and as, in some sense, the founder of the form of Pragmatism which James first made his own, and then developed so independently and so significantly. But by a small and grateful company of philosophical students, Mr. Peirce is prized, not solely, and not, I think, mainly for his part in the early history of Pragmatism, but for his contributions to Logic, and for those remarkable cosmological speculations which James also, in his lectures on the *Pluralistic Universe* (as some of you will remember), heartily acknowledged.

Those ideas of Charles Peirce about Interpretation to which I shall here

---

1. Of the early papers of Mr. Charles Peirce to which reference is here made, the most important are:—
- In the *Proceedings of the American Academy of Arts and Sciences*, a paper: "On a New List of Categories," May 14, 1867.
- In the *Journal of Speculative Philosophy*, Vol. II (1868–1869): "Questions concerning Certain Faculties claimed for Man."
- *Id.:* "Some Consequences of Four Incapacities."
- *Id.:* "Grounds of the Validity of the Laws of Logic; Further Consequences of Four Incapacities."

    In addition to these early papers we may mention:—
- Article "Sign" in Baldwin's "Dictionary of Philosophy and Psychology,"—a brief statement regarding an important point of Peirce's theory.

refer, never, so far as I know, attracted William James's personal attention at any time. I may add that, until recently, I myself never appreciated their significance. In acknowledging here my present indebtedness to these ideas, I have to add that, in this place, there is no room to expound them at length. The context in which these views appear, both in the earliest of the published logical papers of Peirce (about 1868), and in many of his later discussions, is always very technical, and is such that no adequate discussion of the issues involved could be presented in a brief statement. Moreover, it is proper to say that Charles Peirce cannot be held responsible for the use that I shall here make of his opinions, or for any of the conclusions that I base upon them.

There is one additional matter which should be emphasized at the outset. Peirce's opinions as to the nature of interpretation were in no wise influenced by Hegel, or by the tradition of German idealism. He formed them on the basis of his own early scientific studies, and of his extensive, although always very independent, interest in the history of scholastic logic. With recent idealism this "father of Pragmatism" has always felt only a very qualified sympathy, and has frequently expressed no little dissatisfaction. Some twelve years ago, just after I had printed a book on general philosophy, Mr. Charles Peirce wrote to me, in a letter of kindly acknowledgment, the words: "But, when I read you, I do wish that you would study logic. You need it so much."

Abandoning, then, any effort to state Peirce's case as he stated it, let me next call attention to matters which I should never have viewed as I now view them without his direct or indirect aid.

IV

The contrast between the cognitive processes called, respectively, perception and conception, dominates a great part of the history of philosophy. This contrast is usually so defined as to involve a dual classification of our cognitive processes. When one asks which of the two processes, perception or conception, gives us the more significant guidance, or is the original from which the other is derived, or is the ideal process whereof the other is the degenerate fellow, such a dual classification is in possession of the field.

This classic dual opposition was expressed, in characteristically finished fashion, at the outset of the lectures which Professor Bergson read, in May of last year, at the invitation of the University of Oxford. You all remember his words: "If our power of external and internal perception were unlimited, we should never make use of our power to conceive, or of our power to reason. To conceive is a makeshift in the cases where one cannot perceive; and one reasons only in so far as one needs to fill gaps in our outer or inner perception, or to extend the range of perception.''

Here, as is obvious, there is no recognition of the possible or actual existence of a third type of cognitive process, which is neither perception nor conception. The assertion that conception is our makeshift when perception is limited, and that unlimited perception, by rendering conception superfluous, would supply us with that grade of intuition which we, in ideal, attribute to a divine being, involves the postulate that we face the alternative: Either perception, or else conception.

But if one were to oppose the thesis just cited by declaring in favor of conception as against perception; if one were to assert that perception deceives us with vain show, and that conception alone can bring us face to face with reality; if, in short, one were to prefer Plato to Bergson,—one would not thereby necessarily be led to abandon,—one might, on the contrary, all the more emphasize this dual classification of the possible cognitive processes. In such a predominantly dualistic view of the classification of knowledge, both rationalism and empiricism have, on the whole, agreed, throughout the history of thought. Kant and James, Bergson and Mr. Bertrand Russell, are, in this respect, at one.

To be sure, in addition to perception and conception, reason and the reasoning process have been very frequently recognized as having some sort of existence for themselves, over and above the processes of simple perception and conception. Yet when Bergson speaks of reasoning, in the passage just cited from his Oxford lecture, reasoning, for him, means a special form or grade of the conceptual process itself, and is therefore no third type of cognition. When Kant made his well-known triadic distinctions of sense, understanding, and reason, assigning to sense the power of perceiving, to understanding the power to form and to use concepts, and to reason a third function which Kant did not always define in the same way,—he did not really succeed in escaping from the classical dualism with regard to the processes of cognition. For Kant's account of reason assigns to it, in general, a high grade of conceptual functions, as opposed to perceptual functions; and thus still depends upon the dual contrast between perception and conception. Kant is nearest to defining a third type of cognitive process in many of his accounts of what he calls the *Urtheilskraft*. But he never consistently maintains a triadic classification of the cognitive processes.

V

Despite this prevalence of the dual classification of our cognitive processes, most of us will readily acknowledge that, in our real life, we human beings are never possessed either of pure perception or of pure conception. In ideal, we can define an intuitive type of knowledge, which should merely see, and which should never think. In an equally ideal fashion, we can imagine the possibility of a pure thought, which should be wholly absorbed in conceptions, which should have as its sole real object a realm of universals, and which should ignore all sensible data. But we mortals live the intelligent part of our lives through some sort of more or less imperfect union or synthesis of conception and perception.

In recent discussion it has become almost a commonplace to recognize this union as constantly exemplified in human experience. In this one respect, to-day, empiricists and rationalists, pragmatists and intellectualists, are accustomed to agree, although great differences arise with regard to *what* union of perception and conception constitutes such knowledge as we human beings can hopefully pursue or actually possess.

Kant, assuring us that conceptions without perceptions are "empty," and that perceptions without conceptions are "blind," sets forth, in his theory of knowledge, the well-known account of how the "spontaneity" of the intellect actively combines the perceptual data, and brings the so-called "manifold of sense" to "unity of conception."

Recent pragmatism, laying stress upon the "practical" character of every human cognitive process, depicts the life of knowledge as a dramatic pursuit of perceptions,—a pursuit guided by the "leadings" which our conceptions determine, and which, in some sense, simply constitute our conceptions, in so far as these have genuine life.

When, a number of years ago, I began a general metaphysical inquiry by defining an idea as a "plan of action," and thereupon developed a theory of knowledge and of reality, upon bases which this definition helped me to formulate, I was making my own use of thoughts which, in their outlines, are at the present day common property. The outcome of my own individual use of this definition was a sort of absolute pragmatism, which has never been pleasing either to rationalists or to empiricists, either to pragmatists or to the ruling type of absolutists. But in so far as I simply insisted upon the active meaning of ideas, my statement had something in common with many forms of current opinion which agree with one another in hardly any other respect. Only the more uncompromising of the mystics still seek for knowledge in a silent land of absolute intuition, where the intellect finally lays down its conceptual tools, and rests from its pragmatic labors, while its works do not follow it, but are simply forgotten, and are as if they never had been. Those of us who are not such uncompromising mystics, view accessible human knowledge neither as pure perception nor as pure conception, but always as depending upon the marriage of the two processes.

VI

Yet such a recognition of an active synthesis of perception and conception does not by itself enable us to define a genuinely triadic classification of the types of knowing processes. Let me illustrate this fact by another quotation from Bergson. In a passage in the first of his two Oxford lectures, our author says: "I do not deny the usefulness of abstract and general ideas,—any more than I question the value of bank-notes. But just as the note is only a promise to pay cash, so a conception has value only by virtue of the eventual perceptions for which it stands."

In these words, as you see, the antithesis, "conception," "perception," corresponds to the antithesis, "bank-note" and "cash," and the other antithesis, "credit-value," "cash-value." All these corresponding antitheses involve or depend upon dual classifications. Now it is true, and is expressly pointed out by Bergson, that the members of each of these pairs,—the credit-value, and the cash-value,—as well as the bank-note and its equivalent in gold,—are brought into a certain synthesis by the existence of a process of promising, and of redeeming the promise. A promise, however, involves a species of activity. In case of the bank-note, this activity may express whatever makes some vast commercial system solvent, or may be based upon the whole power of a great modern state.

In very much the same way, many philosophers of otherwise widely different opinions recognize that conception and perception are, in live cognitive processes, brought into synthesis by some sort of activity,—the activity of the mind whose cognitions are in question. This activity may be one of attention. Or it may consist of a series of voluntary deeds.

But in each of these cases, the members of a pair, "bank-note and cash," or "conception and perception," are first antithetically opposed to each other; and then a third or active element, a promise, a volition, or what you will, is mentioned as that which brings the members of the pair into synthesis. But this third or synthetic factor is not thus coordinated with the two opposed members of the pair.

If action, or activity, is the name given to whatever brings perceptions and conceptions into synthesis, then this third factor is not hereby set side by side, both with perception and with conception as a third form of cognitive activity. For action may be viewed as a non-cognitive function,—and classified as "conation." Or, on the contrary, action may be viewed as that grade of cognition which, being neither conception alone, nor perception alone, but the synthesis of the two, is the *only* mature and successfully completed cognitive process. Both of these views have been asserted. We need not discuss them here. But, in any case, "action" or "activity" is not itself hereby defined as a third type of cognition; any more than the activity of promising to pay, in Bergson's illustration, is defined as a third sort of currency which is neither gold nor bank-notes.

Thus far, then, the classification of the cognitive processes as being either perceptions or else conceptions remains triumphant, and is not superseded by regarding genuine knowledge as a synthesis of these two. For the dual contrast between perception and conception dominates all such opinions.

VII

Yet cognition may be considered from a slightly different point of view.

It is natural to classify cognitive processes by their characteristic objects. The object of a perception is a datum of some sort, a *thing*, or perhaps, as Bergson insists, a *change*, or whatever else we may be able immediately to apprehend. The object of a conception is an *universal* of some sort, a *general* or *abstract character*, a *type*, a *quality*, or some complex object based upon such universals. Now do all objects of cognition belong to one of these two classes? If so, in which of these classes will you place your neighbor's mind, or any of the conscious acts of that mind? Is your neighbor's mind a *datum* that you could, were your perception "unlimited," simply find *present* to you, as *red* or as a "change" can be present? Is your neighbor's mind, on the contrary, an abstraction, a mere *sort* of being, an *universal* which you merely conceive? If a conception resembles a banknote in being a promise to pay, which needs to be redeemed in the gold of perception,—then what immediate perception of your own could ever render to you the "cash-value" of your idea of your neighbor's mind? On the other hand, your present and personal idea of your neighbor's mind is certainly not itself such a perceptual "cash-value" for you. Your neighbor's mind is no mere *datum* to your sense at any time.

If, then, there be any cognitive process whose proper object is your neighbor's mind, this process is neither a mere conception nor yet a mere perception. Is it, then, some synthesis or combination of perceptions and conceptions? Or is it, finally, some third form of cognitive process, which is neither perception nor conception, and which cannot be completely describable in terms of combined perceptions and conceptions? Now it appears that the word "interpretation" is a convenient name for a process which at least aims to be cognitive. And the proper object of an interpretation, as we usually employ the name, is either something of the nature of a mind, or else is a process which goes on in a mind, or, finally, is a sign or expression whereby some mind manifests its existence and its processes. Let us consider, then, more closely, whether the process of interpretation, in so far as its proper object is a mind, or is the sign of a mind, can be reduced to a pure perception, or to pure conception, or to any synthesis which merely involves these two.

VIII

We shall here be aided by a very familiar instance, suggested by the very illustration which Bergson uses in pointing out the contrast between perception and conception, and in emphasizing the secondary and purely instrumental character of the process of conception. Gold coin, as Bergson reminds us, corresponds, in its value for the ordinary business of buying and selling, to perceptions as they appear in our experience. Bank-notes correspond, in an analogous fashion, to conceptions. The notes are promises to pay cash. The conceptions are useful guides to possible perceptions. The link between the note and its cash-value is the link which the activity of making and keeping the promises of a solvent bank provides. The link between the conception and its corresponding perception is the link which some active synthesis, such as voluntary seeking, or creative action, or habitual conduct, or intention, supplies. The illustration is clear. In a special way perceptions do indeed correspond to cash-values, and conceptions to credit-values. But in the world of commercial transactions there are other values than simple cash-values and credit-values. Perhaps, therefore, in the realm of cognitive processes there may be analogous varieties.

Recall the familiar case wherein a traveller crosses the boundary of a foreign country. To the boundary he comes provided, let us say, with the gold and with bank-notes of his own country, but without any letter of credit. This side of the boundary his bank-notes are good because of their credit-value. His gold is good because, being the coinage of the realm, it possesses cash-value and is legal tender. But beyond the boundary, in the land to which he goes, the coin which he carries is no longer legal tender, and possibly will not pass at all in ordinary transactions. His bank-notes may be, for the moment, valueless, not because the promise stamped upon their face is irredeemable, but because the gold coin itself into which they could be converted upon presentation at the bank in question, would not be legal tender beyond the boundary.

Consequently, at the boundary, a new process may be convenient, if not, for the traveller's purpose, indispensable. It is the process of exchanging coin of the realm which he leaves for that of the foreign land which he enters. The process may be easy or difficult, may be governed by strict rules or else may be capricious, according to the conditions which prevail at the boundary. But it is a third process, which consists neither in the presentation of cash-values nor in the offering or accepting of credit-values. It is a process of interpreting the cash-values which are recognized by the laws and customs of one realm in terms of the cash-values which are legal tender in another country. It is also a process of proceeding to act upon the basis of this interpretation. We are not concerned with the principles which make this interpretation possible, or which guide the conduct either of the traveller or of the money-changer at the boundary. What interests us here is simply the fact that a new type of transaction is now in question. It is a process of money-changing,—a special form of exchange of values, but a form not simply analogous to the type of the activities whereby conceptions are provided with their corresponding perceptions. And this form is not reducible to that of the simple contrast between credit-values and cash-values.

IX

Each of us, in every new effort to communicate with our fellow-men, stands, like the traveller crossing the boundary of a new country, in the presence of a largely strange world of perceptions and of conceptions. Our neighbor's perceptions, in their immediate presence, we never quite certainly share. Our neighbor's conceptions, for various reasons which I need not here enumerate, are so largely communicable that they can often be regarded, with a high degree of probability, as identical, in certain aspects of their meaning, with our own. But the active syntheses, the practical processes of seeking and of construction, the volitions, the promises, whereby we pass from our own concepts to our own percepts, are often in a high degree individual. In that case it may be very difficult to compare them to the corresponding processes of our neighbors; and then a mutual understanding, in respect of our activities and their values, is frequently as hard to obtain as is a direct view of one another's sensory perceptions. "I never loved you," so says Hamlet to Ophelia. "My lord, you made me believe so." Here is a classic instance of a problem of mutual interpretation. Who of us can solve this problem for Hamlet and Ophelia?

Therefore, in our efforts to view the world as other men view it, our undertaking is very generally analogous to the traveller's financial transactions when he crosses the boundary. We try to solve the problem of learning how to exchange the values of our own lives into the terms which can hope to pass current in the new or foreign spiritual realms whereto, when we take counsel together, we are constantly attempting to pass. Both the credit-values and the cash-values are not always easily exchanged.

I have no hope of showing, in the present discussion, how and how far we can make sure that, in a given case of human social intercourse, we actually succeed in fairly exchanging the coinage of our perceptions and the bank-notes of our conceptions into the values which pass current in the realm beyond the boundary. What measure of truth our individual interpretations possess, and by what tests we verify that truth, I have not now to estimate. But I am strongly interested in the fact that, just as the process of obtaining cash for our bank-notes is not the same as the process of exchanging our coins for foreign coins when we pass the border, precisely so the process of verifying our concepts through obtaining the corresponding percepts is not the same as the process of interpreting our neighbors' minds.

A philosophy which, like that of Bergson, defines the whole problem of knowledge in terms of the classic opposition between conception and perception, and which then declares that, if our powers of perception were unlimited, the goal of knowledge would be reached, simply misses the principal problem, both of our daily human existence and of all our higher spiritual life, as well as of the universe. And in bidding us seek the solution of our problems in terms of perception, such a doctrine simply forbids us to pass any of the great boundaries of the spiritual world, or to explore the many realms wherein the wealth of the spirit is poured out. For neither perception nor conception, nor any combination of the two, nor yet their synthesis in our practical activities, constitutes the whole of any interpretation. Interpretation, however, is what we seek in all our social and spiritual relations; and without some process of interpretation, we obtain no fulness of life.

X

It would be wrong to suppose, however, that interpretation is needed and is used only in our literal social relations with other individual human beings. For it is important to notice that one of the principal problems in the life of each of us is the problem of interpreting himself. The bare mention of Hamlet's words reminds us of this fact. Ophelia does not understand Hamlet. But does he understand himself?

In our inner life it not infrequently happens that we have—like the traveller, or like Hamlet in the ghost-scene, or like Macbeth when there comes the knocking on the gate—to pass a boundary, to cross into some new realm, not merely of experience, but of desire, of hope, or of resolve. It is then our fortune not merely that our former ideas, as the pragmatists say, no longer ''work,'' and that our bank-notes can no longer be cashed in terms of the familiar inner perceptions which we have been accustomed to seek.

Our situation is rather this: that *both* our ideas *and* our experiences, both our plans and our powers to realize plans, both our ideas with their "leadings" and our intuitions, are in process of dramatic transformation. At such times we need to know, like Nebuchadnezzar, both our dream and its interpretation.

Such critical passing of a boundary in one's own inner world is a well-known event in youth, when what Goethe called:—

Neue Liebe, neues Leben,
Neue Hoffnung, neues Sehnen,

makes one say to one's heart:—

Ich erkenne dich nicht mehr.

Yet, not only youth, but personal calamity, or other "moving accident," or, in a more inspiring way, the call of some new constructive task, or, in the extreme case, a religious conversion, may at any time force one or another of us to cross a boundary in a fashion similar to those just illustrated.

At such times we are impressed with the fact that there is no royal road to self-knowledge. Charles Peirce, in the earliest of the essays to which I am calling your attention, maintained (quite rightly, I think) that there is no direct intuition or perception of the self. Reflection, as Peirce there pointed out, involves what is, in its essence, an interior conversation, in which one discovers one's own mind through a process of inference analogous to the very modes of inference which guide us in a social effort to interpret our neighbors' minds. Such social inference is surely no merely conceptual process. But it cannot be reduced to the sort of perception which Bergson invited you, in his Oxford lectures, to share. Although you are indeed placed in the "interior" of yourself, you can never so far retire into your own inmost recesses of intuition as merely to find the true self presented to an inner sense.

XI

So far I have merely sketched, with my own illustrations, a few notable features of Peirce's early opinions about interpretation. We are now ready for his central thesis, which, with many variations in detail, he has retained in all his later discussions of the processes in question. I beg you not to be discouraged by the fact that, since Peirce has always been, first of all, a logician, he states this central thesis in a decidedly formal fashion, which I here somewhat freely imitate. We shall soon see the usefulness of this formal procedure.

Interpretation always involves a relation of three terms. In the technical phrase, interpretation *is* a triadic relation. That is, you cannot express any complete process of interpreting by merely naming two terms,—persons, or other objects,—and by then telling what dyadic relation exists between one of these two and the other.

Let me illustrate: Suppose that an Egyptologist translates an inscription. So far two beings are indeed in question: the translator and his text. But a genuine translation cannot be merely a translation in the abstract. There must be some language into which the inscription is translated. Let this translation be, in a given instance, an English translation. Then the translator interprets something; but he interprets it only to one who can read English. And if a reader knows no English, the translation is for such a reader no interpretation at all. That is, a triad of beings—the Egyptian text, the Egyptologist who translates, and the possible English reader—are equally necessary in order that such an English interpretation of an Egyptian writing should exist. Whenever anybody translates a text, the situation remains, however you vary texts or languages or translators, essentially the same. There must exist some one, or some class of beings, to whose use this translation is adapted; while the translator is somebody who expresses himself by mediating between two expressions of meanings, or between two languages, or between two speakers or two writers. The mediator or translator, or interpreter, must, in cases of this sort, himself know both languages, and thus be intelligible to both the persons whom his translation serves. The triadic relation in question is, in its essence, non-symmetrical,—that is, unevenly arranged with respect to all three terms. Thus somebody (let us say A)—the translator or interpreter—interprets somebody (let us say B) to somebody (let us say C). If you transpose the order of the terms,—A, B, C,—an account of the happening which constitutes an interpretation must be altered, or otherwise may become either false or meaningless.

Thus an interpretation is a relation which not only involves three terms, but brings them into a determinate order. One of the three terms is the interpreter; a second term is the object—the person or the meaning or the text—which is interpreted; the third is the person to whom the interpretation is addressed.

This may, at first, seem to be a mere formality. But nothing in the world is more momentous than the difference between a pair and a triad of terms may become, if the terms and the relations involved are themselves sufficiently full of meaning.

You may observe that, when a man perceives a thing, the relation is dyadic. A perceives B. A pair of members is needed, and suffices, to make the relation possible. But when A interprets B to C, a triad of members (whereof, as in case of other relations, two or all three members may be wholly, or in part, identical) must exist in order to make the interpretation possible. Let illustrations show us how important this formal condition of interpretation may become.

When a process of conscious reflection goes on, a man may be said to interpret himself to himself. In this case, although but one personality, in the usual sense of the term, is in question, the relation is still really a triadic relation. And, in general, in such a case, the man who is said to be reflecting remembers some former promise or resolve of his own, or perhaps reads an old letter that he once wrote, or an entry in a diary. He then, at some present time, interprets this expression of his past self.

But, usually, he interprets this bit of his past self to his future self. "This," he says, "is what I meant when I made that promise." "This is what I wrote or recorded or promised." "Therefore," he continues, addressing his future self, "I am now committed to doing thus," "planning thus," and so on.

The interpretation in question still constitutes, therefore, a triadic relation. And there are three men present in and taking part in the interior conversation: the man of the past whose promises, notes, records, old letters, are interpreted; the present self who interprets them; and the future self to whom the interpretation is addressed. Through the present self the past is so interpreted that its counsel is conveyed to the future self.

XII

The illustration just chosen has been taken from the supposed experience of an individual man. But the relations involved are capable of a far-reaching metaphysical generalization. For this generalization I cannot cite the authority of Peirce. I must deal with just this aspect of the matter in my own way.

The relations exemplified by the man who, at a given present moment, interprets his own past to his own future, are precisely analogous to the relations which exist when any past state of the world is, at any present moment, so linked, through a definite historical process, with the coming state of the world, that an intelligent observer who happened to be in possession of the facts could, were he present, interpret to a possible future observer the meaning of the past. Such interpretation might or might not involve definite predictions of future events. History or biography, physical or mental processes, might be in question; fate or free will, determinism or chance, might rule the region of the world which was under consideration. The most general distinctions of past, present, and future appear in a new light when considered with reference to the process of interpretation.

In fact, what our own inner reflection exemplifies is outwardly embodied in the whole world's history. For what we all mean by past time is a realm of events whose historical sense, whose records, whose lessons, we may now interpret, in so far as our memory and the documents furnish us the evidences for such interpretation. We may also observe that what we mean by future time is a realm of events which we view as more or less under the control of the present will of voluntary agents, so that it is worth while to give to ourselves, or to our fellows, counsel regarding this future. And so, wherever the world's processes are recorded, wherever the records are preserved, and wherever they influence in any way the future course of events, we may say that (at least in these parts of the world) the present potentially interprets the past to the future, and continues so to do *ad infinitum*.

Such, for instance, is the case when one studies the crust of a planet. The erosions and the deposits of a present geological period lay down the traces which, if read by a geologist, would interpret the past history of the planet's crust to the observers of future geological periods.

Thus the Colorado Cañon, in its present condition, is a geological section produced by a recent stream. Its walls record, in their stratification, a vast series of long-past changes. The geologist of the present may read these traces, and may interpret them for future geologists of our own age. But the present state of the Colorado Cañon, which will ere long pass away as the walls crumble, and as the continents rise or sink, will leave traces that may be used at some future time to interpret these now present conditions of the earth's crust to some still more advanced future, which will come to exist after yet other geological periods have passed away.

In sum, if we view the world as everywhere and always recording its own history, by processes of aging and weathering, or of evolution, or of stellar and nebular clusterings and streamings, we can simply define the time order, and its three regions,—past, present, future,—as an order of possible interpretation. That is, we can define the present as, potentially, the interpretation of the past to the future. The triadic structure of our interpretations is strictly analogous, both to the psychological and to the metaphysical structure of the world of time. And each of these structures can be stated in terms of the other.

This analogy between the relational structure of the whole time-process and the relations which are characteristic of any system of acts of interpretation seems to me to be worthy of careful consideration.

XIII

The observation of Peirce that interpretation is a process involving, from its very essence, a triadic relation, is thus, in any case, no mere logical formalism.

Psychologically speaking, the mental process which thus involves three members differs from perception and conception in three respects. First, interpretation is a conversation, and not a lonely enterprise. There is some one, in the realm of psychological happenings, who addresses some one. The one who addresses interprets some object to the one addressed. In the second place, the interpreted object is itself something which has the nature of a mental expression. Peirce uses the term "sign" to name this mental object which is interpreted. Thirdly, since the interpretation is a mental act, and is an act which is expressed, the interpretation itself is, in its turn, a Sign. This new sign calls for further interpretation. For the interpretation is addressed to somebody. And so,—at least in ideal,—the social process involved is endless. Thus wealthy, then, in its psychological consequences, is the formal character of a situation wherein any interpretation takes place.

Perception has its natural terminus in some object perceived; and therewith the process, as would seem, might end, were there nothing else in the world to perceive. Conception is contented, so to speak, with defining the universal type, or ideal form which chances to become an object of somebody's thought. In order to define a new universal, one needs a new act of thought whose occurrence seems, in so far, an arbitrary additional cognitive function. Thus both perception and conception are, so to speak, self-limiting processes. The wealth of their facts comes to them from without, arbitrarily.

But interpretation both requires as its basis the sign or mental expression which is to be interpreted, and calls for a further interpretation of its own act, just because it addresses itself to some third being. Thus interpretation is not only an essentially social process, but also a process which, when once initiated, can be terminated only by an external and arbitrary interruption, such as death or social separation. By itself, the process of interpretation calls, in ideal, for an infinite sequence of interpretations. For every interpretation, being addressed to somebody, demands interpretation from the one to whom it is addressed.

Thus the formal difference between interpretation on the one hand, and perception and conception on the other hand, is a difference involving endlessly wealthy possible psychological consequences.

Perception is indeed supported by the wealth of our sensory processes; and is therefore rightly said to possess an endless fecundity.

But interpretation lives in a world which is endlessly richer than the realm of perception. For its discoveries are constantly renewed by the inexhaustible resources of our social relations, while its ideals essentially demand, at every point, an infinite series of mutual interpretations in order to express what even the very least conversational effort, the least attempt to find our way in the life that we would interpret, involves.

Conception is often denounced, in our day, as "sterile." But perception, taken by itself, is intolerably lonesome. And every philosophy whose sole principle is perception invites us to dwell in a desolate wilderness where neither God nor man exists. For where either God or man is in question, interpretation is demanded. And interpretation,—even the simplest, even the most halting and trivial interpretation of our daily life,—seeks what eye hath not seen, and ear hath not heard, and what it hath not entered into the heart of man to conceive,—namely, the successful interpretation of somebody to somebody.

Interpretation seeks an object which is essentially spiritual. The abyss of abstract conception says of this object: It is not in me. The heaven of glittering immediacies which perception furnishes answers the quest by saying: It is not in me. Interpretation says: It is nigh thee,—even in thine heart; but shows us, through manifesting the very nature of the object to be sought, what general conditions must be met if any one is to interpret a genuine Sign to an understanding mind. And withal, interpretation seeks a city out of sight, the homeland where, perchance, we learn to understand one another.

XIV

Our first glimpse of Charles Peirce's neglected doctrine of the logic of signs and of interpretations necessarily gives us extremely inadequate impressions. But in pointing out the parallelism between the relational characters of the time-process and those of the process of interpretation, I have already shown that the questions at issue are neither merely intellectual, nor purely conceptual, and concern many matters which are confined neither to logic nor to descriptive psychology. As a fact, to conceive the cognitive process in terms of such a threefold division, and also in terms of such a triadic relation, as the division and the relation which Peirce brings to our attention,—to view cognition thus throws light, I believe, upon all the principal issues which are now before us.

Recent pragmatism, both in the form emphasized by James and (so far as I know) in all its other now prominent forms, depends upon conceiving two types of cognitive processes, perception and conception, as mutually opposed, and as in such wise opposed that conception merely defines the bank-notes, while only perception can supply the needed cash. In consequence of this dualistic view of the cognitive process, and in view of other considerations recently emphasized, the essential doctrine of pragmatism has come to include the two well-known theses: That truth is mutable; and that the sole criterion of the present state of the truth is to be found in the contents of particular perceptions.

Corresponding to this form of epistemology we have, in the metaphysic of Bergson, a doctrine of reality based upon the same dual classification of the cognitive processes, and upon the same preference for perception as against its supposed sole rival.

But if we review the facts in the new light which Peirce's views about interpretation enable us, I think, to use, we shall reach results, that, as I close, I may yet barely hint.

XV

Reality, so Bergson tells us,—Reality, which must be perceived just as artists perceive its passing data, and thereby teach us to perceive what we never saw before,—Reality is essentially change, flow, movement. In perceptual time, if you abstract from the material limitations which the present bondage of our intellect forces upon us, both present and past interpenetrate, and all is one ever present duration, consisting of endless qualitatively various but coalescing changes.

But a recognition of the existence, and a due understanding of the character of the process of interpretation, will show us, I believe, that the time-order, in its sense and interconnection, is known to us through interpretation, and is neither a conceptual nor yet a perceptual order. We learn about it through what is, in a sense, the conversation which the present, in the name of the remembered or presupposed past, addresses to the expected future, whenever we are interested in directing our own course of voluntary action, or in taking counsel with one another. Life may be a colloquy, or a prayer; but the life of a reasonable being is never a mere perception; nor a conception; nor a mere sequence of thoughtless deeds; nor yet an active process, however synthetic, wherein interpretation plays no part. Life is essentially, in its ideal, social. Hence interpretation is a necessary element of everything that, in life, has ideal value.

But when the time-process is viewed as an interpretation of the past to the future by means of our present acts of choice, then the divisions and the successions which are found in the temporal order are not, as Bergson supposes, due to a false translation of the perceived temporal flow into a spatial order. For every present deed interprets my future; and therefore divides my life into the region of what I have already done, and the region of what

I have yet to accomplish. This division is due, not to the geometrical de-generation which Bergson refers to our intellect, but to one of the most sig-nificant features of the spiritual world,—namely, to the fact that we interpret all past time as irrevocable. So to interpret our past is the very foundation of all deliberate choice. But the irrevocable past changes no more. And the stupendous spiritual significance which this interpretation introduces into our view of our lives, of history, of nature, and of God, we have already had occasion to consider in the first part of this course. The philosophy of change, the perception of an universe where all is fluent, can be interpreted only through recognizing that the past returns not; that the deed once done is never to be recalled; that what has been done is at once the world's safest treasure, and its heaviest burden.

Whoever insists upon the mutability of truth, speaks in terms of the dual classification of cognitive processes. But let one learn to know that our very conception of our temporal experience, as of all happenings, is neither a conception nor a perception, but an interpretation. Let one note that every present judgment bearing upon future experience is indeed, as the prag-matists tell us, a practical activity. But let one also see that, for this very reason, every judgment, whose meaning is concrete and practical, so in-terprets past experience as to counsel a future deed. Let one consider that when my present judgment, addressing my future self, counsels: "Do this," this counsel, if followed, leads to an individual deed, which hence-forth irrevocably stands on the score of my life, and can never be removed therefrom.

Hence, just as what is done cannot be undone, just so what is truly or falsely counselled by any concrete and practical judgment remains perma-nently true or false. For the deed which a judgment counsels remains forever done, when once it has been done.

XVI

Let me summarize the main results of this lecture:—
1. In addition to the world of conception and to the world of percep-tion, we have to take account of a world of interpretation.
2. The features that distinguish from one another the three proc-esses—perception, conception, and interpretation—have to do with their logical and formal characteristics, with their psychological motives and ac-companiments, and with the objects to which they are directed.
3. Logically and formally considered, interpretation differs from per-ception and from conception by the fact that it involves relations which are essentially triadic.

4. Psychologically, interpretation differs from perception and from conception by the fact that it is, in its intent, an essentially social process. It accompanies every intelligent conversation. It is used whenever we acknowledge the being and the inner life of our fellow-men. It transforms our own inner life into a conscious interior conversation, wherein we interpret ourselves. Both of ourselves and of our neighbors we have no merely intuitive knowledge, no complete perception, and no adequate conception. Reflection is an effort at self-interpretation.

5. Both logically and psychologically, interpretation differs from perception and from conception in that each of these latter processes derives the wealth of its facts from a world which, at least in seeming, is external to itself. Were there but one object to perceive, and one universal to conceive, one act of perception and one of conception would be, in the abstract, possible and required. The need for new acts of perception and of conception seems to be, in so far, arbitrarily determined by the presence of new facts which are to be perceived or conceived. But interpretation, while always stimulated to fresh efforts by the inexhaustible wealth of the novel facts of the social world, demands, by virtue of its own nature, and even in the simplest conceivable case, an endless wealth of new interpretations. For every interpretation, as an expression of mental activity, addresses itself to a possible interpreter, and demands that it shall be, in its turn, interpreted. Therefore it is not the continuance, but the interruption, of the process of interpretation which appears to be arbitrary; and which seems to be due to sources and motives foreign to the act of interpretation.

6. Metaphysically considered, the world of interpretation is the world in which, if indeed we are able to interpret at all, we learn to acknowledge the being and the inner life of our fellow-men; and to understand the constitution of temporal experience, with its endlessly accumulating sequence of significant deeds. In this world of interpretation, of whose most general structure we have now obtained a glimpse, selves and communities may exist, past and future can be defined, and the realms of the spirit may find a place which neither barren conception nor the chaotic flow of interpenetrating perceptions could ever render significant.

7. Bergson has eloquently referred us to the artists, as the men whose office it is to teach us how to perceive. Let the philosophers, he tells us, learn from the methods of the artists. In reply we can only insist, in this place, that the sole office of the artists has always been to interpret. They address us, so as to interpret to us their own perceptions, and thereby their own lives and deeds. In turn, they call upon us to renew the endless life of the community of the spirits who interpret. The artists do not do their work for "nothing," nor yet for "pleasure." They do their work because they

love the unity of spirit which, through their work, is brought into the life of mankind. The artists are in this respect not alone.

The prophets, the founders of religions, the leaders of mankind: they do not merely see; nor do they merely think; nor yet are they mere pragmatists hovering between abstract conceptions which they dislike, and particular experiences which they indeed desire, but so view that therein they find *only* the particular. Those for whom the sole contrast in the world of cognitions is that between conception and perception, stand in Faust's position. Their conceptions are indeed mere bank-notes. But alas! their perceptions are, at best, mere cash. So in desire they hasten to enjoyment, and in enjoyment pine to feel desire.

Such find indeed their "cash" of experience in plenty. But they never find what has created all the great religions, and all the deathless loyalties, and all the genuinely true insights of the human world,—namely, that interpretation of life which sends us across the borders both of our conceptual and of our perceptual life, to lay up treasures in other worlds, to interpret the meaning of the processes of time, to read the meaning of art and of life.

8. Do you ask what this process is which thus transcends both perception and conception, I answer that it is the process in which you engage whenever you take counsel with a friend, or look in the eyes of one beloved, or serve the cause of your life. This process it is which touches the heart of reality. Let the philosophers, then, endeavor to avoid "sterile" conceptions. Let them equally avoid those wanton revels in mere perception which are at present the bane of our art, of our literature, of our social ideals, and of our religion. Let the philosophers learn from those who teach us, as the true artists do, the art of interpretation.

A few fragmentary indications of the principles of this art we may hope, at the next time, to set forth upon the bases which Charles Peirce's theory has suggested.

THE WORLD OF INTERPRETATION

In the closing lecture of a course delivered a few years since, on the "Problem of Age, Growth, and Death," Professor Charles S. Minot, of Harvard University, in summarizing the results of his studies, used these words: "I do not wish to close without a few words of warning explanation. For the views which I have presented before you in this series of lectures, I personally am chiefly responsible. Science consists in the discoveries made by individuals, afterwards confirmed and correlated by others, so that they lose their personal character. You ought to know that the interpretations which I have offered you are still largely in the personal stage. Whether my colleagues will think that the body of conceptions which I have presented are fully justified or not, I cannot venture to say."

This was the word of a distinguished leader of research in Comparative Anatomy. It expressed, in passing, a view about the general character of scientific method which the same author, not very long afterwards, set forth at much greater length in a lecture before his own section at a meeting of the American Association for the Advancement of Science. In that lecture "On the Method of Science" Professor Minot carefully expounded, and very extensively illustrated, the thesis that, while natural science is dependent upon the experiences of individuals for every one of its advances in the knowledge of the facts of nature, no experience of any individual man can count as a scientific discovery until it has been sufficiently confirmed by other and by independent observers. Professor Minot speaks of this confirmation by fellow workers as constituting a sort of "depersonalizing" of the discoveries of each individual observer.

The thesis here in question is familiar. I cite Professor Minot's words, not as if he himself thought them at all novel, but merely in order to bring at the moment as directly as possible to your minds what we all know to be an essential feature of the methods of natural science.

300

I

For my own part, I should not say, as Dr. Minot does, that the discoveries of the individual worker in a natural science "lose their personal character" by receiving the confirmation which makes them possessions of science. I think that I understand what my colleague means by calling this process a "depersonalizing" of the individual's contributions to scientific work. But I should myself prefer to express this well-known maxim of method by saying that the individual observer's discoveries have first to be interpreted to the scientific community, and then substantiated by the further experience of that community, before they belong to the science. In still other words, the work of science is what, in the athletic phrase, is called team-work. The spirit of science is one of loyalty to a Community of Interpretation. The term Community of Interpretation I here use in the technical sense defined in the foregoing lecture.

But however you choose to formulate the rule, the lesson of which it reminds us is one which concerns philosophers quite as much as it does the students of nature. Let us attempt to read this lesson, and to generalize it. We shall find it to be a lesson in metaphysics.

Our knowledge of nature depends upon experience. An experience, in order to be useful for the purposes of physical science, must involve the testing, or at all events the present success, of an idea. In this experience percepts and concepts must be brought into synthesis. Some idea about nature, as the pragmatists tell us, must be found to "work," at least in the one case which is first in question when a new natural fact is found. A scientific discovery consists in the observation of such a "working." And so far all who have learned how the study of the physical world is carried on, will agree regarding the bases of scientific knowledge.

II

Discoveries, however, are made by individuals. The individual discoverer, then, must be the one who first finds that, at a certain moment, and for him personally, concepts and percepts meet thus and thus. Some question of his is answered, and, in general, some hypothesis of his is for the moment verified. The individual observer finds that "cash" is rendered to correspond to certain "credit-values" which he has previously possessed only in conceptual form. Some interest of his in the search for percepts is, at least momentarily, fulfilled. Unless at least so much takes place in the life of somebody, science is not enriched by a new discovery.

Such, then, are the necessary conditions which must be met if a scientific advance is to take place. But are these conditions sufficient? Does every case wherein the individual finds novel "cash payment" rendered for some of his own "credit-values," and new perceptual answers given to his conceptual questions, and "workings" crowning with at least momentary success an idea of his own about nature,—an idea which has heretofore "worked" for no other man,—does every such case involve a genuine scientific discovery? Can the individual simply turn over to his science the "cash" which his percepts have now rendered? Can he address all who are concerned thus?—"Lo, I have indeed found a new scientific fact. Scientific facts are facts of experience. I have had an experience. True ideas are ideas which 'work.' Here is an idea of mine; and this time it 'works,' for I have seen its 'working.' You want in science, not mere concepts, but percepts. I have a percept. You want, not mere credit, but cash. I have the cash; and here it is."

Is this the sole way in which the individual wins access to new scientific facts? And is this the spirit in which the trained scientific observer— for instance, the colleague whom I have just cited—reports his discoveries?

No, these conditions of a scientific discovery are necessary, but not sufficient. The individual has made his discovery; but it is a scientific discovery only in case it can become, through further confirmation, the property and the experience of the community of scientific observers. The process whereby the transition is made from the individual observation to the needed confirmation is one whose technical details, as they appear in the life of any one special science, interest us here not at all. But what does interest us, first of all, is the fact that this confirmation always involves a typical instance, or a series of instances, of Peirce's cognitive process called interpretation. What further concerns us is that this interpretation is guided by principles which are, in their bearings, both very general and highly metaphysical. One needs no other principles than these for dealing with all the central problems of philosophy.

I am far from accusing my colleague, Professor Minot, of any conscious intention to express an opinion about a problem of metaphysics when he uttered his loyal word of warning regarding his own scientific discoveries. But none the less, this appeal to the scientific community implies a belief that there is such a community. This belief is due not to perception or to conception alone. This belief in the reality of the scientific community is itself no belief in a fact which is open to the scientific observations of any individual. No observer of nature has ever discovered, by the methods used in his or in any natural science, that there exists any such community. The existence of the community of scientific observers is known through interpretation. This interpretation expresses essentially social motives, as well as profoundly ethical motives. And this interpretation is also of a type which we are obliged to use in dealing with the whole universe.

III

Let me illustrate the thesis which I have just expressed. Let us first consider why the individual observer must await the confirmation of others before his discovery can get its place as a contribution to a physical science. Let us use our foregoing study of the cognitive process of interpretation as a further aid towards the understanding of the relations between an individual scientific man and the work of the natural science to which he may contribute.

There is a well-known maxim of common sense which tells us that no man should be judge in his own case. The patient does ill who attempts to be his own physician. The litigant, even if he happens to be a lawyer, needs somebody besides himself as his counsel. The judge on the bench may not undertake to try a suit in which he is plaintiff or defendant. Even a great statesman needs aid when his own fitness for office is in question. The artist, however original, may be an untrustworthy critic of his own genius.

This maxim of common sense, at least in its application to patients, to litigants, to office-seekers, or to artists, seems to be somewhat remote from the maxim of scientific method which Professor Minot formulated. And yet, in both maxims, essentially the same principle is in question. Why is a man in so many cases so poor a judge of his own case? Why ought not the most expert of judges to undertake to decide a case in which he is plaintiff or defendant? Why is it, in general, true, as they say, that the man who is his own lawyer has a fool for a client? Why is every one of us disqualified from self-estimate in respect of some of the matters which personally concern us most of all?

IV

The general answers to these questions are easy. A man's own case is usually not *merely* his own. It also concerns some social order to which he belongs. The litigant stands in presence, not merely of his own rights and wrongs, but of the whole social will. The decision of his case will affect many besides himself, and sometimes might save or wreck a nation. The patient's illness is not merely a medical phenomenon, and not merely an individual misfortune, but also is an event of social moment. His family, and perhaps his country, may be affected by what is done with this single case. Napoleon's state of health, during the later years of his power, probably influenced the course of all future European history. And the obscurest victim of the plague may prove to be a centre of infection for a whole continent. Hence, when anybody is ill, his case is not merely his own.

When a man's affairs deeply concern other people besides himself, the only way to deal justly with the case is to interpret this man's own individual views and interests to some fitting representative of the social will, in order that the matter may be arbitrated, or in order that the wills of all concerned may be, as far as possible, both harmonized and expressed. A Community of Interpretation must exist or must be formed.

The sufferer who is ill, or the man who is haled into court, needs, then, not only to be an object of perception or of conception. It is not enough to wait in order to see whether his ideas "work" or not. What is needed is the triadic process of mediating between his mind and some other mind, between his ideas and other men's ideas.

And no interpreter who merely blended with the mind and the ideas of the one whom he is to interpret, or with the interests of those whom he is to address, could do the work. The distinction of the persons, or of the personal functions involved, is as essential to a Community of Interpretation as is the common task in which these three persons engage, or in which these three distinct ideas or personal functions coöperate.

Now it is indeed perfectly possible for a man to undertake the task of interpreting his own case. There are instances in which we all of us wisely attempt some form of self-interpretation. There are callings, such as those of the trained administrators and of the sea-captains, in which it becomes a regular part of a man's duty, even at moments when great and novel emergencies arise, to interpret his own duty to himself.

In a previous lecture, we have seen how such enterprises of self-interpretation are actually carried out. At some present moment, a man may interpret his past plans, his habits, his resolutions, his ideals, his obligations, to his future self, and thereupon may give commands to himself.

The psychology of such processes is simply that of comparison, when comparison is taken in Peirce's sense, as a triadic mode of cognition. In such instances a man discovers a third or mediating idea, whereby two of his own distinct ideas are, within the limits of his individual consciousness, woven into a threefold unity. Now that this can sometimes be accomplished with success, the sea-captain—who, while on the bridge, faces a great emergency and consults no other man, yet gives fitting orders and succeeds—well illustrates. The captain's task, of course, concerns the interests of a social order. But his training has prepared him to unite in his own person certain functions of a community.

From one essential feature of his self-imposed task, however, the man who acts as his own adviser in any socially significant situation, cannot be relieved. He attempts, at such a moment, to do the work of three men at once. The three personal functions which must be brought into unity if the work is to be successfully done, remain distinct. They must not blend. If they actually blend, the whole affair becomes a blind product of instinct or of routine, and not any genuine self-direction whatever. As a fact, there are some callings which train a man for such a threefold task. There are some situations in life wherein any mature man who knows his own business has to act as his own adviser. But the task has its difficulty determined by its form. An individual has, in all such instances, to do the work of a community.

Now in case of illness, of legal peril, or of the personal estimate to which the artist or the statesman is subjected by the social will, experience shows that a man is seldom, and, in sufficiently great emergencies, is never able to act with success as his own adviser. The reasons for this sort of defect are two: First, the question at issue concerns the interests of at least two distinct individuals; and hence, whether the patient or the litigant, or other man in question endeavors to be his own director or not, the task is essentially such that it can be accomplished only by the aid of an interpreter. For just because more than one individual must be rightly treated, there exists some social boundary which must be crossed. Therefore neither the "cash-values" nor the "credit-values" of individual ideas are mainly in question. The "exchange-values" of two distinct forms of ideal coinage are to be considered. And so the adjustment required has to be triadic in its inmost form. But secondly, while this process of interpretation, this crossing of our ideal boundary, can indeed be undertaken within the limits of an individual man's consciousness, as it is undertaken whenever we compare two distinct ideas of our own,—experience shows that the effort to fill at once the functions of three distinct persons does not succeed with the patients and with the litigants, although analogous threefold functions may succeed in case of the sea-captains and the great administrators.

V

Let us return to the case of the scientific observer,—not because the maxim defined by my colleague is either obscure or doubtful, but because the underlying principle needs to be brought clearly to our consciousness.

Common sense regards the physical world as a realm whose objects can be experienced in common by many observers. We have not here to inquire into the origin of this special belief. But the belief can be readily illustrated by the way in which two men who row in the same boat regard the boat and the oars which they see and touch, and the water over which they fly.

Each man views the boat and the oars and the water as objects which he experiences for himself. At the same time, each of the two men believes that both of them are experiencing, while they row together, the *same* external facts,—the *same* boat, the *same* oars, the *same* water.

It is important for our purposes to notice that, while each individual, as he pulls his oar, verifies some of his own ideas, and finds them "working" in his own individual experience, neither of them individually verifies the "workings" of the other man's ideas. Consequently, when each man believes that the boat in which he observes himself to be rowing is the same boat as the one which the other man also finds as an object in his own experience,—this belief, as each of the men possesses it, is *not* a perception, and is not verified by the individual "workings" of the ideas of either of the men.

This belief in the common object is, for each of the men, an interpretation, which he may address to the other man, or may regard the other as in turn addressing to him.

The cognitive process involved is through and through triadic.

The boat which each man finds, sees, touches, and feels himself pull, appears to him as verifying his own ideas. The common boat, the boat which each man regards as an object not only for his own, but also for his neighbor's experience, is essentially an object of interpretation.

The real boat may indeed actually be what each of the two men takes it to be; and it may be the same boat as that boat which each man verifies in his own experience. But if this is the case, and if the boat is really a common object of experience for both the oarsmen, then the community of interpretation into which the two men enter whenever they talk about their boat or about their rowing, is a community which even now views both itself and its boat as it would view both of them in case its goal were actually attained, and in case the interpretation had been transformed into a perfectly clear vision of a comparison of ideas.

In any case, however, it is useless to attempt to express the community of experience which the two oarsmen possess in terms of the separate "workings" of the ideas of either of them or of both, taken as mutually detached individuals.

Each rower verifies his own idea of the boat. Neither of them, as an individual, verifies the other's idea of this boat. Each of them, as interpreter, either of himself or of the other man, believes that their two individual experiences have a common object. Ncither can (merely as this individual) verify this idea. Neither could, as an individual, ever verify his belief in the interpretation, even although they two should row in the same boat together until doomsday.

If the common interpretation is true, then the two oarsmen actually form a community of interpretation, and are even now believing what would be seen to be true if, and only if, this community of interpretation were actually to reach its goal.

Pragmatism, whose ideas, like those of the bewitched Galatians, are fain to be saved solely by their own "works," is, as I believe, quite unable to define in its own dyadic terms, the essentially spiritual sense in which any interpretation can be true, and the sense in which any community of interpretation could reach its goal. Nothing, however, is better known to us, or is more simply empirical, than is the reaching of such a limited but determinate goal of interpretation, whenever we ourselves compare two distinct ideas of our own, and survey with clearness the union of the mediating or third idea with those whose contrasts it interprets. The oarsmen who not only row in the same boat, but who are able to talk over together their boat and their rowing, interpret their united life and work as such a real community of interpretation.

They constantly interpret themselves as the members, and their boat as the empirical object of such a community. And they constantly define what could be actually verified only if the goal of the community were reached. By merely rowing they will indeed never reach it. But does the real world anywhere or anyhow contain the actual winning of the goal by the community? If not, then the ideas of the interpreters are actually and always quite unverifiable. Yet their community, by hypothesis, is real. But if the real world contains the actual winning of the goal by the community, then the verifying experience is not definable in the terms which pragmatism uses.

For such a goal is essentially the experience of a community; and the success,—the salvation,—the final truth of each idea, or of each individual person, that enters into this community, is due (when the goal is reached) neither to its "works" nor to its workings, but to its essentially spiritual unity in and with the community.

VI

The case of the two men rowing together in the same boat is a case in which common sense raises no question regarding the physical reality of the boat. Such a question is, for common sense, unnecessary, simply because the interpretation of the boat as the common object of the experience of both the rowers is already made obvious by the essentially social nature and training of all of us. Our social consciousness is, psychologically speaking, the most deeply rooted foundation of our whole view of ourselves and of the world; and we therefore tend from the outset to make interpretation, rather than perception or conception, our ruling cognitive process whenever explicitly social relations are concerned. And so, for common sense, the physical objects, especially when they appear to us in the field of our experience of sight and of touch, are regarded as essentially common objects,—the same for all men. For do we not appear to see men dealing together with these common objects?

This is an interpretation; but it is an early and a natural interpretation. So long as we are untrained to reflection, we remain indeed unaware of the principles which lie at the basis of such common-sense opinions about natural facts.

These principles come to a clearer consciousness only when scientific methods, or similarly critical undertakings, have made us sceptical in our scrutiny of experience.

Professor Minot's maxim expresses one result of such criticism. This maxim simply generalizes the view which the two men rowing in the boat naturally take.

VII

If physical objects are especially to be viewed as objects which are or which can become common objects of experience for various men, then whoever says, "I have discovered a physical fact," is not merely reporting the workings of his own individual ideas. He is interpreting. He is therefore appealing to a community of interpretation.

If he has found a really novel object in his own individual experience, then this object has not already won its place, as the boat and the oars and the water have long since done, among the recognized objects of common experience. If hereupon the discoverer persists, as an individual, in interpreting his own experience; if he says, with direct confidence, "Since my ideas here work in this novel way, I have found a new physical fact,"— then the discoverer is attempting to be judge in his own cause. His perils are, therefore, quite analogous to those which the patient faces who attempts to be his own physician, or to the dangers which the man encounters who enters court as his own counsel.

The source and the limitations of these perils we now know. The observer of a new fact may justly be, at least for the time, his own interpreter, in case his training has rightly prepared him for the scientific emergency of a notable discovery made by him while he is working alone. For in such a case the discoverer has already become expert in the arts of his community. Yet always the scientific discoverer is, in principle, subject to Professor Minot's maxim. Isolated observations of individuals, even when these individuals are of the highest grade of expertness, are always unsatisfactory. And the acknowledged facts of a natural science are the possessions of the community.

That the scientific community itself exists, is therefore one of the most important principles used in the natural sciences. Often this principle is more or less subconscious. It is seldom adequately analyzed.

VIII

Our previous study has prepared us to understand the constitution of the scientific community of interpretation more precisely than would be possible without such a basis as we now possess. The scientific community consists, at the least, of the original discoverer, of his interpreter, and of the critical worker who tests or controls the discoverer's observations by means of new experiences devised for that purpose.

Usually, of course, in case the discovery has attracted much attention, the critic whose control is in question is no one individual man. For then the work of testing the discovery is done by a large body of individual workers.

In many cases, in the routine work of the highly developed sciences, the interpreter's task takes, in large part, the form of simply reporting and recording the discoverer's observations.

But Professor Minot calls attention to another and a very important part of the office of mediating between the discoverer and his community. Professor Minot speaks of the way in which scientific discoveries are "correlated" by others than those who made them. This process of correlation involves, upon its higher levels, elaborate comparisons. How complex and how significant, for the advance of science, this aspect of the process of interpretation may be, the historical instance of Clerk Maxwell's theoretical interpretation of Faraday's discoveries in Electricity and Magnetism will suggest sufficiently for our present purpose.

As for the work of criticism and of control to which the interpretation leads, it is not only capable of infinite complexity, but involves various reversals in the direction of the process of interpretation. Criticism and control often come from those who, as in the typical case of the discoveries of Darwin, address the discoverer, and arouse him to make new discoveries.

But however complex the processes which arise in the course of such undertakings, the essential structure of the community of scientific interpretation remains definitely the same. The existence of this community is presupposed as a basis of every scientific inquiry into natural facts. And the type of truth which is sought by scientific investigators is one which indeed includes, but which simply cannot be reduced to, the dyadic type to which pragmatism devotes its exclusive attention. For everybody concerned, while he indeed aims to have his own ideas "work," is also concerned with the truth of his interpretations, and of those which are addressed to him. And such truth can be fully tested, under our human conditions, only in the cases wherein, for the interpretation of another human individual's mind, the comparison of distinct ideas is substituted, while these ideas fall within the range of our individual insight.

In all other cases, just as in our ordinary social dealings with one another, we aim towards the goal of the community of interpretation. Our will is the "will to interpret." We do not reach the goal in any one moment, so long as we are dealing with other human beings. Yet we interpret the goal. For the goal of the community is always precisely that luminous knowledge which we do, in a limited but in a perfectly definite form, possess, within the range of our own individual life whenever our comparisons of distinct ideas are made with clearness.

We define the facts of the common social experience in terms of this perfectly concrete and empirical goal of the scientific community of interpretation. This goal is a certain type of spiritual unity. All scientific research depends upon loyalty to the cause of the scientific community of interpretation.

IX

But how—so one may still insist—should we know that any community of interpretation exists?

This question brings us indeed to the very centre of metaphysics. From this point outwards we can survey all the principal problems about reality. The will to interpret, in all of its forms, scientific or philosophical or religious, presupposes that somehow, at some time, in some fitting embodiment, a community of interpretation exists, and is in process of aiming towards its goal. Any conversation with other men, any process of that inner conversation whereof, as we have seen, our individual self-consciousness consists, any scientific investigation, is carried on under the influence of the generally subconscious belief that we all are members of a community of interpretation. When such enterprises are at once serious and reasonable and truth-loving, the general form of any such community, as we have already observed, is that of the ideal Pauline Church. For there is the member whose office it is to edify. There is the brother who is to be edified. And there is the spirit of the community, who is in one aspect the interpreter, and in another aspect the being who is interpreted. Now what is the warrant for believing in the reality of such a community?

For a general answer to this question let us hereupon consult the philosophers. The philosophers differ sadly amongst themselves. They do not at present form a literal human community of mutual enlightenment and of growth in knowledge, to any such extent as do the workers in the field of any one of the natural sciences. The philosophers are thus far individuals rather than consciously members one of another. The charity of mutual interpretation is ill developed amongst them. They frequently speak with tongues and do not edify. And they are especially disposed to contend regarding their spiritual gifts. We cannot expect them, then, at present to agree regarding any one philosophical opinion. Nevertheless, if we consider them in a historical way, there is one feature about their work to which, at this point, I need to call especial attention.

I have already more than once asserted that the principal task of the philosopher is one, not of perception, not of conception, but of interpretation. This remark refers in the first place to the office which the philosophers have filled in the history of culture.

X

Common opinion classes philosophy among the humanities. It ought so to be classed. Philosophers have actually devoted themselves, in the main, neither to perceiving the world, nor to spinning webs of conceptual theory, but to interpreting the meaning of the civilizations which they have represented, and to attempting the interpretation of whatever minds in the universe, human or divine, they believed to be real. That the philosophers are neither the only interpreters, nor the chiefs among those who interpret, we now well know. The artists, the leaders of men, and all the students of the humanities, make interpretation their business; and the triadic cognitive function, as the last lecture showed, has its applications in all the realms of knowledge. But in any case the philosopher's ideals are those of an interpreter. He addresses one mind and interprets another. The unity which he seeks is that which is characteristic of a community of interpretation.

The historical proofs of this thesis are manifold. A correct summary of their meaning appears in the common opinion which classes philosophy amongst the humanities. This classification is a perfectly just one. The humanities are busied with interpretations. Individual illustrations of the historical office of philosophy could be furnished by considering with especial care precisely those historical instances which the philosophers furnish who, like Plato or like Bergson, have most of all devoted their efforts to emphasizing as much as possible one of the other cognitive processes, instead of interpretation. For the more exclusively such a philosopher lays stress upon perception alone, or conception alone, the better does he illustrate our historical thesis.

Plato lays stress upon conception as furnishing our principal access to reality. Bergson has eloquently maintained the thesis that pure perception brings us in contact with the real. Yet each of these philosophers actually offers us an interpretation of the universe. That is, each of them begins by taking account of certain mental processes which play a part in human life. Each asks us to win some sort of touch with a higher type of consciousness than belongs to our natural human existence. Each declares that, through such a transformation of our ordinary consciousness, either through a flight from the vain show of sense into the realm of pure thought, or else through an abandonment of the merely practical labors of that user of tools, the intellect, we shall find the pathway to reality. Each in his own way interprets our natural mode of dealing with reality to some nobler form of insight which he believes to be corrective of our natural errors, or else, in turn, interprets the supposed counsels of a more divine type of knowledge to the blindness or to the barrenness or to the merely practical narrowness of our ordinary existence.

Each of these philosophers mediates, in his own way, between the spiritual existence of those who sit in the darkness of the cave of sense, or who, on the other hand, wander in the wilderness of evolutionary processes and of intellectual theories;—he mediates, I say, between these victims of error on the one hand, and that better, that richer, spiritual life and the truer insight, on the other hand, of those who, in this philosopher's opinion, find the homeland—be that land the Platonic realm of the eternal forms of being, or the dwelling-place which Bergson loves,—where the artists see their beautiful visions of endless change.

In brief, there is no philosophy of pure conception, and there is no philosophy of pure perception. Plato was a leader of the souls of those men to whom he showed the way out of the cave, and in whom he inspired the love of the eternal. Bergson winningly devotes himself to saying, as any artist says, "Come and intuitively see what I have intuitively seen."

Such speech, however, is the speech neither of the one who trusts to mere conception, nor of one who finds the real merely in perception. It is the speech of an interpreter, who, addressing himself to one form of personality or of life, interprets what he takes to be the meaning of some other form of life.

This thesis, that the philosopher is an interpreter, simply directs our attention to the way in which he is required to define his problems. And the universality of these problems makes this purely elementary task of their proper definition at once momentous and difficult. We shall not lose by any consideration which rightly fixes our attention upon an essential aspect of the process of knowledge which the philosopher seeks to control. For the philosopher is attempting to deal with the world as a whole, with reality in general.

Why is it that the philosopher has to be an interpreter even when, like Bergson or like Plato, he tries to subordinate interpretation either to conception alone or to perception alone? Why is it that when, in his loftiest speculative flights, he attempts to seize upon some intuition of reason, or upon some form of direct perception, which shall reveal to him the inmost essence of reality, he nevertheless acts as interpreter?

The answer to this question is simple.

XI

If, as a fact, we could, at least in ideal, and as a sort of speculative experiment, weld all our various ideas, our practical ideas as well as our theoretical ideas, together into some single idea, whose "leading" we could follow wherever it led, from concept to percept, or from percept to concept; and if we could reduce our problem of reality simply to the question, Is this one idea expressive of the nature of reality?—then indeed some such philosophy as that of Bergson, or as that of Plato, might be formulated in terms either of pure perception or of pure conception. Then the philosopher who thus welded his ideas into one idea, and who then assured himself of the success of that one idea, would no longer be an interpreter.

Thus, let us imagine that we could, with Spinoza, weld together into the one idea of Substance, the totality of ideas, that is of pragmatic leadings, which all men, at all times, are endeavoring to follow through their experience, or to express through their will. Suppose that this one idea could be shown to be successful. Then our philosophy could assume the well-known form which Spinoza gave to his own:—

By substance, Spinoza means that which is "in itself" and which needs no other to sustain or in any ideal fashion to contain it. Hereupon the philosopher finds it easy to assert that whatever is in any sense real must indeed be either "in itself" or "in another." No other idea need be used in estimating realities except the idea thus defined. The only question as to any object is: Is this a substance or not? A very brief and simple process of conceptual development, then, brings us to Spinoza's result that whatever is "in another" is not in the highest sense real at all. Therefore there remains in our world only that which is real "in itself." The one idea can be realized only in a world which is, once for all, the Substance. The tracks of all finite creatures that are observed near the edge of the cave of this Substance lead (as was long ago said of Spinoza's substance) only inwards. The world is defined in terms of the single idea, all other human ideas or possible ideas being but special cases of the one idea. The real world is purely conceptual, and is also monistic.

Suppose, on the other hand, that we indeed recognize with Bergson, and with the pragmatists, an endless and empirical wealth of ideas which, in practical life, lead or do not lead from concepts to percepts, as experience may determine. Suppose, however, that, with Bergson, we first notice that all these ideal leadings of the intellect constitute, at best, but an endlessly varied using of tools. Suppose that hereupon, with Bergson and with the mystics, we come to regard all this life of the varied ideas, this mechanical using of mere tools, this mere pragmatism, as an essentially poorer sort of life from which nature has long since delivered the nobler of the insects, from which the artists can and do escape, and from which it is the loftiest ideal of philosophy to liberate those who are indeed to know reality.

Then indeed, though not at all in Spinoza's way, all the ideal leadings which the philosopher has henceforth to regard as essentially illuminating, will simply blend into a single idea. This idea will be the one idea of winning a pure intuition. We shall define reality in terms of this pure intuition. And hereupon a purely perceptual view of reality will result.

If, then, all the ideas of men, if all ideas of reality, could collapse or could blend or could otherwise be ideally welded into a single idea, then this idea could be used to define reality, just as pragmatism has come to define all the endless variety of forms of "truth" in terms of the single idea which gets the name "success" or "working" or "expediency" or "cash-value," according to the taste of the individual pragmatist.

XII

As a fact, however, the genuine problem, whether of reality, or of truth, cannot be faced by means of any such blending of all ideal leadings into a single ideal leading.

We all of us believe that there is any real world at all, simply because we find ourselves in a situation in which, because of the fragmentary and dissatisfying conflicts, antitheses, and problems of our present ideas, an interpretation of this situation is needed, but is not now known to us. *By the "real world" we mean simply the "true interpretation" of this our problematic situation.* No other reason can be given than this for believing that there is any real world at all. From this one consideration, vast consequences follow. Let us next sketch some of these consequences.

Whoever stands in presence of the problem of reality has, at the very least, to compare two essential ideas. These ideas are, respectively, the idea of present experience and the idea of the goal of experience. The contrast in question has countless and infinitely various forms. In its ethical form the contrast appears as that between our actual life and our ideal life. It also appears as the Pauline contrast between the flesh and the spirit; or as the Stoic contrast between the life of the wise and the life of fools. It is also known to common sense as the contrast between our youthful hopes and our mature sense of our limitations. The contrast between our future life, which we propose to control, and our irrevocable past life which we can never recall, presents the same general antithesis. In the future, as we hopefully view it, the goal is naturally supposed to lie. But the past, dead as it is often said to be, determines our present need, and sets for us our ideal task.

In the world of theory the same contrast appears as that between our ignorance and our possible enlightenment, between our endlessly numerous problems and their solutions, between our innumerable uncertainties and those attainments of certainty at which our sciences and our arts aim. For our religious consciousness the contrasts between nature and grace, between good and evil, between our present state and our salvation, between God and the world, merely illustrate the antithesis.

One can also state this antithesis as that between our Will (which, as Schopenhauer and the Buddhists said, is endlessly longing) and the Fulfilment of our will. Plato, on the one hand, and the mystics on the other, attempt to conceive or to perceive some such fulfilment, according as Plato, or as some mystic, emphasizes one or the other of the two cognitive processes to which the philosophers have usually confined their attention.

This antithesis between two fundamental ideas presents to each of us the problem of the universe, and dominates that problem. For by the "real world" we mean the true interpretation of the problematic situation which this antithesis presents to us in so far as we compare what is our ideal with what is so far given to us. Whatever the real world is, its nature has to be expressed in terms of this antithesis of ideas.

Two such ideas, then, stand in contrast when we face our problem of reality. They stand as do plaintiff and defendant in court, or as do the ideas of the suffering patient and his hopes of recovery, or as do the wrongs which the litigant feels and the rights or the doom which the law allows him. The empirical shapes which the antithesis takes are simply endless in their wealth. They furnish to us the special topics which science and common sense study. But the general problem which the antithesis presents is the world-problem. *The question about what the real world is, is simply the question as to what this contrast is and means.* Neither of the two ideas can solve its own problem or be judge in its own case. Each needs a counsel, a mediator, an interpreter, to represent its cause to the other idea.

In the well-known metaphysical expression, this contrast may be called that between appearance and reality. The antithesis itself is in one sense the appearance, the phenomenon, the world-problem. The question about the real world is that furnished to us by our experience of this appearance. When we ask what the real world is, we simply ask what this appearance, this antithesis, this problem of the two contrasting ideas both is and means. So to ask, is to ask for the solution of the problem which the antithesis presents. That is, we ask: "What is the interpretation of this problem, of this antithesis?" The real world is that solution. Every special definition of reality takes the form of offering such a solution. Whether a philosopher calls himself realist or idealist, monist or pluralist, theist or materialist, empiricist or rationalist, his philosophy, wherever he states it, takes the form of saying: "The true, the genuine interpretation of the antithesis is such and such."

If you say that perhaps there is no solution of the problem, that hypothesis, if true, could be verified only by an experience that in itself would constitute a full insight into the meaning of the real contrast, and so would in fact furnish a solution. In any case, the real world is precisely that whose nature is expressed by whatever mediating idea is such that, when viewed in unity with the two antithetical ideas, it fully compares them, and makes clear the meaning of the contrast. *But an interpretation is real only if the appropriate community is real, and is true only if that community reaches its goal.*

In brief, then, the real world is the Community of Interpretation which is constituted by the two antithetic ideas, and their mediator or interpreter, whatever or whoever that interpreter may be. If the interpretation is a reality, and if it truly interprets the whole of reality, then the community reaches its goal, and the real world includes its own interpreter. *Unless both the interpreter and the community are real, there is no real world.*

XIII

After the foregoing discussion of the nature and the processes of interpretation, we are now secure from any accusation that, from this point of view, the real world is anything merely static, or is a mere idea within the mind of a finite self, or is an Absolute that is divorced from its appearances, or is any merely conceptual reality, or is "out of time," or is a "block universe," or is an object of a merely mystical intuition.

Interpretation, as we have seen in our general discussion of the cognitive process in question, demands that at least an infinite series of distinct individual acts of interpretation shall take place, unless the interpretation which is in question is arbitrarily interrupted. If, then, the real world contains the Community of Interpretation just characterized, this community of interpretation expresses its life in an infinite series of individual interpretation, each of which occupies its own place in a perfectly real order of time.

If, however, this community of interpretation reaches its goal, this whole time-process is in some fashion spanned by one insight which surveys the unity of its meaning. Such a viewing of the whole time-process by a single synopsis will certainly not be anything "timeless." It will not occur, on the other hand, at any one moment of time. But its nature is the one empirically known to us at any one moment when we clearly contrast two of our own ideas and find their mediator.

XIV

Nothing is more concretely known to us than are the nature, the value, and the goal of a community of interpretation. The most ideal as well as the most scientifically exact interests of mankind are bound up with the existence, with the purposes, with the fortunes, and with the unity of such communities.

The metaphysical doctrine just set forth in outline can be summed up thus: The problem of reality is furnished to us by a certain universal antithesis of two Ideas, or, if one prefers the word, by the antithesis of two Selves. The first thesis of this doctrine is that Reality—the solution of this problem—is the interpretation of this antithesis, the process of mediating between these two selves and of interpreting each of them to the other. Such a process of interpretation involves, of necessity, an infinite sequence of acts of interpretation. It also admits of an endless variety within all the selves which are thus mutually interpreted. These selves, in all their variety, constitute the life of a single Community of Interpretation, whose central member is that spirit of the community whose essential function we now know. In the concrete, then, the universe is a community of interpretation whose life comprises and unifies all the social varieties and all the social communities which, for any reason, we know to be real in the empirical world which our social and our historical sciences study. The history of the universe, the whole order of time, is the history and the order and the expression of this Universal Community.

XV

The method by which this doctrine has been reached may also be summarily stated thus: We began with a sketch of the essentially social character which belongs to our human knowledge of the physical world. Here one of our guides was the way in which common sense interprets the being of material objects. Our other guide was the maxim of scientific method which Professor Minot, wholly without any technically metaphysical purpose, has stated. The result of regarding our human experience of nature from these two points of view was that we found our belief in the reality of the physical world to be inseparable from our belief in the reality of a community of interpretation. The rest of our discussion has been a metaphysical generalization of this first result.

Turning from these special instances to the general philosophical problem of reality, we next noticed the historical fact that philosophers have never been able to define a theory of the universe in purely conceptual terms, and have been equally unable to state their doctrines about the world in purely perceptual terms. The philosophers have always been interpreters, in our technical sense of that term.

Is this limitation of the philosophers (if you call it a limitation) due to the fact that they have been, themselves, human beings, busied with interpreting life to their fellow-men, and unable therefore to dwell exclusively either upon perception or upon conception?

To this question we have answered that the philosopher's office as interpreter is not forced upon him merely by the fact that he is appealing, as man, to other men. The source of his task as interpreter lies deeper. Reality cannot be expressed exclusively either in perceptual or in conceptual form. Nor can its nature be described in terms of the ''leadings'' which any one idea can express. However you attempt to weld all ideas into one idea (such as Spinoza's idea of substance), and then to hold that reality is the expression of this one idea, you stand in presence of a contrast, an antithesis of at least two ideas, ''Appearance and Reality,'' ''Actual and Possible,'' ''Real and Ideal,'' or some other such pair. If you succeed in reducing this antithesis to its simplest statement, the world-problem then becomes the problem of defining the mediating idea in terms of which this contrast or antithesis can be and is interpreted. If you define, however tentatively, such a mediating idea, and then offer the resulting interpretation as an account of what the real world is, your philosophy becomes an assertion that the universe itself has the form and the real character of a community of interpretation. You have no reason for believing that there is any world whatever, except a reason which implies that some interpretation of the antithesis both exists and is true. A real and a true interpretation occur only in case the corresponding community exists and wins its goal.

In brief, if any single idea endeavors to define in terms of its own "leadings" the whole nature of things, that idea is in the position of the man who undertakes to be judge of his own cause. For it belongs to the nature of things to involve an interpretation of its own contrasts, and a mediation of its own antitheses. To the world, then, belongs an Interpreter of its own life. In this sense, then, the world is the process and the life of the Spirit and of the Community.

SUMMARY AND CONCLUSION

In beginning these lectures I said that I should undertake the task neither of the apologist nor of the hostile critic of Christianity.

I

Some of my hearers may have thought this statement to be modelled after the word of "jesting Pilate," who asked, "What is truth?" but "stayed not for an answer." When I added, at the same time, that I should also avoid the position, not only of the hostile, but of the indifferent critic of Christianity, the paradox of this initial definition of our undertaking may have appeared to become hopeless. "What?"—so my hearer may have inwardly exclaimed,—"neither apologist, nor hostile critic, nor yet indifferent? What manner of philosophy of the Christian religion can such a student propound? A Pilate,—but a Pilate who adds that he is not even indifferent,—who shall assume and maintain this character?"

I was willing, at the outset of our course, to accept the risk of such a judgment. I then justified my position merely in so far as the emphasis upon our title: "The Problem of Christianity," enabled me to remind you from the outset that problems ought to be considered, if possible, with an open mind. Yet you will also have felt that whoever discusses a problem hopes to reach some result; and that whoever invites others to take part with him in such a discussion is responsible for showing in the end, to those who listen, some outcome which will make the quest seem to them worth while. And if indeed we are to get any result from the study of the problem of Christianity, must not such a result take the form either of a defence or of an attack, or of a counsel to regard the whole topic with indifference? With

320

such obvious objections in mind some of you may have listened to our first lecture.

But now that our inquiry is completed, and now that we come to summarize its results, are we not prepared to return to our initial statement, and to see why, despite its paradox, it was justified, and has not proved fruitless? Nothing is farther from my wish than to magnify unduly the extremely modest office of the philosophical inquirer. But when I now ask, not: "What have I, in all my weakness as a student of philosophy, accomplished in the course of these few lectures?" but "What word would an ideally trustworthy teacher, if such were accessible to us, address to the modern man concerning the problem of Christianity?" I have to remember that not merely Pontius Pilate, but quite another man, is reported to have said something that bears upon this very problem. Let my words, so far as they are mine, be forgotten. But let us remember that John the Baptist, according to the gospel story, was no apologist for the teaching of the Kingdom of Heaven, and was still less its hostile critic, and was least of all an indifferent critic. What the burden of his preaching was, we all know: "The axe is laid at the root of the tree. The Kingdom of Heaven is at hand." John did not create a new sect. He did not preach a new creed. He did not himself undertake to found a new religion. He did not defend; he did not assail the Kingdom of Heaven. He announced that a religion, long needed, was yet to come. His references to the early end of all things, and to the imminence of the final transformation of human affairs, may well have been, like all other Apocalyptic announcements of those days, only symbols. But the deeper meaning that lay beneath his teaching was none the less true. I hold that this deeper meaning is still true. The Kingdom of Heaven is still at hand in precisely the sense in which every temporal happening is, in its own way, and, according to its special significance, a prophecy of the triumph of the spirit, and a revelation of the everlasting nearness of the insight which interprets, and of the victory which overcomes the world.

II

The essential message of Christianity has been the word that the sense of life, the very being of the time process itself, consists in the progressive realization of the Universal Community in and through the longings, the vicissitudes, the tragedies, and the triumphs of this process of the temporal world. Now this message has been historically expressed through the symbols, through the traditions, and through the concrete life of whatever human communities have most fully embodied the essential spirit of Christianity. We know not in what non-human forms the spiritual life may now or hereafter find its temporal embodiment. Our metaphysical doctrine, dealing, as it does, with universal issues, is quite unable to extend our vision to any heavenly realm of angelic powers. We have undertaken merely to defend a thesis regarding the form in which the life of the community, whether human or non-human, finds its conscious expression.

On earth, as we have seen, the universal community is nowhere visibly realized. But in the whole world, the divine life is expressed in the form of a community. Herewith, in teaching us this general but intensely practical truth, the "kindly light" seems also to show us not, in its temporal details, "the distant scene," but the "step" which we most need to see "amid the encircling gloom." And our little task it has been to learn whether, for our special purpose, that step is not, in just our present sense, "enough."

III

This is why we have been right to take, not Pilate indeed, but John the Baptist, for our guide. The Kingdom of Heaven is "at hand." For, in the true unity of the spirit, we always stand in the presence of the divine interpretation of the whole temporal process, and are members, if we choose, of the truly universal community. Yet, since only the whole of time can express the whole of the ideal, and can exhaust the meaning of the process of the spirit, no one event constitutes "the coming of the end," and the true church never yet has become visible to men. And that is true simply because the meaning of the whole of time can never become adequately visible at any one moment of time. Whoever preaches the Kingdom must accept this limitation of every finite and temporal being. He must not say: Lo here! and Lo there! Signs and wonders will not be vouchsafed to him, or to his hearers, as sufficient to present any immediate vision of the divine presence. The truth of the word: "Lo, I am with you alway, even unto the end of the world," will never be merely perceived; just as this same truth will never be expressible in terms of the abstract conceptions which James found to be so "sterile." This truth is simply the truth of an interpretation. What it means is that, for every estrangement that appears in the order of time, there somewhere is to be found, and will be found, the reconciling spiritual event; that for every wrong there will somewhere appear the corresponding remedy; and that for every tragedy and distraction of individual existence the universal community will find the way—how and when we know not—to provide the corresponding unity, the appropriate triumph. We are saved through and in the community. There is the victory which overcomes the world. There is the interpretation which reconciles. There is the doctrine which we teach. This, so far as we have had time, in these brief lectures, to state our case, is our philosophy, and this doctrine, as we assert, is in agreement with what is vital in Christianity.

The apologists for Christian tradition generally fail to express such a doctrine, because they misread the symbols which tradition has so richly furnished. The assailants of Christianity are generally ignorant of the meaning of the ideal of the universal and beloved community. Those who are indifferent to Christianity are generally unaware of what salvation through loyalty signifies. Hence it has been necessary for us to refuse to take part with any of the parties to the traditional controversies. Hereby we have been able to interpret, however, what the apologists and the critics of Christianity equally need to recognize. Therefore I submit that our quest has not been fruitless.

IV

Our last words must include two final attempts to set our case before you for your judgment. The first of these attempts will be an effort to furnish one more illustration of our philosophy. The second attempt will endeavor to point out a practical application of our foregoing teaching.

Let me briefly indicate what each of these closing considerations will be. First, let me speak of the illustration of our philosophy which I here propose to offer.

I have already said that we cannot, like the founders of new religious faiths, point to any sign or wonder as the evidence that we have rightly interpreted the divine process of which the world is the expression. Yet, as I leave our argument, in its incomplete statement, to produce, if possible, some effect upon your future thoughts about these matters, I wish to call your attention,—not to a further technical proof of our philosophy of interpretation, but to a closing exemplification of its main doctrine. This example may serve to bring our philosophy, which many of you will have found too recondite and too speculative, into closer touch with certain thoughtful interests which not only our own age, but many future ages of human inquiry, are certain to cherish.

I wish, namely, to indicate that our main thesis concerning the World of Interpretation is not only in harmony with the spirit which guides the researches of the empirical natural sciences, but is, in a very striking way, suggested to us afresh when we ponder the meaning which the very existence and the successes of the empirical sciences seem to imply. In other words, I wish to show you that our theory of the World of Interpretation, and our doctrine that the whole process of the temporal order is the progressive expression of a single spiritual meaning, is—not indeed proved—

but lighted up, when we reconsider for a moment the question: ''What manner of natural world is this in which the actual successes of our inductive sciences are possible?''

You will understand that what I say in this connection is a mere hint, and is not intended as a demonstrative argument. Our philosophy of interpretation teaches that the whole of time is a manifestation of a world-order which contains its own interpreter. But the illustration to which I shall call your attention shows us a connection between philosophical idealism and natural science such as few have ever recognized. Once more I have here to express my indebtedness to Charles Peirce. For it is he who has repeatedly pointed out that this matter to which I shall call your attention has a deep meaning, and tends to make probable a thesis about the nature of things which we shall find to be in close harmony with our doctrine of the world as a progressively realized Community of Interpretation.

So much for a hint of the first of the two matters which these closing words will call to your notice. The second matter will concern the practical outcome of our quest. I have no new faith to preach, and no ambition to found either a sect or a party. But it is fair to ask yet one question as the last issue which we have time to face. If our account of the Problem of Christianity is true, what ought we to do for the furtherance of our common religious interests? With a summary formulation of that question, and with a very little counsel regarding its answer, my lecture, and this course, will end.

V

Next, then, let me sketch my closing illustration of our philosophy of interpretation. Let me show you that there is a harmony, unexpected and interesting, between the view of the universe which the general philosophy of these lectures defends, and the result to which we are led when we ponder, as Charles Peirce has taught us to ponder, upon the conditions which make the actual successes of our natural sciences possible.[1]

Every one knows that the natural sciences depend, for their existence, upon inductive inquiries. And all of us are aware, in a general way, of what is meant by induction. When one collects facts of experience and then in-

---

1. Charles Peirce has repeatedly given expression to the thoughts about the nature and conditions of the inductive sciences to which I here, in passing, shall refer. A notable expression of opinion upon the subject occurs in a brief passage contained in his extremely interesting essay entitled ''A Neglected Argument for the Being of God,'' published in the *Hibbert Journal* during 1908.

fers, with greater or less probability, that some proposition relating to facts not yet observed, or relating to the laws of nature, is a true proposition, the thinking process which one uses is called inductive reasoning. The conditions which make a process of reasoning inductive are thus twofold. First, inductive reasoning is based upon an experience of particular facts. That is, inductions depend upon observations or experiments. Secondly, what one concludes or infers, from the observations or experiments in question, follows from these facts not necessarily, but with some more or less precisely estimable degree of probability. The terms "inductive inference" and "probable inference" are almost precisely equivalent terms.[1] If you draw from given premises or presuppositions a conclusion such that, *in case* the premise is true, the conclusion *must* be true, the process of reasoning which is in question is called "necessary inference" or "deductive inference" (these two terms being, for our present purposes, equivalent). But if, upon assuming certain premises to be true, you find that they merely make a given conclusion *probable,* the inference which guides you to the conclusion is an inductive inference.

Examples of such inference may easily be mentioned. Thus a life insurance company, in assuming new risks, and in computing premiums, is guided by mortality tables. Such tables summarize, in a statistical fashion, facts which previous experience has furnished regarding the ages at which men have died. The insurance actuaries compute, upon the basis of the tables, the mortalities of men who are yet to be insured. The results of the tables and of the computations are probable inferences to the effect that of a certain number of men, who are now in normal condition and who are of a given age, a certain proportion will die within a year, or within ten years, or within some other chosen interval of time. Such probable inferences are used, by the insurance company, in determining the rate at which it is safe to insure a given applicant who appears to be, upon examination, a "good risk" for his age. Nobody can know when any one individual man will die; and the insurance company draws as few inferences as possible regarding the case of any one individual man. But the premium charged to the individual man who wishes to insure his life is determined by the fact that the company is insuring, not this man alone, but a large number of men at about the same time; and inferences about the proportion of some large number of men who will die within a year, or within ten years, can be rendered, through the use of good methods, very highly probable. Now the insurance company's processes of inference include some numerical computations

---

1. Objections to an assertion of the *precise* equivalence of the terms "inductive inference" and "probable inference" exist, but need not be discussed in the present connection, since they are irrelevant to the matter which Charles Peirce's comment here calls to our notice.

which, within certain limits, remain mainly deductive. For the outcome of a correct numerical computation is, when considered in itself, a necessary inference. But the principal and decisive basis of the insurance company's inferences is such that the inferences drawn are inductive and not deductive. That is, the reasoning of the insurance company is based upon particular observed facts, and the conclusions drawn are merely probable conclusions. If the mortality tables are correct, these conclusions, when applied to large numbers of insured persons, are highly probable. They are never certain.

What the insurance companies do when they reason about taking new risks is an example of a method widely used in the natural sciences. A collection of facts of observation, a statistical study of these facts, and a probable inference based upon such statistics,—these, in many cases, make up a great part of the work of an inductive science.

VI

But the statistical methods used by the insurance companies are not the only methods known to natural science. Another sort of probable inference is also known, and is, in many cases, of much more importance for natural science than is the more directly statistical method which the insurance companies use. This other method is known to you all. It is the method of forming hypotheses and of testing these hypotheses by comparing their results with experience. Let me mention a well-known instance of this method. We can then see how it contrasts with the methods most frequently used by the insurance companies, and why it is a valuable method.

An enthusiastic student of antiquity, the now celebrated Schliemann, was deeply influenced, a half century ago, by the hypothesis that the story of the Trojan war, as told in the "Iliad," had a substantial basis in historical fact. This hypothesis was not new; but just at that time it was in disfavor when judged in the light of the prevailing opinions of the classical historians. Schliemann gave to this hypothesis a new vividness; for he was an imaginative man. But in making the hypothesis vivid, he made it more and more improbable by adding to it the further hypothesis that the ancient tradition as to the site of Troy was also historically well founded. Having formed his hypothesis, he reasoned in a way that, for our momentary purpose, we may roughly summarize thus: "If the Homeric story of the Trojan war was historically well founded, and if the ancient traditions about the site of the real Troy were also true, and if nothing has since occurred to render unrecognizable the ruins which were left when Troy was burned,— then, in case I dig in just that mound, yonder, I shall find the ruins of a large city, which once contained palaces and treasures, and which will show signs of having been burned.''

Now this hypothesis of Schliemann about Troy was, when he formed or reformed his conjectures upon the topic, a seemingly very unlikely hypothesis. But Schliemann dug, and the now well-known ruins came to light.

Hereupon you will all agree that, from the facts of experience which were thus presented for further judgment, no important conclusion could be said to follow deductively and as a necessary condition. And as a fact Schliemann is known to have overestimated both the probability and the importance of the conclusions which he himself drew from his discoveries. Later research corrected his conclusions in many respects. But all of us will agree that in one respect Schliemann's success when his excavations were made very greatly changed the probability of his own assertion that the Homeric story of the Trojan war had some basis in historical facts. What he said was: ''If this old story is true, and if I dig in yonder mound, such and such things will come to light.'' The success of his excavations, the fact that such things as he had predicted actually came to light when he dug,— all this did not demonstrate, but did make probable, the assertion: ''This old story has a real basis in historical truth.'' The very fact that, before the excavation was tried, Schliemann's hypothesis about the truth of the old story of the sack of Troy seemed improbable, and that his expectations of success in digging for the ruins appeared extravagant and unwarranted,— this very fact made his actual success all the more significant. Common sense at once commented: What could lead to such an antecedently unlikely success as that of Schliemann, unless the idea which guided Schliemann's excavations had some basis in fact? Nothing was demonstrated by Schliemann's first discoveries. But a new probability had henceforth to be assigned to the hypothesis which had led to Schliemann's predictions and discoveries,—namely, that some historical foundation existed for the story of the Trojan war.

VII

Schliemann's triumph, such as it was, is familiar. It furnishes a typical instance of the second of the two leading processes of inductive reasoning. This second method is that of hypothesis and test. Suppose that we make some hypothesis A. Hereupon suppose that we are able to reason, in advance of further experience, that if A is true, some fact, let us say E, will be observed, in case we meet certain conditions of observation or of experiment. Then, the more unlikely it is, in the light of previous knowledge, that the fact E should be observable under the mentioned conditions, the more does our actual success in finding the fact of experience, E, at the place and time where the hypothesis had led us to look for it, render probable the assertion that there is at least some measure of truth about the hypothesis A.

The method used by the insurance companies, when they apply facts which are summarized in the mortality tables as a guide for future insurance transactions, depends upon reasoning from experiences which we have already collected, to the probability of assertions about facts which are as yet unobserved. The other method of induction,—the method which, in his own way, Schliemann exemplified, follows an order which is, in part, the reverse of the order of the reasoning process which the insurance companies emphasize. This second method of induction consists in first inventing some hypothesis A, which is adapted to the purpose of the investigator. Then the user of this method discovers, usually by some process of deductive reasoning, that, if the hypothesis A is true, some determinate fact of experience E will be found under certain conditions. The investigator hereupon looks for this predicted fact E. If he fails to find it, his hypothesis is refuted, and he must look for another. But if he finds E where his hypothesis had bidden him to look for E, then the hypothesis A begins to be rendered probable. And the more frequently A is verified, and the more unexpected and antecedently improbable are these verifications, the more probable does the hypothesis A become.

The most important and exact results of the inductive sciences are reached by methods in which the verification of hypotheses plays a very large part. Galileo used hypotheses, computed what the results would be in case the hypotheses were true, and then by further experience verified the hypotheses. So did Newton; so in a very different age, and in a very different field, did Darwin. Upon the process of inventing hypotheses, of computing their consequences, and of then appealing to experience to confirm or refute the hypotheses, the greatest single advances in physical science rest.

And the principle used in this branch of induction may be stated thus:—

When without any antecedent knowledge that the consequences of a given hypothesis are true, we find, upon a fair examination of the facts, that these consequences are unexpectedly verified, then the hypothesis in question becomes, not certainly true, but more and more probable.

VIII

These general remarks about the inductive methods used in science may seem to some of you to be mere commonplaces. But they have been needed to bring us to the point where Charles Peirce's remark about the significance of the actual successes of scientific method can at length be appreciated.

If the only methods followed by the natural sciences were the statistical methods of the insurance companies; if all the work of scientific induction were done, first by making collections of facts, such as mortality tables exemplify, and secondly by making probable predictions about the future based mainly upon the already observed facts, as the insurance companies issue new policies on the basis of the already existing tables, then indeed the work of the inductive sciences would be progressive, but it would not be nearly as creative as it actually is.

In fact, however, the inductive sciences owe their greatest advances to their greatest inventors of hypotheses,—to men such as Galileo or as Darwin. To be sure, when the inventors of scientific hypotheses are in question, these inventors must also be not only inventors, but also verifiers, and must be willing readily to abandon any hypothesis whose consequences conflict with experience. But since it is the actually successful, while far-reaching, hypothesis which adds the most new probabilities to science, the art of making great advances, especially in the most exact branches of physical science, must especially depend upon the power to invent fitting hypotheses.

Now a very good hypothesis depends, in general, for its high value, first upon its novelty; secondly, upon the fact that, when duly tested, it is verified. If it is not novel, the verification of its consequences will make comparatively little difference to the science in question. If it cannot be verified, and especially if experience refutes it, it does not directly contribute to the progress of science. But the more novel an hypothesis is, the more in advance of verification must it appear improbable; and the greater are the risks which its inventor seems to run when he first proposes it.

IX

Now in what way shall a good inventor of hypotheses be guided to his invention? Shall he confine himself only to the hypotheses which, when first he proposes them, seem antecedently probable? If he does this, he condemns himself to relative infertility. For the antecedently probable hypothesis is precisely the hypothesis which lacks any very notable novelty. Even if such an hypothesis bears the test of experience, it therefore adds little to knowledge. Worthless for the purposes of any more exact natural science until it has been duly verified, the hypothesis which is to win, in the advancement of science, a really great place, must often be, at the moment of its first invention, an apparently unlikely hypothesis,—a poetical creation, warranted as yet by none of the facts thus far known, and subject to all the risks which attend great human enterprises in any field. In such a position was Darwin's hypothesis regarding the origin of species through natural selection, when first he began to seek for its verification.

This, however, is not all. A highly significant scientific hypothesis must not only be a sort of poetic creation. There is another consideration to be borne in mind. The number of possible new hypotheses, in any large field of scientific inquiry, is, like the number of possible new poems, often very great. The labor of testing each one of a number of such hypotheses, sufficiently to know whether the hypothesis tested is or is not probably true, is frequently long. And the poetic skill with which the hypotheses are invented, as well as their intrinsic beauty, gives, in advance of the test, no assurance that they will succeed in agreeing with experience. The makers of great scientific hypotheses,—the Galileos, the Darwins,—are, so to speak, poets whose inventions must be submitted to a very stern critic, namely, to the sort of experience which their sciences use. And no one can know in advance what this critic's verdict will be. Therefore, if it were left to mere chance to determine what hypotheses should be invented and tested, scientific progress would be very slow. For each new hypothesis would involve new risks, would require lengthy new tests, and would often fail.

As a fact, however, the progress of natural science, since Galileo began his work, and since the new inductive methods were first applied, has been (so Charles Peirce asserts) prodigiously faster than it could have been had mere chance guided the inventive processes of the greater scientific thinkers. In view of these facts, Charles Peirce reasons that the actual progress of science, from the sixteenth century until now, could not have been what it is, had not the human mind been, as he says, in some deep way attuned to the nature of things. The mind of man must be peculiarly fitted to invent new hypotheses such that, when tested by experience, they bear the test, and turn out to be probably true. The question hereupon arises, "To what is this aptness of the human mind for the invention of important and successful scientific hypotheses due?"

X

This question is not easy to answer. Were new hypotheses in science framed simply by processes analogous to those which the insurance companies employ when they take new risks, the matter would be different. For the insurance companies adapt the existing tables of mortality to their new undertakings, or else obtain modified tables gradually, by a mere process of collection and arrangement. And all the statistical sciences make use of this method; and there is, of course, no doubt that this method of gradual advance, through patient collection of facts, is one of the two great sources of scientific progress.

But the other method, the method of inventing new hypotheses which go beyond all results thus far obtained,—the method which first proposes and then tests these hypotheses,—involves at every stage a venture into an unknown sea. Unless some deep-lying motive guides the inventor, he will go uselessly astray, and will waste his efforts upon inventions which prove to be failures.

In many branches of science such fortunes have in fact long barred the way. Consider, for instance, the fortunes of modern pathological research, up to the present moment, in dealing with the problem furnished by the existence of cancer. The most patient devotion to details, the most skilful invention of hypotheses, has so far led only to defeat regarding some of the most central problems of the pathology of cancer. These problems may be solved at any moment in the near future. But up to this time it seems— according to what the leading pathologists tell us—as if the human mind had not been attuned to the invention of fitting hypotheses regarding the most fundamental problems of the "cancer-research."

How different, on the other hand, were the fortunes of mechanics from Galileo's time to that of Newton. What wonderful scientific inventiveness guided the early stages of electrical science. How rapidly some portions of pathological research have advanced. And, according to Charles Peirce, in all these most successful instances it is the happy instinct for inventing the hypotheses which has shortened a task that, if left to chance and to patience, would have proved hopelessly slow. If science had advanced mainly by the successive testing of all the possible hypotheses in any given field, the cancer research, in its period of tedious trials and errors, and not the physical science of Galileo, with its dramatic swiftness of progress, nor yet the revolutionary changes due to the influence of Darwin, would exemplify the ruling type of scientific research. But as a fact, the great scientific advances have been due to a wonderful skill in the art of Galileo, and of the other leading inventors of new scientific ideas.

The present existence, then, and the rapid progress of the inductive sciences, have been rendered possible by an instinctive aptitude of the human mind to shorten the labors of testing hypothesis through some sort of native skill in the invention of hypotheses such as are capable of bearing the test of experience.

XI

Now one cannot explain the existence of such an aptitude for inventing good hypotheses by pointing out that the processes of science are simply a further development of that gradual adaptation of man to his environment which has enabled our race to survive, and which has moulded us to our natural conformity to the order of nature. For the aptitude to invent scientific hypotheses is not like our power to find our way in the woods, or to get our food, or even to create and to perpetuate our ordinary social orders. Each new scientific hypothesis of high rank is a new creation which is no mere readapting of habits slowly acquired. The conditions which enable the creator of the hypothesis to invent it never existed before his time. Human beings could have continued to exist indefinitely had Galileo never appeared. Science gets what may be called its "survival value" only after its hypotheses have been invented and tested. Without science, the race could have found its food, and been moulded to its environment, for indefinitely numerous future ages. Natural selection could never, by itself, have produced, through merely favoring the survival of skilful warriors or of industrious artisans, the genius which was so attuned to the whole nature of things as to invent the atomic hypothesis, or to discover spectrum-analysis, or to create electrical science. Our science invents hypotheses about phenomena which are, in appearance, utterly remote from our practical life. Only after a new science, such as that of electricity, has grown out of this mysterious attuning of man's creative powers to the whole nature of the physical universe, then, and only then, does this science prove, in its applications, to be useful.

We can therefore here sum up the matter by saying that the natural world has somehow created, in man, a being who is apt for the task of interpreting nature. Man's interpretation is halting and fallible; but it has shown itself, since Galileo's time, too rapidly progressive in its invention of successful hypotheses to permit us to regard this aptitude as the work of chance. Man's gradual adjustment to his natural environment may well explain his skill as artisan, or as mere collector and arranger of natural facts, but cannot explain the origin of his power to invent, as often and as wonderfully as he has invented, scientific hypotheses about nature which bear the test of experience.

XII

If, then, you seek for a sign that the universe contains its own interpreter, let the very existence of the sciences, let the existence of the happy inventive power which has made their progress possible, furnish you such a sign. A being whom nature seems to have intended, in the first place, simply to be more crafty than the other animals, more skilful in war and in hunting, and in the arts of living in tribal unities, turns out to be so attuned to the whole of nature that, when he once gets the idea of scientific research, his discoveries soon relate to physical matters as remote from his practical needs as is the chemical constitution of the nebulæ, or as is the origin and destiny of this earth, or as is the state of the natural universe countless ages ago in the past. In brief, man is not what he seems, a creature of a day, but is known to be an interpreter of nature. He is full of aptitudes to sound the depths of time and of space, and to invent hypotheses which it will take ages to verify, but which will, in a vast number of cases, be verified. Full of wonders is nature. But the most wonderful of all is man the interpreter,— a part and a member (if our philosophy is right) of the world's infinite Community of Interpretation.

The very existence of natural science, then, is an illustration of our thesis that the universe is endlessly engaged in the spiritual task of interpreting its own life.

XIII

The older forms of teleology, often used by the theologians of the past, frequently missed the place where the empirical illustrations of the workings of intelligence, in the universe, and where the signs of the life of the divine spirit are most to be sought. The teleology of the future will look for illustrations of the divine, and of design, neither in miracles nor in the workings of any continuously striving "will" or "vital impulse" which from moment to moment moulds things so as to meet present needs, or to guide present evolution.

Man, as we have seen, has an aptitude to invent hypotheses that, when once duly tested, throw light on things as remote in space as are the nebulæ, as distant in time as is the origin of our whole stellar system. This aptitude lies deep in human nature. Its existence is indeed no miraculous event of to-day. Man's power to interpret his world has somehow evolved with man. The whole natural world of the past has been needed to produce man the interpreter. On the other hand, this power of man cannot have been the result of any "vital impulse" "canalizing" matter or otherwise blindly striving continuously and tentatively for light. For this scientific aptitude of man links him even now with the whole time-order. He is so attuned by nature that, imperfect as he now is, he is adapted to be or to become, in his own halting way, but not in totally blind fashion, an interpreter of the meaning of the whole of time. Now such a teleological process as this which man's scientific successes express, illustrates the teleology of a spiritual process which does not merely, from moment to moment, adapt itself to a preëxistent world. Nor does this process appear as merely one whereby an unconscious impulse squirms its way through the "canals" which it makes in matter. No, this teleology appears to illustrate a spiritual process which, in its wholeness, interprets at once the endless whole of time.[1]

XIV

I have spent most of our brief time, in our closing lecture, in illustrations of our metaphysical doctrine. For it is needful to leave this doctrine

---

1. While I write these words, a colleague of mine, Professor L. J. Henderson, is publishing a book, entitled "The Fitness of the Environment," wherein he points out that however we may interpret the facts, there exists, in the natural world, an instance of apparent adaptation which has never before been clearly apprehended and described. This instance, viewed by itself, furnishes no proof of our present philosophy, and no proof of any other philosophy; but it furnishes an illustration of the sort of evidence for teleology which, as I believe, the teleologically disposed philosophers of the future will ponder, and will interpret.

What Professor Henderson points out is that the physico-chemical constitution of the whole natural world, so far as that world is accessible to scientific study, is "preadapted," is "fitted" to be an environment for living beings. This "fitness" is of a nature which cannot have resulted from the processes whereby life has been evolved. The same fitness involves an union of many different physico-chemical properties of the environment of living beings,— an union so complicated that one cannot suppose it due to chance. And finally the origin of this fitness must have preceded by countless ages any physical event of which we now have any probable knowledge. If life itself ever had an origin, the physical world was thus, in a manner which is new to us, inexplicably preadapted to the coming life for an indefinitely vast period before the life appeared. If life had (as Arrhenius has supposed) no origin whatever, the fitness of the environment which is here in question, being due neither to life nor to chance, remains a problem requiring scientific study, but at present promising no scientific solution.

As Professor Henderson points out, the "fitness of the environment" which he has thus discovered is so vast and pervasive, and so incapable of explanation in "vitalistic" terms as to render all forms of vitalism (including that of Bergson) superfluous as explanations of the true mutual fitness of organism and environment. In a natural world which is once for all, as Professor Henderson points out, "biocentric," why seek any longer after special vitalistic explanations for special instances of adaptation?

My own view of the relation of Professor Henderson's discovery to the sort of philosophy which these lectures have defended, is that here we have just that sort of preadaptation of earlier stages of the time-process to later stages which of course does not prove, but does illustrate, our own view of the time-process. Professor Henderson's "fitness of the environment" is analogous to Charles Peirce's "attuning" of the human mind to the universe which our sciences progressively interpret. Whatever else life is, it contains the natural conditions for an interpretation of the world. What Professor Henderson's facts, and Charles Peirce's facts, do not prove, but illustrate, is our philosophical thesis that the time-world viewed as a whole, or in very long stretches, is a process which possesses, and includes, not mere miracles and efforts and vital impulses, but a total meaning and a coherent interpretation.

in your minds as one which calls attention to an essentially new aspect of philosophical idealism, as well as to a doctrine of Life.

Time, Interpretation, and the Community, and finally, The World as a Community,—these have been the central ideas of the metaphysical portion of our course. We have everywhere pointed out, as we went, the connection between these ideas and the ethical and religious interests which we have also expounded and defended. Our last words of all must relate to the practical consequences which follow for us, and for our present age, if our view of the historical mission of Christianity is true, and if the form of idealism, which we have here expounded, rightly states the relation of the Christian ideas to the real world. Let me sum up these practical consequences as briefly as I can. In sum, they amount to two maxims.

In the past, the teaching of Christian doctrine has generally depended upon some form of Christology. In recent times the traditional problems of Christology have become, in the light of our whole view of the world, of mankind, and of history, increasingly difficult and perplexing. Whoever asserts that, at one moment of human history, and only at that one moment, an unique being, at once an individual man, and at the same time also God, appeared, and performed the work which saved mankind,—whoever, I say, asserts this traditional thesis, involves himself in historical, in metaphysical, in technically theological, and in elementally religious problems, which all advances in our modern sciences and in our humanities, in our spiritual life and in our breadth of outlook upon the universe, have only made, for the followers of tradition, constantly harder to face and to solve. The first of our practical maxims is: *Simplify your traditional Christology, in order thereby to enrich its spirit. The religion of loyalty has shown us the way to this end.*

Henceforth our religion must more and more learn to look upon the natural world as infinite both in space and in time, and upon the salvation of man as something bound up with the interpretation of an infinitely rich realm of spiritual life,—a realm whose character the legends of early Christian tradition did not portray with literal truth. Therefore, if religious insight is indeed to advance, and if the spirit of Christianity is to keep in touch with the growing knowledge of mankind, *the Christology of the future cannot permanently retain the traditional forms which have heretofore dominated the history both of dogma, and of the visible Christian church.*

And yet, if our previous account of the Christian ideas has been sound, the Christology of the past has been due to motives which are perfectly verifiable in human religious experience, and which can be interpreted in terms of a rationally defensible philosophy both of life and of the universe. As a fact, whatever Christology Paul, or any later leader of Christian faith, has taught, and whatever religious experience has been used by the historical church, or by any of its sects or of its visible forms, as giving warrant for the Christological opinions, *the literal and historical fact has always been this, that in some fashion and degree those who have thus believed in the being whom they called Christ, were united in a community of the faithful, were in love with that community, were hopefully and practically devoted to the cause of the still invisible, but perfectly real and divine Universal Community, and were saved by the faith and by the life which they thus expressed.*

Now in general, whatever else they held to be true, all the communities of Christian believers have viewed their Christ as the being whose life was a present fact in their community, inspiring its doings, uniting its members, and pointing beyond the little company of the present believers to the ideal communion of all the saints, and to the triumph of the Spirit.

Now if my account of the matter is well founded, the fact that believers have expressed their views about Christ in terms which involved symbols, legends, doubtful dogmas, and endlessly perplexing theological problems need not obscure from us any longer a truth which is verifiable, is literal, and is saving. This is the one truth which has always been grasped, in a concrete and practical form, whenever the religion of loyalty has found on earth its own. *The name of Christ has always been, for the Christian believers, the symbol for the Spirit in whom the faithful—that is to say the loyal—always are and have been one.*

Now the first practical result of recognizing that in this faith lies the genuine meaning which has lain beneath all the various and perplexing Christologies of the past is, otherwise, expressed thus: It is unwise to try to express this genuinely catholic faith of all the loyal by attempting to form one more new sect. I do not wish to see any such new sect, or to hear of one. It is needless to expect that those whom tradition now satisfies will at present first abandon tradition in order to learn the truth which, in their heart of hearts, they know that tradition has always symbolized. If men are loyal, but are in doubt as to traditional theology, it is a waste of time to endeavor to prove the usual theses of dogmatic Christology by any collection of accessible historical evidences. Such historical evidences are once for all insufficient. The existing documents are too fragmentary. The historical hypotheses are too shifting and evanescent. And if it is faith that is to be, in Christological matters, the real substance of things hoped for and the evidence of things not seen, what faith has ever been more Christian in spirit, more human in its verifiability, more universal, more saving, more concrete, than the faith of the Pauline churches? Our practical maxim is: *Hold fast by that faith.*

What is practically necessary is therefore this: Let your Christology be the practical acknowledgment of the Spirit of the Universal and Beloved

Community. This is the sufficient and practical faith. Love this faith, use this faith, teach this faith, preach this faith, in whatever words, through whatever symbols, by means of whatever forms of creeds, in accordance with whatever practices best you find to enable you with a sincere intent and a whole heart to symbolize and to realize the presence of the Spirit in the Community. All else about your religion is the accident of your special race or nation or form of worship or training or accidental personal opinion, or devout private mystical experience,—illuminating but capricious. The core, the center of the faith, is not the person of the individual founder, and is not any other individual man. Nor is this core to be found in the sayings of the founder, nor yet in the traditions of Christology. The core of the faith is the Spirit, the Beloved Community, the work of grace, the atoning deed, and the saving power of the loyal life. There is nothing else under heaven whereby men have been saved or can be saved. To say this is to found no new faith, but to send you to the heart of all true faith.

This is no vague humanitarianism, is no worship of the mere natural being called humanity, and is no private mystic experience. This is a creed at once human, divine, and practical, and religious, and universal. Assimilate and apply this creed, and you have grasped the principle of Christian institutional life in the past, and the principle which will develop countless new religious institutions in the future, *and which will survive them.*

The first of my practical concluding maxims may be stated thus: Interpret Christianity and all the problems of its Christology in this spirit, and you will aid towards the one crowning office of all human religion. You will win membership in the one invisible church.

My second maxim is this: *Look forward to the human and visible triumph of no form of the Christian church.* Still less look to any sect, new or old, as the conqueror. Henceforth view the religious ideal as one which, in the future, is to be won, if at all, by methods distinctively analogous to the methods which now prevail in the sciences of nature. It is not my thought that natural science can ever displace religion or do its work. But what I mean is that since the office of religion is to aim towards the creation on earth of the Beloved Community, the future task of religion is the task of inventing and applying the arts which shall win men over to unity, and which shall overcome their original hatefulness by the gracious love, not of mere individuals, but of communities. Now such arts are still to be discovered. Judge every social device, every proposed reform, every national and every local enterprise by the one test: *Does this help towards the coming of the universal community.* If you have a church, judge your own church by this standard; and if your church does not yet fully meet this standard, aid towards reforming your church accordingly. If, like myself, you hold the true church to be invisible, require all whom you can influence to help to render it visible. To do that, however, does not mean that you shall either conform to the church as it is, or found new sects. If the spirit of scientific investigation, or of learned research, shows signs—as it already does—of becoming one of the best of all forms of unifying mankind in free loyalty, then regard science not merely as in possible harmony with religion, but as itself already one of the principal organs of religion. Aid toward the coming of the universal community by helping to make the work of religion not only as catholic as is already the true spirit of loyalty, but as inventive of new social arts, as progressive as is now natural science. So shall you help in making, not merely happy individuals (for no power can render detached individuals permanently happy, or save them from death or from woe). You shall aid towards the unity of spirit of those who shall be at once free and loyal.

We can look forward, then, to no final form, either of Christianity or of any other special religion. But we can look forward to a time when the work and the insight of religion can become as progressive as is now the work of science.

INDEX